Tamaki Nozomu Presents Dance In The Vampire Bund 5

ダンス イン ザ ヴァンパイアバンド

5

環 望

Das Firmament blaut ewig und die Erde
Wird lange fest stehen und aufblühn im Lenz. Du aber, Mensch, wie lang lebst denn du?
Nicht hundert Jahre darfst du dich ergötzen
An all dem morschen Tande dieser Erde!

Seht dort hinab!
Im Mondschein auf den Gräbern Hockt eine wildgespenstische Gestalt!
Ein Aff ist's! Hört ihr, wie sein Heulen Hinausgellt in den süssen Duft
des Lebens!

Jetzt nehmt den Wein! Jetzt ist es Zeit, Genossen!
Leert eure goldnen Becher zu Grund! Dunkel ist das Leben, ist der Tod!

The firmament in its eternal blue, and the earth
These will long endure, will blossom in springtime.
But thou, O man, what is the span of thy life?
Not a hundred years art thou permitted
To enjoy the idle vanities of this earth!

Look there below! In the moonlight upon the graves
There crouches a wild, ghostly figure.
An ape, it is! Hark how his howling

come, my comrades!
s to the dregs!
death!

Gustav Mahler, Das Lied von der Erde

Dance In The Vampire Bund 5

Contents

*Weil lange fest stehen und
schön im Lenz die schön
Nach, ich lang lebst denn du?
hundert Jahre darfst du dich
im Mosat dem morschen Tande
Erde! Seht dort hinab! Im
solchein auf den Gräbern
kommt schlagsgeistische Gestalt!
Afficts! Horche wie am
se Hinausgellt in den einer
des Lebens! Setzt nehmt den
Jetzt ist es Zeit Genossen!
ere geleiten Becher zu Grund!
el ist das Leben ist der Tod?
Firmament blaut ewig
die Erde Wird lange fest
en und aufblühn im Lenz.
ber, Mensch, wie lang
denn du? Nicht hundert
darfst du dich ergötzen
I dem morschen Tande
r Erde! Seht dort hinab!
ondschein auf den
ern Hockt eine
gespenstische Gestalt! Ein
's! Hört ihr, wie sein
n Hinausgellt in den
Duft des Lebens! Jetzt
t den Wein! Jetzt ist es
Genossen! Leert eure
en Becher zu Grund!
el ist das Leben, ist der*

*Firmament blaut ewig
ie Erde Wird lange fest
n und aufblühn im Lenz.
ber, Mensch, wie lang
denn du? Nicht hundert
darfst du dich ergötzen
I dem morschen Tande
Erde! Seht dort
Im Mondschein auf
rÄbern Hockt eine
spenstische Gestalt!
aff ist's! Hört ihr, wie
Heulen Hinausgellt in
sen Duft des Lebens!
chmt den Wein! Jetzt
Zeit, Genossen! Leert
oldnen Becher zu
! Dunkel ist das
, ist der Tod!*

*Firmament blaut
und die Erde
I lange fest stehen
aufblühn im Lenz.
ber, Mensch, wie
lebst denn du?
t hundert Jahre
t du dich ergötzen
I dem morschen
e dieser Erde!
dort hinab! Im*

Tamaki Nozomu Presents Dance In The Vampire Bund

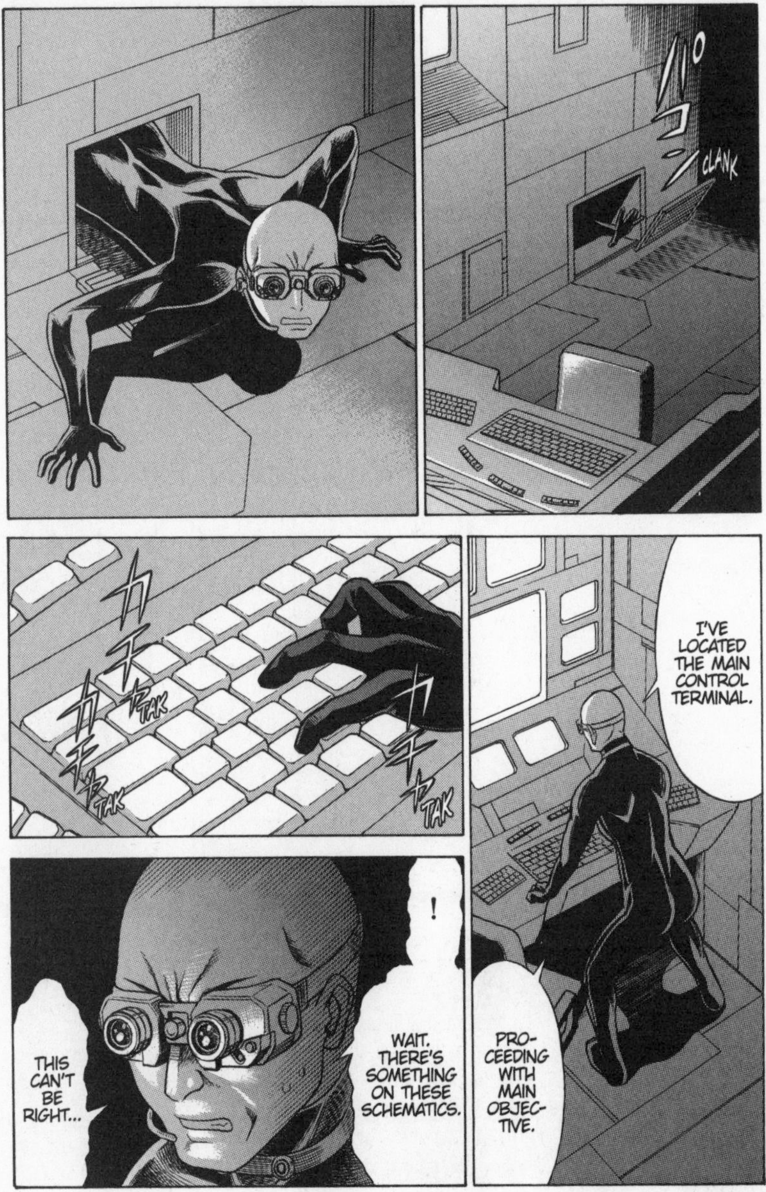
CLANK
I'VE LOCATED THE MAIN CONTROL TERMINAL.
PRO-CEEDING WITH MAIN OBJEC-TIVE.
TAK
TAK
TAK
!
WAIT. THERE'S SOMETHING ON THESE SCHEMATICS.
THIS CAN'T BE RIGHT...

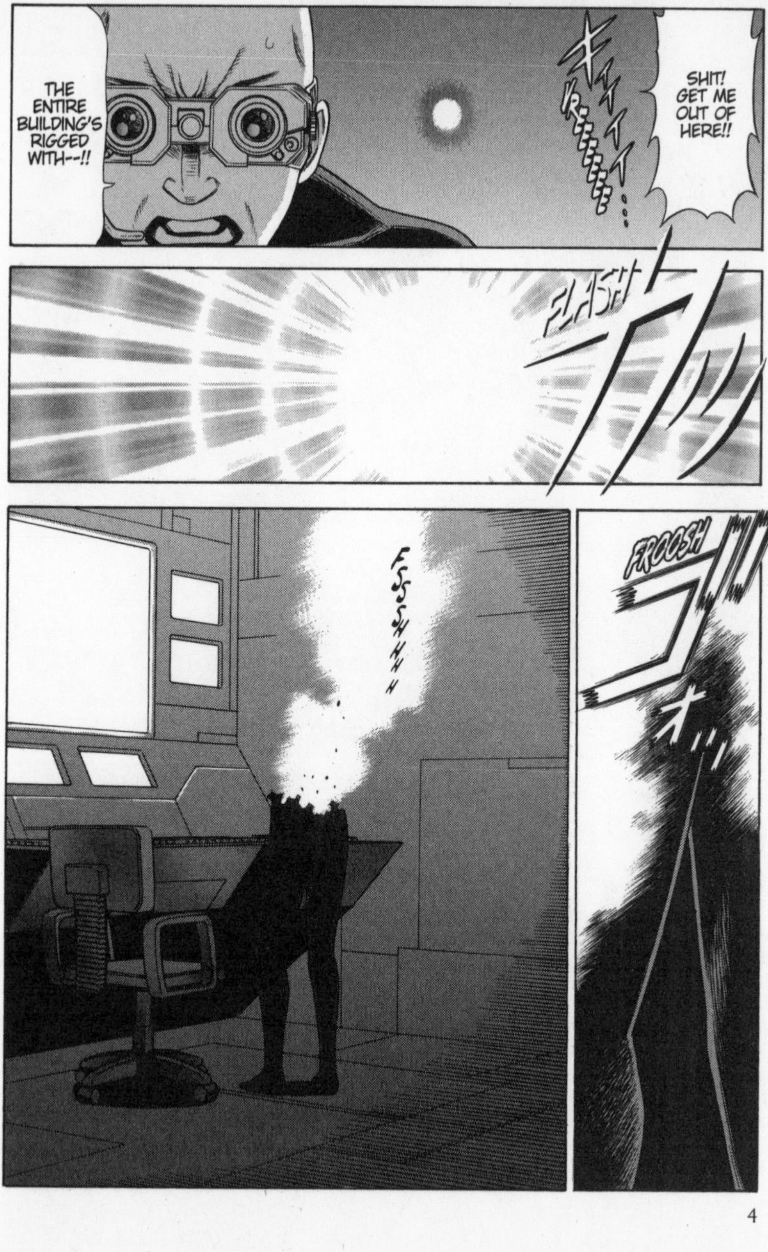
SHIT! GET ME OUT OF HERE!!
KREEEEEEEE...
THE ENTIRE BUILDING'S RIGGED WITH--!!
FLASH
FROOSH
FSSSHHHH

Chapter 25: Two in the Darkness

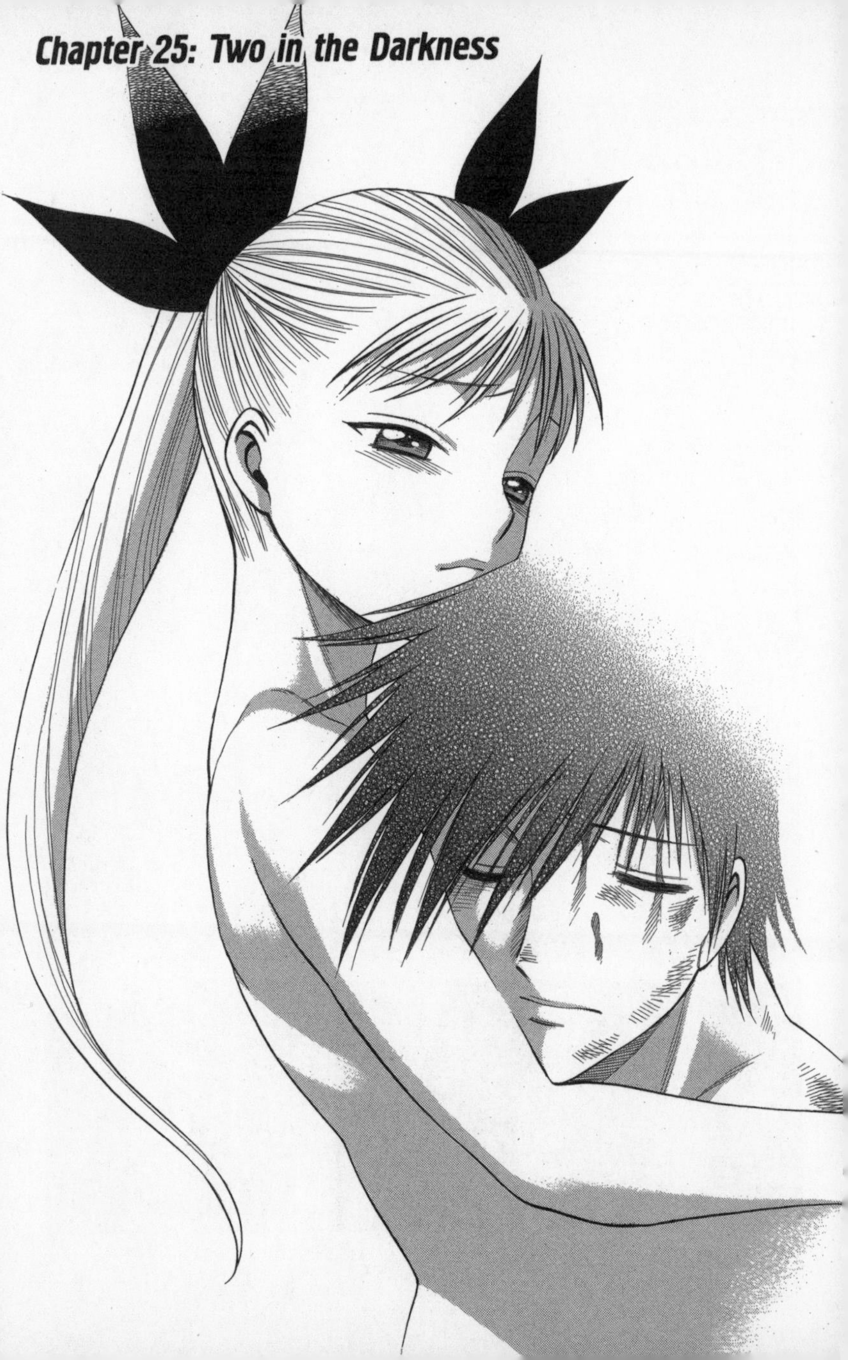

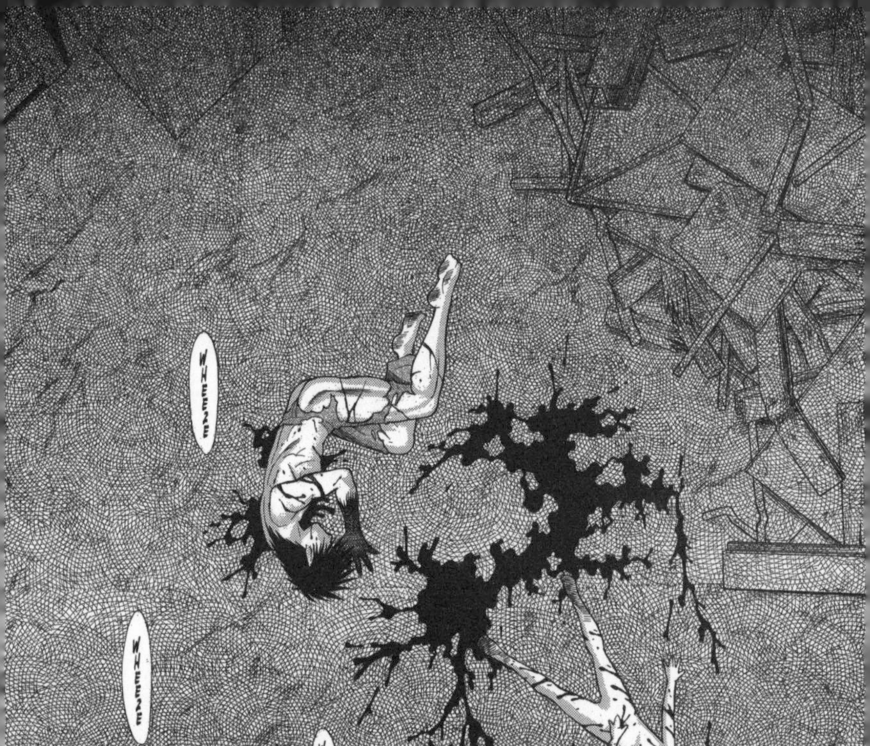
WHEEZE
WHEEZE
WHEEZE
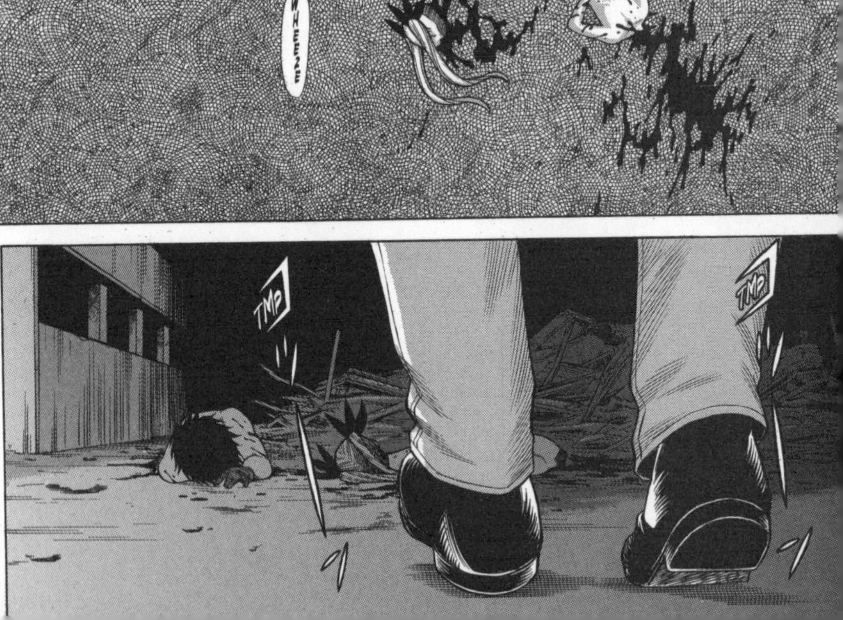
TMP
TMP

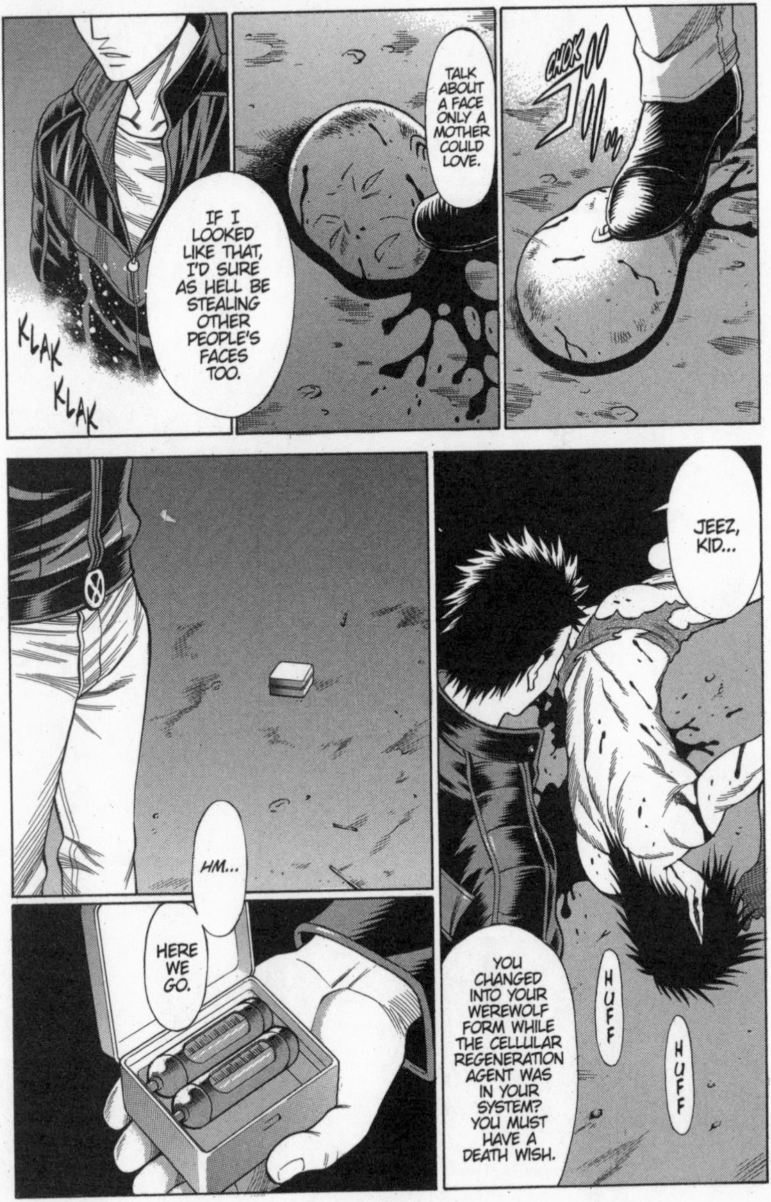
CHOK
TALK ABOUT A FACE ONLY A MOTHER COULD LOVE.
IF I LOOKED LIKE THAT, I'D SURE AS HELL BE STEALING OTHER PEOPLE'S FACES TOO.
KLAK KLAK
JEEZ, KID...
YOU CHANGED INTO YOUR WEREWOLF FORM WHILE THE CELLULAR REGENERATION AGENT WAS IN YOUR SYSTEM? YOU MUST HAVE A DEATH WISH.
HUFF
HUFF
HM...
HERE WE GO.

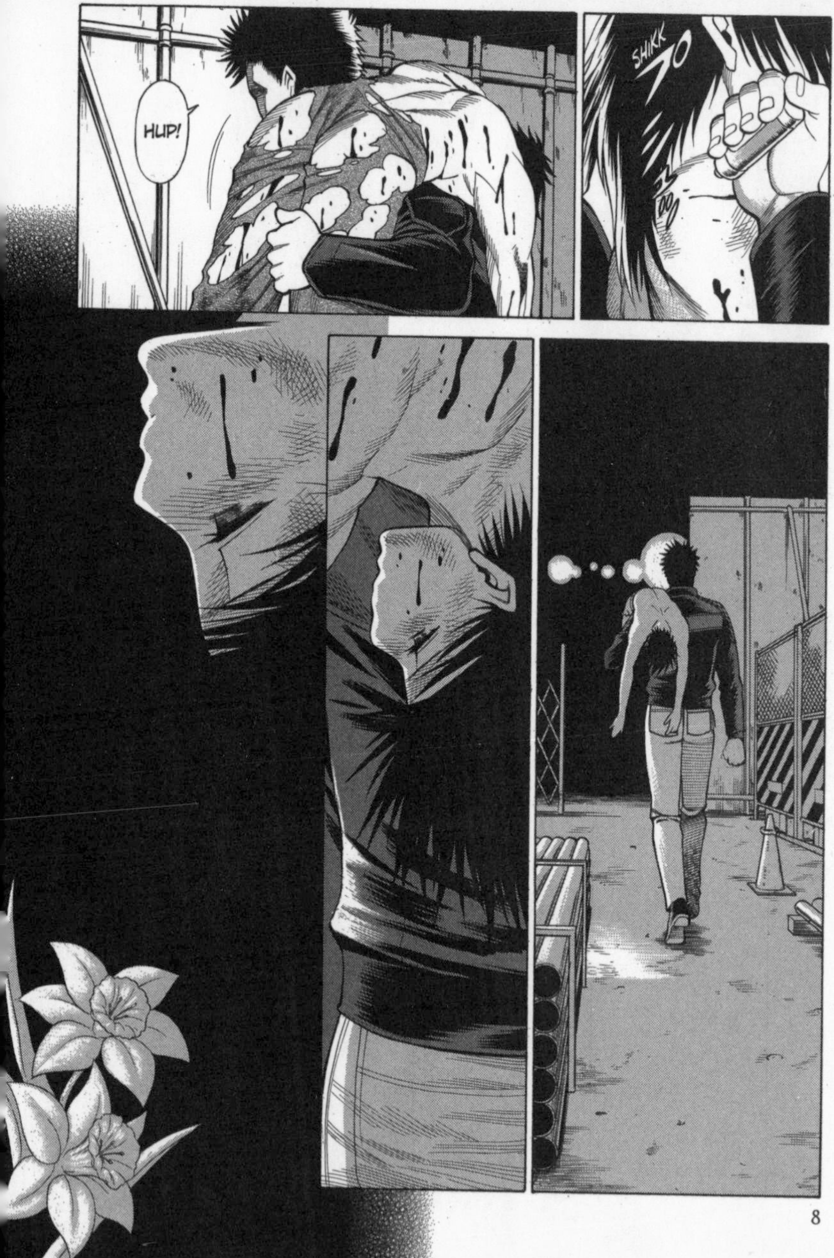
SHIKK
HUP!

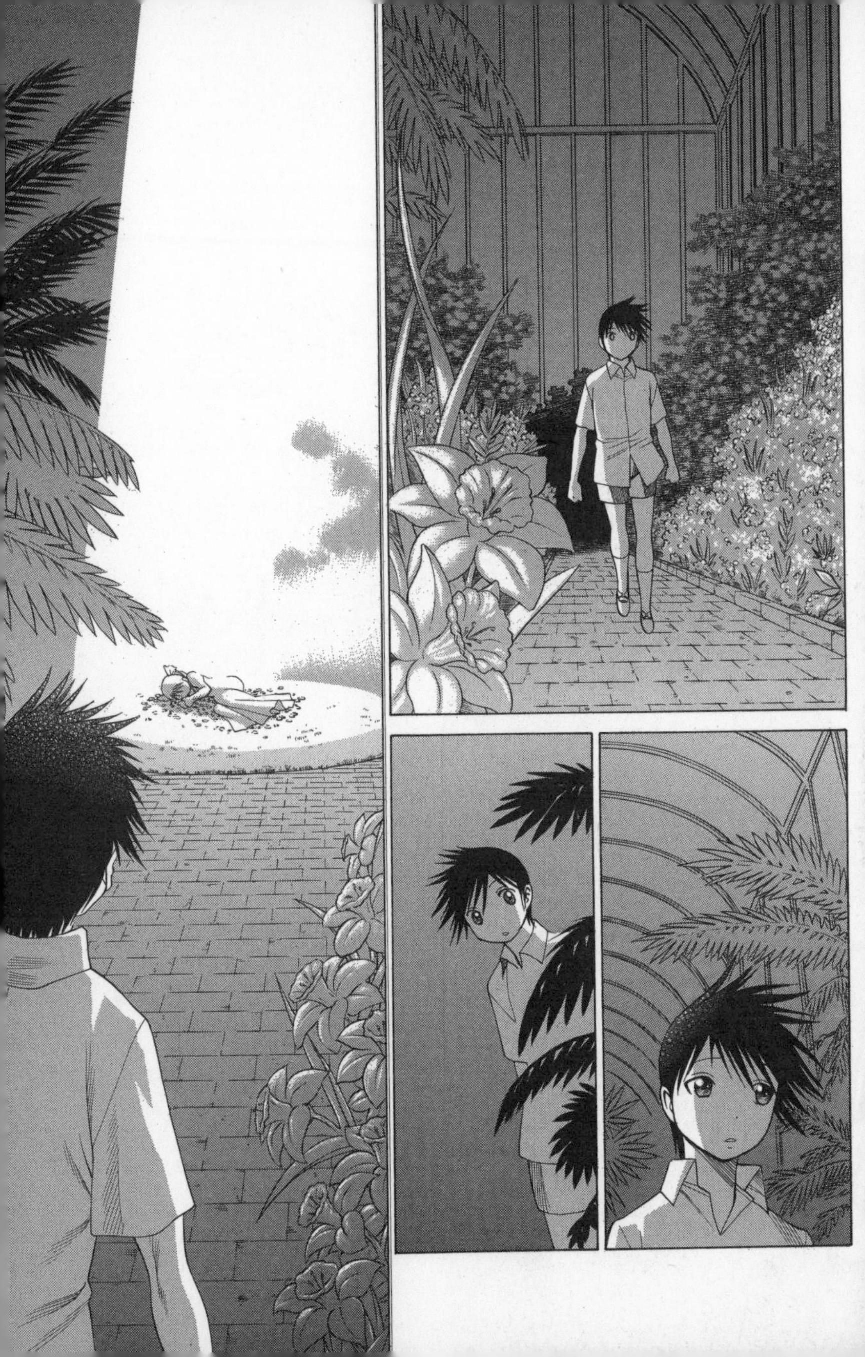

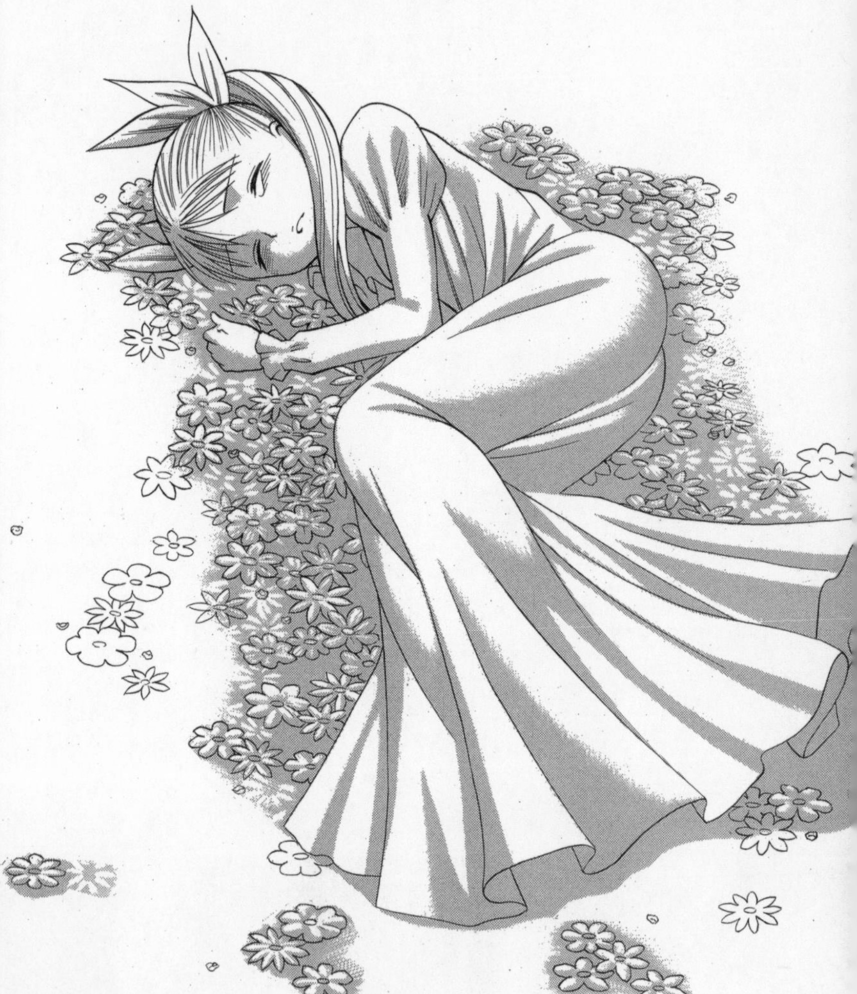

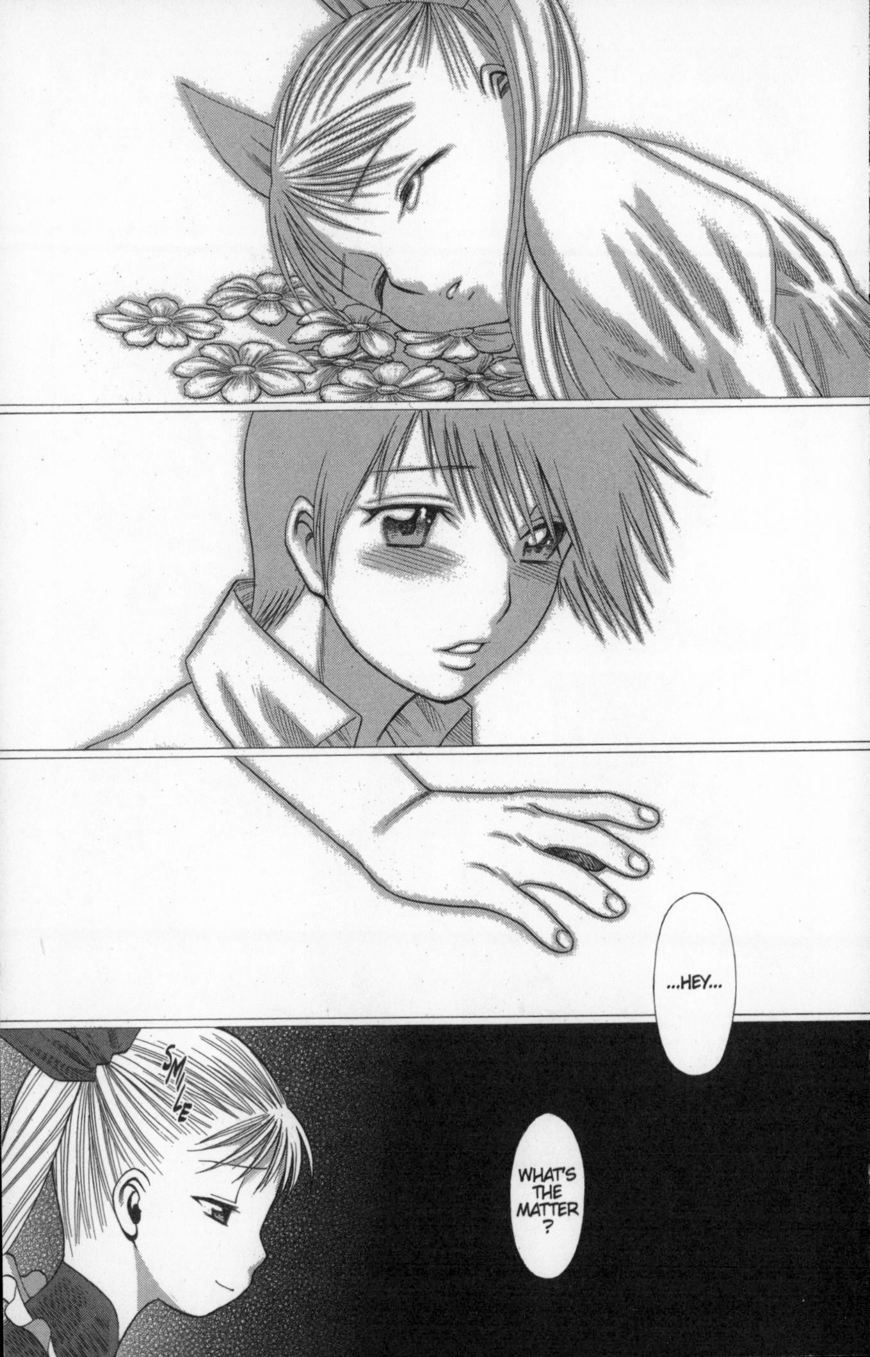
...HEY...
SMILE
WHAT'S THE MATTER?

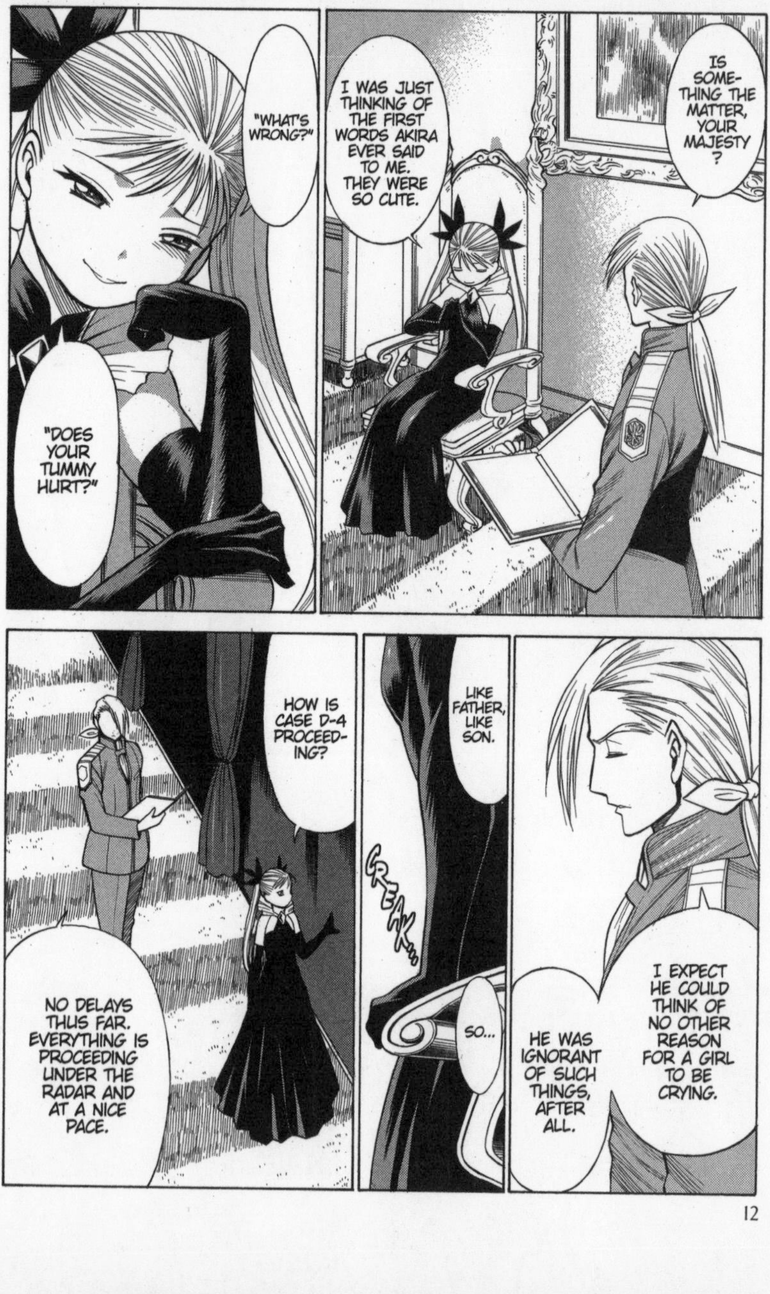
IS SOMETHING THE MATTER, YOUR MAJESTY?
I WAS JUST THINKING OF THE FIRST WORDS AKIRA EVER SAID TO ME. THEY WERE SO CUTE.
"WHAT'S WRONG?"
"DOES YOUR TUMMY HURT?"
I EXPECT HE COULD THINK OF NO OTHER REASON FOR A GIRL TO BE CRYING.
HE WAS IGNORANT OF SUCH THINGS, AFTER ALL.
LIKE FATHER, LIKE SON.
CREAK...
SO...
HOW IS CASE D-4 PROCEEDING?
NO DELAYS THUS FAR. EVERYTHING IS PROCEEDING UNDER THE RADAR AND AT A NICE PACE.

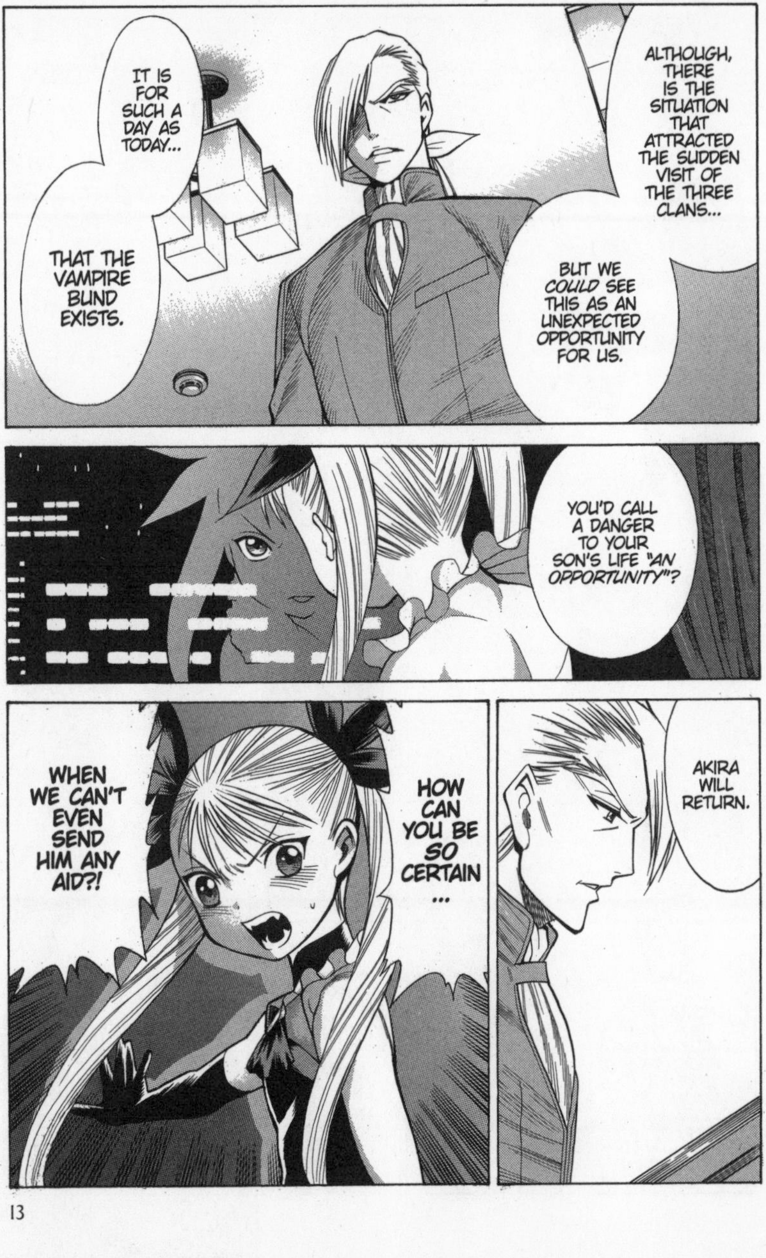
ALTHOUGH, THERE IS THE SITUATION THAT ATTRACTED THE SUDDEN VISIT OF THE THREE CLANS...
BUT WE COULD SEE THIS AS AN UNEXPECTED OPPORTUNITY FOR US.
IT IS FOR SUCH A DAY AS TODAY...
THAT THE VAMPIRE BUND EXISTS.
YOU'D CALL A DANGER TO YOUR SON'S LIFE "AN OPPORTUNITY"?
AKIRA WILL RETURN.
HOW CAN YOU BE SO CERTAIN...
WHEN WE CAN'T EVEN SEND HIM ANY AID?!

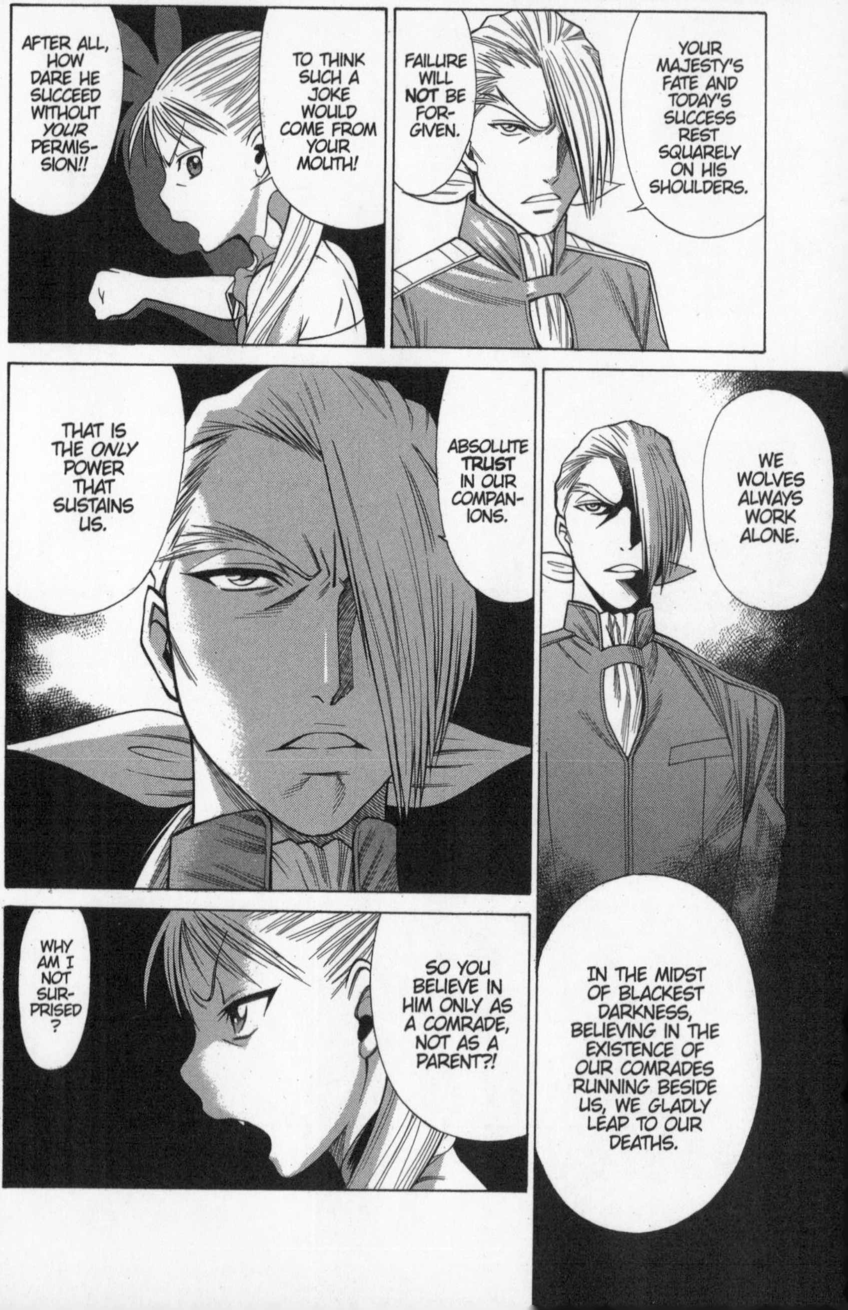
YOUR MAJESTY'S FATE AND TODAY'S SUCCESS REST SQUARELY ON HIS SHOULDERS.
FAILURE WILL NOT BE FORGIVEN.
TO THINK SUCH A JOKE WOULD COME FROM YOUR MOUTH!
AFTER ALL, HOW DARE HE SUCCEED WITHOUT YOUR PERMISSION!!
WE WOLVES ALWAYS WORK ALONE.
IN THE MIDST OF BLACKEST DARKNESS, BELIEVING IN THE EXISTENCE OF OUR COMRADES RUNNING BESIDE US, WE GLADLY LEAP TO OUR DEATHS.
ABSOLUTE TRUST IN OUR COMPANIONS.
THAT IS THE ONLY POWER THAT SUSTAINS US.
SO YOU BELIEVE IN HIM ONLY AS A COMRADE, NOT AS A PARENT?!
WHY AM I NOT SURPRISED?

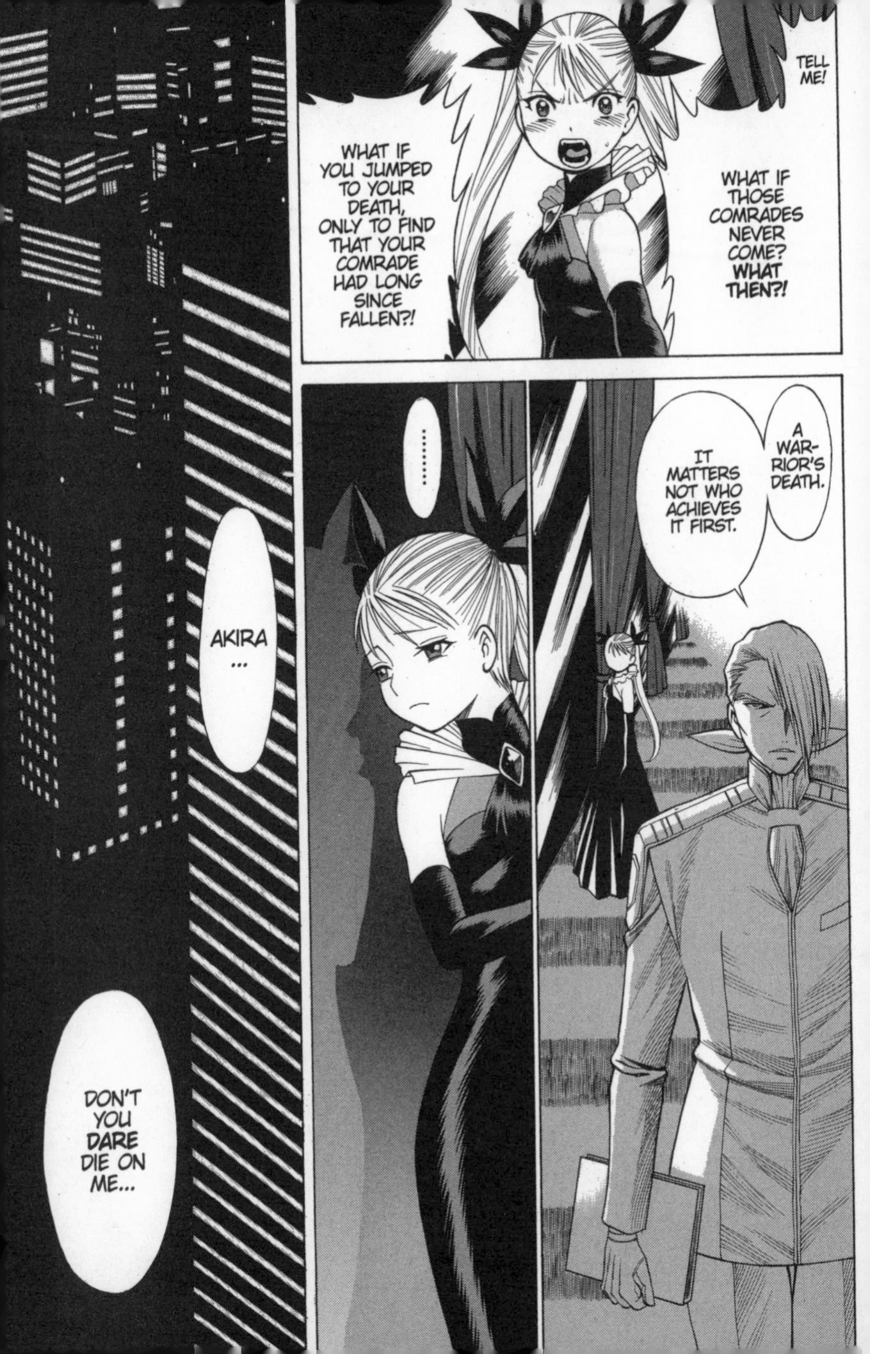
TELL ME!
WHAT IF THOSE COMRADES NEVER COME? WHAT THEN?!
WHAT IF YOU JUMPED TO YOUR DEATH, ONLY TO FIND THAT YOUR COMRADE HAD LONG SINCE FALLEN?!
A WAR-RIOR'S DEATH.
IT MATTERS NOT WHO ACHIEVES IT FIRST.
....
AKIRA ...
DON'T YOU DARE DIE ON ME...

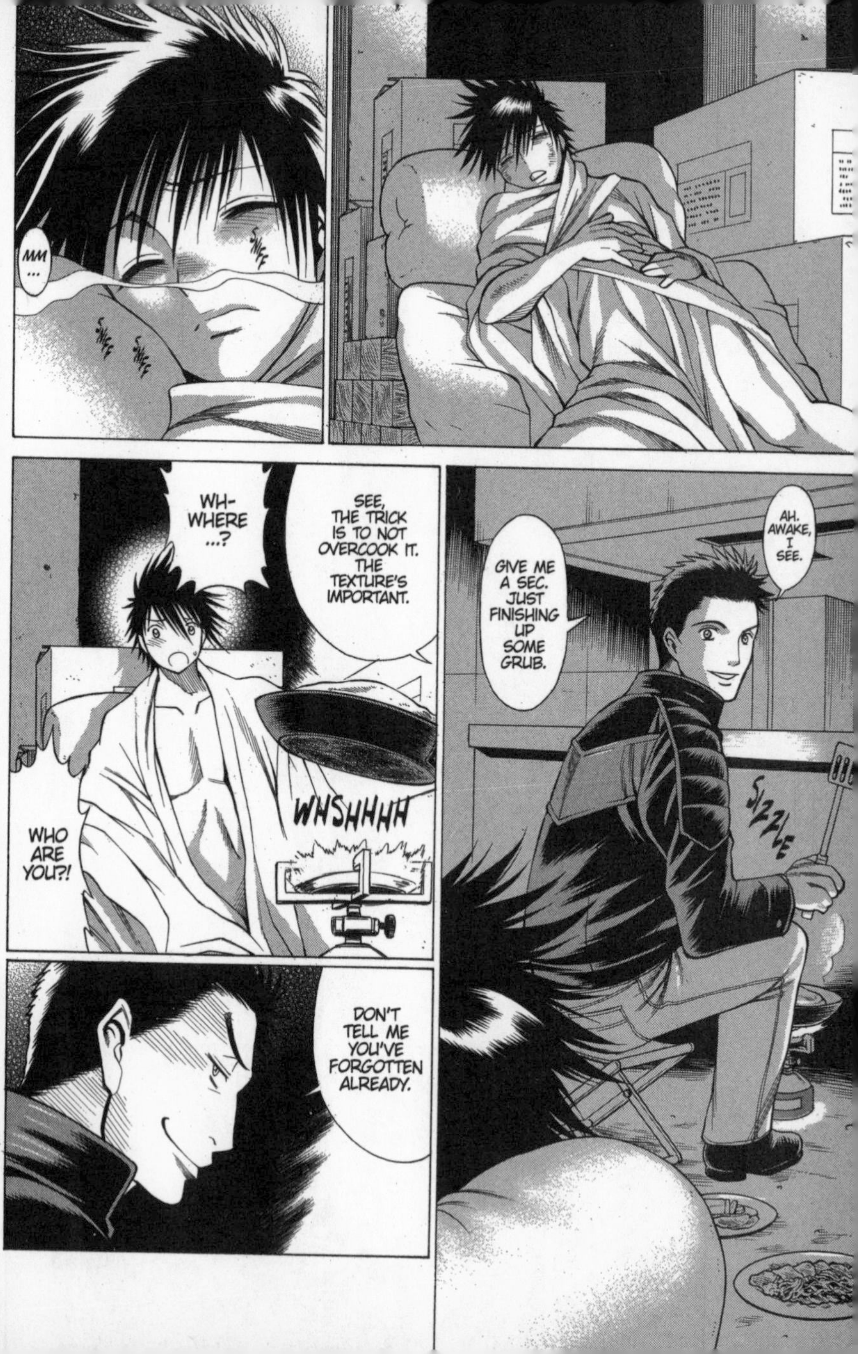
MM ...
SNIFF
SNIFF
SNIFF
AH. AWAKE, I SEE.
GIVE ME A SEC. JUST FINISHING UP SOME GRUB.
SIZZLE
SEE, THE TRICK IS TO NOT OVERCOOK IT. THE TEXTURE'S IMPORTANT.
WH-WHERE ...?
WHSHHHH
WHO ARE YOU?!
DON'T TELL ME YOU'VE FORGOTTEN ALREADY.

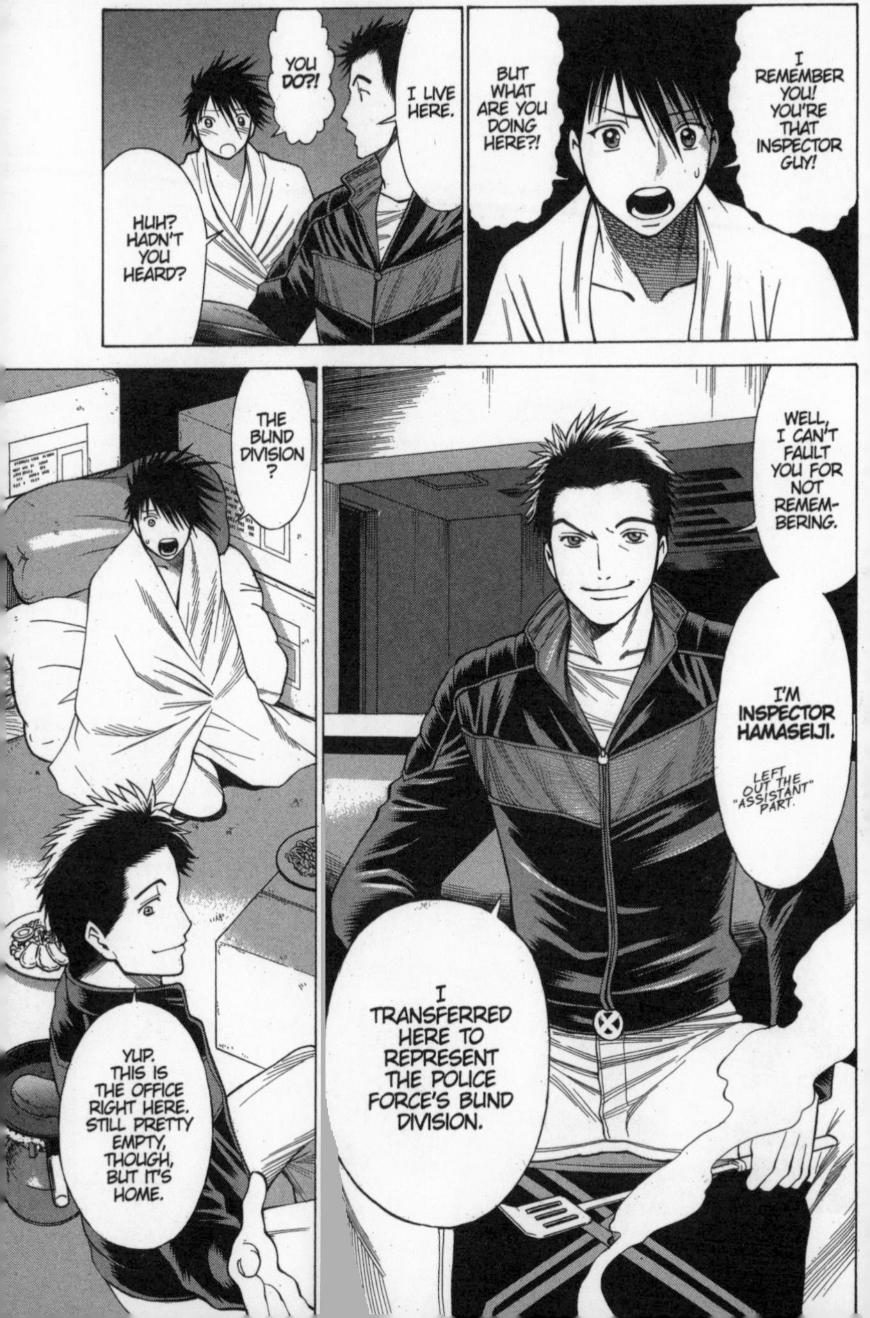
I REMEMBER YOU! YOU'RE THAT INSPECTOR GUY!
BUT WHAT ARE YOU DOING HERE?!
I LIVE HERE.
YOU DO?!
HUH? HADN'T YOU HEARD?
WELL, I CAN'T FAULT YOU FOR NOT REMEMBERING.
I'M INSPECTOR HAMASEIJI.
LEFT OUT THE "ASSISTANT" PART.
I TRANSFERRED HERE TO REPRESENT THE POLICE FORCE'S BUND DIVISION.
THE BUND DIVISION?
YUP. THIS IS THE OFFICE RIGHT HERE. STILL PRETTY EMPTY, THOUGH, BUT IT'S HOME.

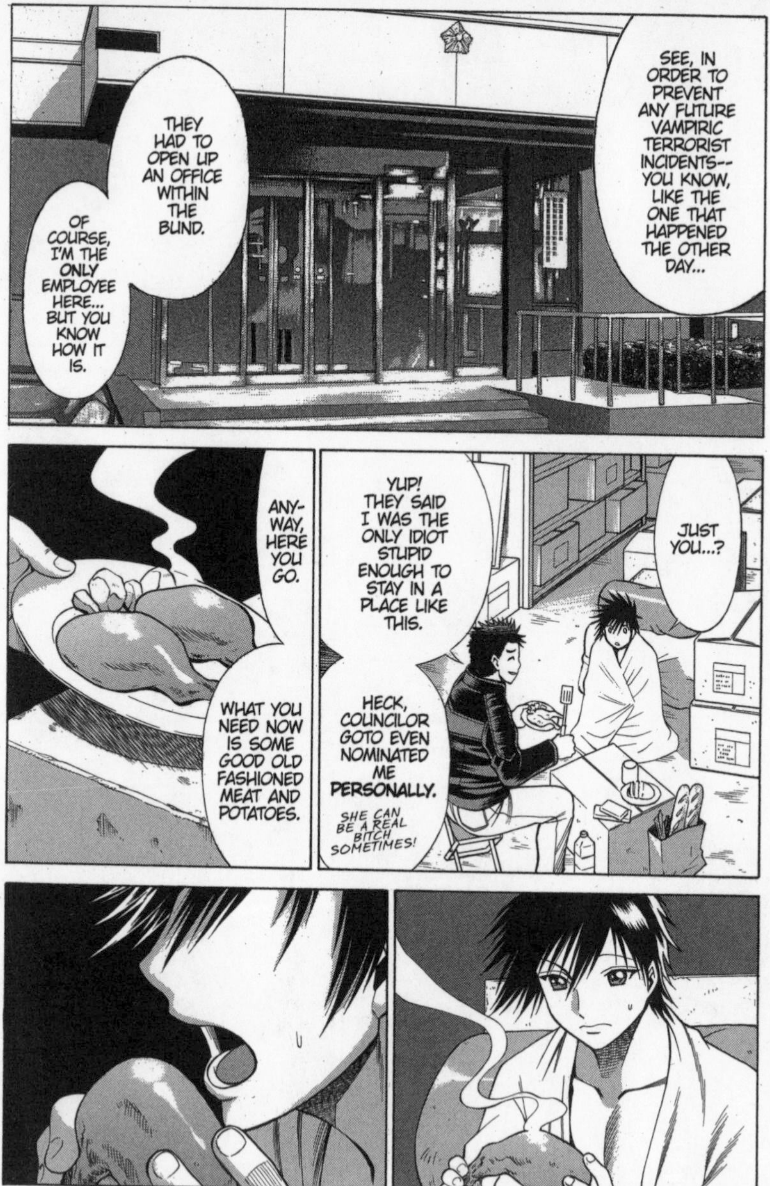
SEE, IN ORDER TO PREVENT ANY FUTURE VAMPIRIC TERRORIST INCIDENTS--YOU KNOW, LIKE THE ONE THAT HAPPENED THE OTHER DAY...
THEY HAD TO OPEN UP AN OFFICE WITHIN THE BUND.
OF COURSE, I'M THE ONLY EMPLOYEE HERE... BUT YOU KNOW HOW IT IS.
JUST YOU...?
YUP! THEY SAID I WAS THE ONLY IDIOT STUPID ENOUGH TO STAY IN A PLACE LIKE THIS.
HECK, COUNCILOR GOTO EVEN NOMINATED ME **PERSONALLY.**
SHE CAN BE A REAL BITCH SOMETIMES!
ANY-WAY, HERE YOU GO.
WHAT YOU NEED NOW IS SOME GOOD OLD FASHIONED MEAT AND POTATOES.

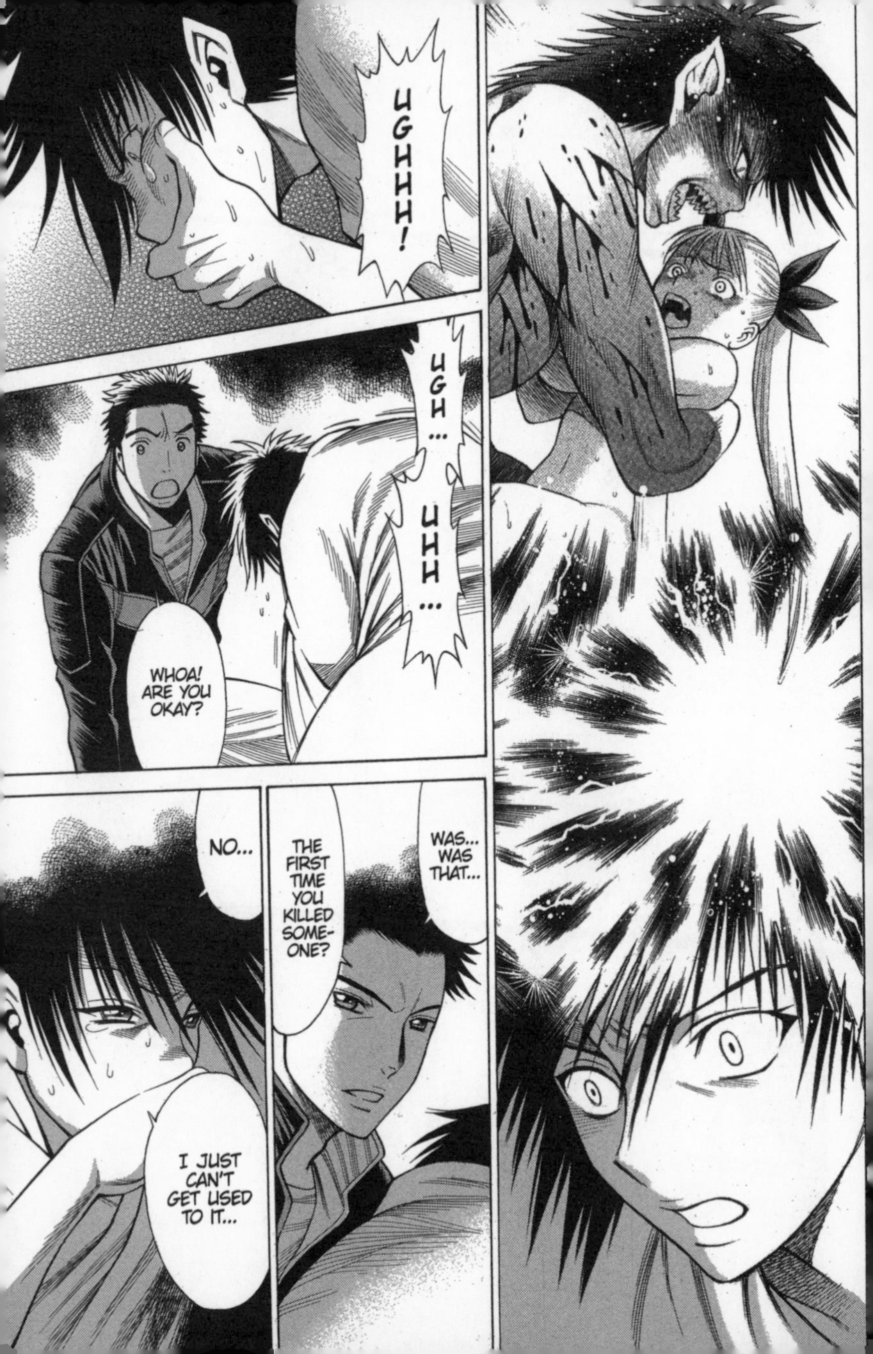
UGHHHH!
UGH... UHH...
WHOA! ARE YOU OKAY?
WAS... WAS THAT...
THE FIRST TIME YOU KILLED SOME-ONE?
NO...
I JUST CAN'T GET USED TO IT...

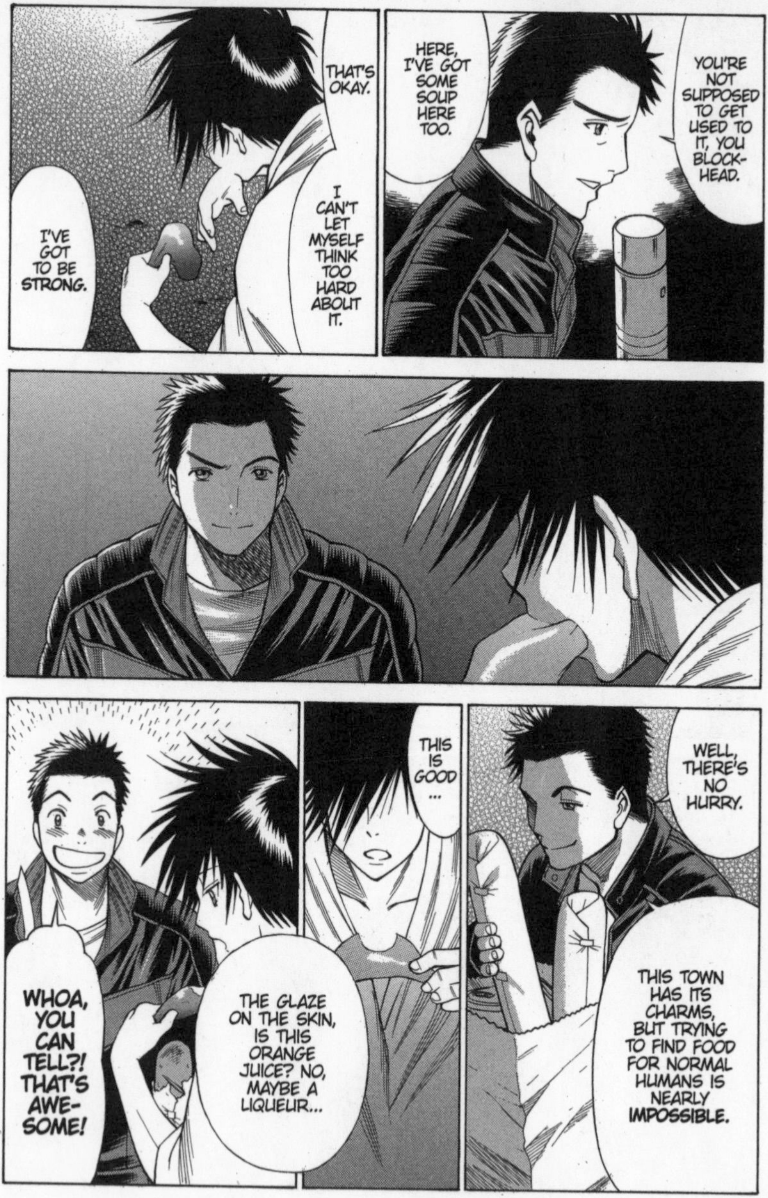

YOU'RE NOT SUPPOSED TO GET USED TO IT, YOU BLOCK-HEAD.
HERE, I'VE GOT SOME SOUP HERE TOO.
THAT'S OKAY.
I CAN'T LET MYSELF THINK TOO HARD ABOUT IT.
I'VE GOT TO BE STRONG.
WELL, THERE'S NO HURRY.
THIS TOWN HAS ITS CHARMS, BUT TRYING TO FIND FOOD FOR NORMAL HUMANS IS NEARLY IMPOSSIBLE.
THIS IS GOOD ...
THE GLAZE ON THE SKIN, IS THIS ORANGE JUICE? NO, MAYBE A LIQUEUR...
WHOA, YOU CAN TELL?! THAT'S AWE-SOME!

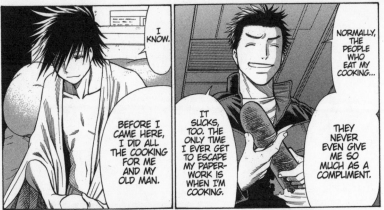

NORMALLY, THE PEOPLE WHO EAT MY COOKING...
THEY NEVER EVEN GIVE ME SO MUCH AS A COMPLIMENT.
IT SUCKS, TOO. THE ONLY TIME I EVER GET TO ESCAPE MY PAPER-WORK IS WHEN I'M COOKING.
I KNOW.
BEFORE I CAME HERE, I DID ALL THE COOKING FOR ME AND MY OLD MAN.
NO MATTER WHAT I MADE, HE NEVER SAID ANYTHING.
I JUST ALWAYS FIGURED HE NEVER HAD ANY INTEREST IN IT.
BUT WE WERE FAMILY, SO I KEPT MAKING IT.
AND NOW THAT I'M HERE, THE MAIDS TAKE CARE OF EVERY-THING...
SO I DON'T EVEN COOK ANYMORE.
......
HEY, THAT MUST BE NICE!
HEH... YEAH, I GUESS.

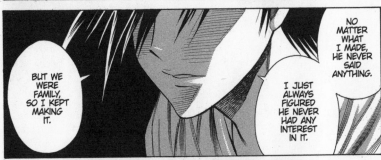

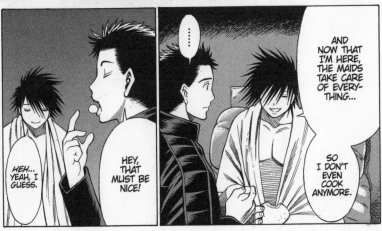

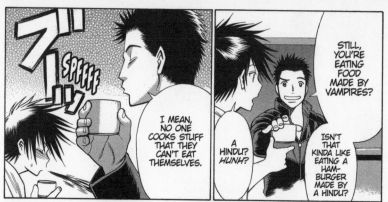

STILL, YOU'RE EATING FOOD MADE BY VAMPIRES?
ISN'T THAT KINDA LIKE EATING A HAM-BURGER MADE BY A HINDU?
A HINDU? *HUNH?*
SPFFFF
I MEAN, NO ONE COOKS STUFF THAT THEY CAN'T EAT THEMSELVES.
HA HA! GET IT? ♡
HARDLY!!
COUGH COUGH
I CHOKED BECAUSE IT WAS SO STUPID!!
......
THANKS FOR THE FOOD.
IT WAS DELI-CIOUS.
WELL, I'D BETTER GET GOING.
DON'T BE AN IDIOT. I KNOW YOU'RE NOT A HUNDRED PERCENT YET.
IF I STAY HERE, IT'LL JUST MAKE PROBLEMS FOR YOU.

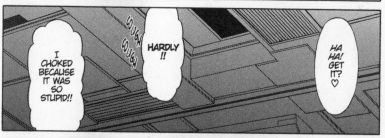

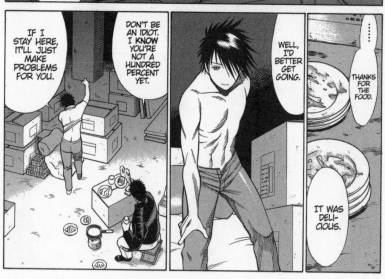

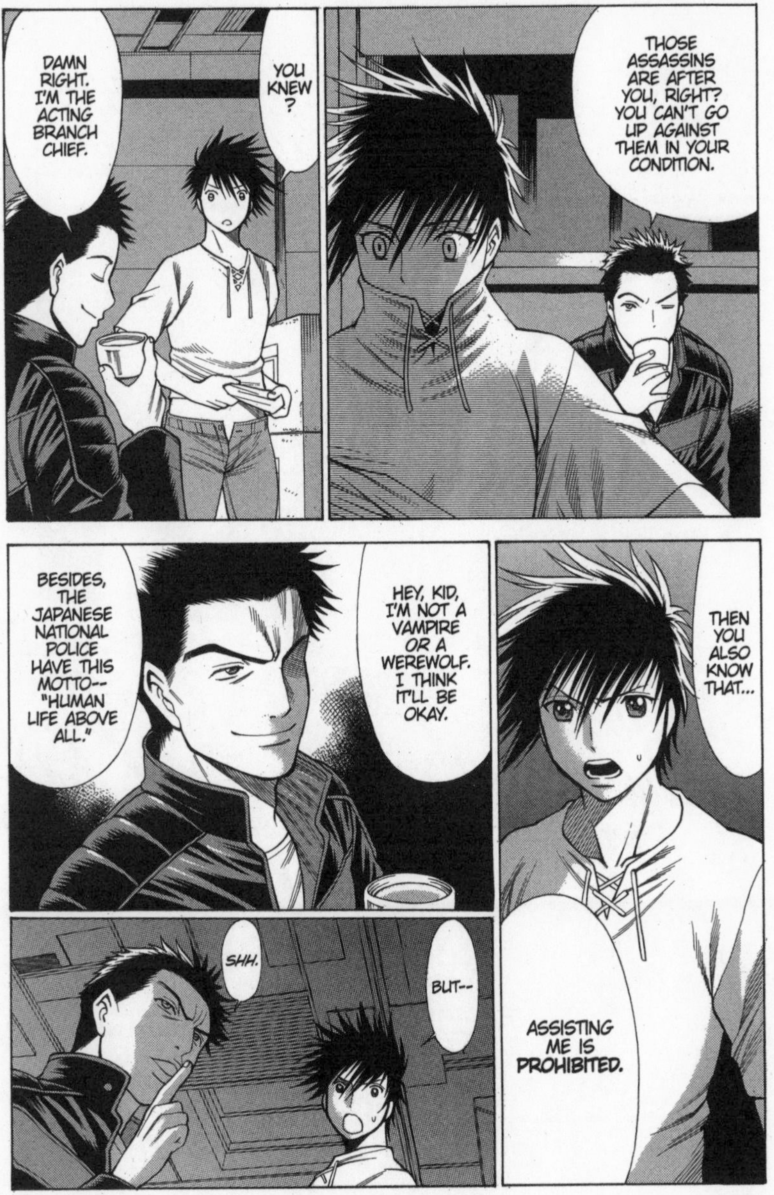
THOSE ASSASSINS ARE AFTER YOU, RIGHT? YOU CAN'T GO UP AGAINST THEM IN YOUR CONDITION.
YOU KNEW?
DAMN RIGHT. I'M THE ACTING BRANCH CHIEF.
THEN YOU ALSO KNOW THAT...
ASSISTING ME IS PROHIBITED.
HEY, KID, I'M NOT A VAMPIRE OR A WEREWOLF. I THINK IT'LL BE OKAY.
BESIDES, THE JAPANESE NATIONAL POLICE HAVE THIS MOTTO-- "HUMAN LIFE ABOVE ALL."
BUT--
SHH.

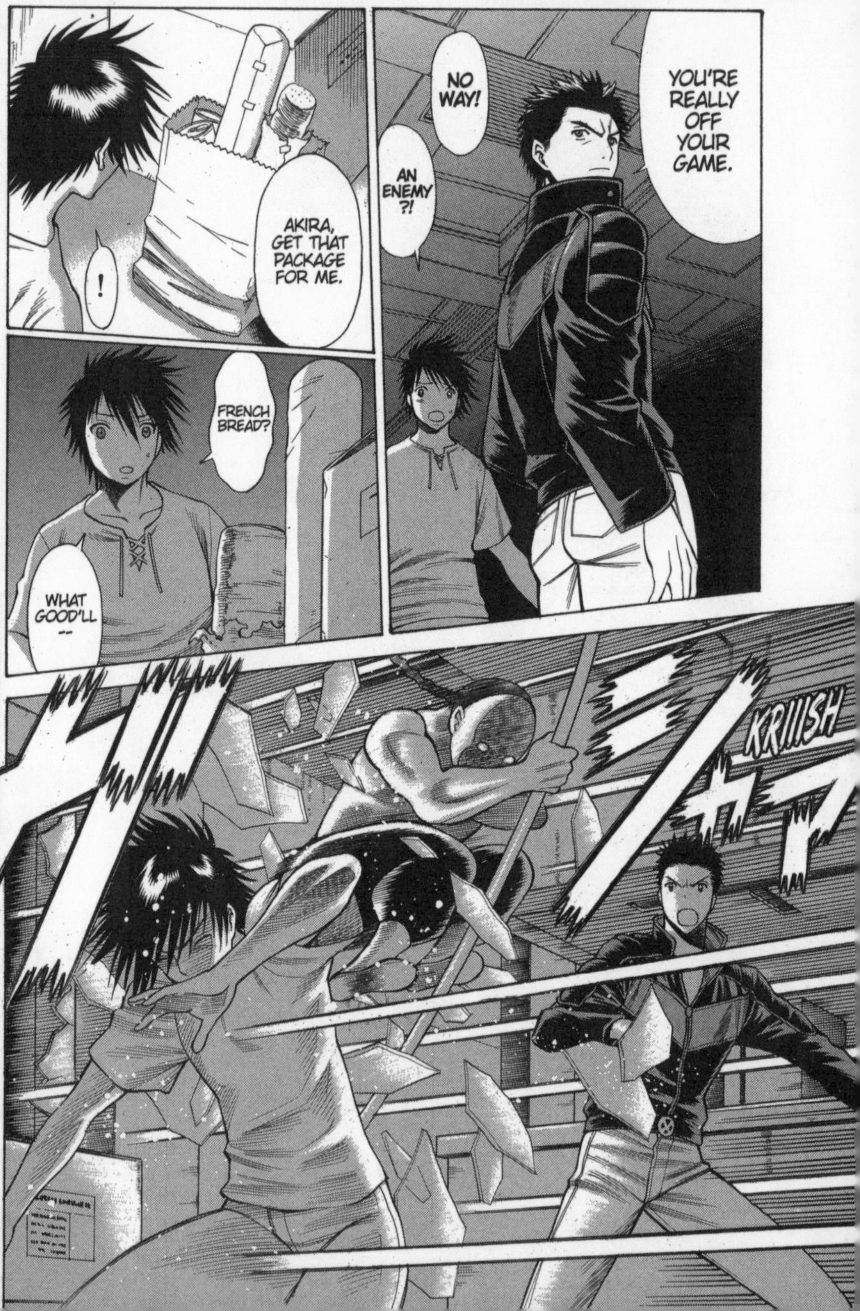
YOU'RE REALLY OFF YOUR GAME.
NO WAY!
AN ENEMY ?!
AKIRA, GET THAT PACKAGE FOR ME.
!
FRENCH BREAD?
WHAT GOOD'LL --
KRIIISH

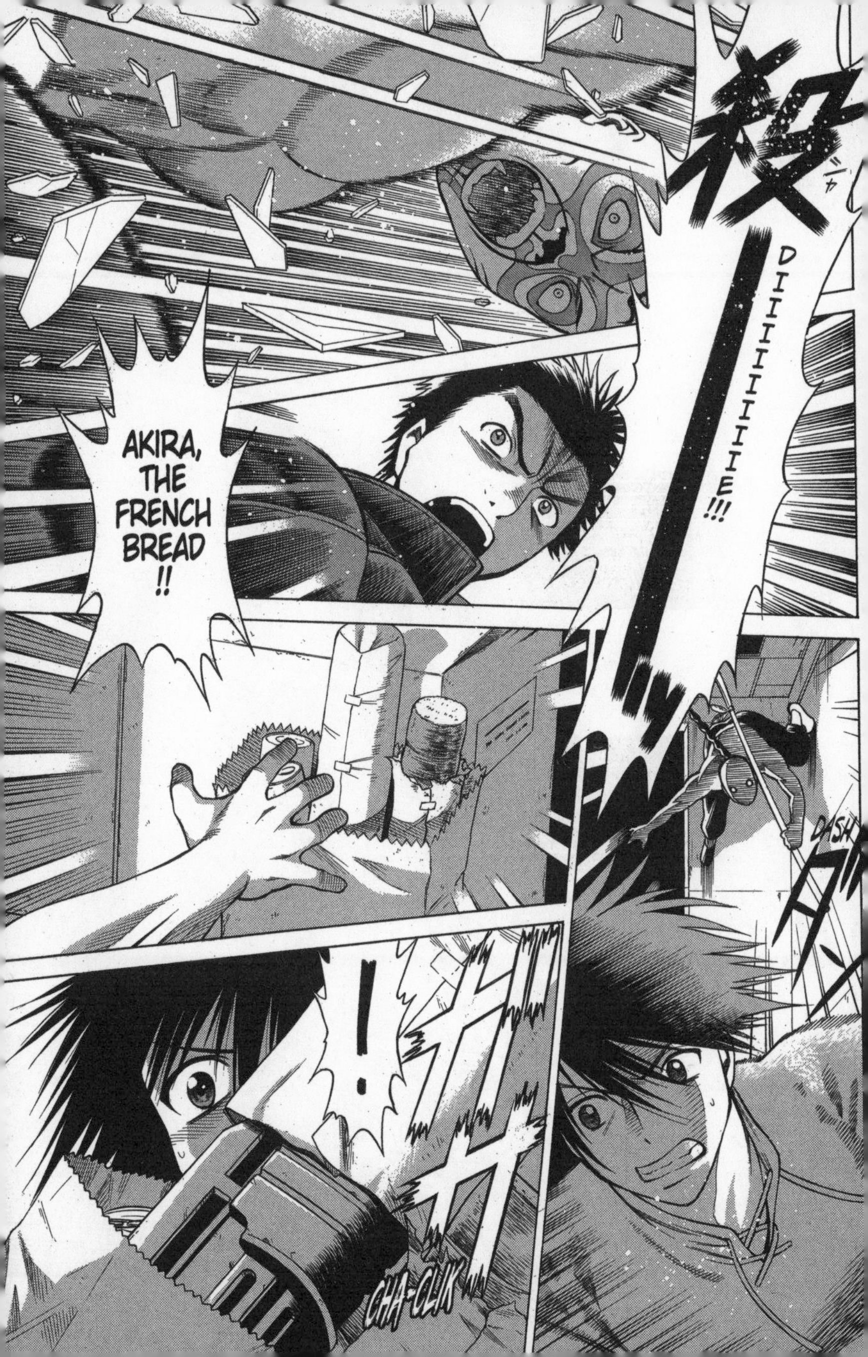
殺
ジャ
DIIIIIIIIE!!!
AKIRA, THE FRENCH BREAD !!
DASH
!
CHA-CLIK

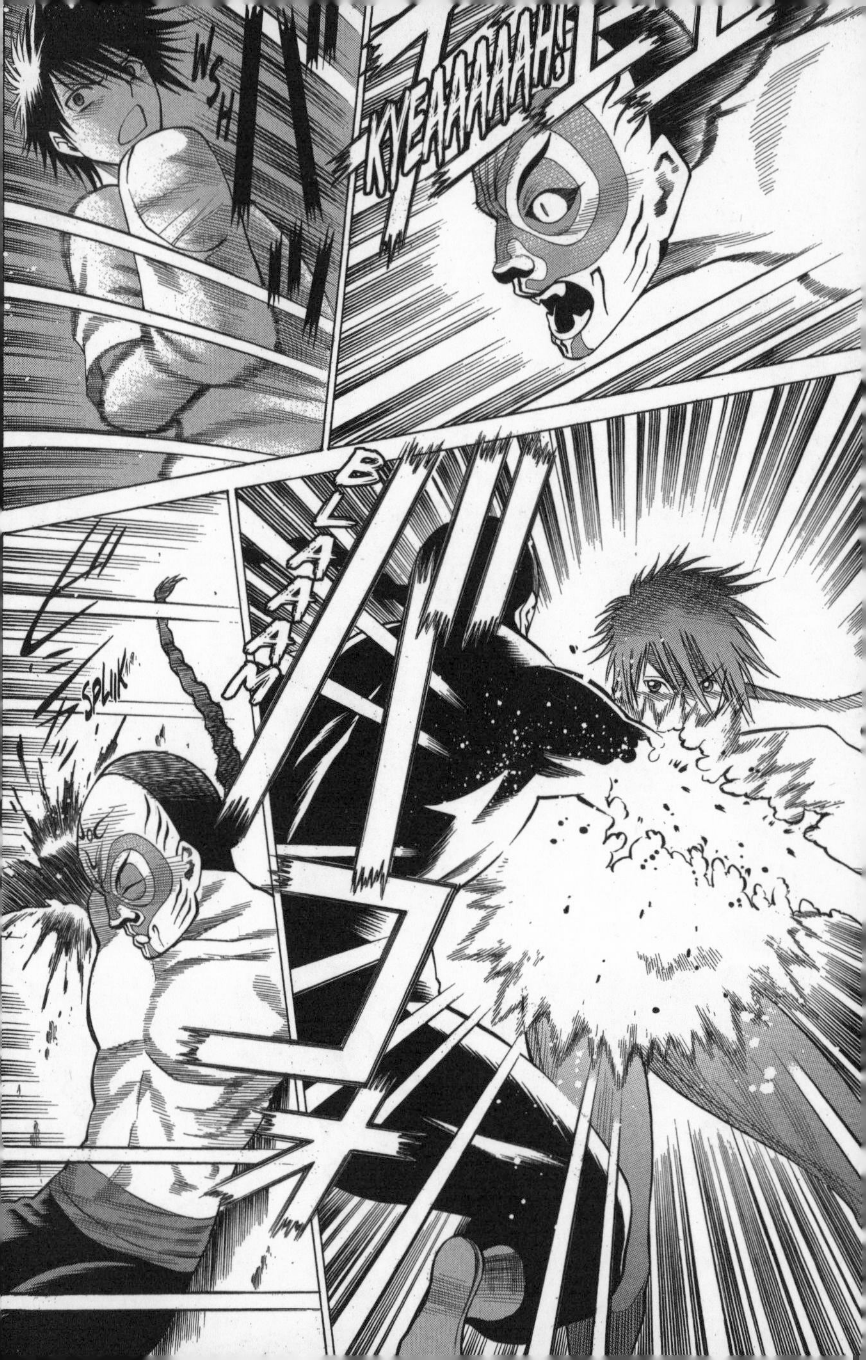
KYEAAAAAAH!
WSH
BLAAAM
SPLIIK

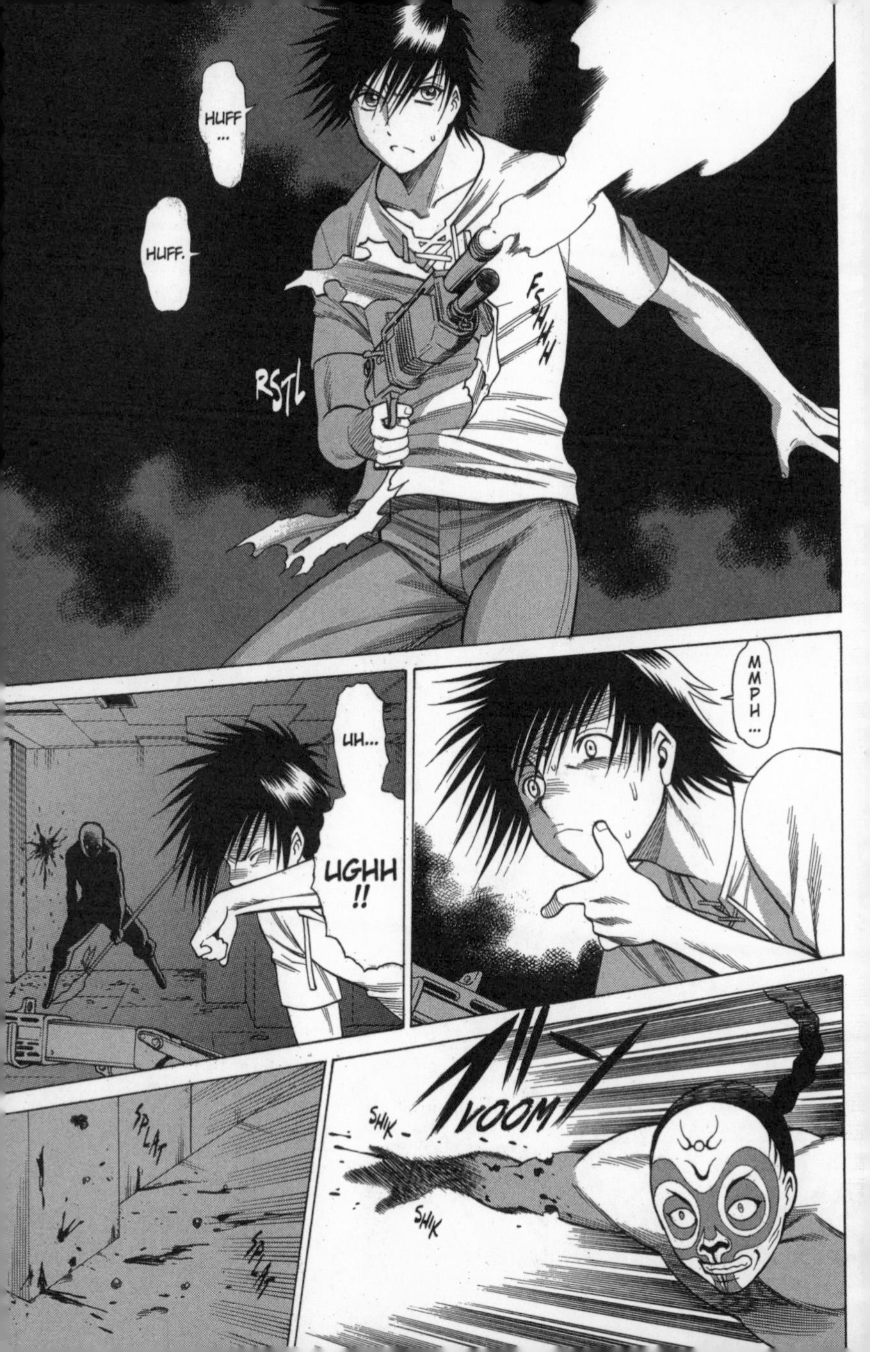
HUFF ...
HUFF.
FSHHH
RSTL
MMPH ...
UH...
UGHH !!
SHIK
VOOM
SHIK
SPLAT
SPLAT

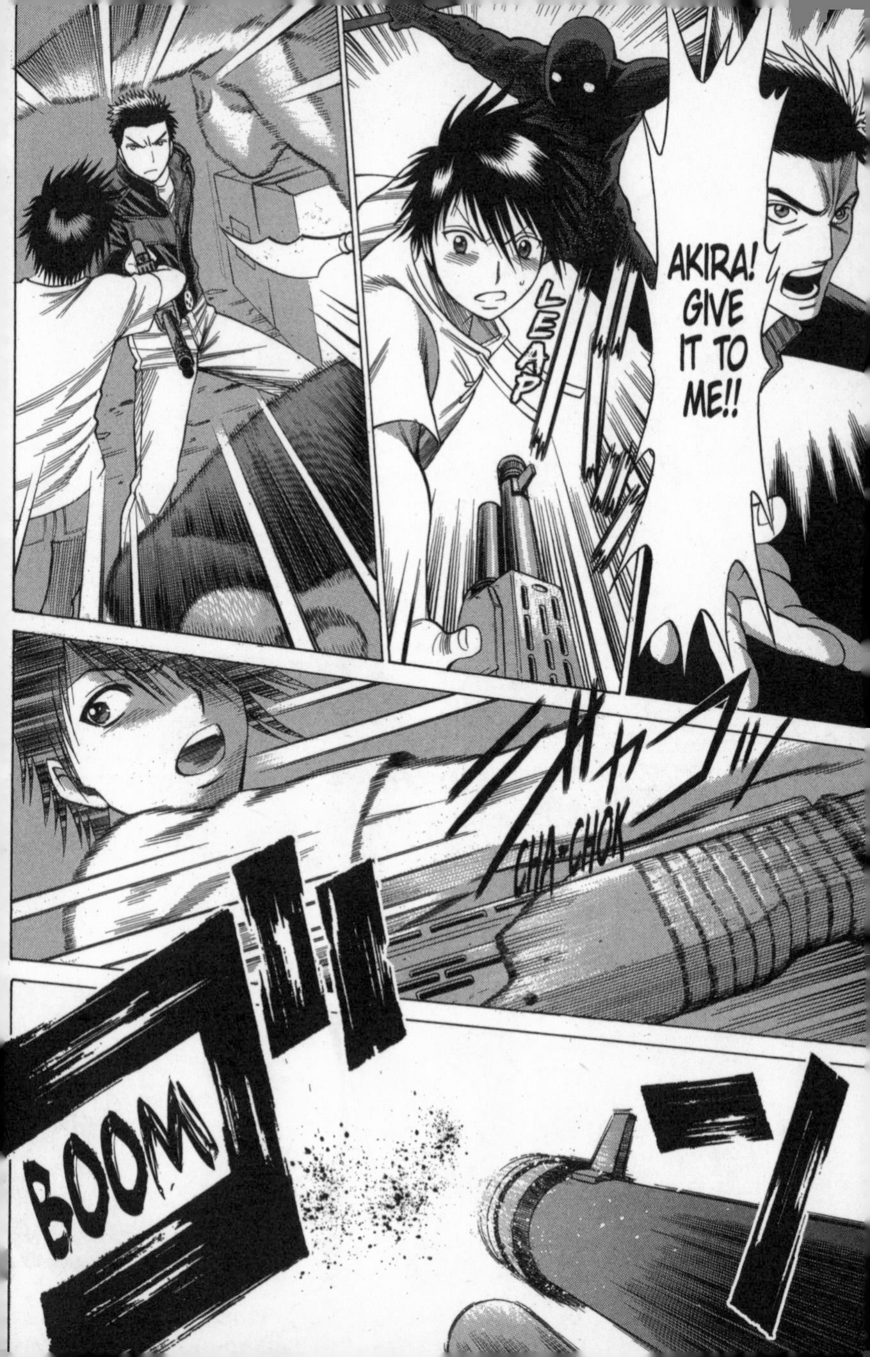
AKIRA! GIVE IT TO ME!!
LEAP
CHA-CHOK
BOOM

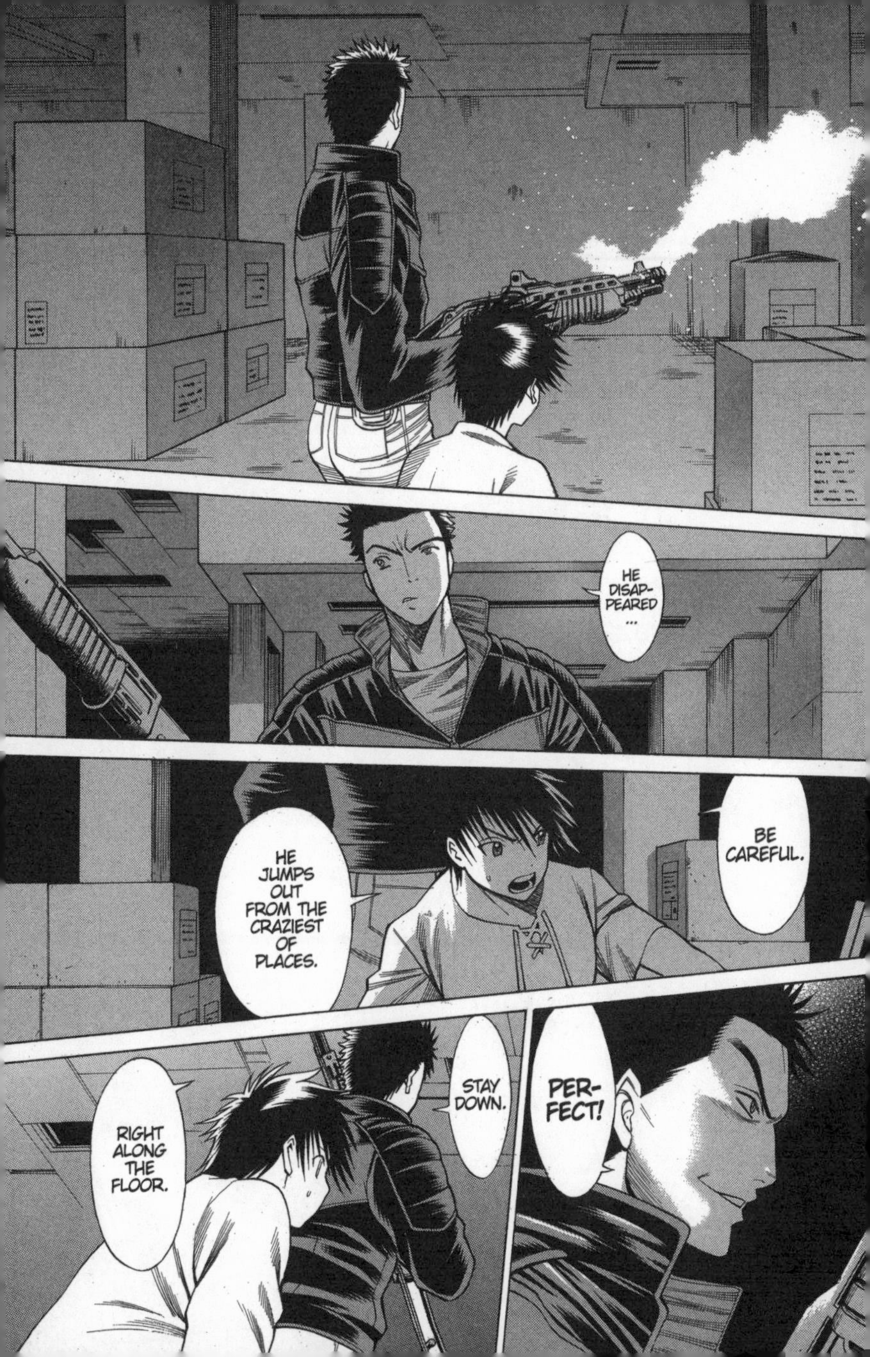
HE DISAP-PEARED ...
BE CAREFUL.
HE JUMPS OUT FROM THE CRAZIEST OF PLACES.
PER-FECT!
STAY DOWN.
RIGHT ALONG THE FLOOR.

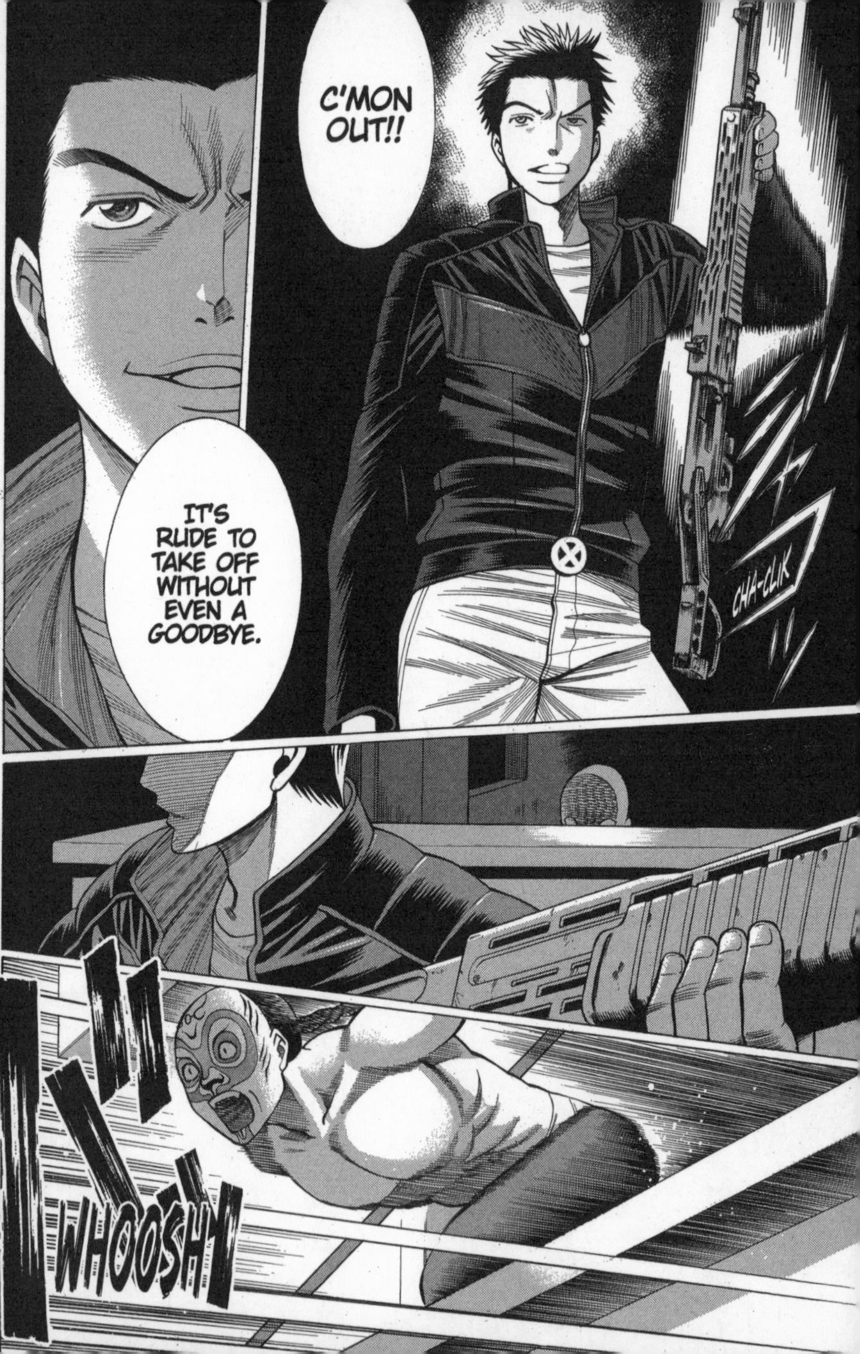
C'MON OUT!!
CHA-CLIK
IT'S RUDE TO TAKE OFF WITHOUT EVEN A GOODBYE.
WHOOSH

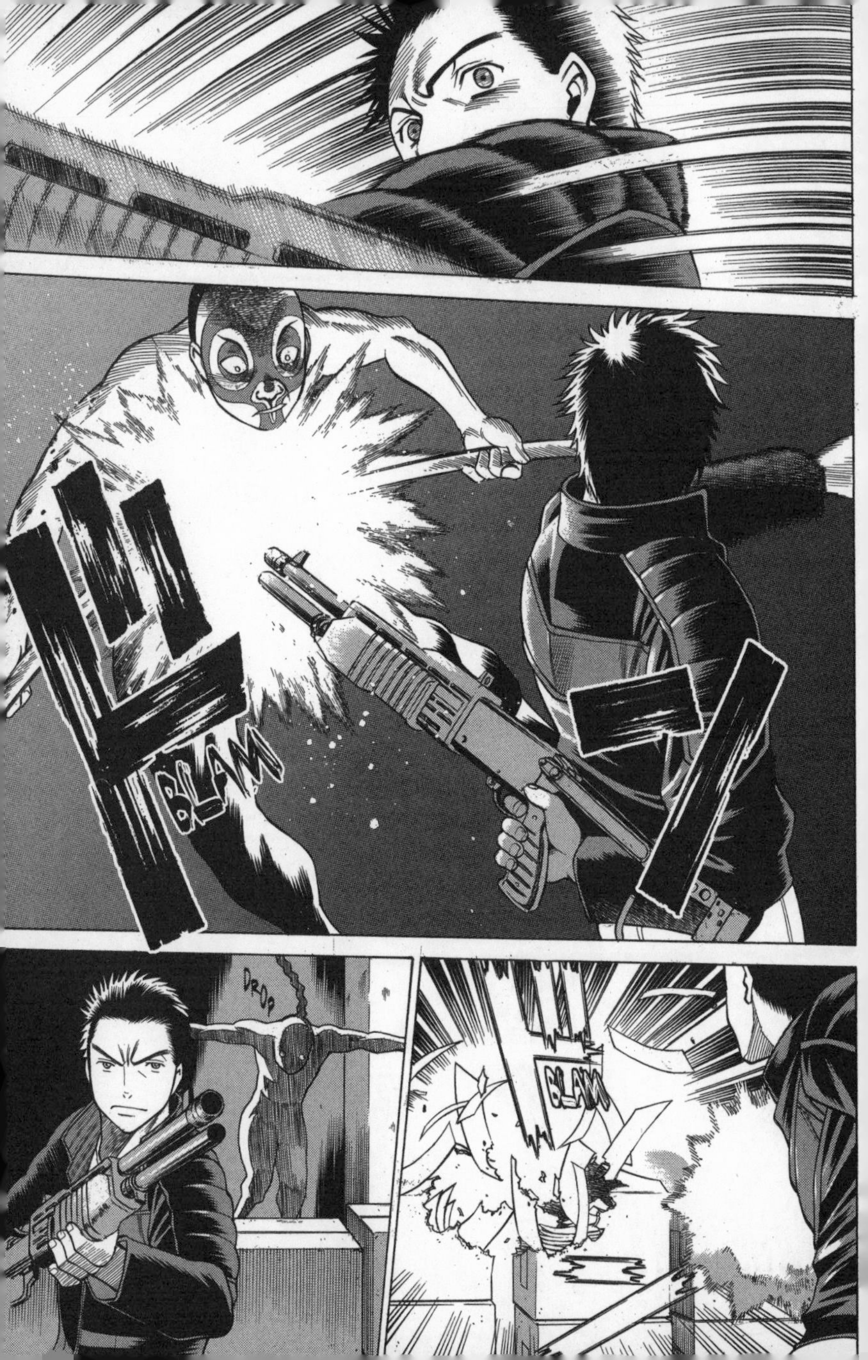
BLAM
BLAM
DROP

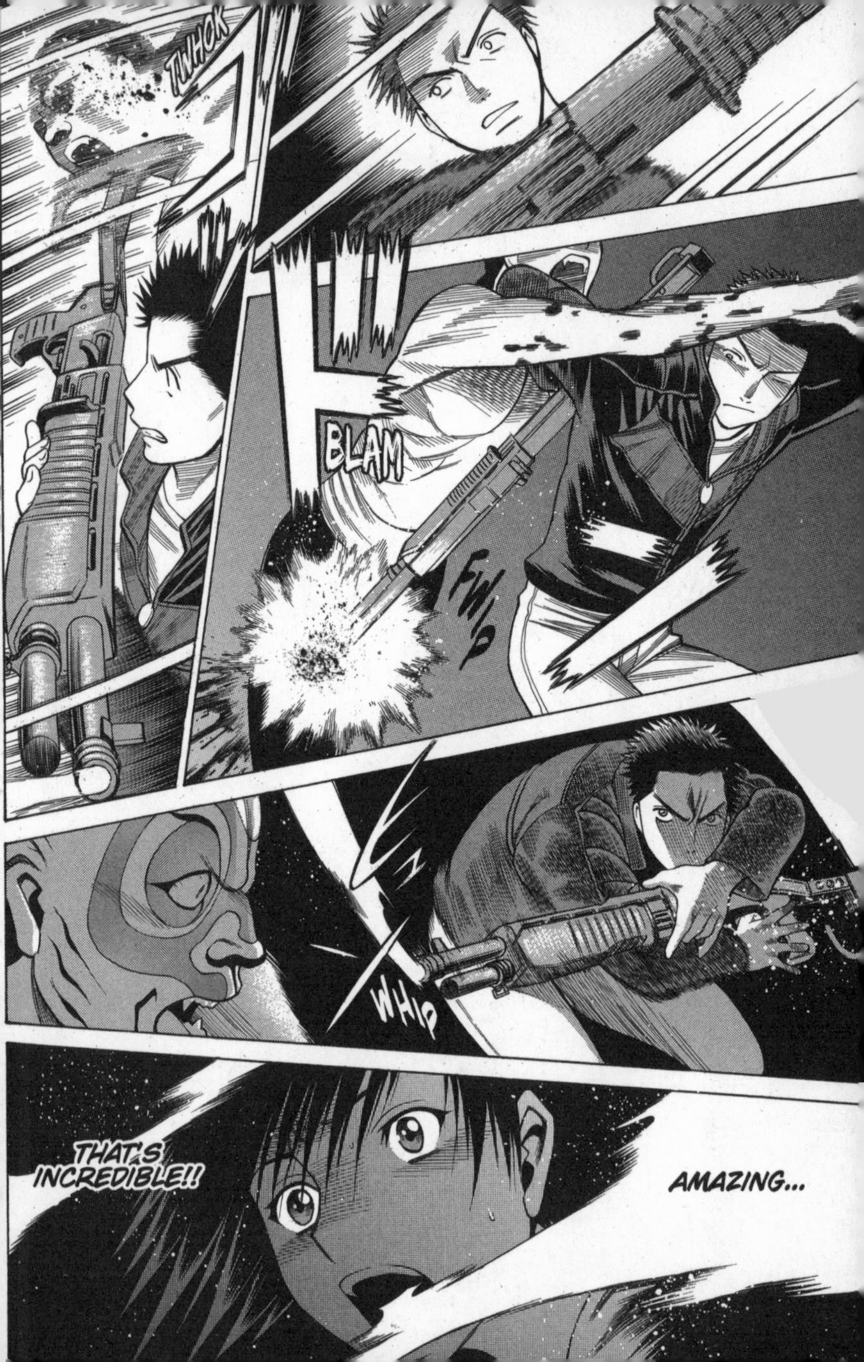
TWHOK
BLAM
FWIP
WHIP
AMAZING...
THAT'S INCREDIBLE!!

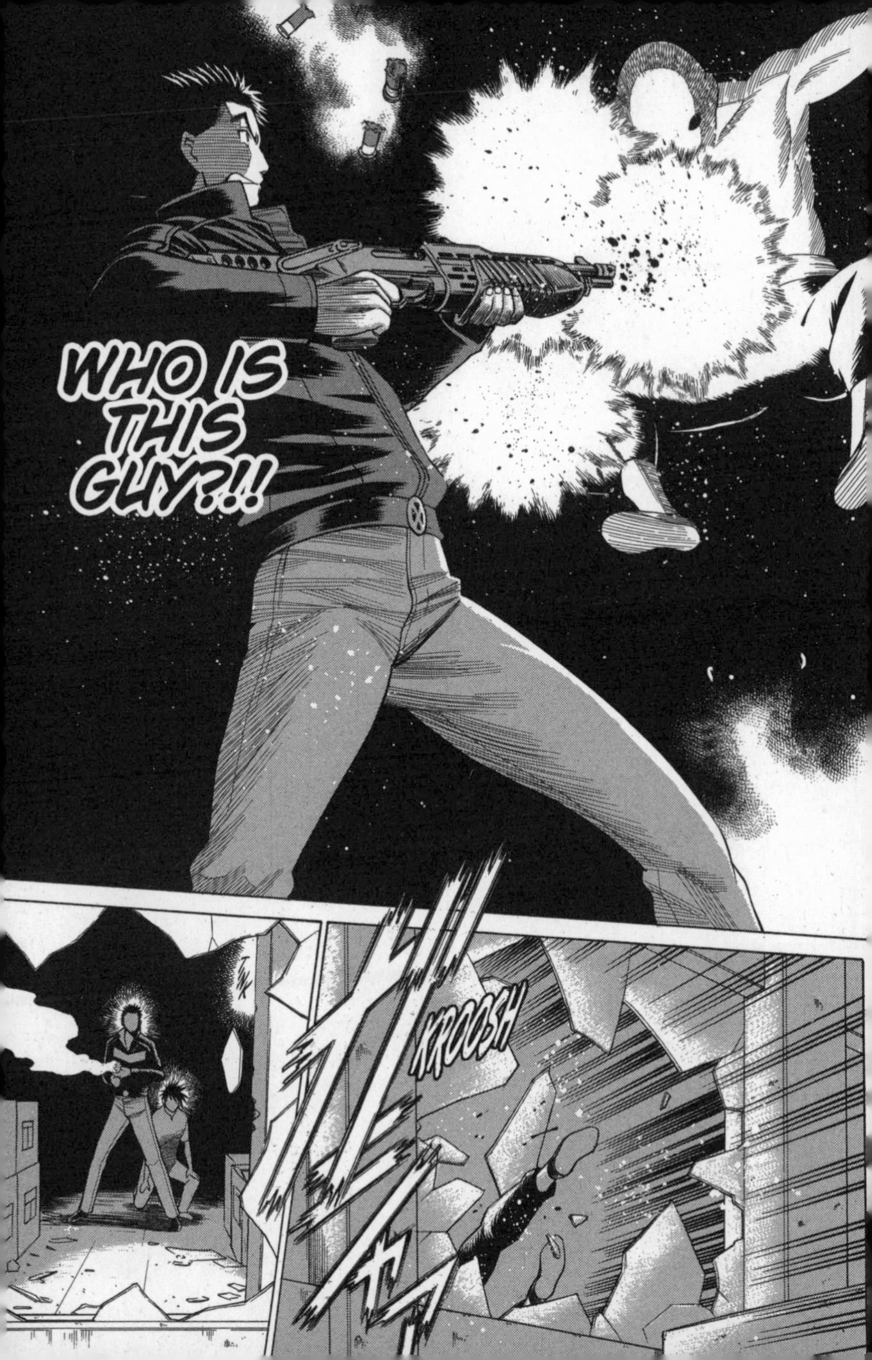
WHO IS THIS GUY?!!
KROOSH
TINK

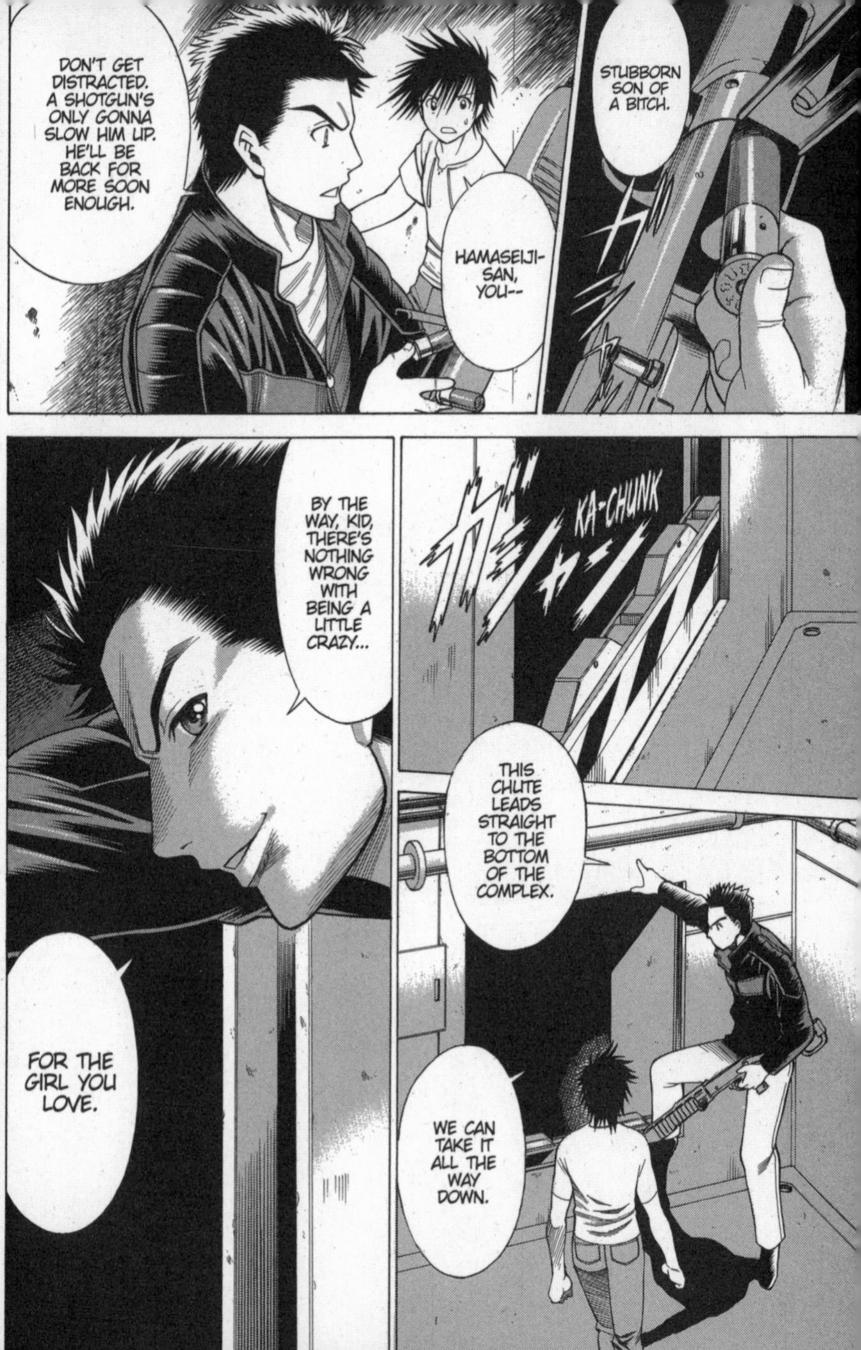
STUBBORN SON OF A BITCH.
HAMASEIJI-SAN, YOU--
DON'T GET DISTRACTED. A SHOTGUN'S ONLY GONNA SLOW HIM UP. HE'LL BE BACK FOR MORE SOON ENOUGH.
KA-CHUNK
THIS CHUTE LEADS STRAIGHT TO THE BOTTOM OF THE COMPLEX.
WE CAN TAKE IT ALL THE WAY DOWN.
BY THE WAY, KID, THERE'S NOTHING WRONG WITH BEING A LITTLE CRAZY...
FOR THE GIRL YOU LOVE.

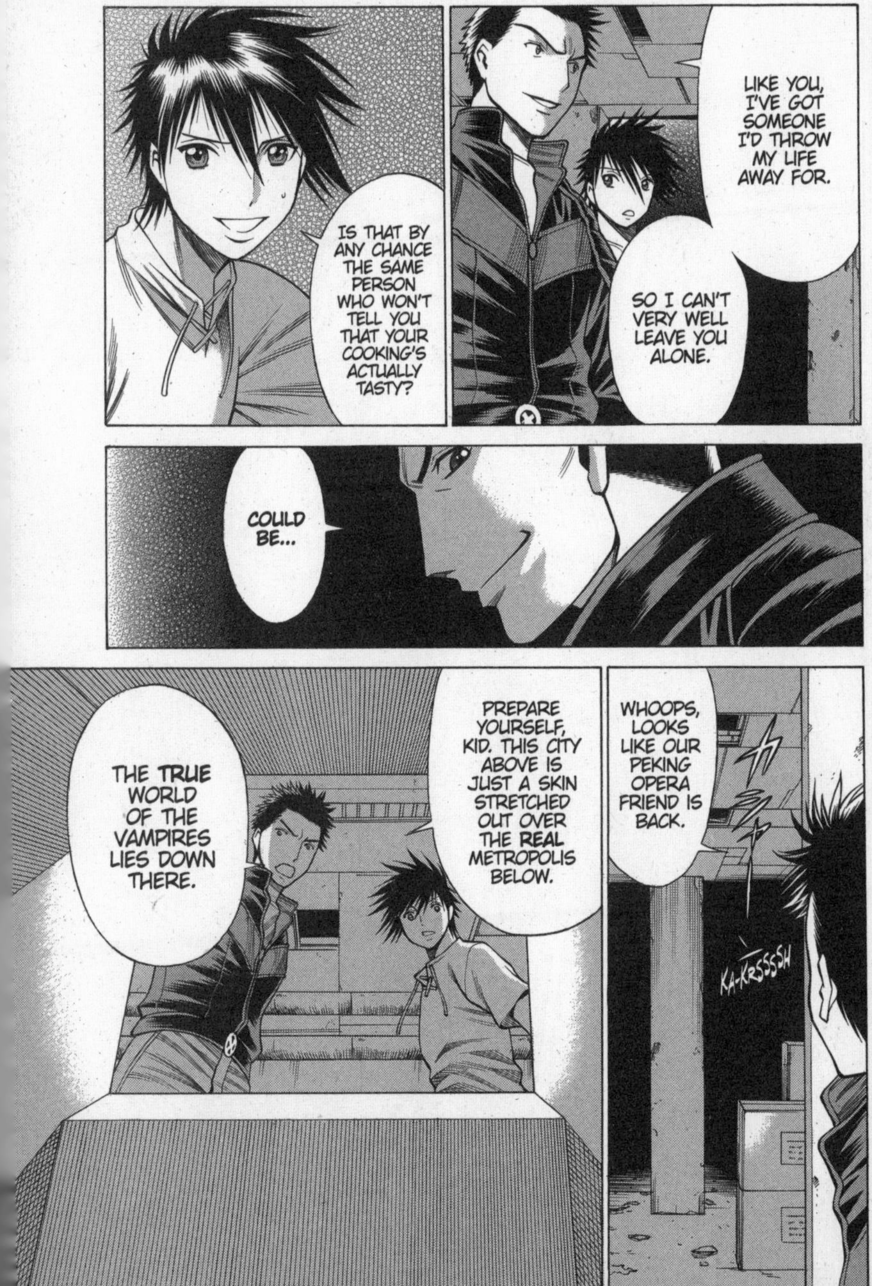
LIKE YOU, I'VE GOT SOMEONE I'D THROW MY LIFE AWAY FOR.
SO I CAN'T VERY WELL LEAVE YOU ALONE.
IS THAT BY ANY CHANCE THE SAME PERSON WHO WON'T TELL YOU THAT YOUR COOKING'S ACTUALLY TASTY?
COULD BE...
WHOOPS, LOOKS LIKE OUR PEKING OPERA FRIEND IS BACK.
KA-KRSSSSH
PREPARE YOURSELF, KID. THIS CITY ABOVE IS JUST A SKIN STRETCHED OUT OVER THE **REAL** METROPOLIS BELOW.
THE **TRUE** WORLD OF THE VAMPIRES LIES DOWN THERE.

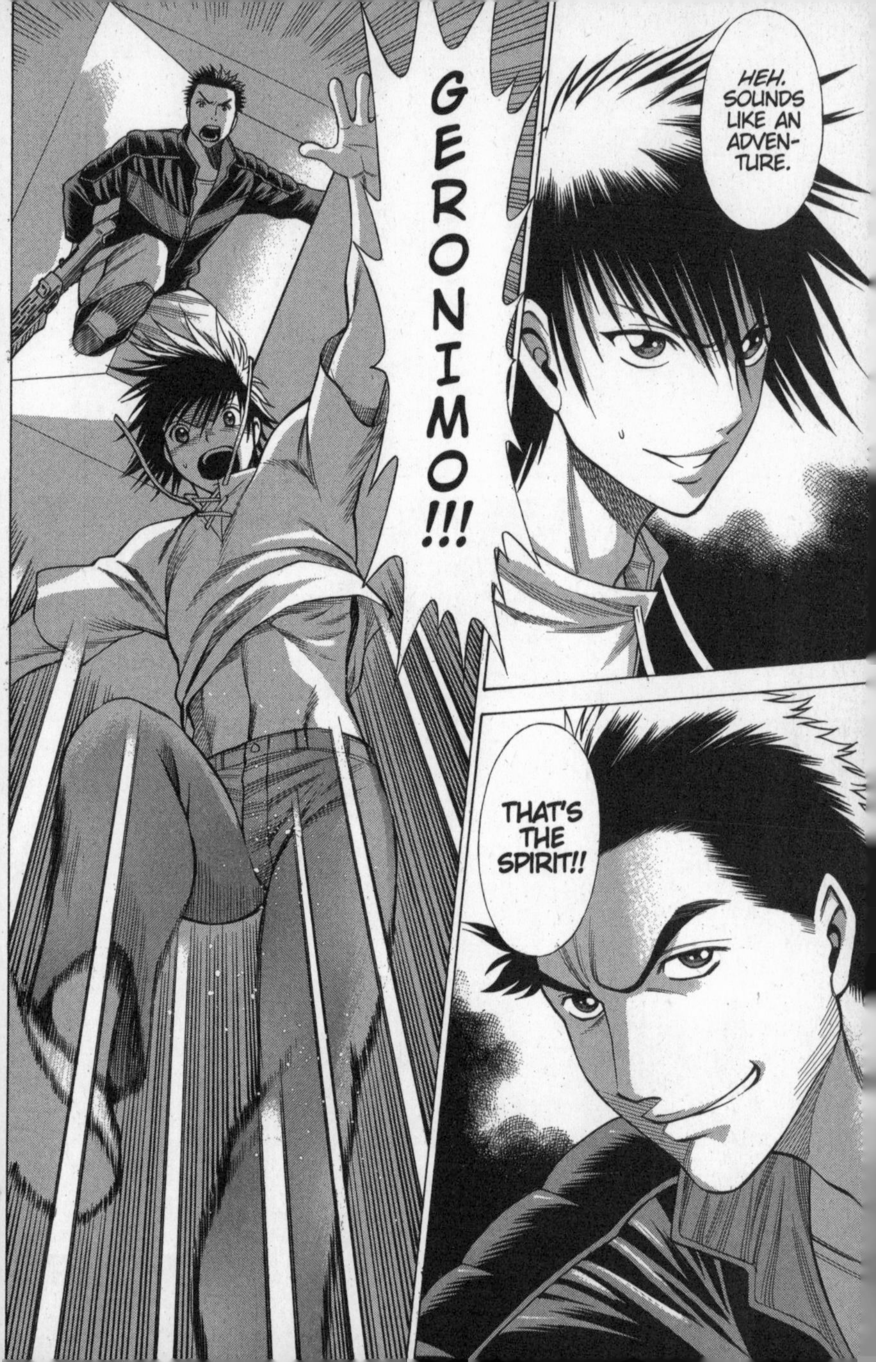
HEH. SOUNDS LIKE AN ADVEN-TURE.
THAT'S THE SPIRIT!!
GERONIMO!!!

Chapter 26: Intermedio

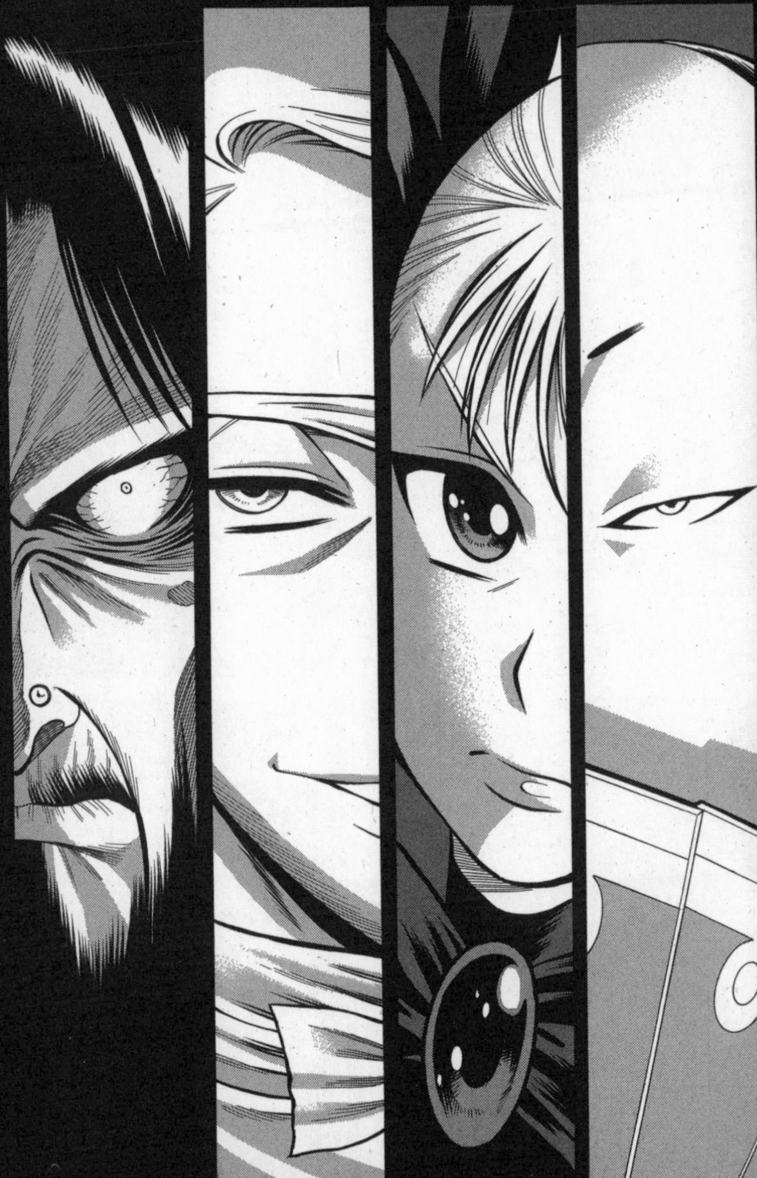

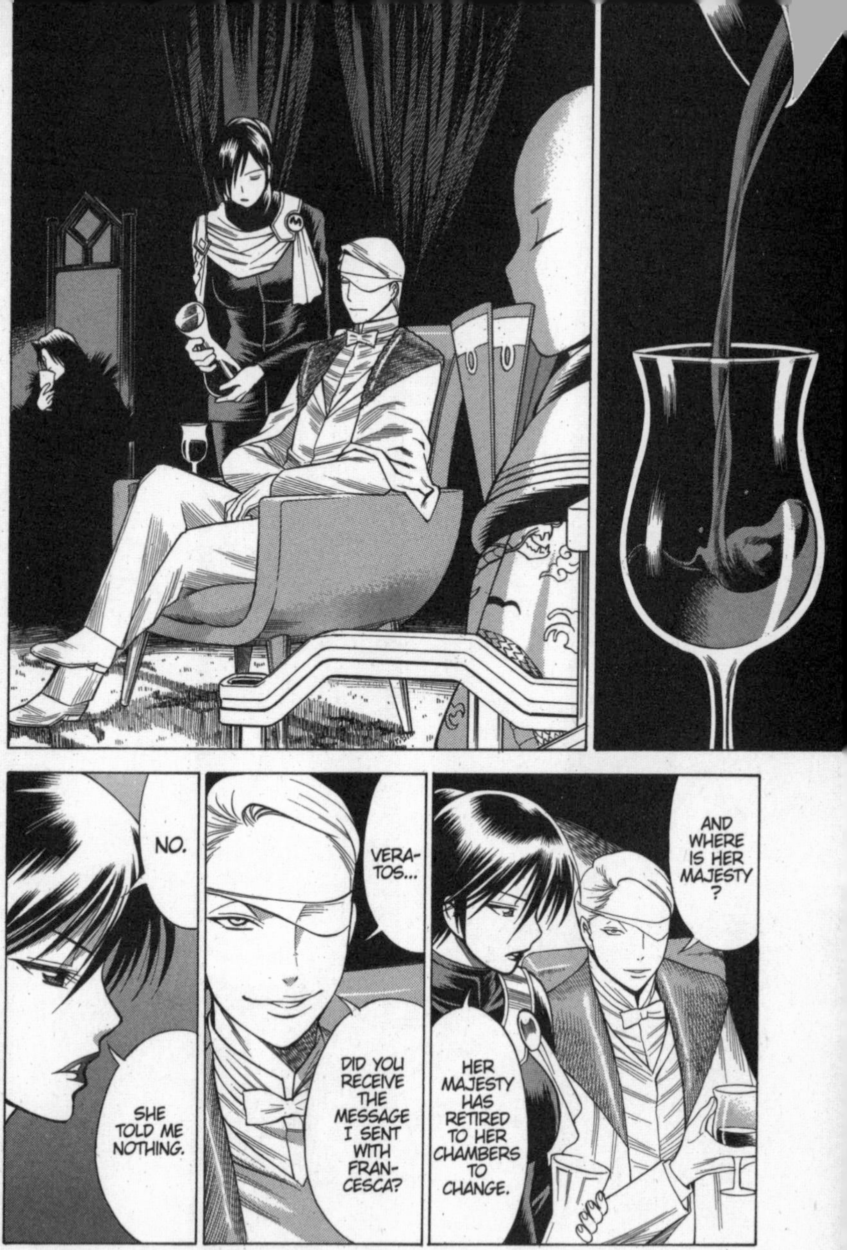
AND WHERE IS HER MAJESTY?
HER MAJESTY HAS RETIRED TO HER CHAMBERS TO CHANGE.
VERATOS...
DID YOU RECEIVE THE MESSAGE I SENT WITH FRANCESCA?
NO.
SHE TOLD ME NOTHING.

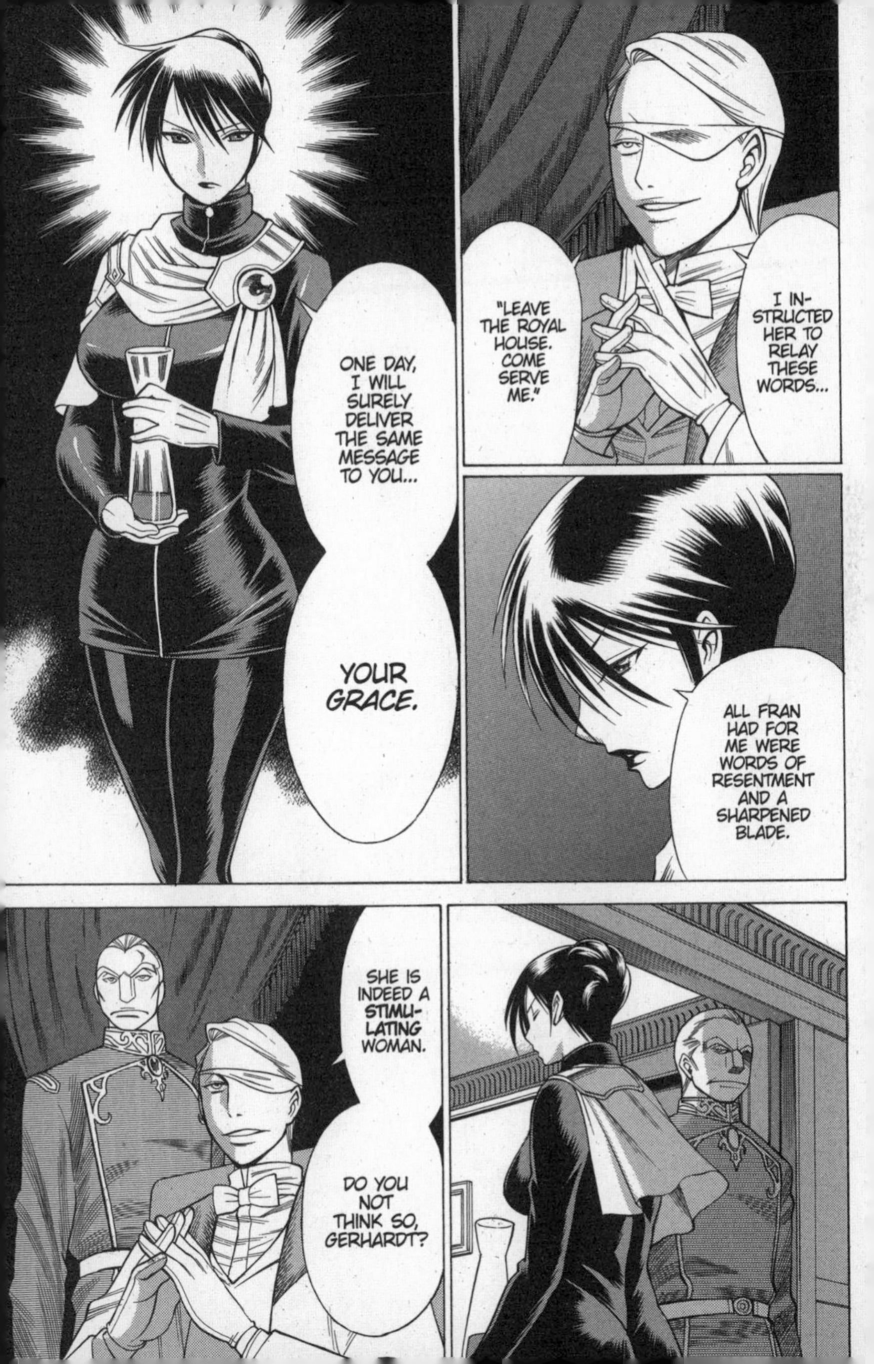
I IN-STRUCTED HER TO RELAY THESE WORDS...
"LEAVE THE ROYAL HOUSE. COME SERVE ME."
ALL FRAN HAD FOR ME WERE WORDS OF RESENTMENT AND A SHARPENED BLADE.
ONE DAY, I WILL SURELY DELIVER THE SAME MESSAGE TO YOU...
YOUR GRACE.
SHE IS INDEED A STIMU-LATING WOMAN.
DO YOU NOT THINK SO, GERHARDT?

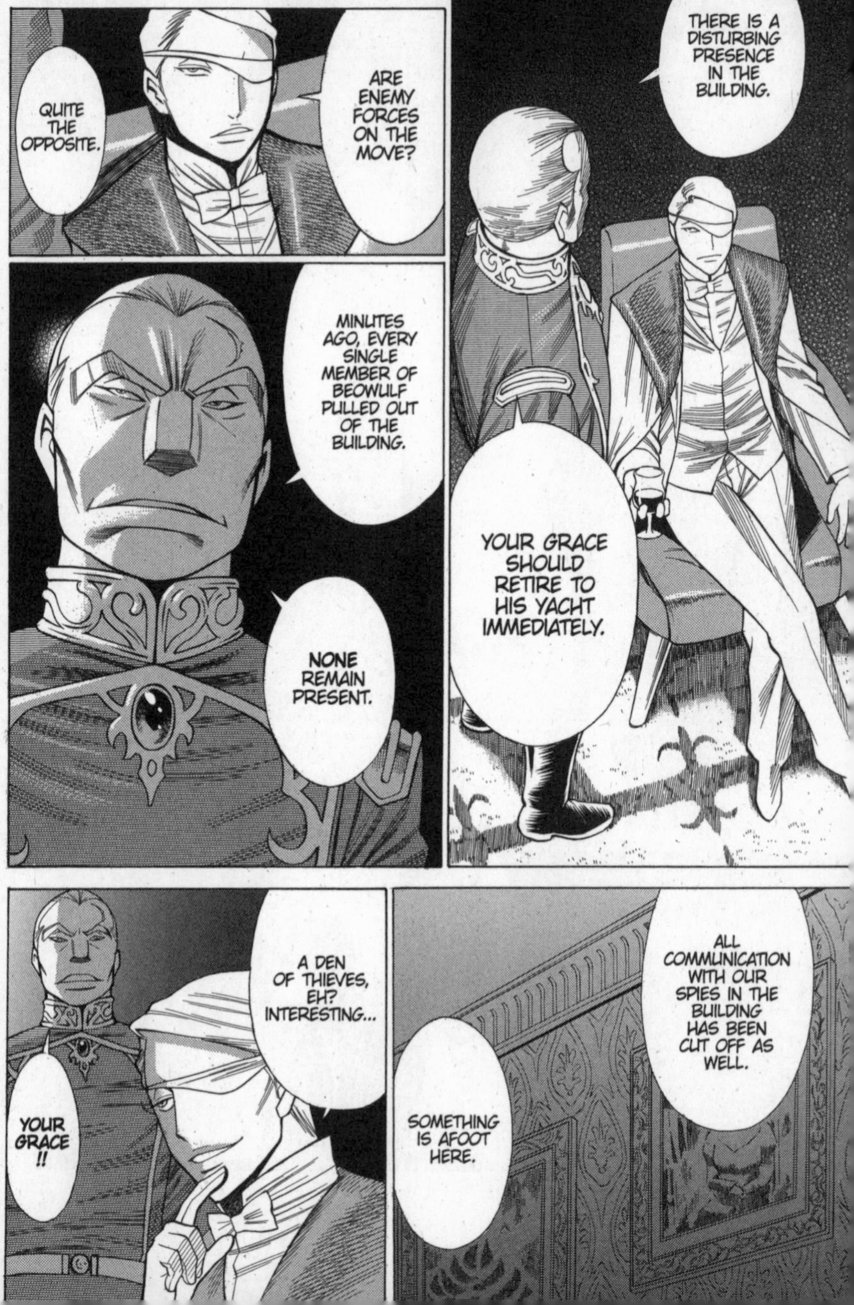
THERE IS A DISTURBING PRESENCE IN THE BUILDING.
YOUR GRACE SHOULD RETIRE TO HIS YACHT IMMEDIATELY.
ARE ENEMY FORCES ON THE MOVE?
QUITE THE OPPOSITE.
MINUTES AGO, EVERY SINGLE MEMBER OF BEOWULF PULLED OUT OF THE BUILDING.
NONE REMAIN PRESENT.
ALL COMMUNICATION WITH OUR SPIES IN THE BUILDING HAS BEEN CUT OFF AS WELL.
SOMETHING IS AFOOT HERE.
A DEN OF THIEVES, EH? INTERESTING...
YOUR GRACE !!

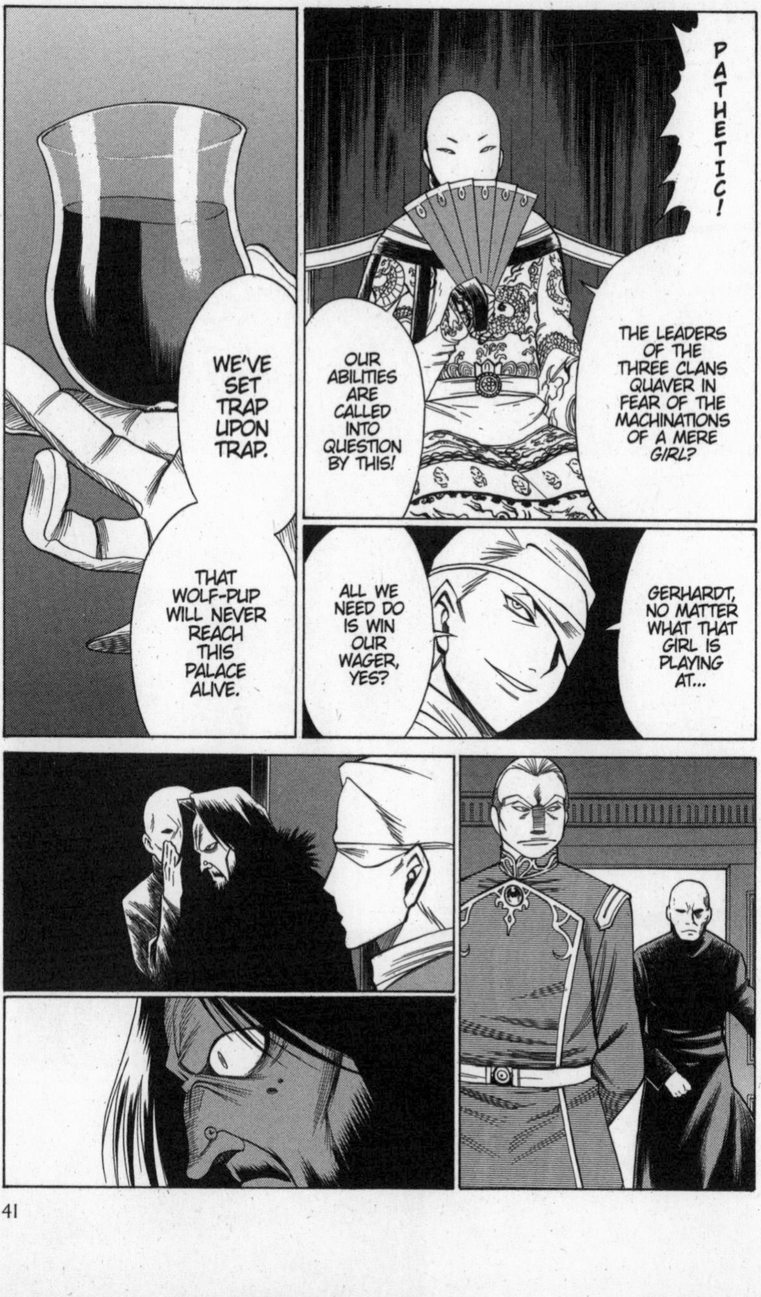
PATHETIC!
THE LEADERS OF THE THREE CLANS QUAVER IN FEAR OF THE MACHINATIONS OF A MERE *GIRL*?
OUR ABILITIES ARE CALLED INTO QUESTION BY THIS!
GERHARDT, NO MATTER WHAT THAT GIRL IS PLAYING AT...
ALL WE NEED DO IS WIN OUR WAGER, YES?
WE'VE SET TRAP UPON TRAP.
THAT WOLF-PUP WILL NEVER REACH THIS PALACE ALIVE.

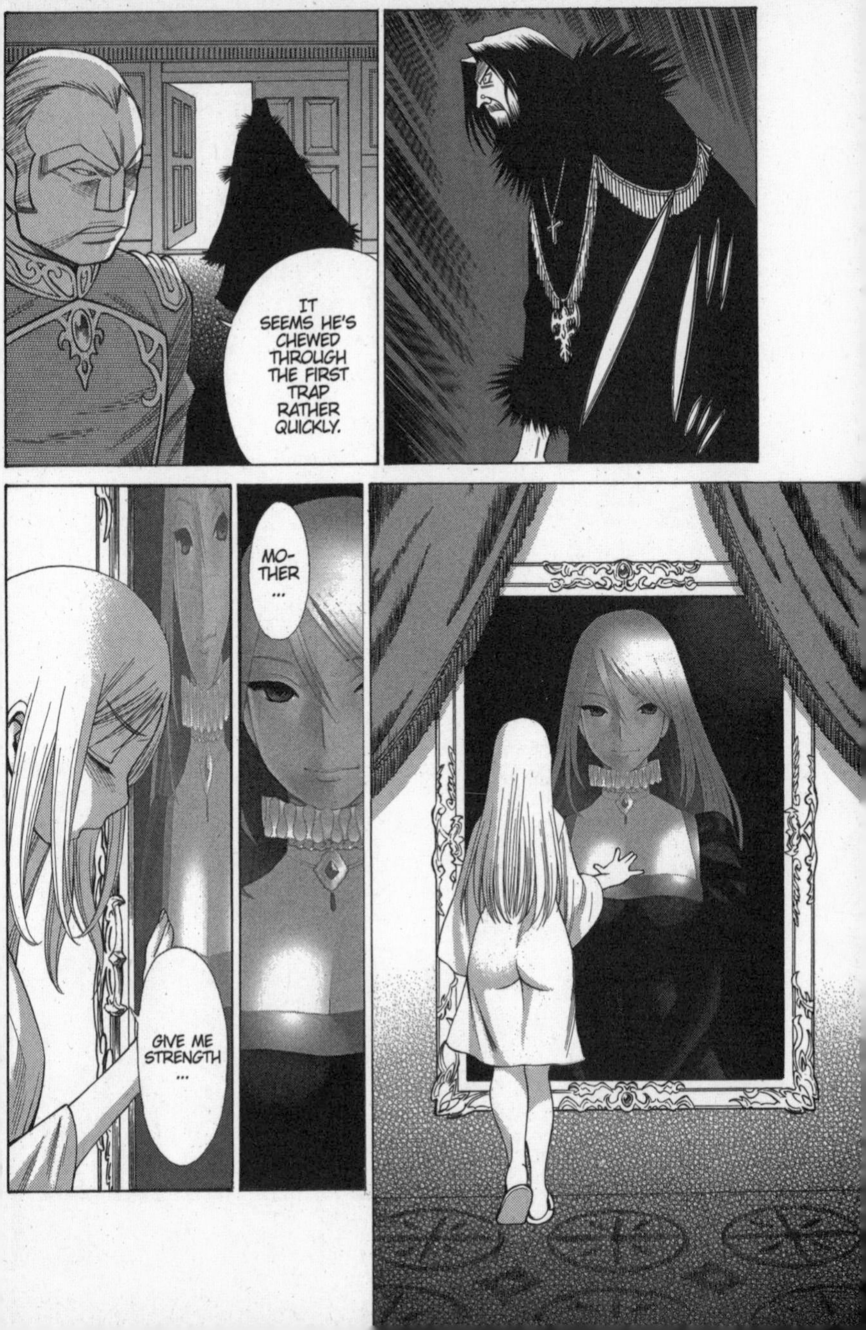
IT SEEMS HE'S CHEWED THROUGH THE FIRST TRAP RATHER QUICKLY.
MO-THER ...
GIVE ME STRENGTH ...

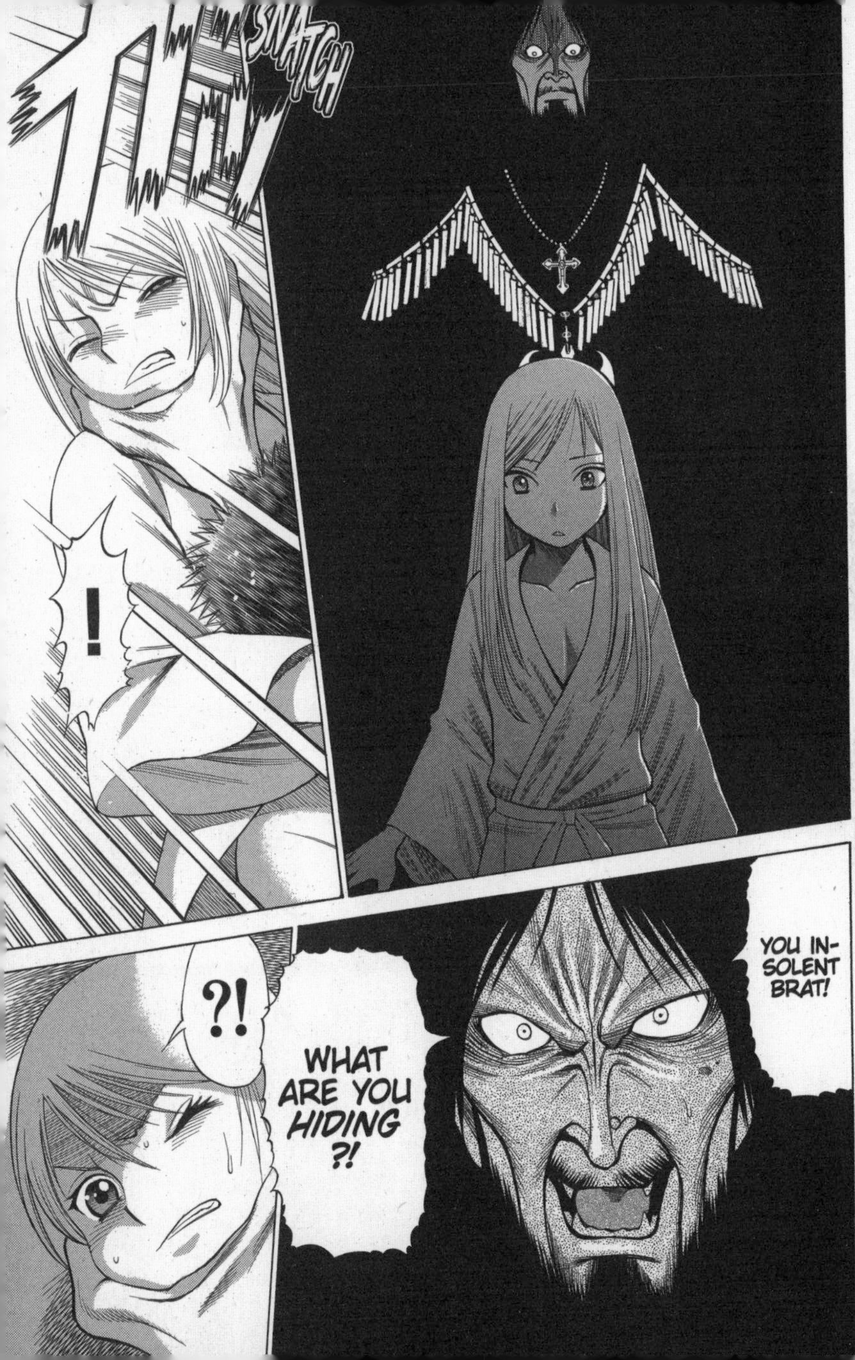
SNATCH
!
YOU IN-
SOLENT
BRAT!
WHAT
ARE YOU
HIDING
?!
?!

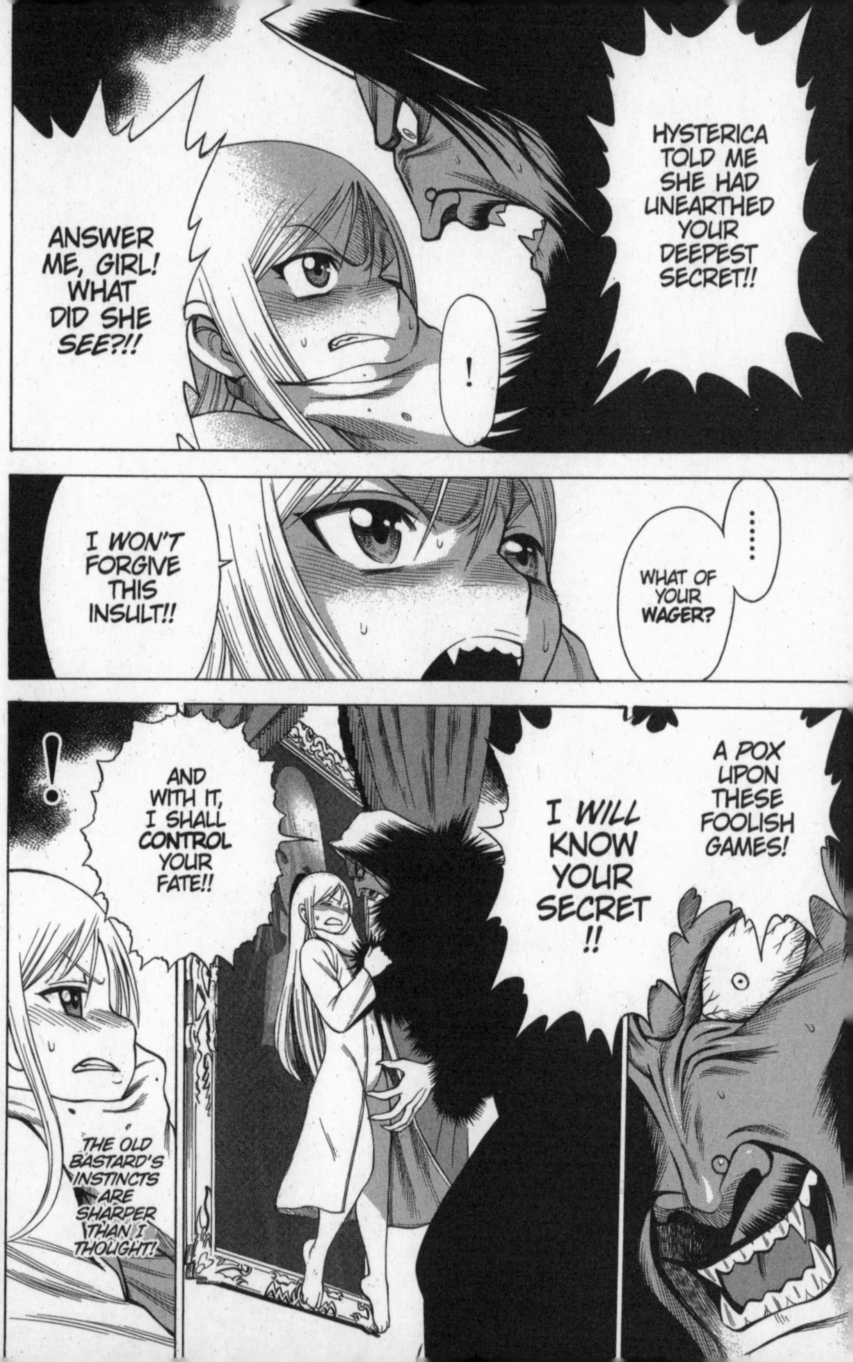
HYSTERICA TOLD ME SHE HAD UNEARTHED YOUR DEEPEST SECRET!!
!
ANSWER ME, GIRL! WHAT DID SHE SEE?!!
......
WHAT OF YOUR WAGER?
I WON'T FORGIVE THIS INSULT!!
A POX UPON THESE FOOLISH GAMES!
I WILL KNOW YOUR SECRET!!
AND WITH IT, I SHALL CONTROL YOUR FATE!!
!
THE OLD BASTARD'S INSTINCTS ARE SHARPER THAN I THOUGHT!

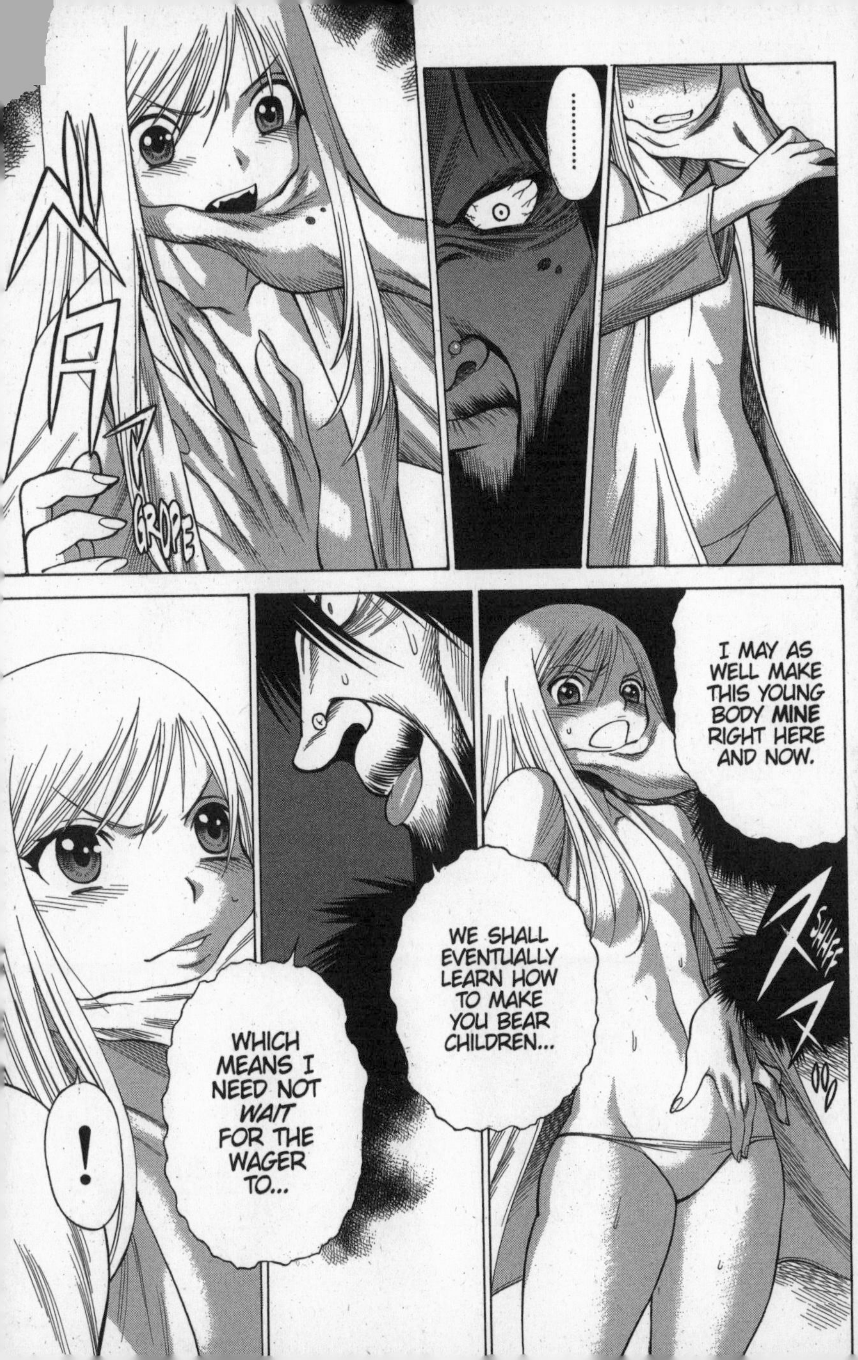
....
GROPE
I MAY AS WELL MAKE THIS YOUNG BODY MINE RIGHT HERE AND NOW.
SHUFF
WE SHALL EVENTUALLY LEARN HOW TO MAKE YOU BEAR CHILDREN...
WHICH MEANS I NEED NOT *WAIT* FOR THE WAGER TO...
!

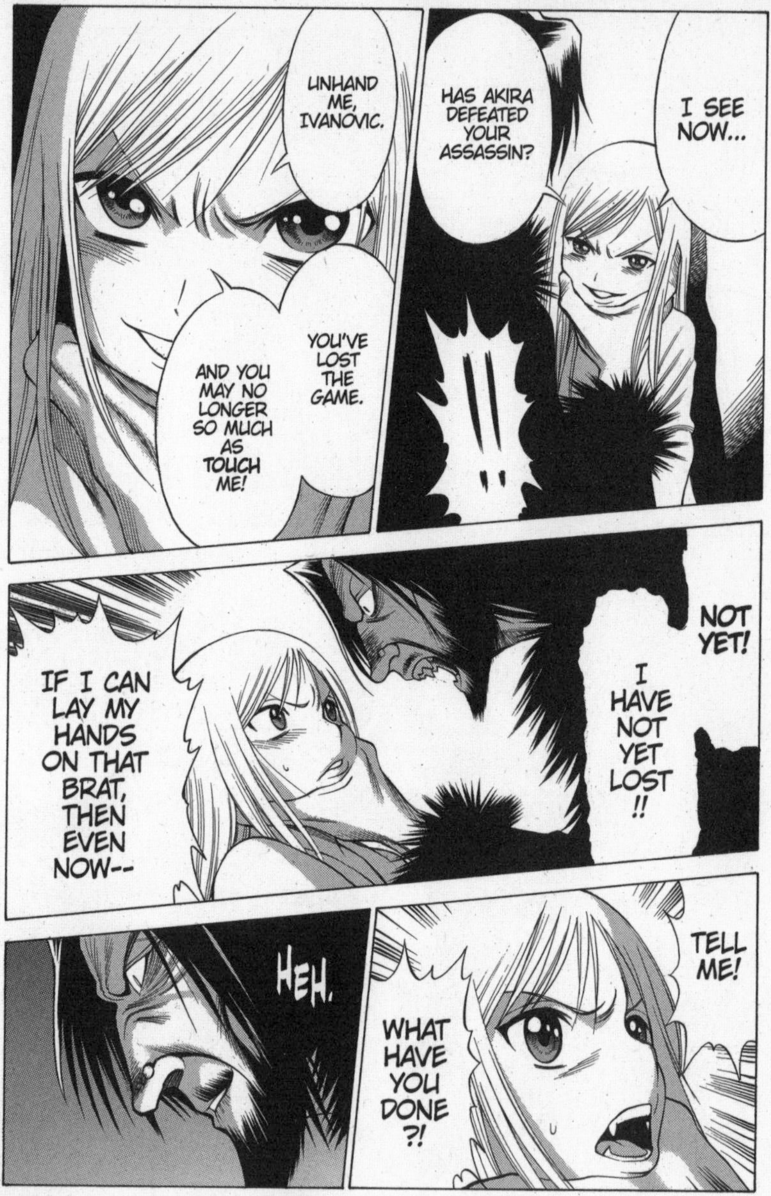
I SEE NOW...
HAS AKIRA DEFEATED YOUR ASSASSIN?
UNHAND ME, IVANOVIC.
YOU'VE LOST THE GAME.
AND YOU MAY NO LONGER SO MUCH AS TOUCH ME!
NOT YET!
I HAVE NOT YET LOST !!
IF I CAN LAY MY HANDS ON THAT BRAT, THEN EVEN NOW--
TELL ME!
WHAT HAVE YOU DONE ?!
HEH.

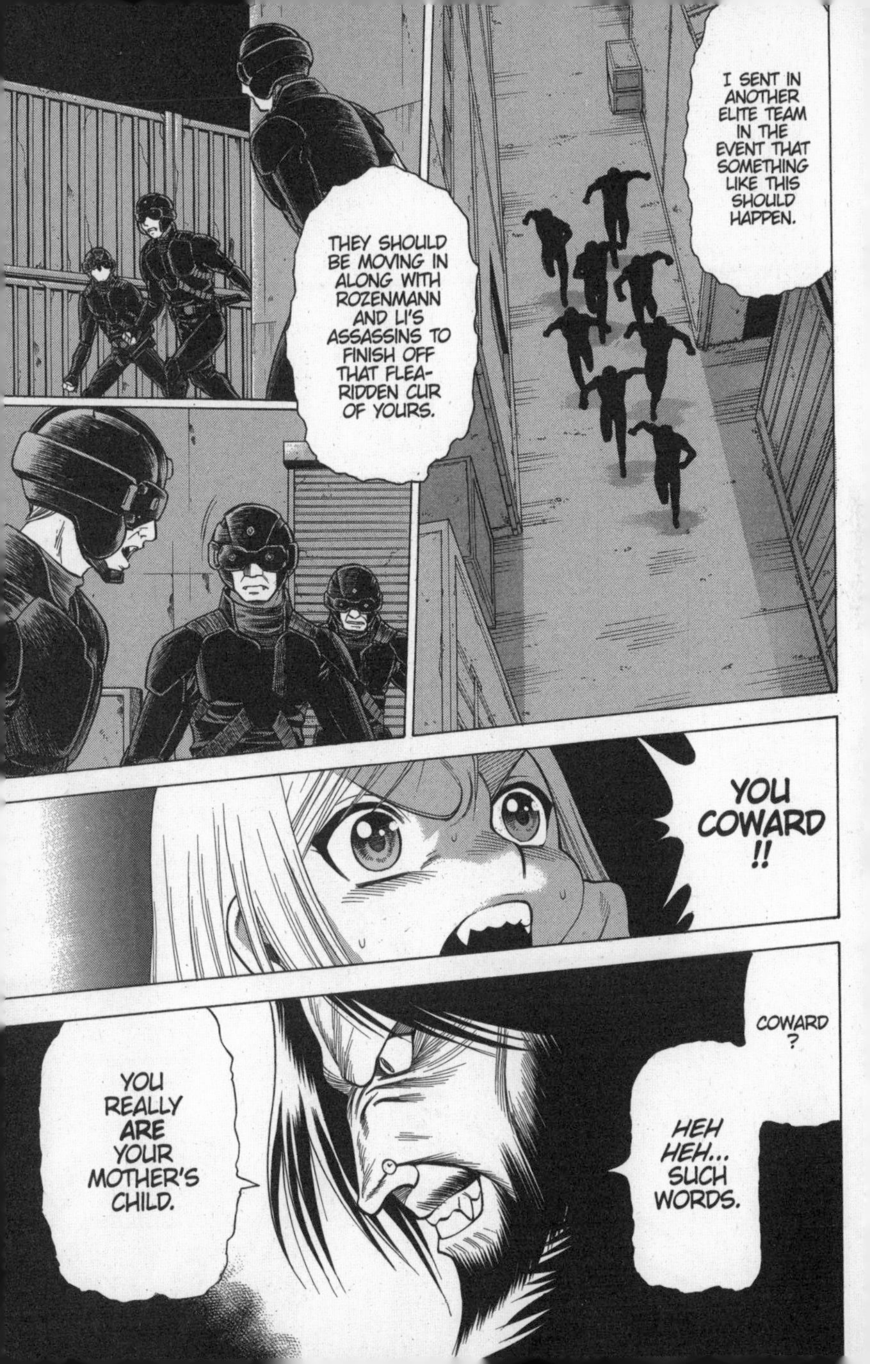
I SENT IN ANOTHER ELITE TEAM IN THE EVENT THAT SOMETHING LIKE THIS SHOULD HAPPEN.
THEY SHOULD BE MOVING IN ALONG WITH ROZENMANN AND LI'S ASSASSINS TO FINISH OFF THAT FLEA-RIDDEN CUR OF YOURS.
YOU COWARD !!
COWARD ?
HEH HEH... SUCH WORDS.
YOU REALLY ARE YOUR MOTHER'S CHILD.

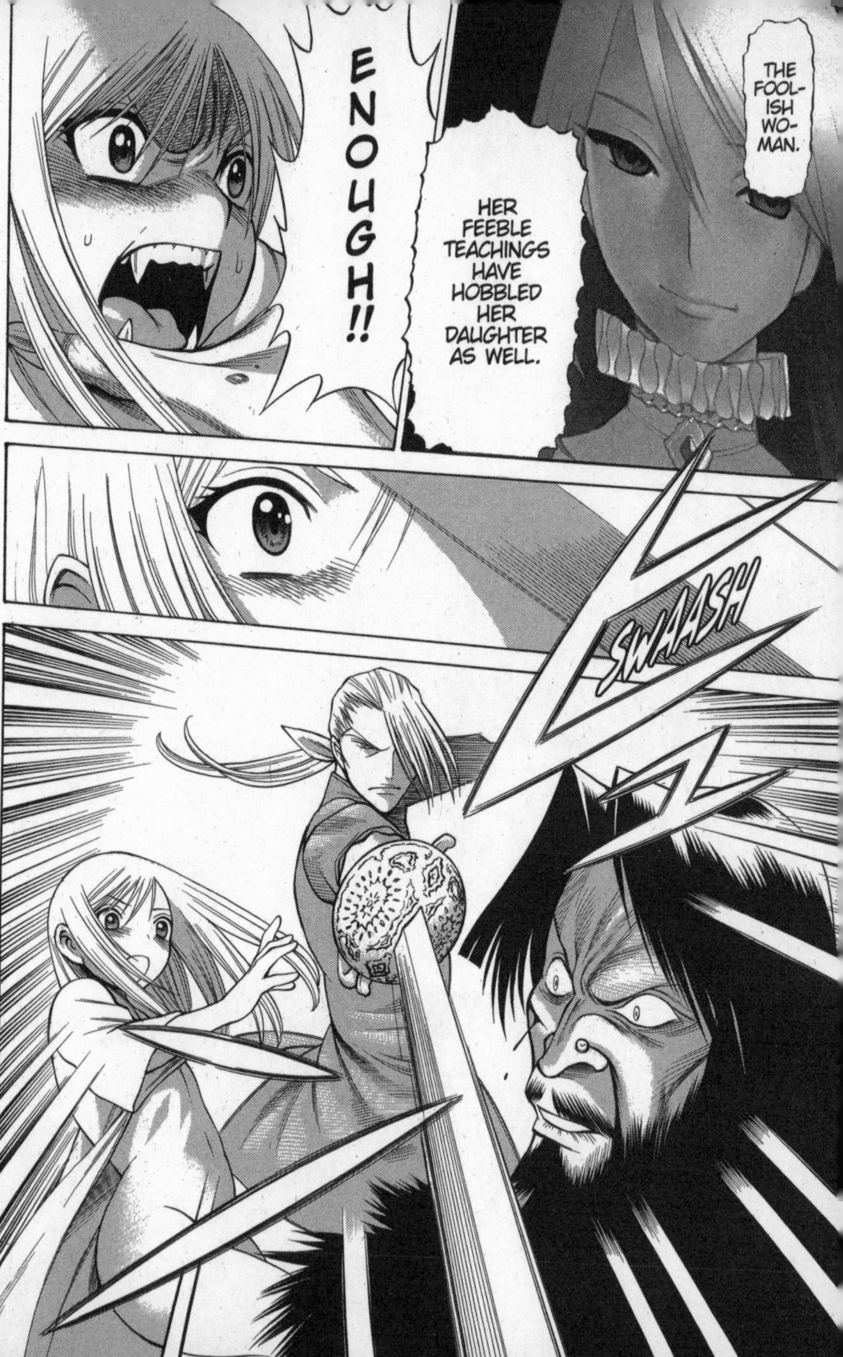
THE FOOL-ISH WO-MAN.
HER FEEBLE TEACHINGS HAVE HOBBLED HER DAUGHTER AS WELL.
ENOUGH!!
SWAASH

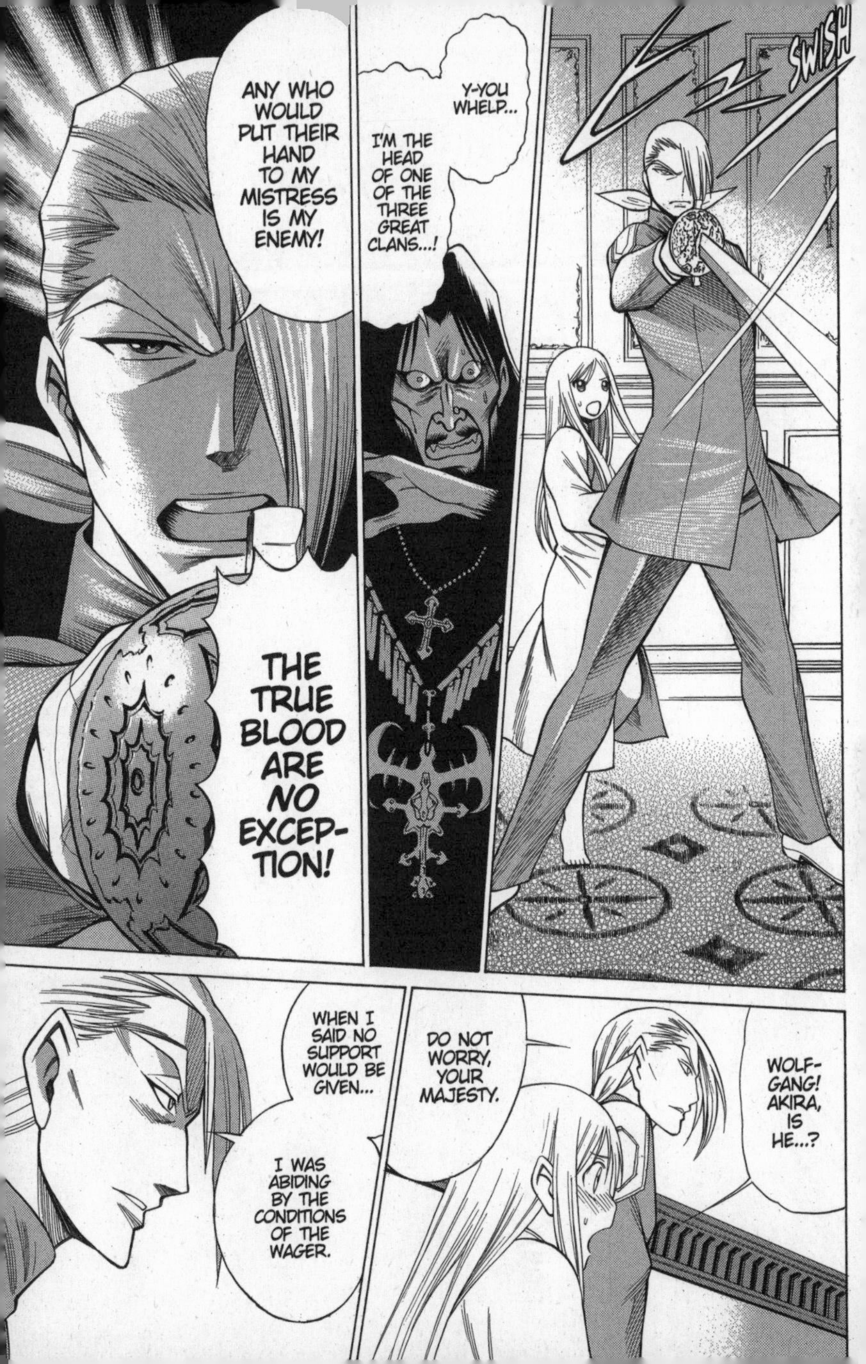
SWISH
Y-YOU WHELP...
I'M THE HEAD OF ONE OF THE THREE GREAT CLANS...!
ANY WHO WOULD PUT THEIR HAND TO MY MISTRESS IS MY ENEMY!
THE TRUE BLOOD ARE NO EXCEPTION!
WOLF-GANG! AKIRA, IS HE...?
DO NOT WORRY, YOUR MAJESTY.
WHEN I SAID NO SUPPORT WOULD BE GIVEN...
I WAS ABIDING BY THE CONDITIONS OF THE WAGER.

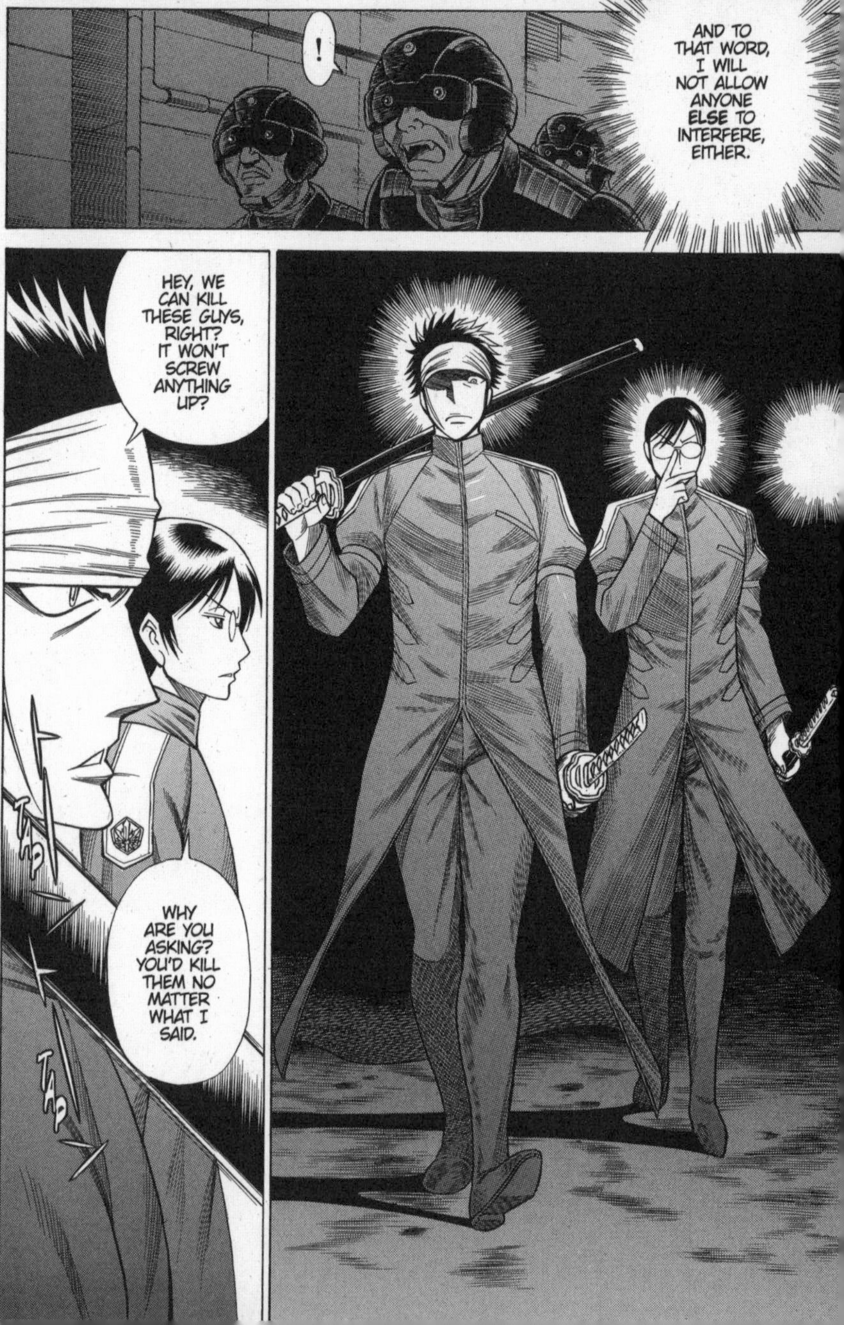
AND TO THAT WORD, I WILL NOT ALLOW ANYONE ELSE TO INTERFERE, EITHER.
!
HEY, WE CAN KILL THESE GUYS, RIGHT? IT WON'T SCREW ANYTHING UP?
TAP
WHY ARE YOU ASKING? YOU'D KILL THEM NO MATTER WHAT I SAID.
TAP

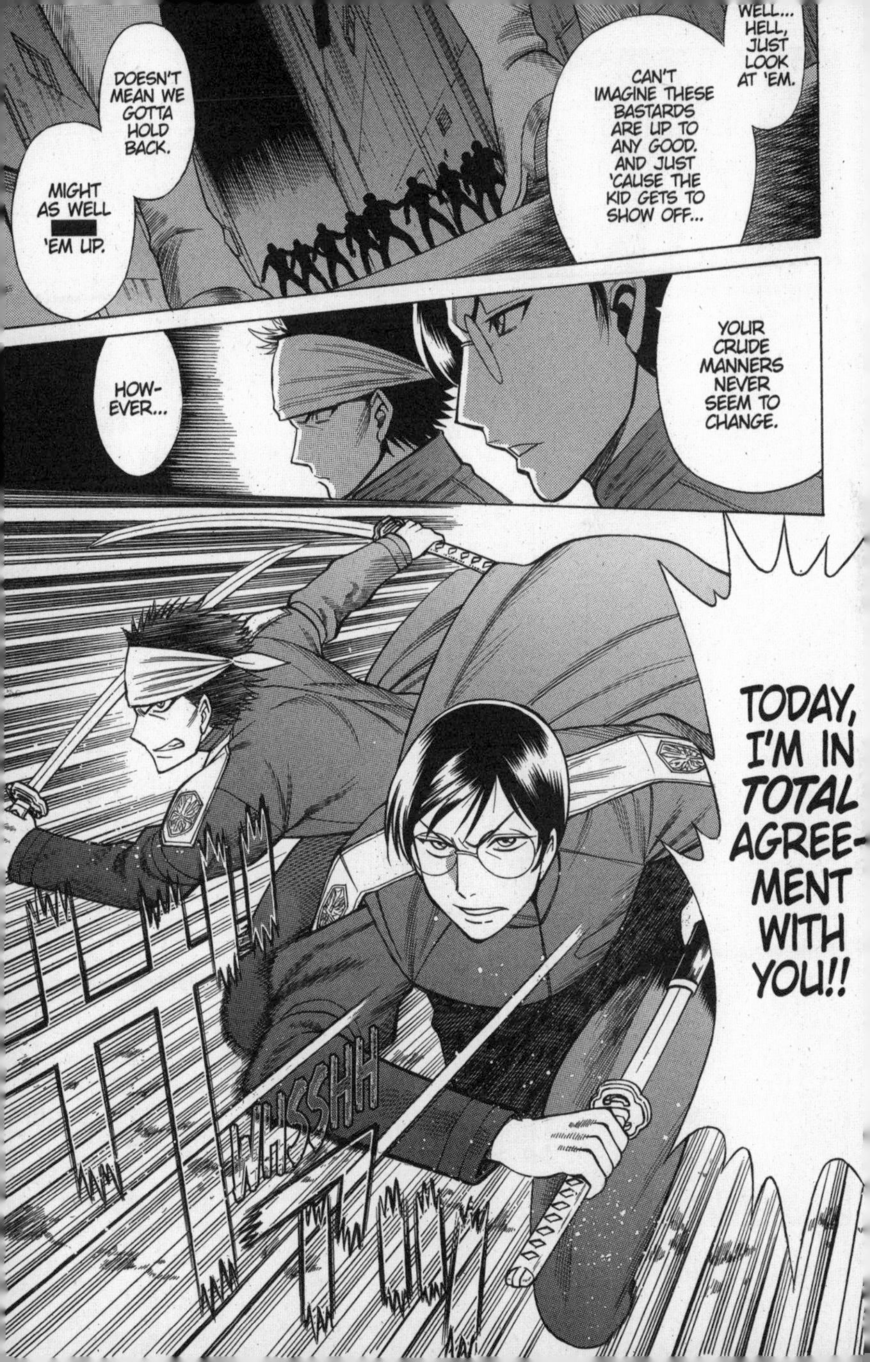

WELL... HELL, JUST LOOK AT 'EM.
CAN'T IMAGINE THESE BASTARDS ARE UP TO ANY GOOD. AND JUST 'CAUSE THE KID GETS TO SHOW OFF...
DOESN'T MEAN WE GOTTA HOLD BACK.
MIGHT AS WELL [redacted] 'EM UP.
YOUR CRUDE MANNERS NEVER SEEM TO CHANGE.
HOW-EVER...
TODAY, I'M IN *TOTAL* AGREE-MENT WITH YOU!!
WHSSHH

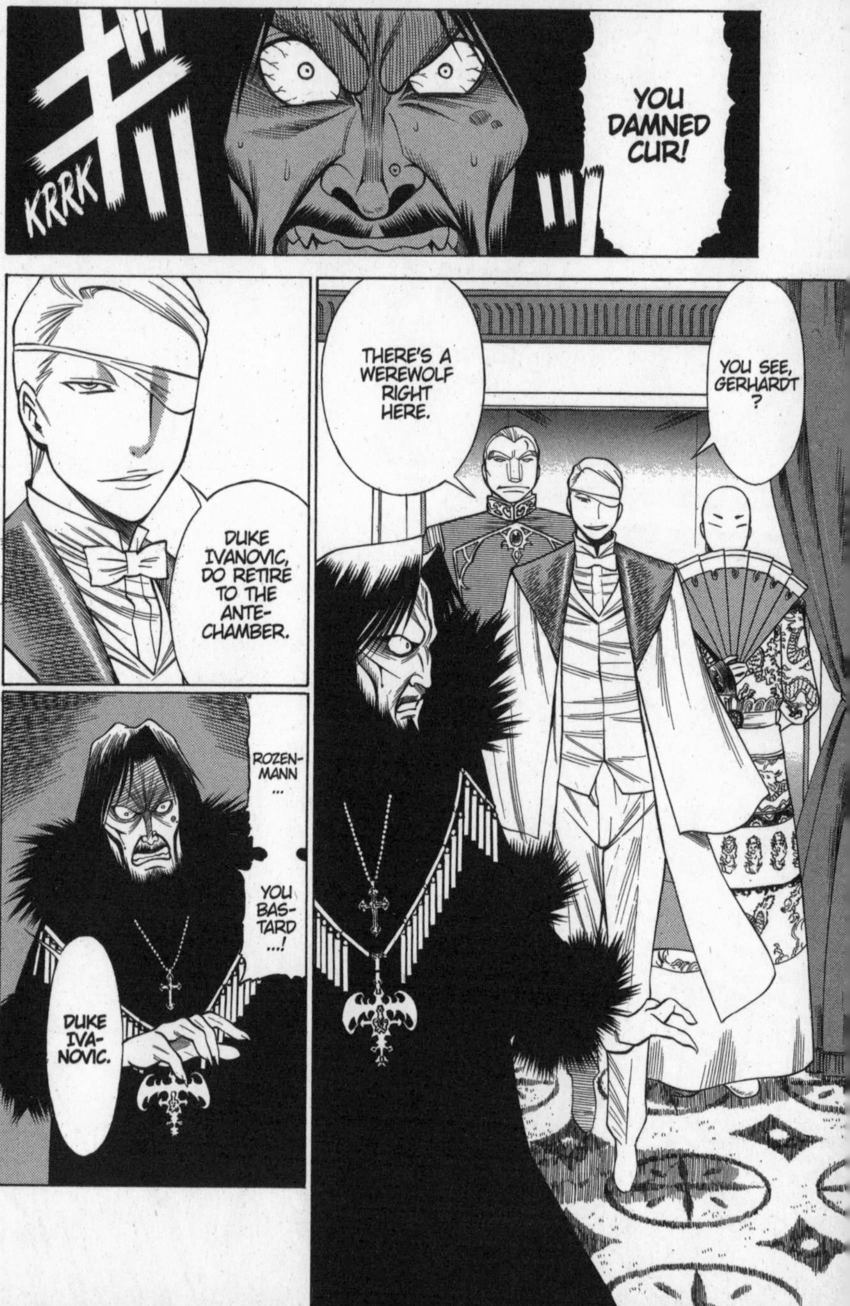
YOU DAMNED CUR!
KRRK
YOU SEE, GERHARDT?
THERE'S A WEREWOLF RIGHT HERE.
DUKE IVANOVIC, DO RETIRE TO THE ANTE-CHAMBER.
ROZEN-MANN...
YOU BAS-TARD...!
DUKE IVA-NOVIC.

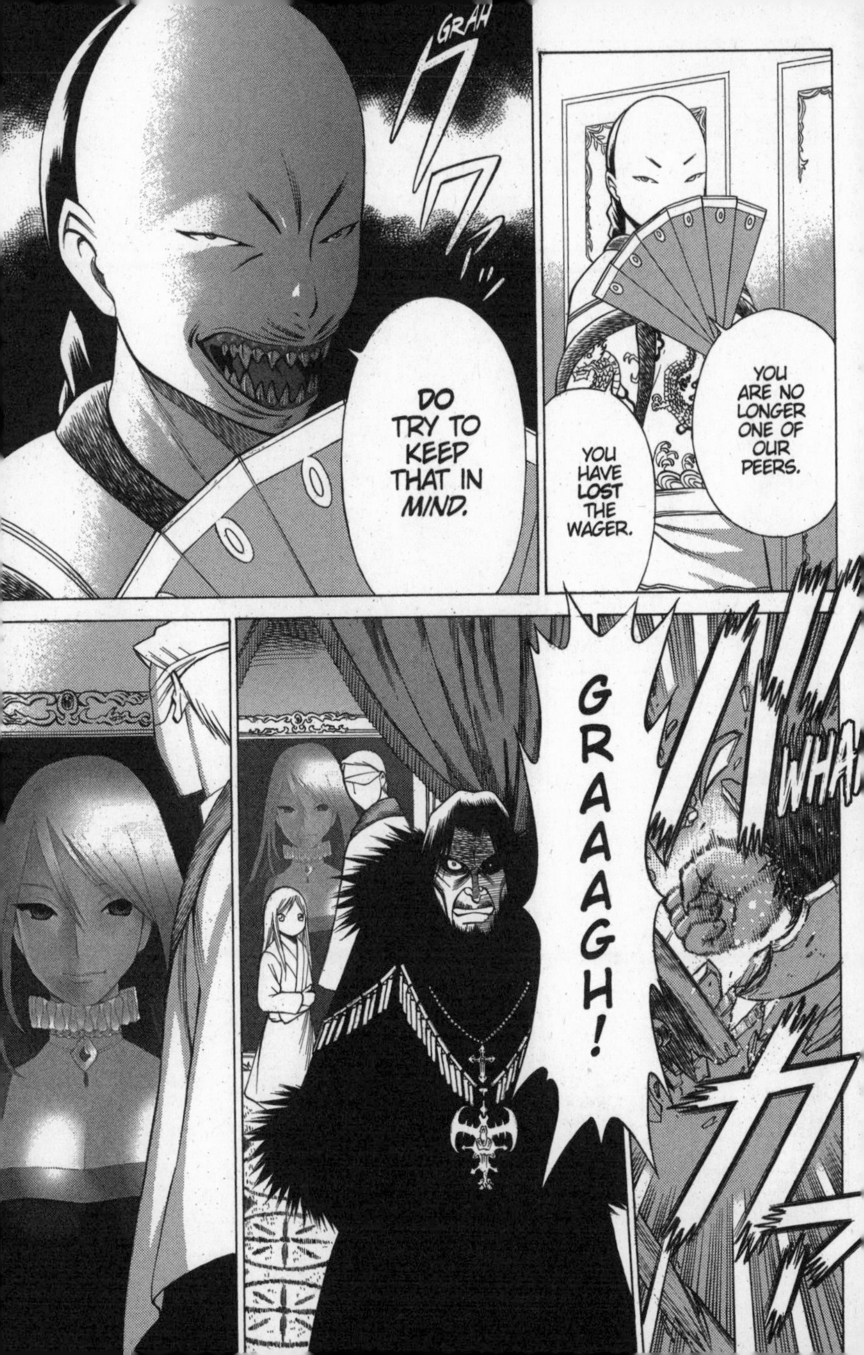
YOU ARE NO LONGER ONE OF OUR PEERS.
YOU HAVE LOST THE WAGER.
GRAH
DO TRY TO KEEP THAT IN *MIND.*
WHA
GRAAAAGH!

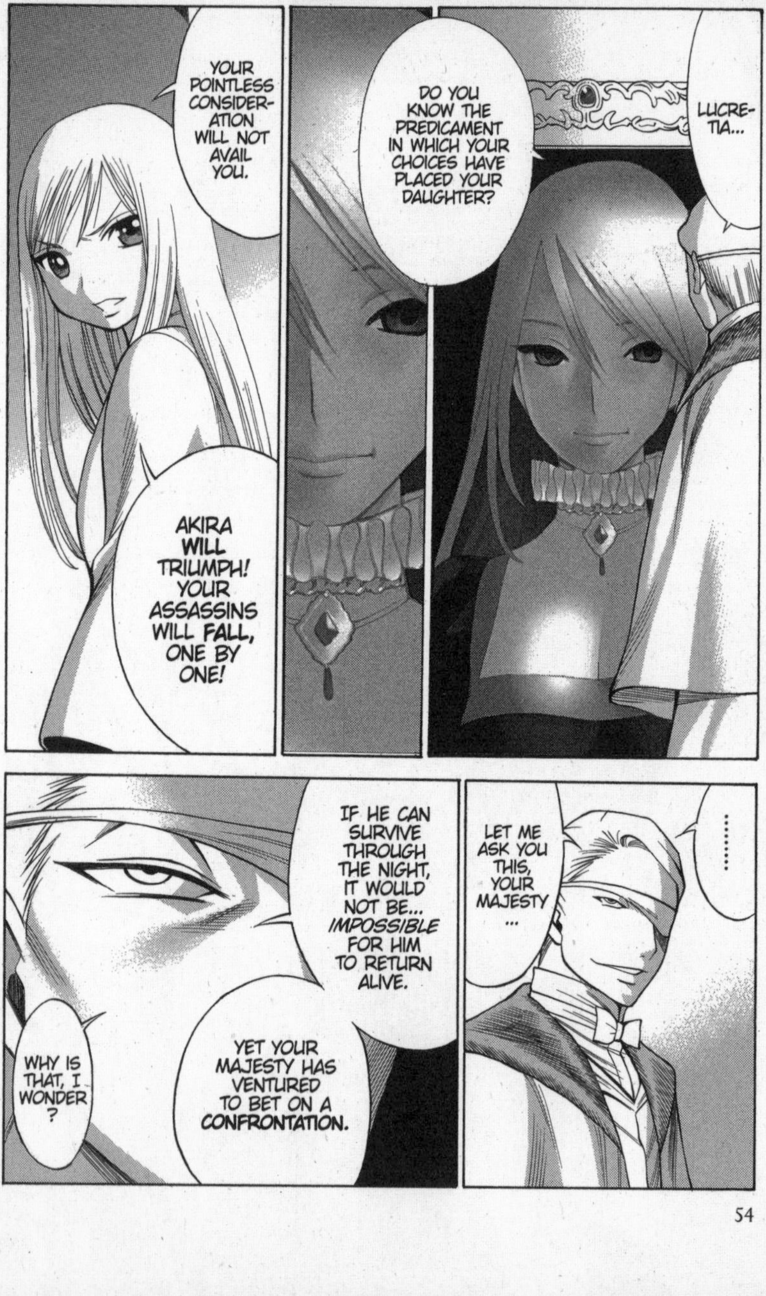
LUCRETIA...
DO YOU KNOW THE PREDICAMENT IN WHICH YOUR CHOICES HAVE PLACED YOUR DAUGHTER?
YOUR POINTLESS CONSIDERATION WILL NOT AVAIL YOU.
AKIRA **WILL** TRIUMPH! YOUR ASSASSINS WILL **FALL**, ONE BY ONE!
......
LET ME ASK YOU THIS, YOUR MAJESTY...
IF HE CAN SURVIVE THROUGH THE NIGHT, IT WOULD NOT BE... *IMPOSSIBLE* FOR HIM TO RETURN ALIVE.
YET YOUR MAJESTY HAS VENTURED TO BET ON A **CONFRONTATION.**
WHY IS THAT, I WONDER?

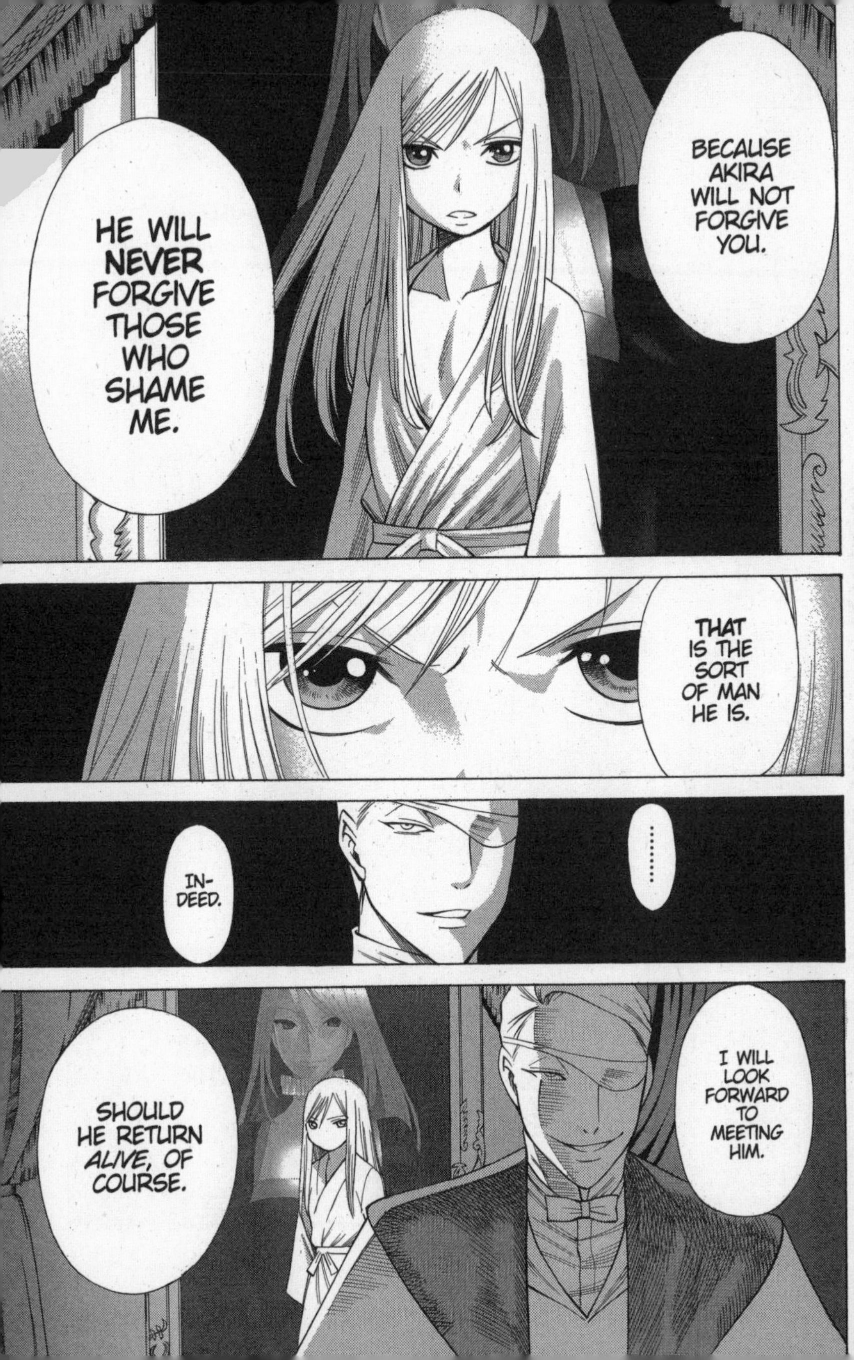
BECAUSE AKIRA WILL NOT FORGIVE YOU.
HE WILL NEVER FORGIVE THOSE WHO SHAME ME.
THAT IS THE SORT OF MAN HE IS.
......
IN-DEED.
I WILL LOOK FORWARD TO MEETING HIM.
SHOULD HE RETURN *ALIVE*, OF COURSE.

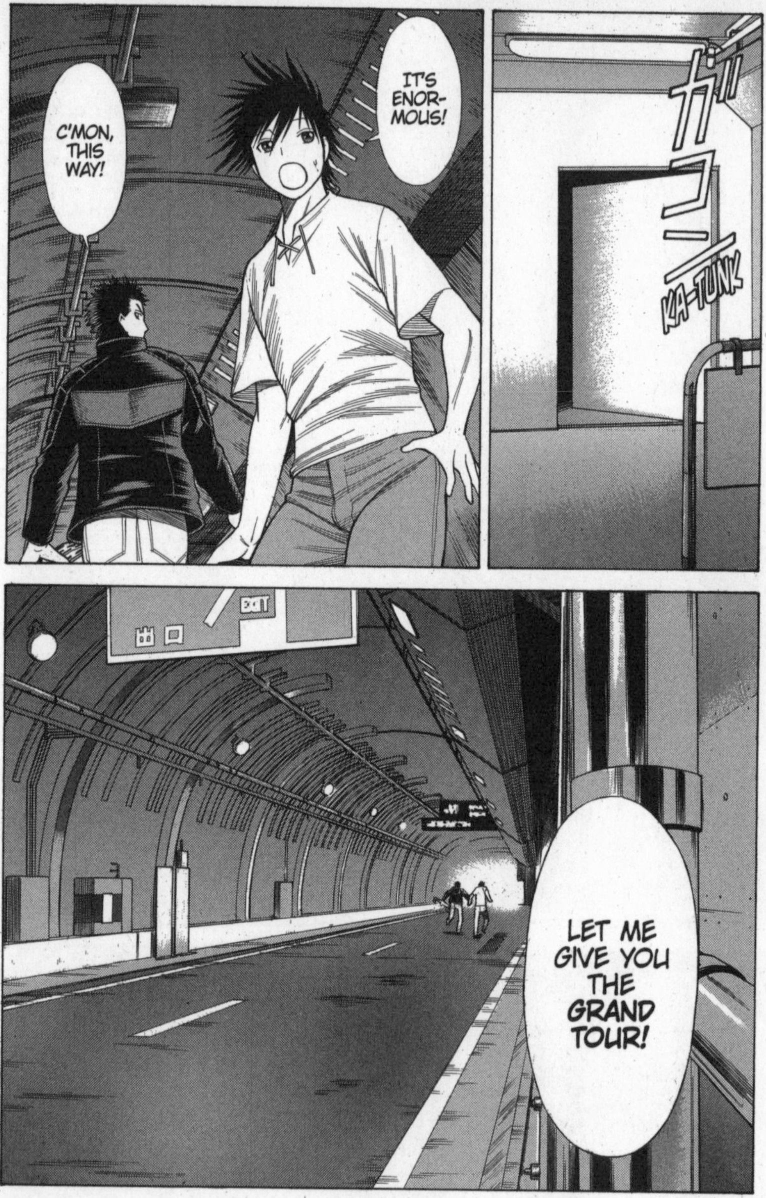
KA-TUNK
IT'S ENORMOUS!
C'MON, THIS WAY!
EXIT
LET ME GIVE YOU THE GRAND TOUR!

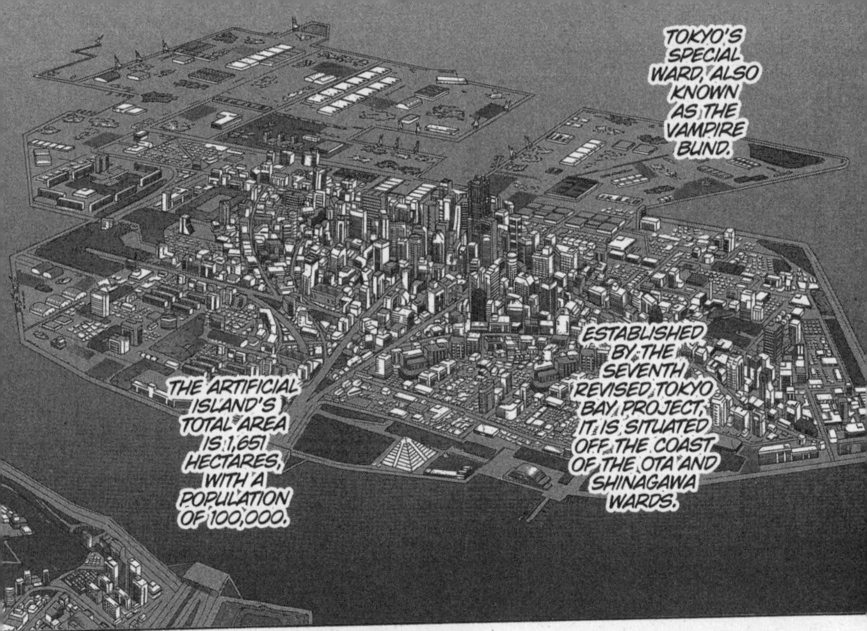
TOKYO'S SPECIAL WARD, ALSO KNOWN AS THE VAMPIRE BUND.
ESTABLISHED BY THE SEVENTH REVISED TOKYO BAY PROJECT, IT IS SITUATED OFF THE COAST OF THE OTA AND SHINAGAWA WARDS.
THE ARTIFICIAL ISLAND'S TOTAL AREA IS 1,651 HECTARES, WITH A POPULATION OF 100,000.

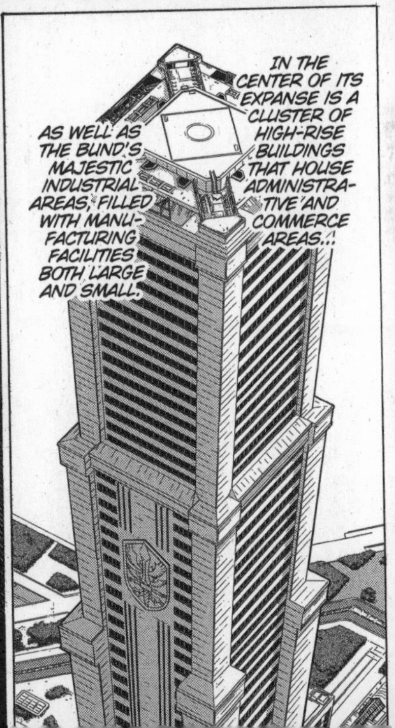
IN THE CENTER OF ITS EXPANSE IS A CLUSTER OF HIGH-RISE BUILDINGS THAT HOUSE ADMINISTRA-TIVE AND COMMERCE AREAS...
AS WELL AS THE BUND'S MAJESTIC INDUSTRIAL AREAS, FILLED WITH MANU-FACTURING FACILITIES BOTH LARGE AND SMALL.

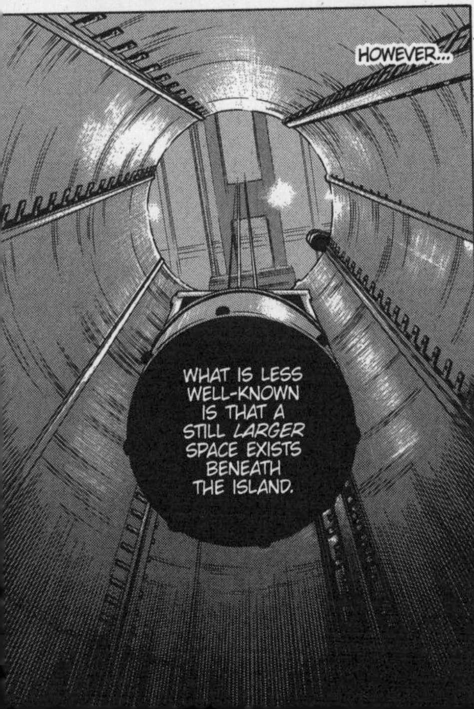
HOWEVER...
WHAT IS LESS WELL-KNOWN IS THAT A STILL *LARGER* SPACE EXISTS BENEATH THE ISLAND.

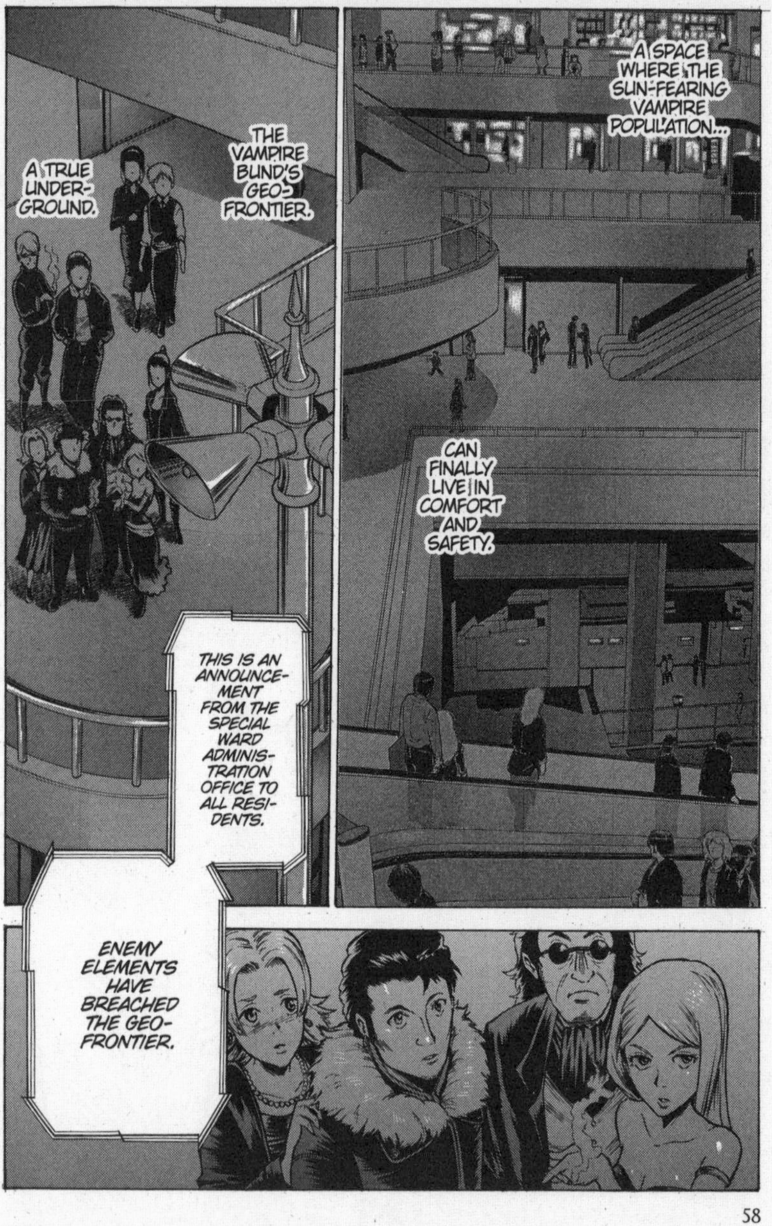
A SPACE WHERE THE SUN-FEARING VAMPIRE POPULATION...
CAN FINALLY LIVE IN COMFORT AND SAFETY.
THE VAMPIRE BUND'S GEO-FRONTIER.
A TRUE UNDER-GROUND.
THIS IS AN ANNOUNCE-MENT FROM THE SPECIAL WARD ADMINIS-TRATION OFFICE TO ALL RESI-DENTS.
ENEMY ELEMENTS HAVE BREACHED THE GEO-FRONTIER.

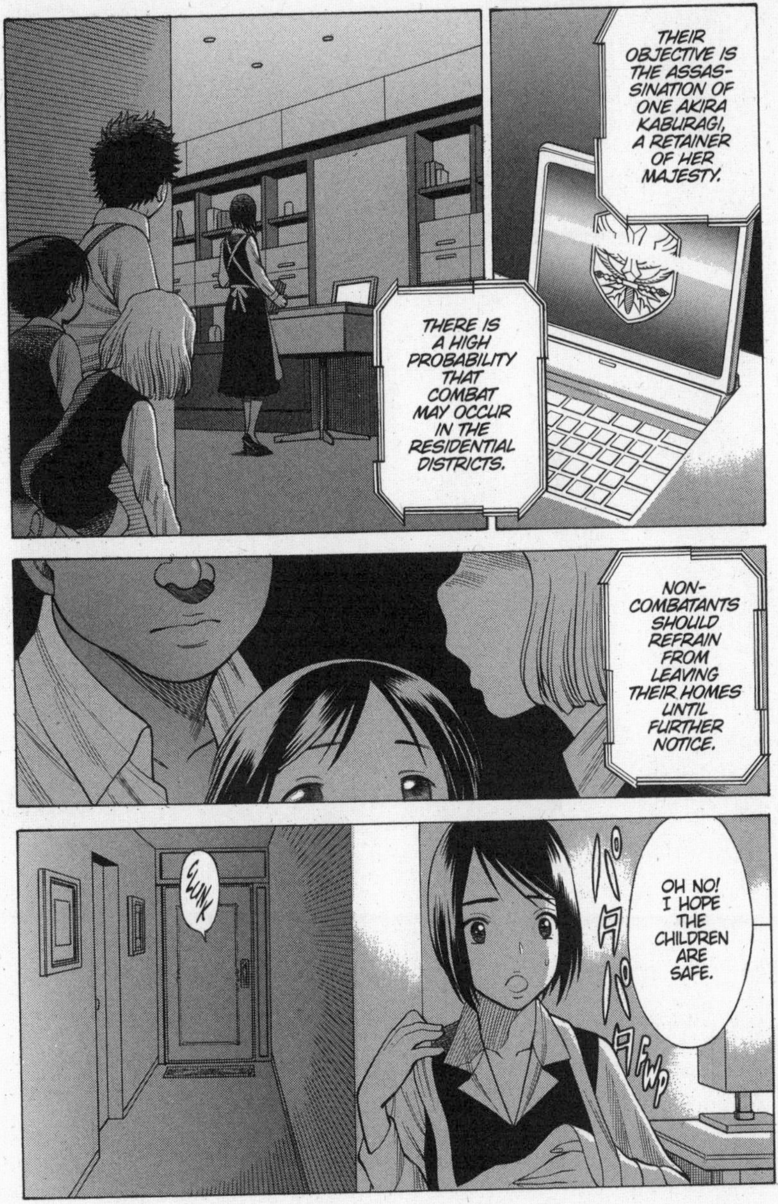
THEIR OBJECTIVE IS THE ASSASSINATION OF ONE AKIRA KABURAGI, A RETAINER OF HER MAJESTY.
THERE IS A HIGH PROBABILITY THAT COMBAT MAY OCCUR IN THE RESIDENTIAL DISTRICTS.
NON-COMBATANTS SHOULD REFRAIN FROM LEAVING THEIR HOMES UNTIL FURTHER NOTICE.
OH NO! I HOPE THE CHILDREN ARE SAFE.
fwp
CLUNK

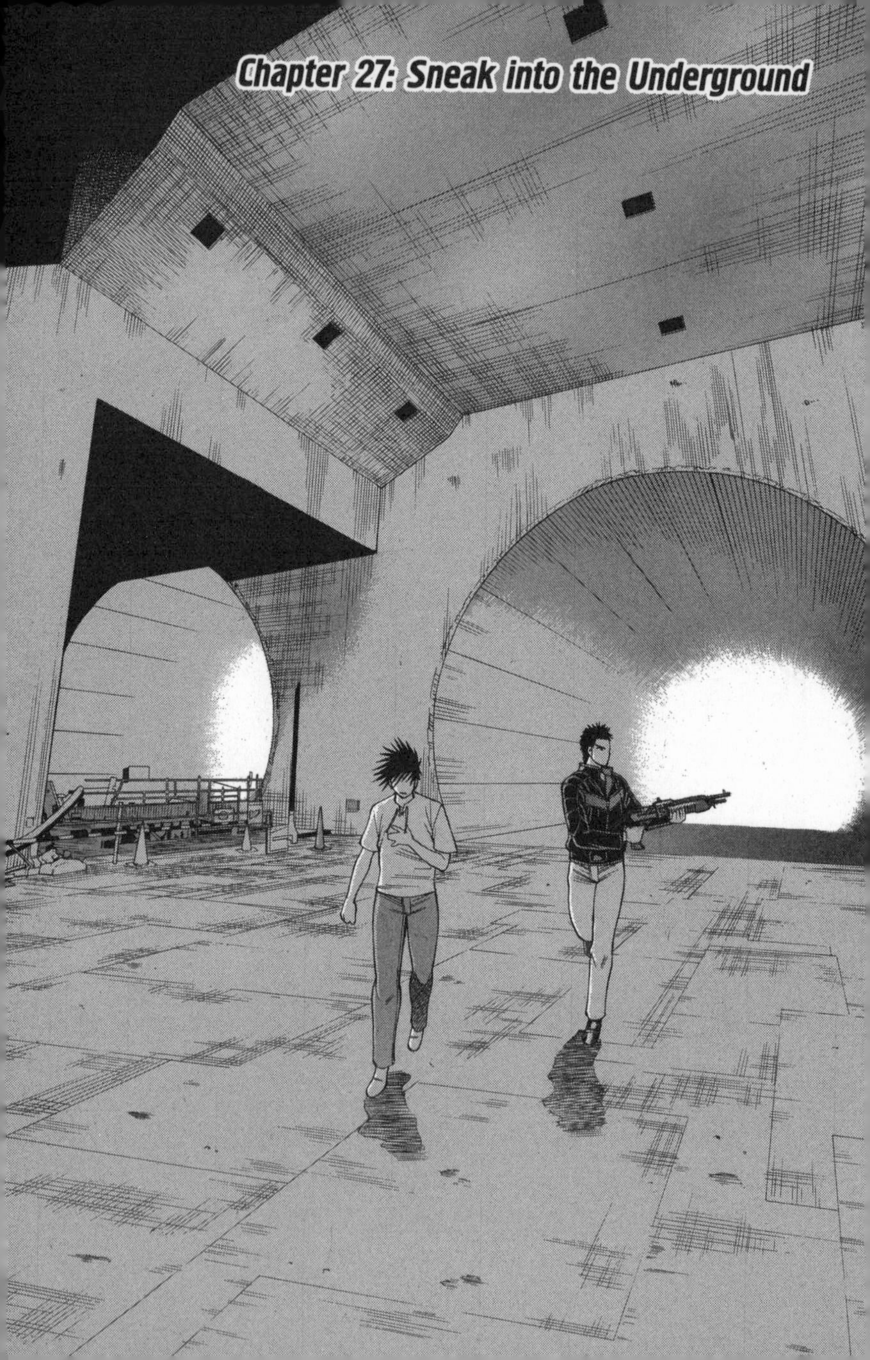
Chapter 27: Sneak into the Underground

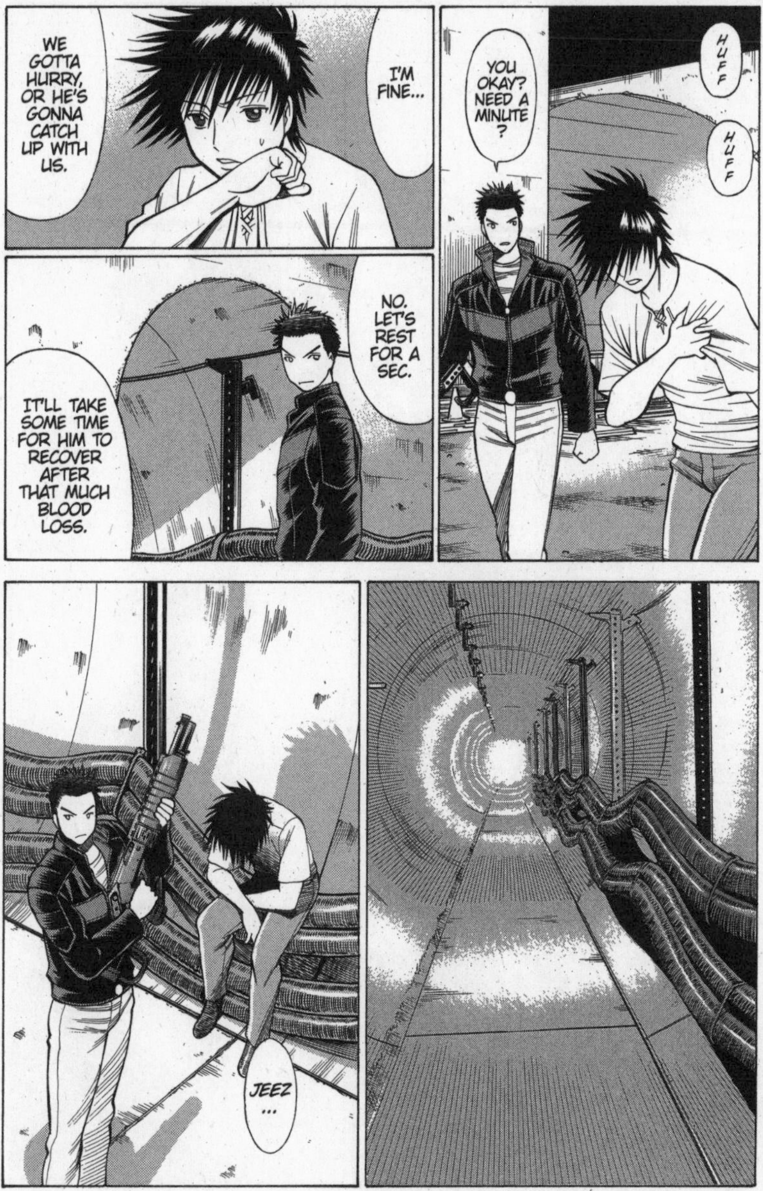
HUFF
HUFF
YOU OKAY? NEED A MINUTE?
I'M FINE...
WE GOTTA HURRY, OR HE'S GONNA CATCH UP WITH US.
NO. LET'S REST FOR A SEC.
IT'LL TAKE SOME TIME FOR HIM TO RECOVER AFTER THAT MUCH BLOOD LOSS.
JEEZ...

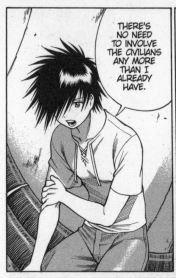

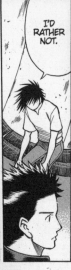

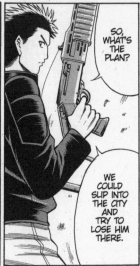

SO, WHAT'S THE PLAN?
WE COULD SLIP INTO THE CITY AND TRY TO LOSE HIM THERE.
I'D RATHER NOT.
THERE'S NO NEED TO INVOLVE THE CIVILIANS ANY MORE THAN I ALREADY HAVE.
……
WHAT?
NOTHING. IF THAT'S WHAT YOU WANT, THEN WE'LL DO IT.
SO YOU SAID THERE'S TWO OF THEM?
YEAH, THE CHINESE OPERA GUY, AND THE POWER RANGER.

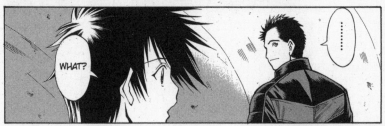

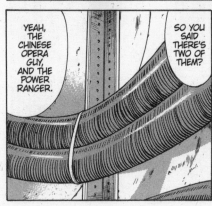

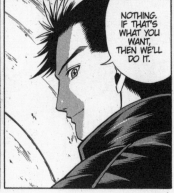

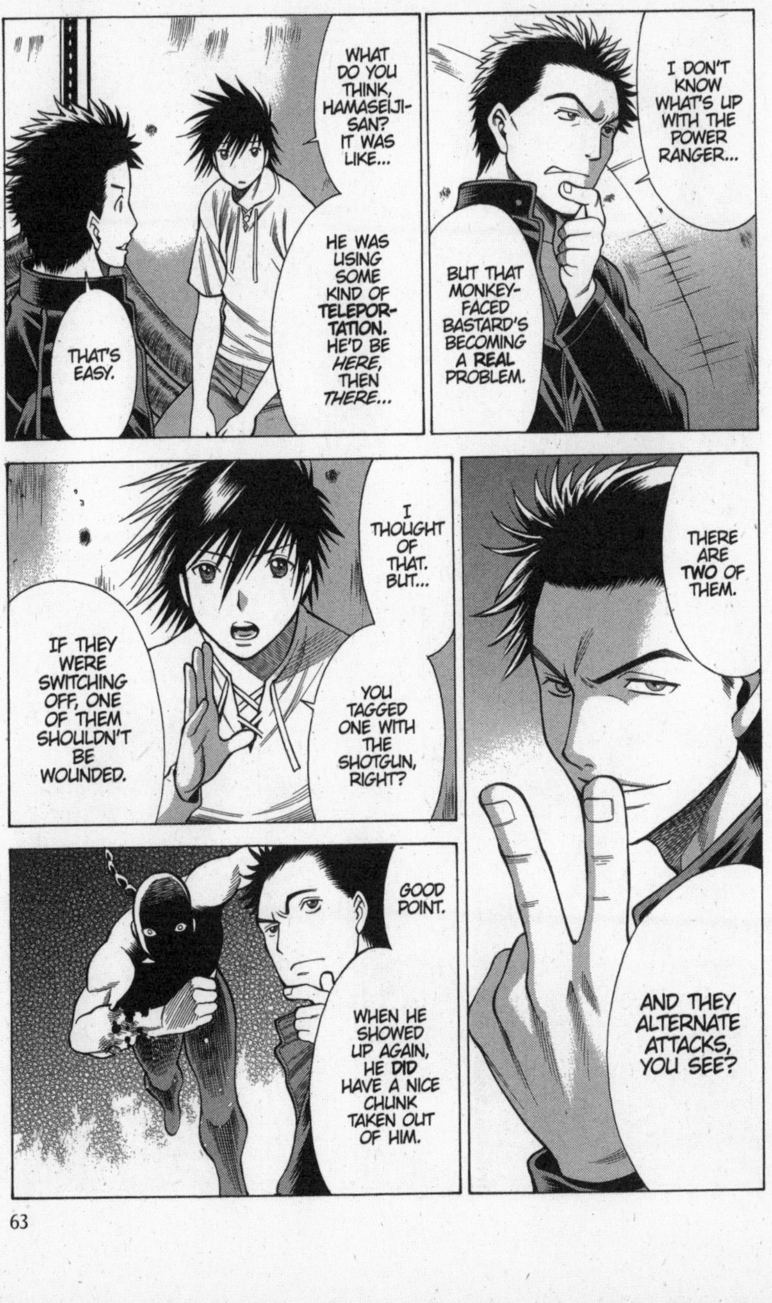
I DON'T KNOW WHAT'S UP WITH THE POWER RANGER...
BUT THAT MONKEY-FACED BASTARD'S BECOMING A REAL PROBLEM.
WHAT DO YOU THINK, HAMASEIJI-SAN? IT WAS LIKE...
HE WAS USING SOME KIND OF TELEPORTATION. HE'D BE HERE, THEN THERE...
THAT'S EASY.
THERE ARE TWO OF THEM.
AND THEY ALTERNATE ATTACKS, YOU SEE?
I THOUGHT OF THAT. BUT...
YOU TAGGED ONE WITH THE SHOTGUN, RIGHT?
IF THEY WERE SWITCHING OFF, ONE OF THEM SHOULDN'T BE WOUNDED.
GOOD POINT.
WHEN HE SHOWED UP AGAIN, HE DID HAVE A NICE CHUNK TAKEN OUT OF HIM.

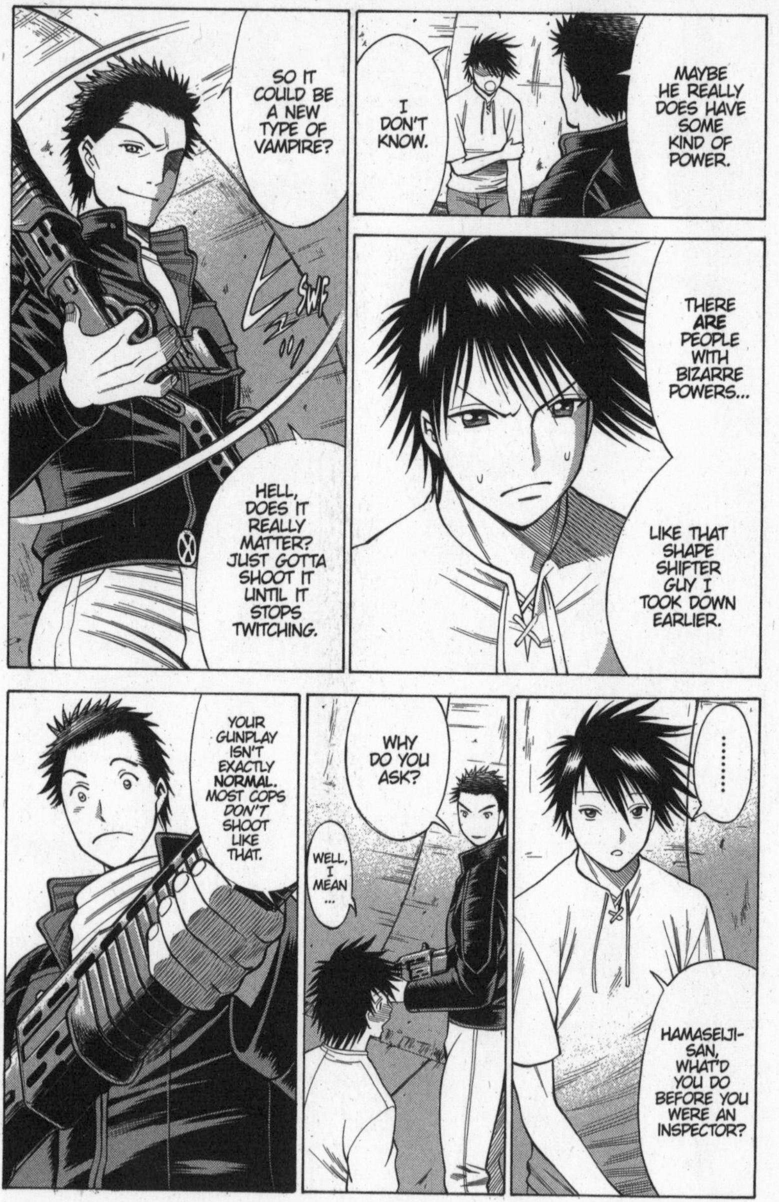
MAYBE HE REALLY DOES HAVE SOME KIND OF POWER.
I DON'T KNOW.
THERE ARE PEOPLE WITH BIZARRE POWERS...
LIKE THAT SHAPE SHIFTER GUY I TOOK DOWN EARLIER.
SO IT COULD BE A NEW TYPE OF VAMPIRE?
SWIP
HELL, DOES IT REALLY MATTER? JUST GOTTA SHOOT IT UNTIL IT STOPS TWITCHING.
....
HAMASEIJI-SAN, WHAT'D YOU DO BEFORE YOU WERE AN INSPECTOR?
WHY DO YOU ASK?
WELL, I MEAN ...
YOUR GUNPLAY ISN'T EXACTLY NORMAL. MOST COPS DON'T SHOOT LIKE THAT.

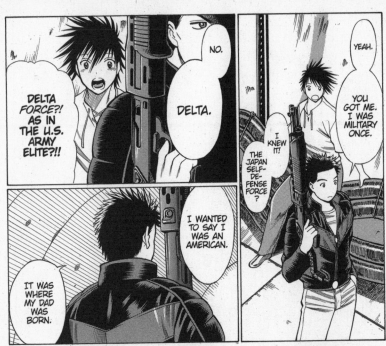

YEAH.
YOU GOT ME. I WAS MILITARY ONCE.
I KNEW IT!
THE JAPAN SELF-DEFENSE FORCE?
NO.
DELTA.
DELTA FORCE?! AS IN THE U.S. ARMY ELITE?!!
I WANTED TO SAY I WAS AN AMERICAN.
IT WAS WHERE MY DAD WAS BORN.
YOUR DAD WAS AMERI-CAN?
HEH, YOU CAN'T TELL, CAN YOU?
I'M HALF NAVAJO. NATIVE AMERICAN.
MY MOM WAS JAPANESE. I WAS BORN OVER HERE.
NAVAJO, REALLY?
IMPRES-SIVE.

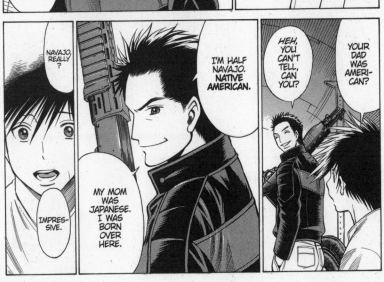

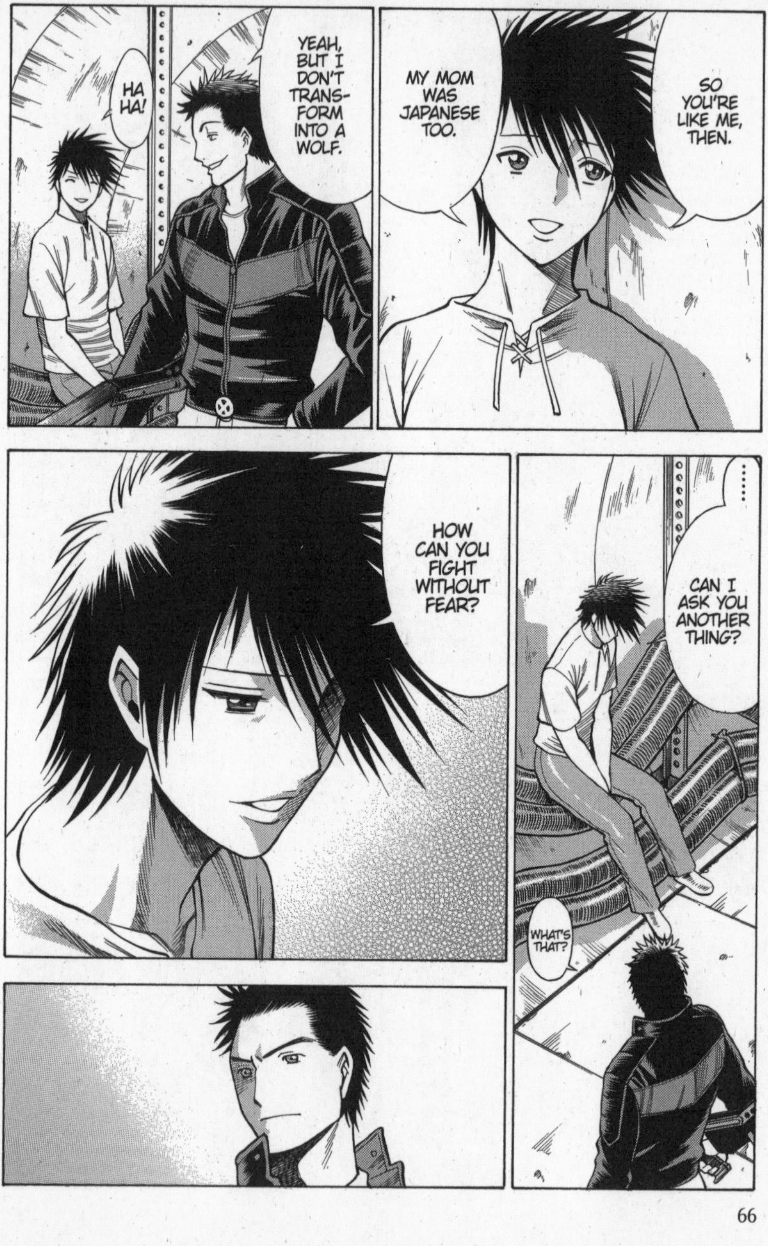
SO YOU'RE LIKE ME, THEN.
MY MOM WAS JAPANESE TOO.
YEAH, BUT I DON'T TRANS-FORM INTO A WOLF.
HA HA!
......
CAN I ASK YOU ANOTHER THING?
WHAT'S THAT?
HOW CAN YOU FIGHT WITHOUT FEAR?

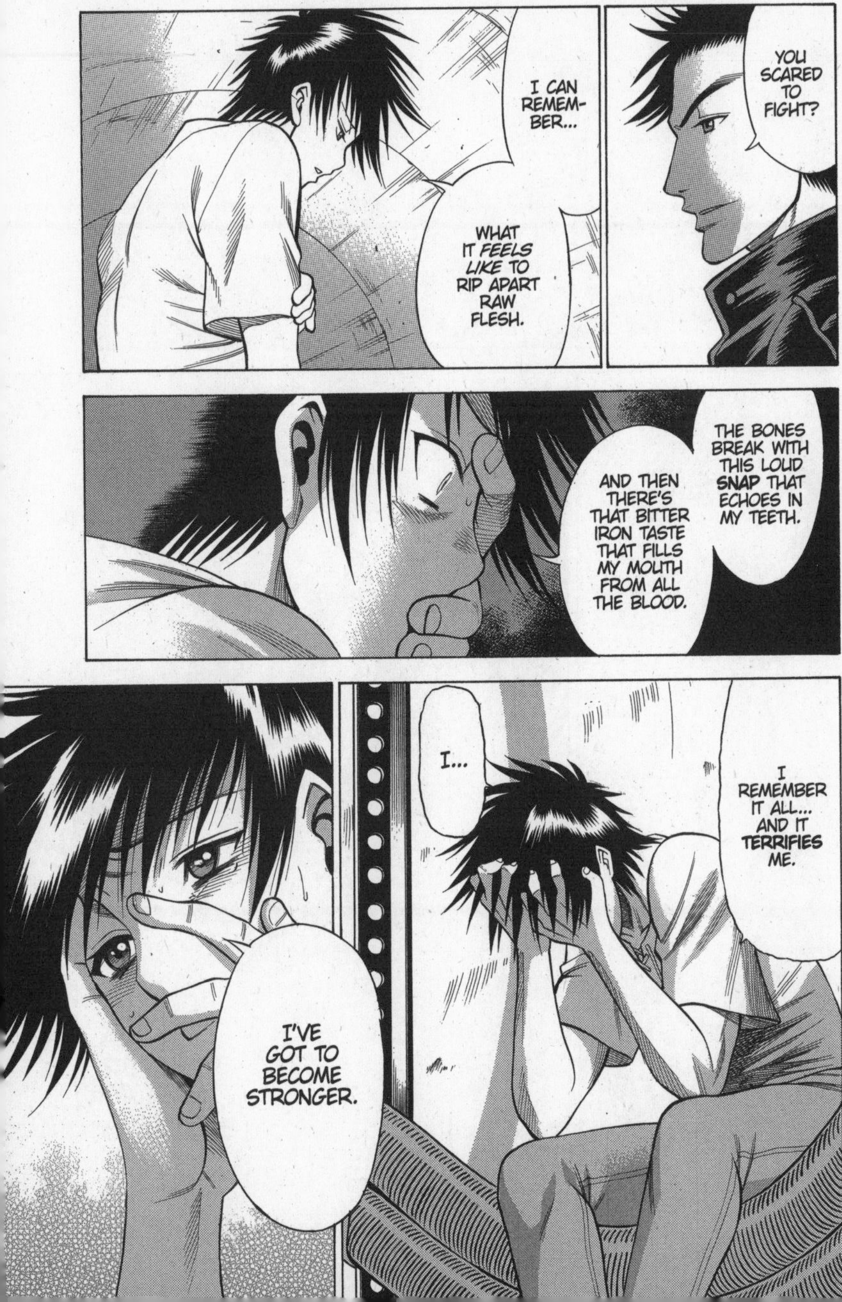
YOU SCARED TO FIGHT?
I CAN REMEMBER...
WHAT IT FEELS LIKE TO RIP APART RAW FLESH.
THE BONES BREAK WITH THIS LOUD SNAP THAT ECHOES IN MY TEETH.
AND THEN THERE'S THAT BITTER IRON TASTE THAT FILLS MY MOUTH FROM ALL THE BLOOD.
I REMEMBER IT ALL... AND IT TERRIFIES ME.
I...
I'VE GOT TO BECOME STRONGER.

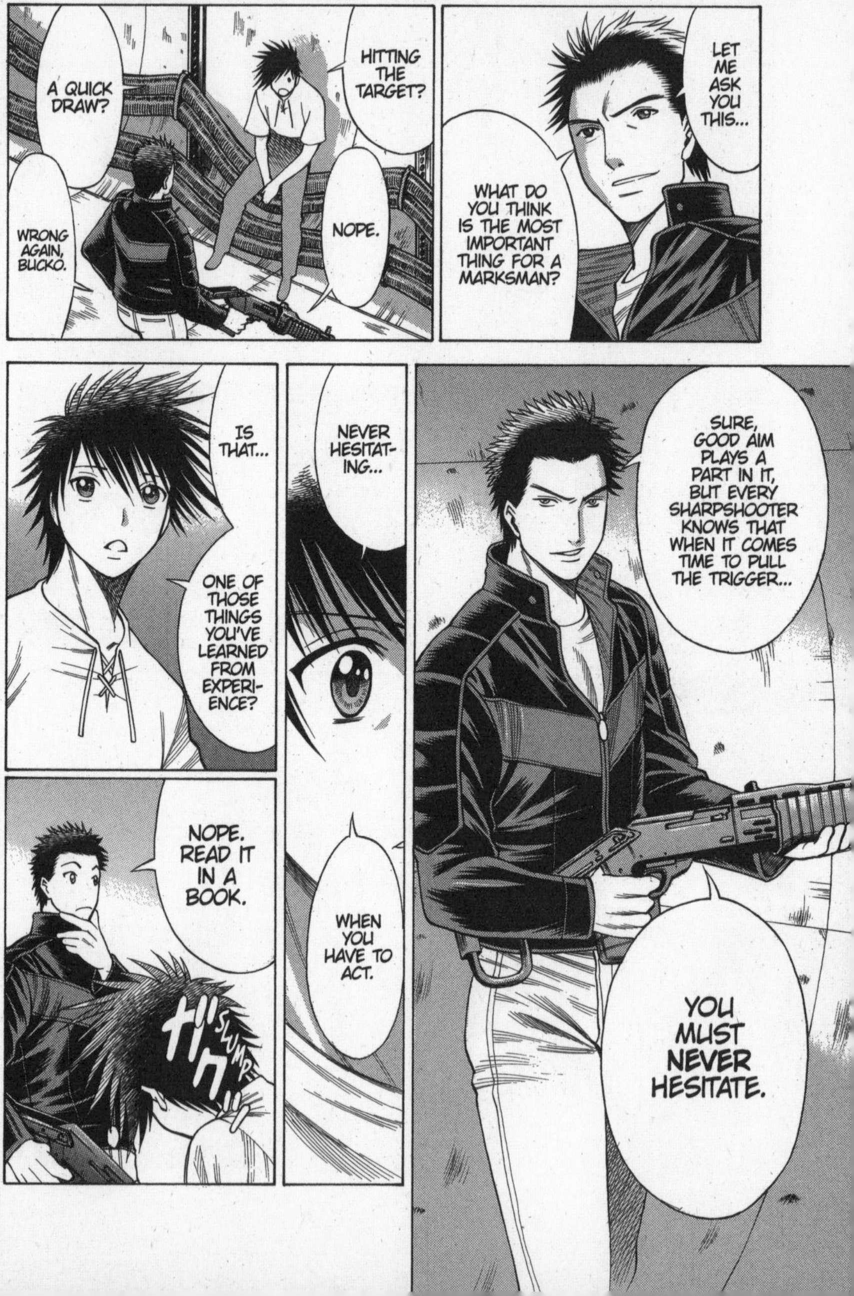
LET ME ASK YOU THIS...
WHAT DO YOU THINK IS THE MOST IMPORTANT THING FOR A MARKSMAN?
HITTING THE TARGET?
A QUICK DRAW?
NOPE.
WRONG AGAIN, BUCKO.
SURE, GOOD AIM PLAYS A PART IN IT, BUT EVERY SHARPSHOOTER KNOWS THAT WHEN IT COMES TIME TO PULL THE TRIGGER...
YOU MUST NEVER HESITATE.
NEVER HESITATING...
WHEN YOU HAVE TO ACT.
IS THAT...
ONE OF THOSE THINGS YOU'VE LEARNED FROM EXPERIENCE?
NOPE. READ IT IN A BOOK.
SLUMP

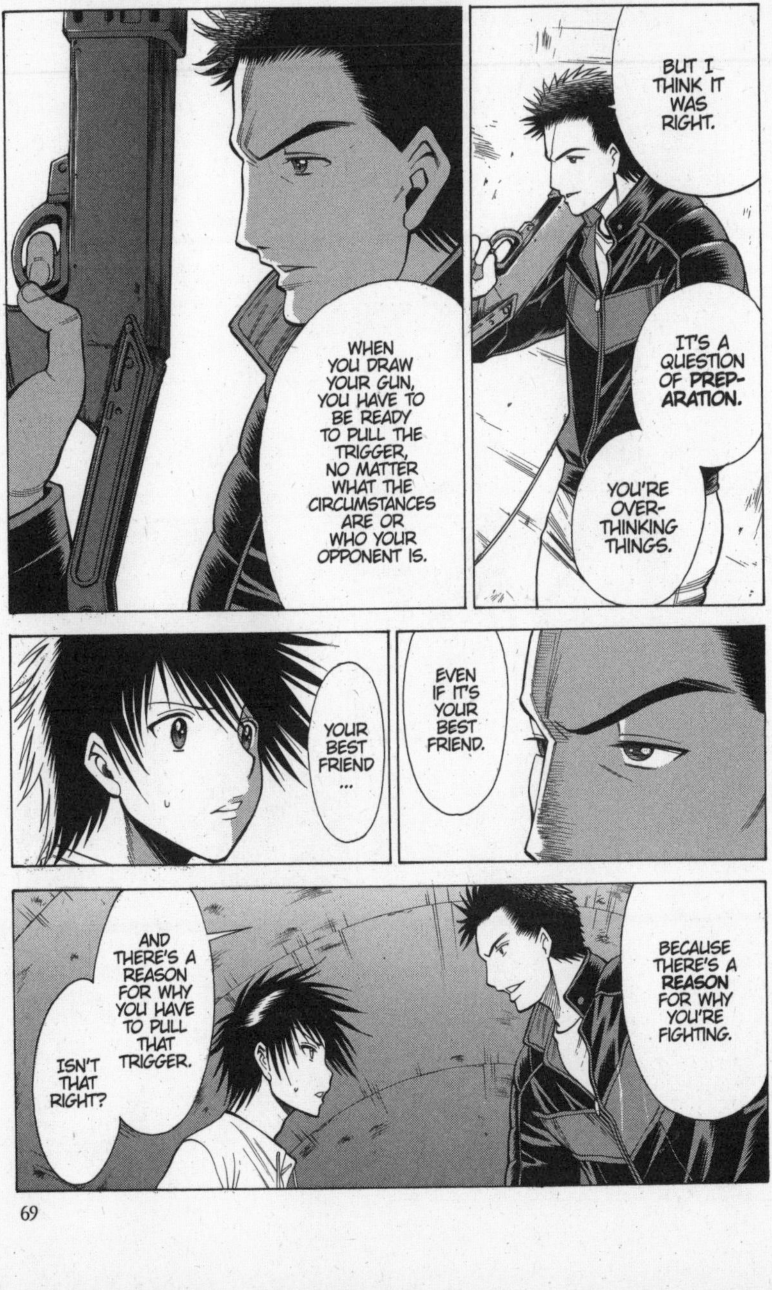
BUT I THINK IT WAS RIGHT.
IT'S A QUESTION OF PREP-ARATION.
YOU'RE OVER-THINKING THINGS.
WHEN YOU DRAW YOUR GUN, YOU HAVE TO BE READY TO PULL THE TRIGGER, NO MATTER WHAT THE CIRCUMSTANCES ARE OR WHO YOUR OPPONENT IS.
EVEN IF IT'S YOUR BEST FRIEND.
YOUR BEST FRIEND ...
BECAUSE THERE'S A REASON FOR WHY YOU'RE FIGHTING.
AND THERE'S A REASON FOR WHY YOU HAVE TO PULL THAT TRIGGER.
ISN'T THAT RIGHT?

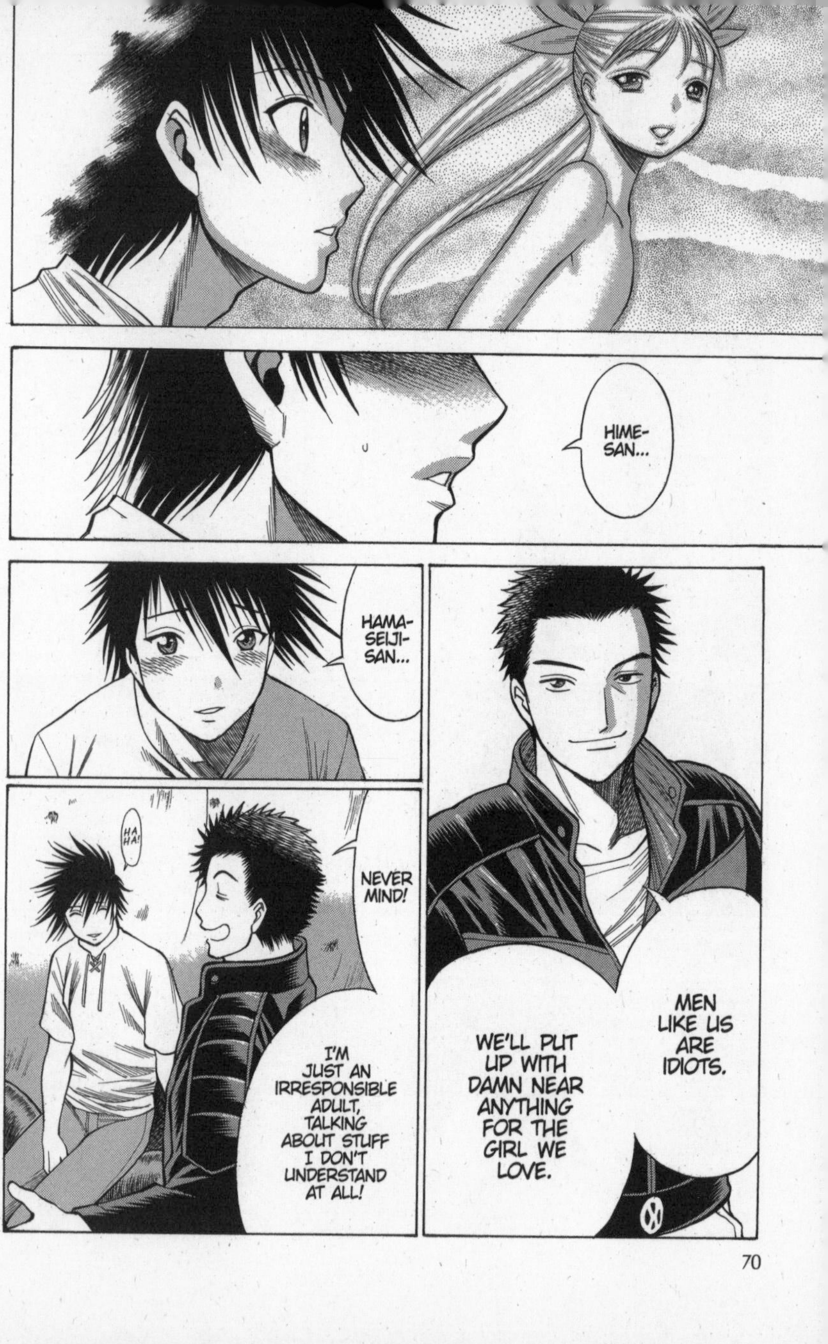
HIME-SAN...
MEN LIKE US ARE IDIOTS.
WE'LL PUT UP WITH DAMN NEAR ANYTHING FOR THE GIRL WE LOVE.
HAMA-SEIJI-SAN...
NEVER MIND!
HA HA!
I'M JUST AN IRRESPONSIBLE ADULT, TALKING ABOUT STUFF I DON'T UNDERSTAND AT ALL!

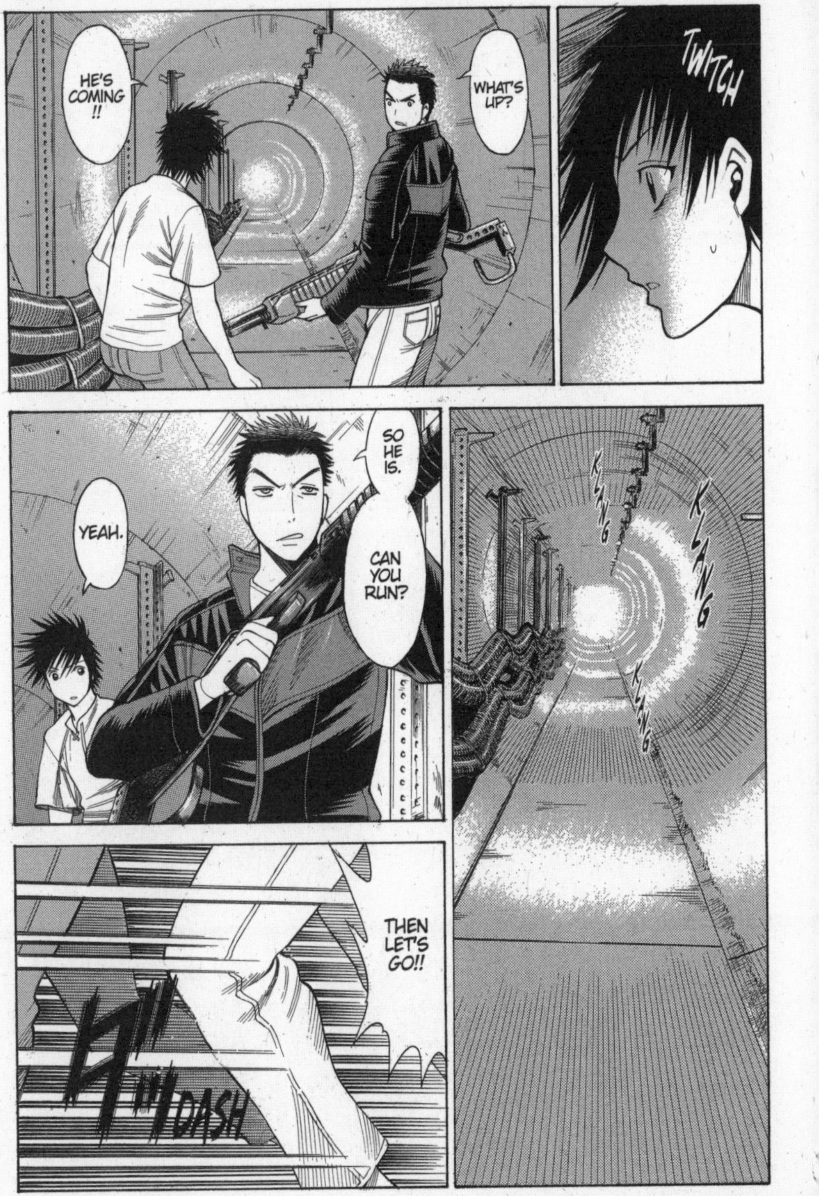
TWITCH
WHAT'S UP?
HE'S COMING!!
KLANG
KLANG
KLANG
SO HE IS.
CAN YOU RUN?
YEAH.
THEN LET'S GO!!
DASH

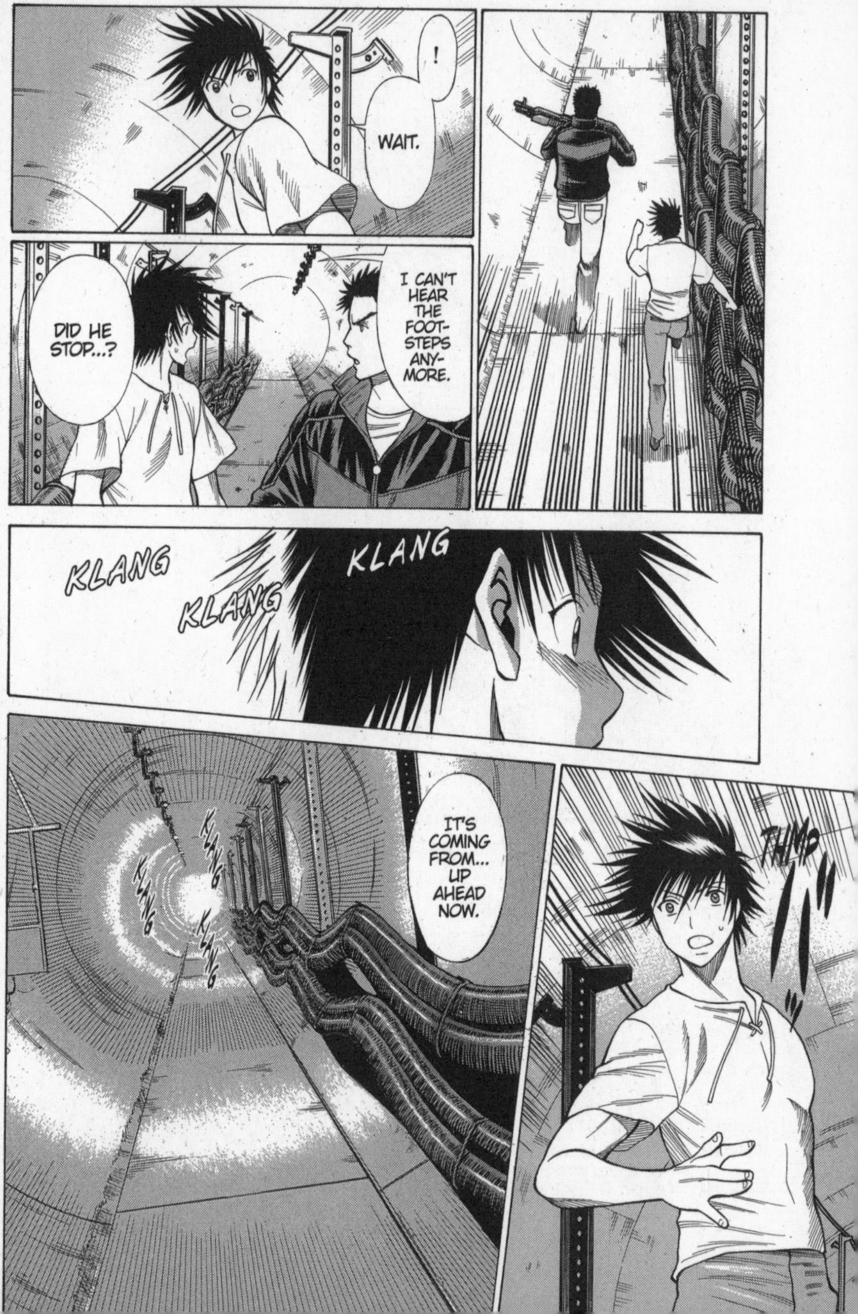
!
WAIT.
I CAN'T HEAR THE FOOT-STEPS ANY-MORE.
DID HE STOP...?
KLANG
KLANG
KLANG
THMP
IT'S COMING FROM... UP AHEAD NOW.
KLANG
KLANG
KLANG
KLANG

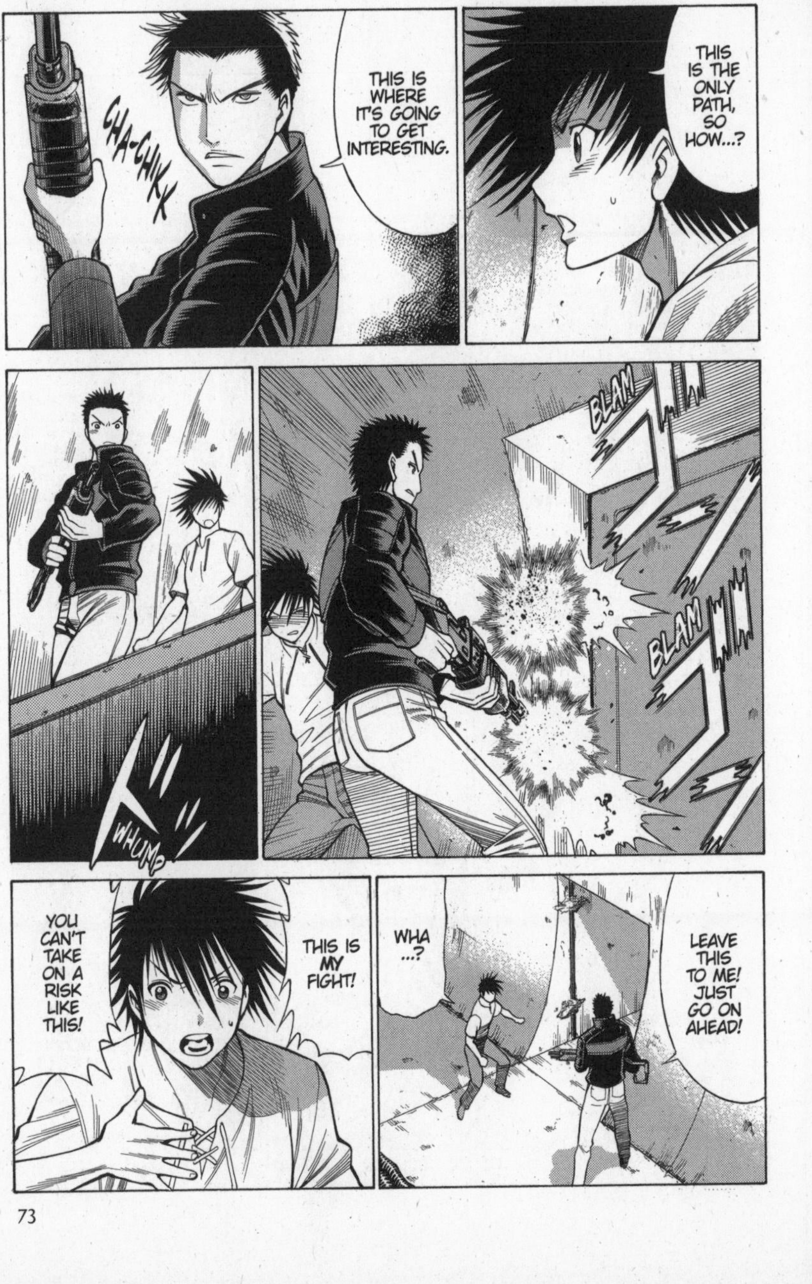
THIS IS THE ONLY PATH, SO HOW...?
CHA-CHIKK
THIS IS WHERE IT'S GOING TO GET INTERESTING.
BLAM
BLAM
WHUMP
LEAVE THIS TO ME! JUST GO ON AHEAD!
WHA ...?
THIS IS MY FIGHT!
YOU CAN'T TAKE ON A RISK LIKE THIS!

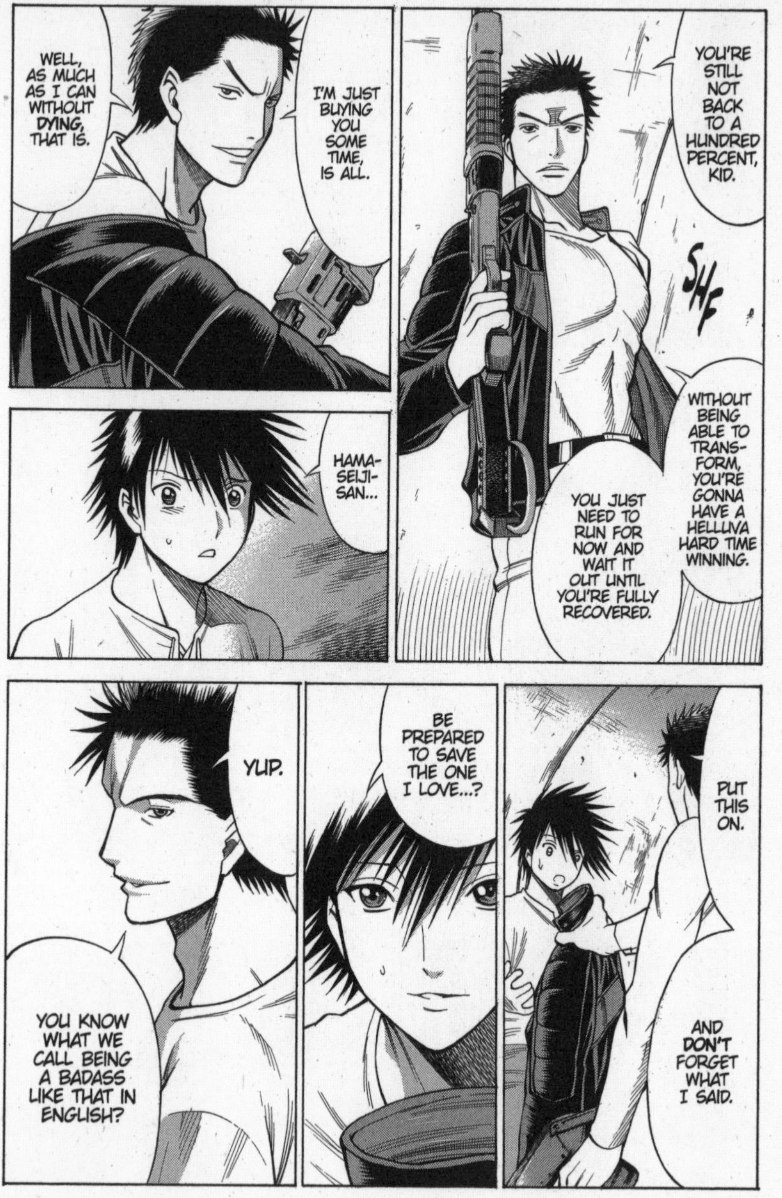
YOU'RE STILL NOT BACK TO A HUNDRED PERCENT, KID.
SHF
WITHOUT BEING ABLE TO TRANS-FORM, YOU'RE GONNA HAVE A HELLUVA HARD TIME WINNING.
YOU JUST NEED TO RUN FOR NOW AND WAIT IT OUT UNTIL YOU'RE FULLY RECOVERED.
I'M JUST BUYING YOU SOME TIME, IS ALL.
WELL, AS MUCH AS I CAN WITHOUT DYING, THAT IS.
HAMA-SEIJI-SAN...
PUT THIS ON.
AND DON'T FORGET WHAT I SAID.
BE PREPARED TO SAVE THE ONE I LOVE...?
YUP.
YOU KNOW WHAT WE CALL BEING A BADASS LIKE THAT IN ENGLISH?

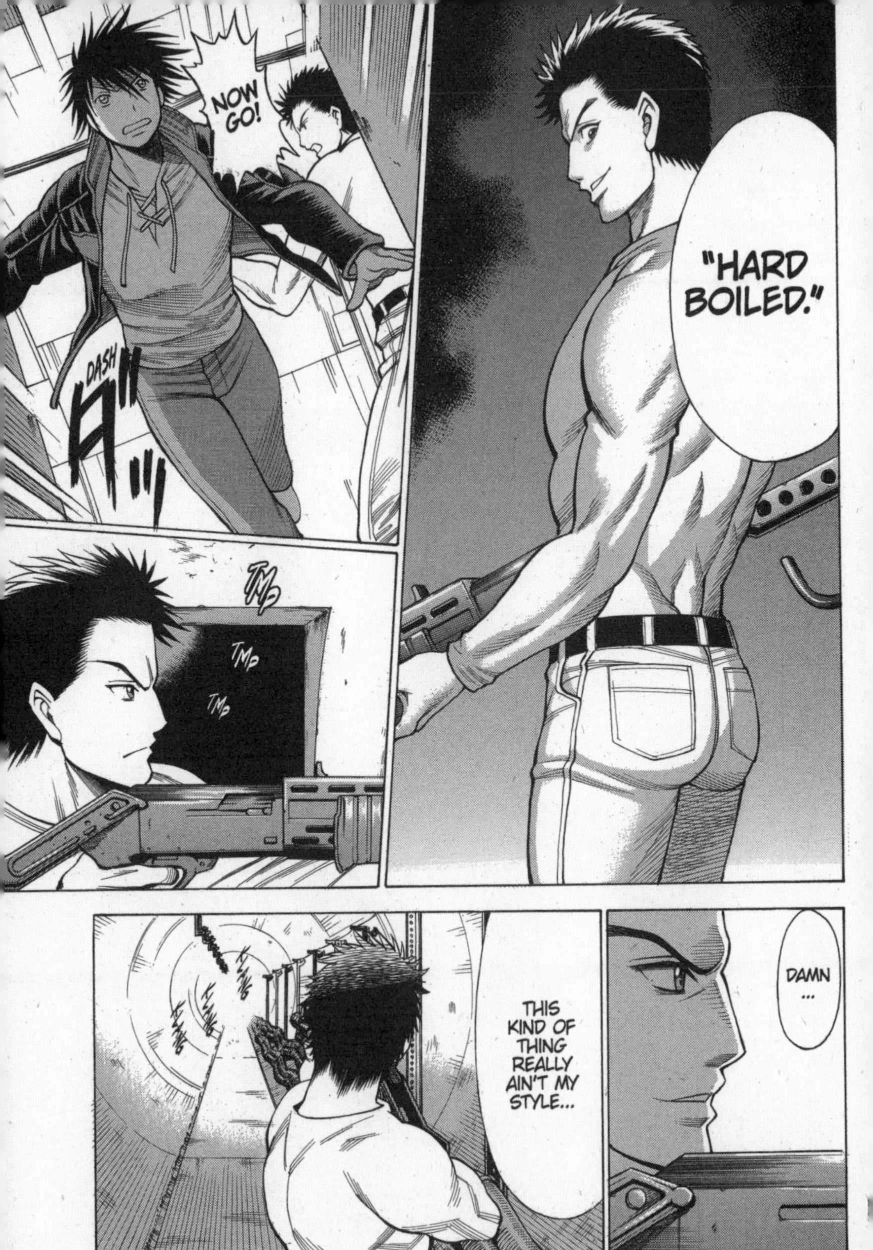
"HARD BOILED."
NOW GO!
DASH
TMP
TMP
TMP
DAMN ...
THIS KIND OF THING REALLY AIN'T MY STYLE...

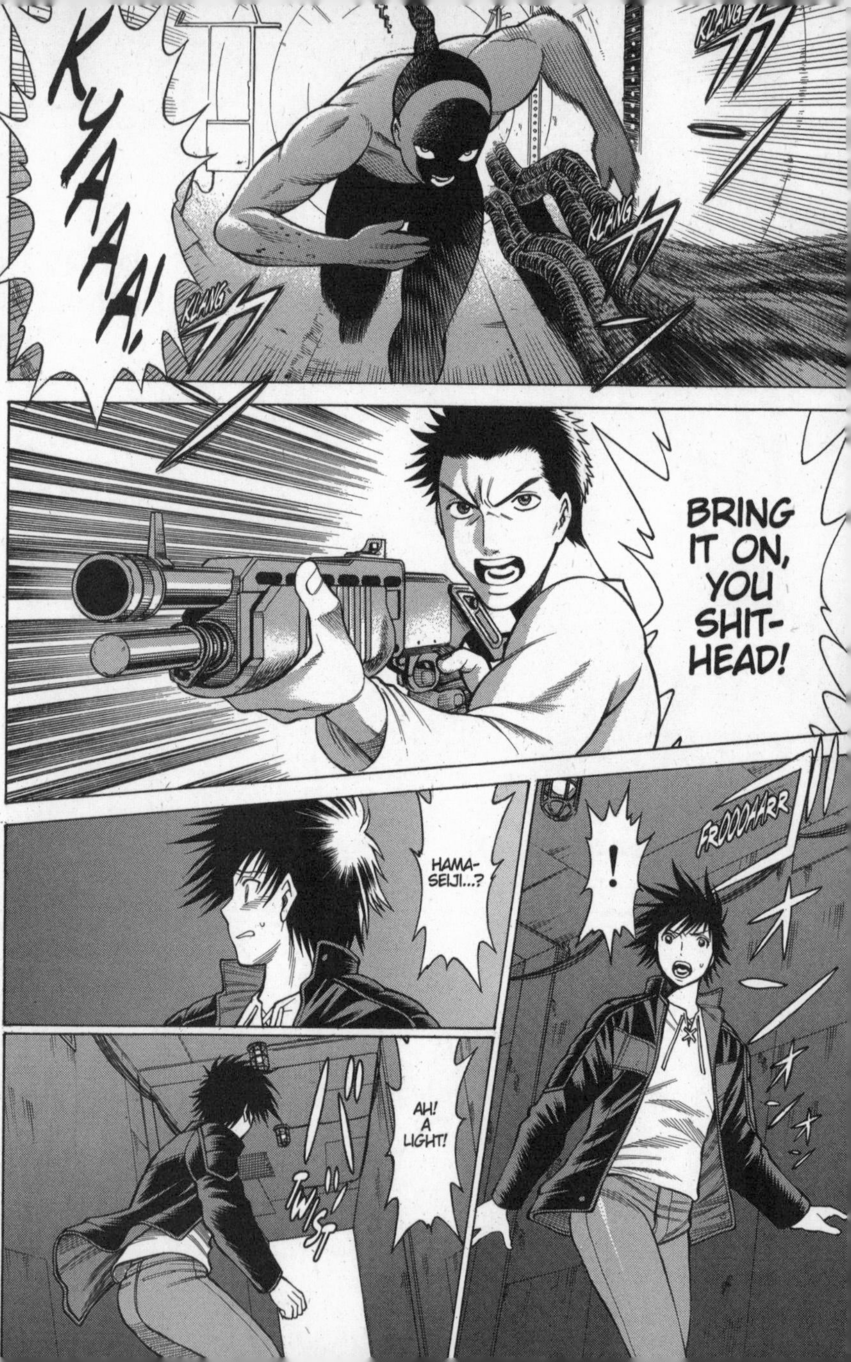
KLANG
KLANG
KYAAAA!
KLANG
BRING IT ON, YOU SHIT-HEAD!
FROOOHARR
!
HAMA-SEIJI...?
AH! A LIGHT!
TWIST

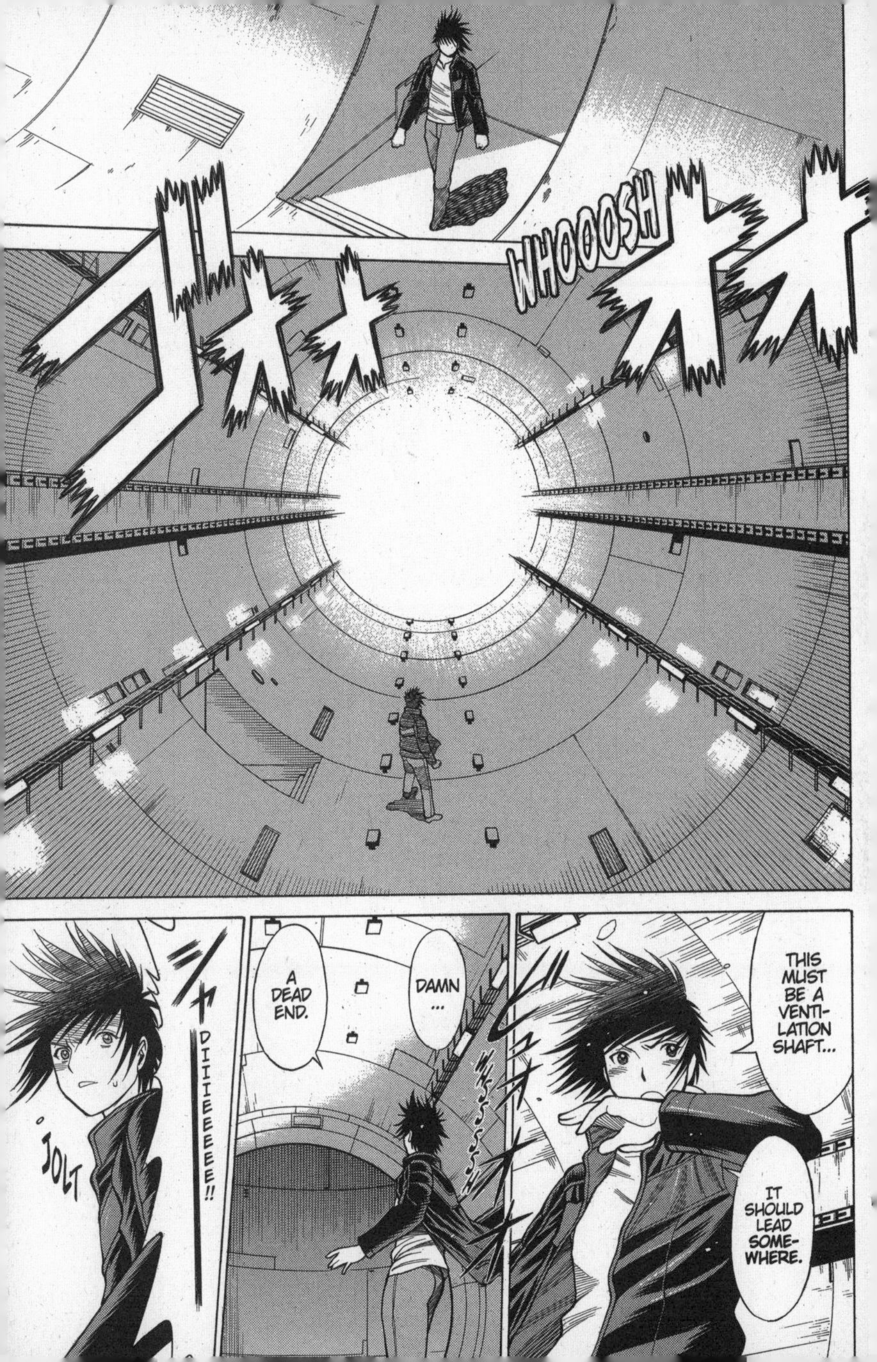

WHOOOSH
THIS MUST BE A VENTI-LATION SHAFT...
IT SHOULD LEAD SOME-WHERE.
DAMN ...
A DEAD END.
DIIIEEEEE!!
JOLT

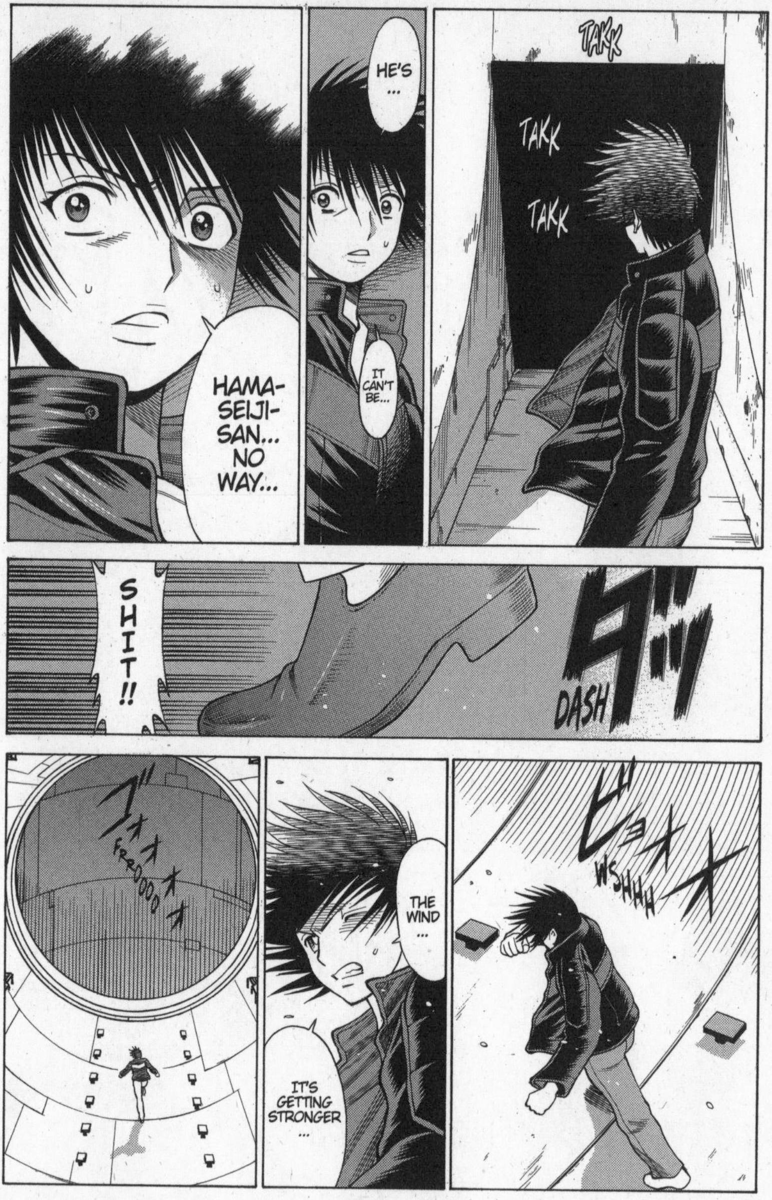
TAKK
TAKK
TAKK
HE'S ...
IT CAN'T BE...
HAMA-SEIJI-SAN... NO WAY...
DASH
SHIT!!
WSHHH
THE WIND ...
IT'S GETTING STRONGER ...
FRROOOD

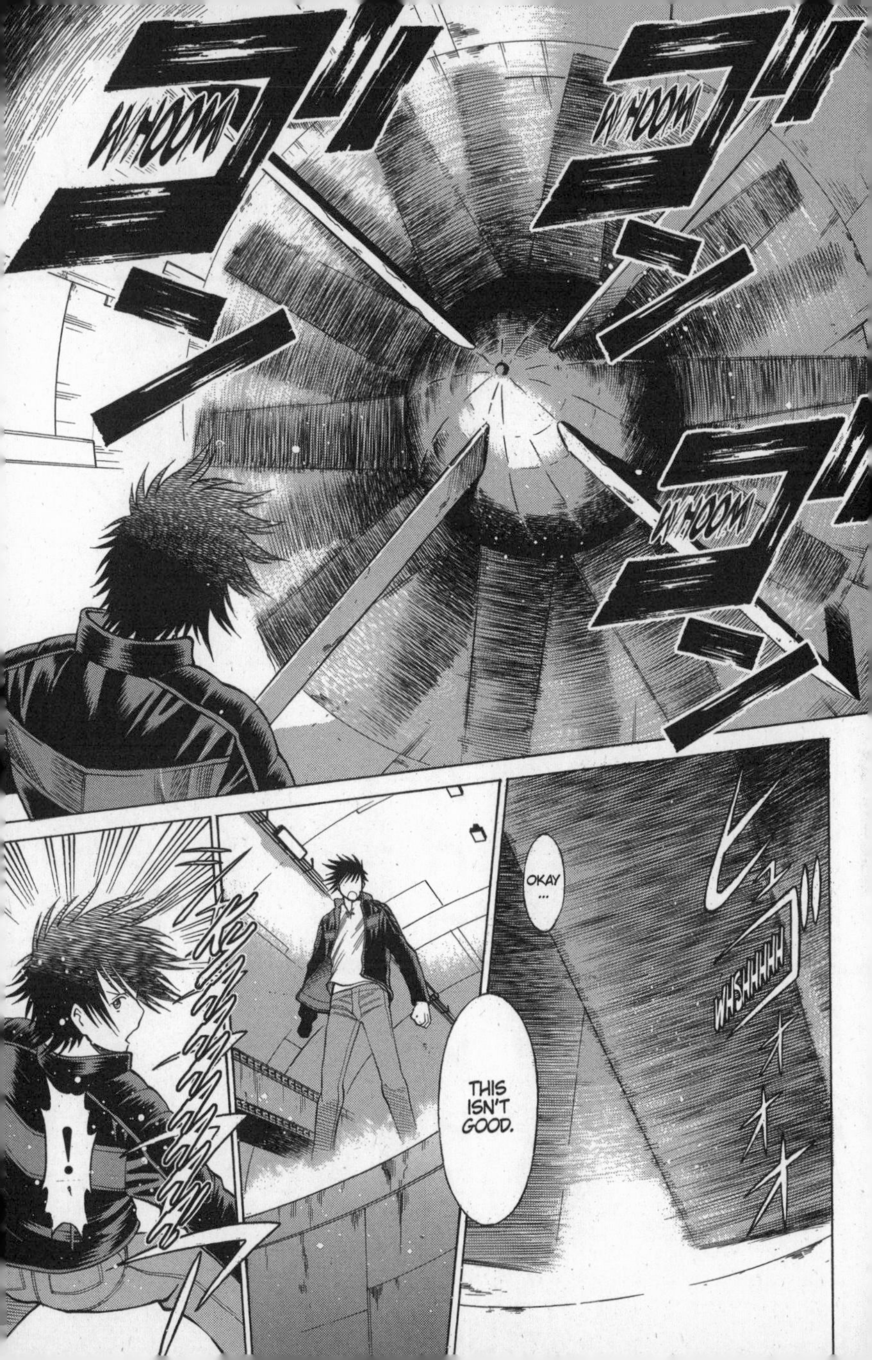
WHOOM
WHOOM
WHOOM
OKAY ...
WHSHHHH
THIS ISN'T GOOD.
!

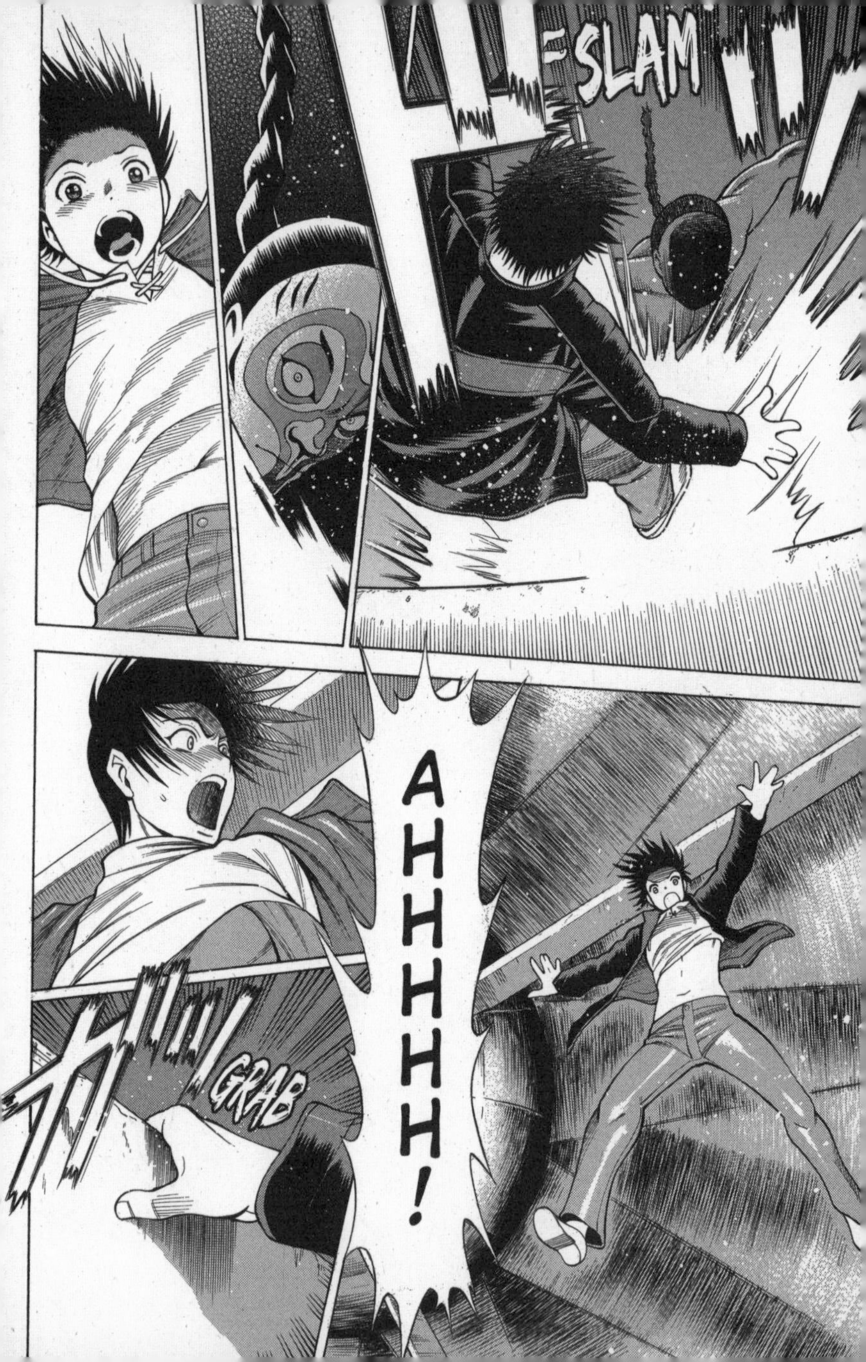
SLAM
AHHHHH!
GRAB

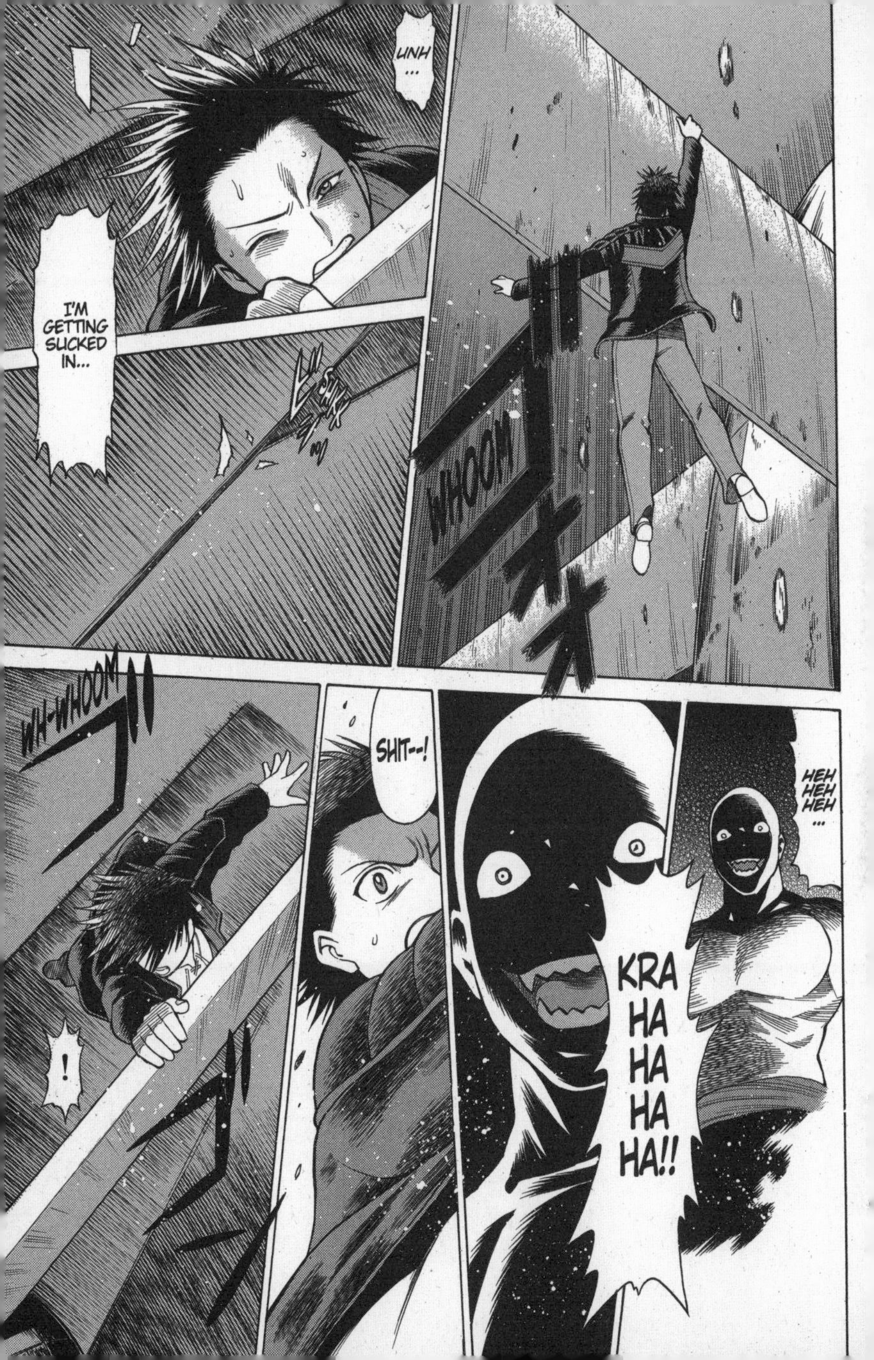
WHOOM
UNH...
I'M GETTING SUCKED IN...
SHIK
HEH HEH HEH...
KRA HA HA HA HA HA!!
SHIT--!
WH-WHOOM
!

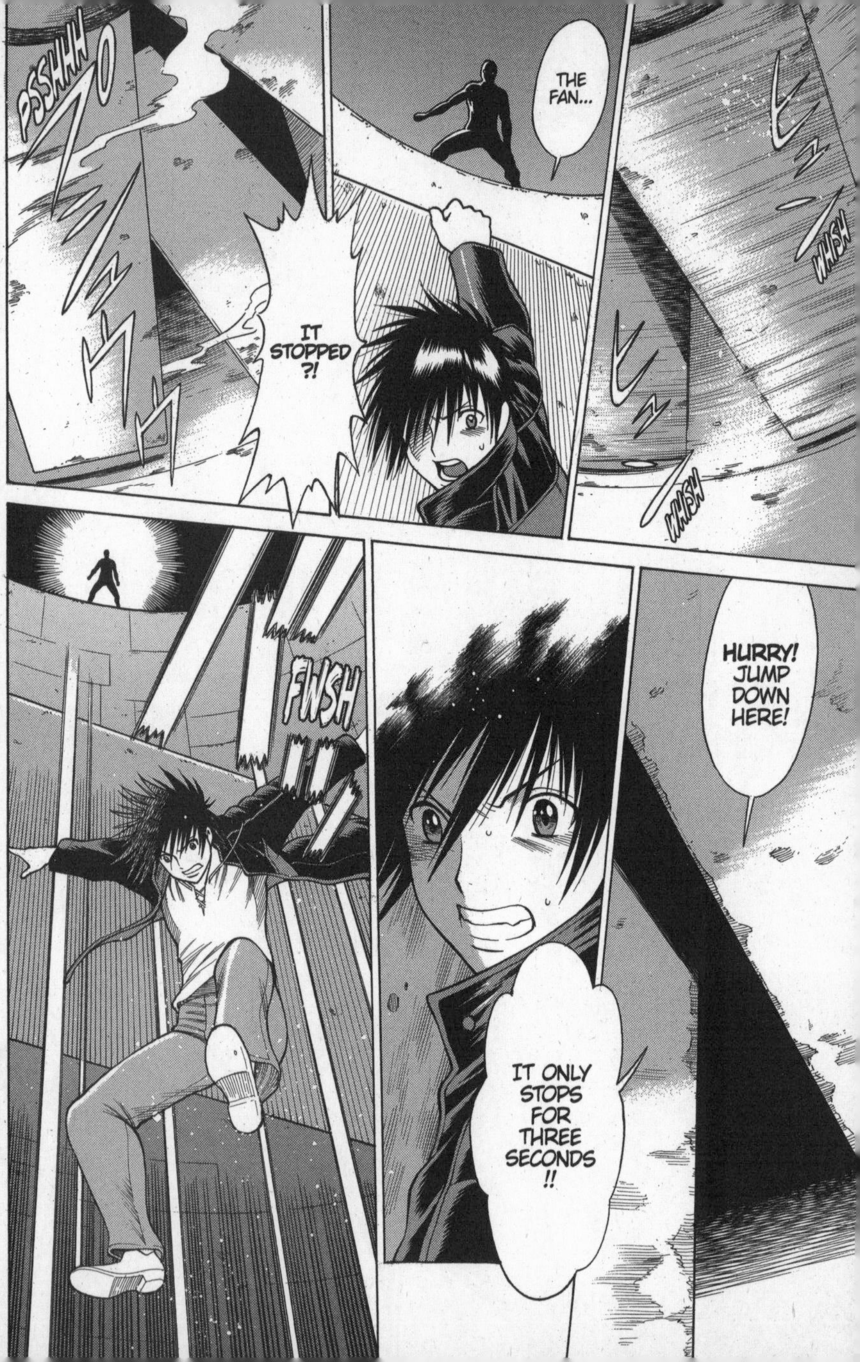
WHSH
WHSH
THE FAN...
IT STOPPED ?!
PSSHHH
HURRY! JUMP DOWN HERE!
IT ONLY STOPS FOR THREE SECONDS !!
FWSH !!

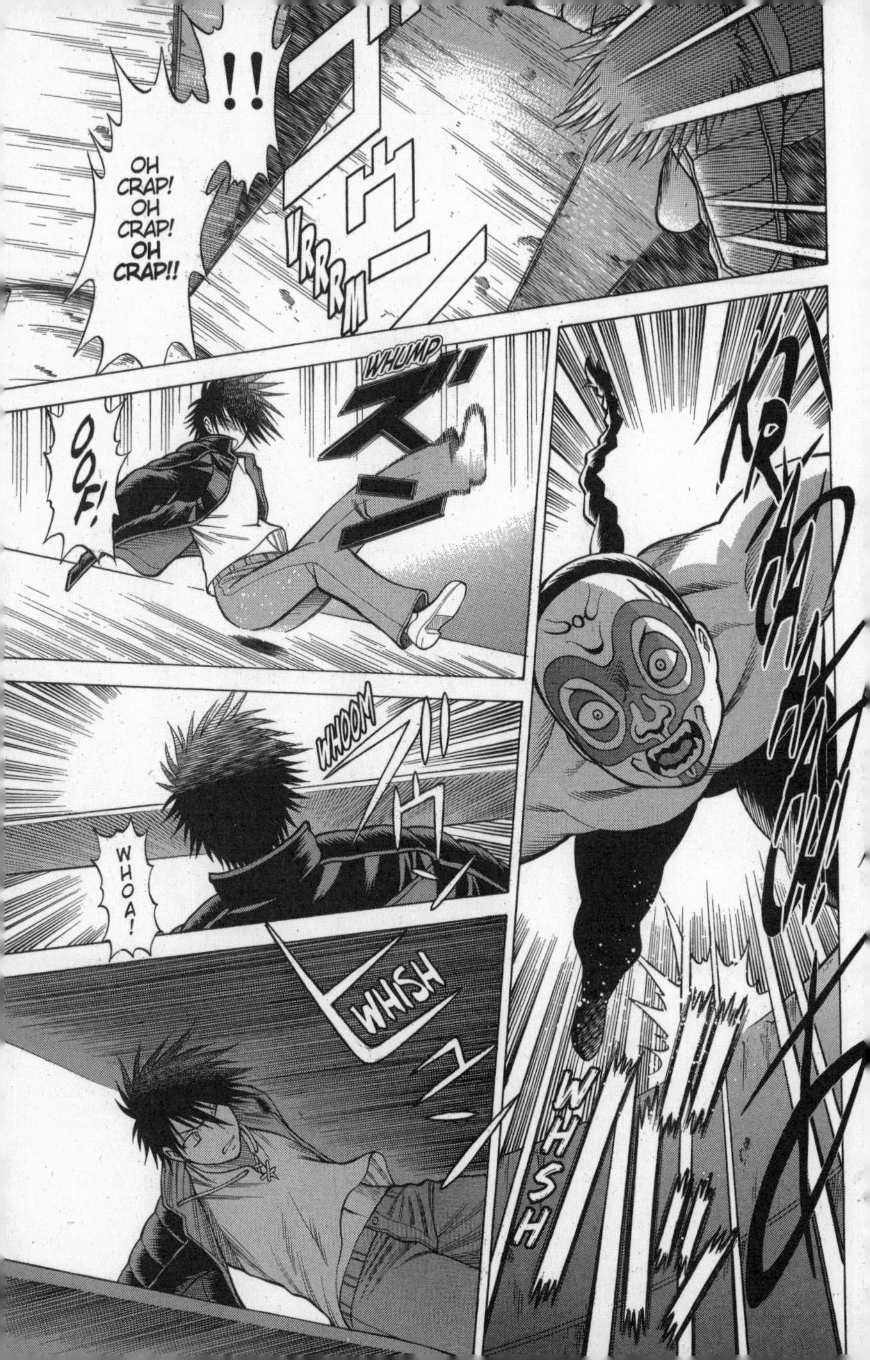
!!
OH CRAP! OH CRAP! OH CRAP!!
VRRRM
WHSH
WHUMP
OOF!
WHOOM
WHOA!
WHSH

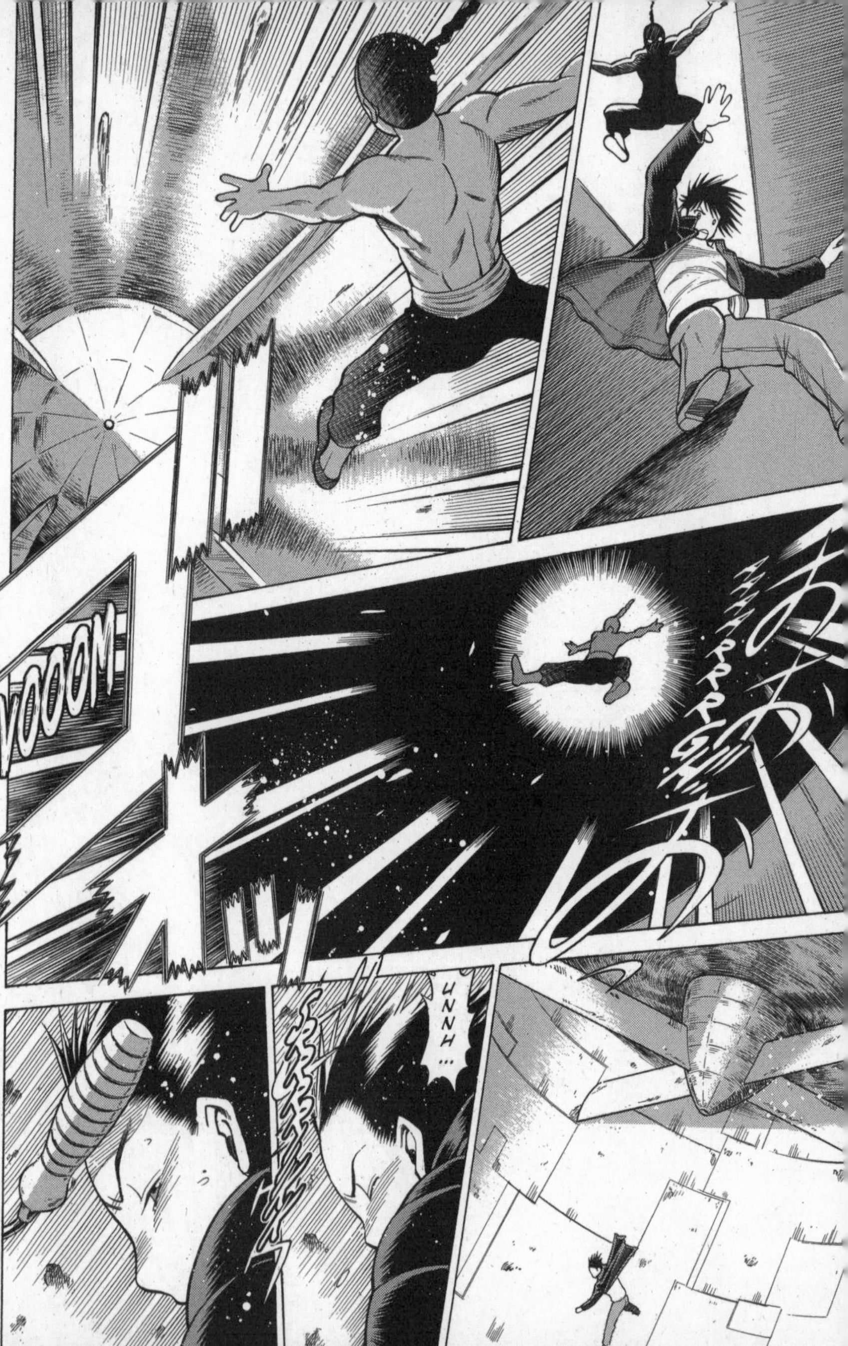
AAAARRRRRGH!!!
VOOOM
UNNH...

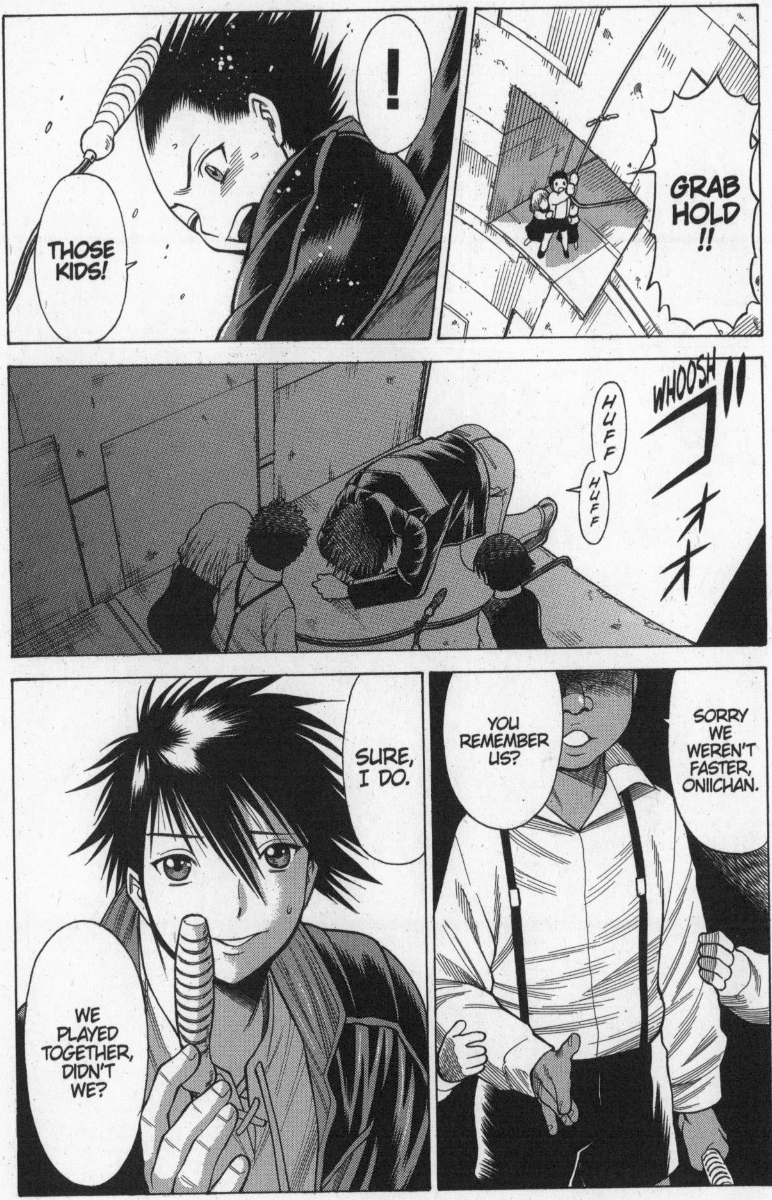
GRAB HOLD !!
!
THOSE KIDS!
WHOOSH
HUFF HUFF
SORRY WE WEREN'T FASTER, ONIICHAN.
YOU REMEMBER US?
SURE, I DO.
WE PLAYED TOGETHER, DIDN'T WE?

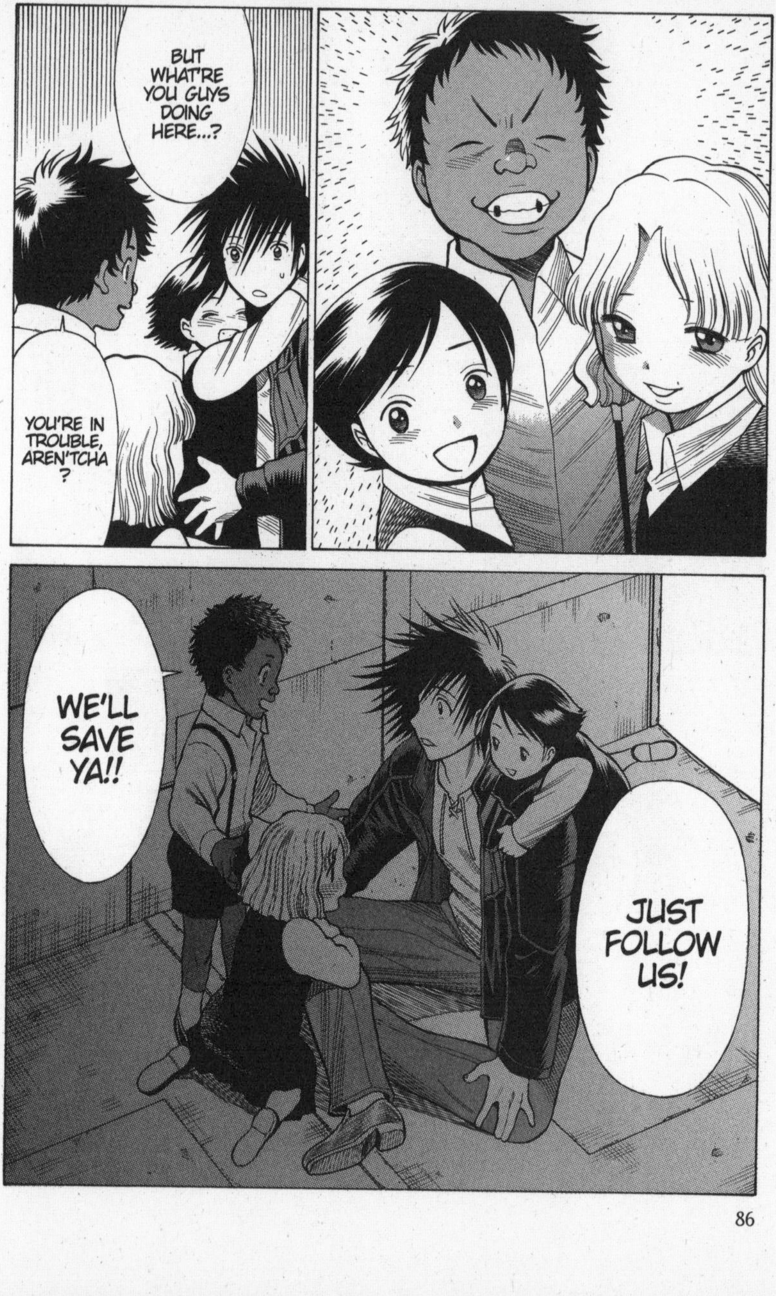
BUT WHAT'RE YOU GUYS DOING HERE...?
YOU'RE IN TROUBLE, AREN'TCHA?
WE'LL SAVE YA!!
JUST FOLLOW US!

Chapter 28: The Honeybee's Whisper

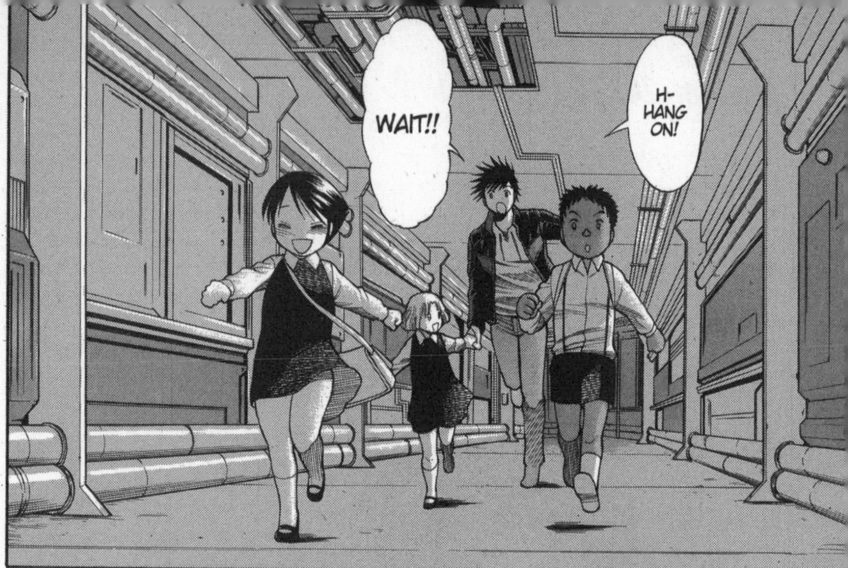
H-HANG ON!
WAIT!!

*The words "assassin" and "rectangle" are both pronounced "shikaku" in Japanese

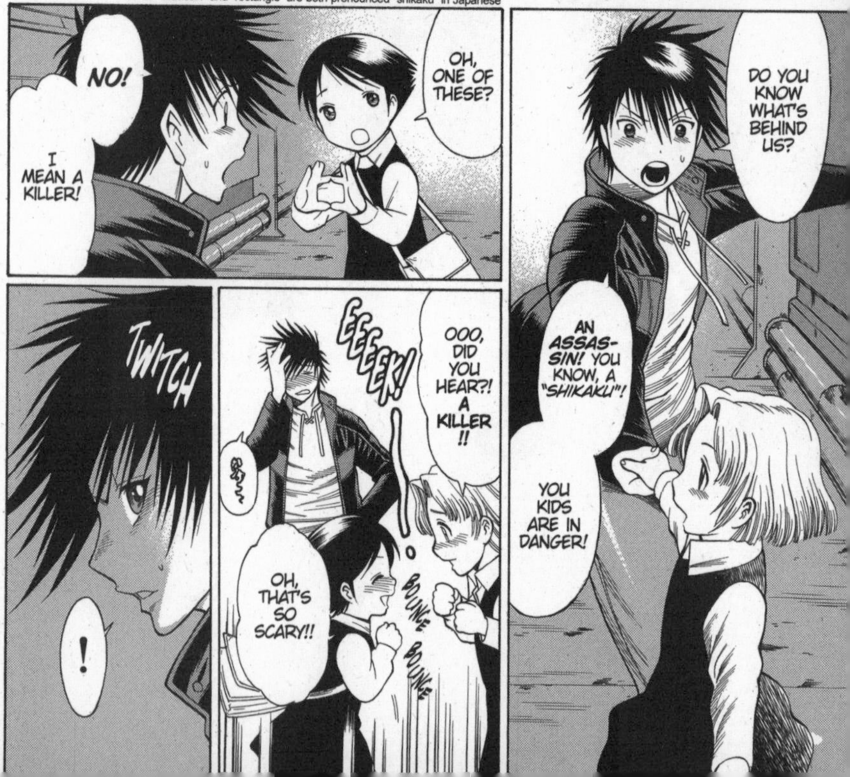
DO YOU KNOW WHAT'S BEHIND US?
AN ASSAS-SIN! YOU KNOW, A "SHIKAKU"!
YOU KIDS ARE IN DANGER!
OH, ONE OF THESE?
NO!
I MEAN A KILLER!
EEEEK!
OOO, DID YOU HEAR?! A KILLER!!
OH, THAT'S SO SCARY!!
BOUNCE
BOUNCE
TWITCH
!

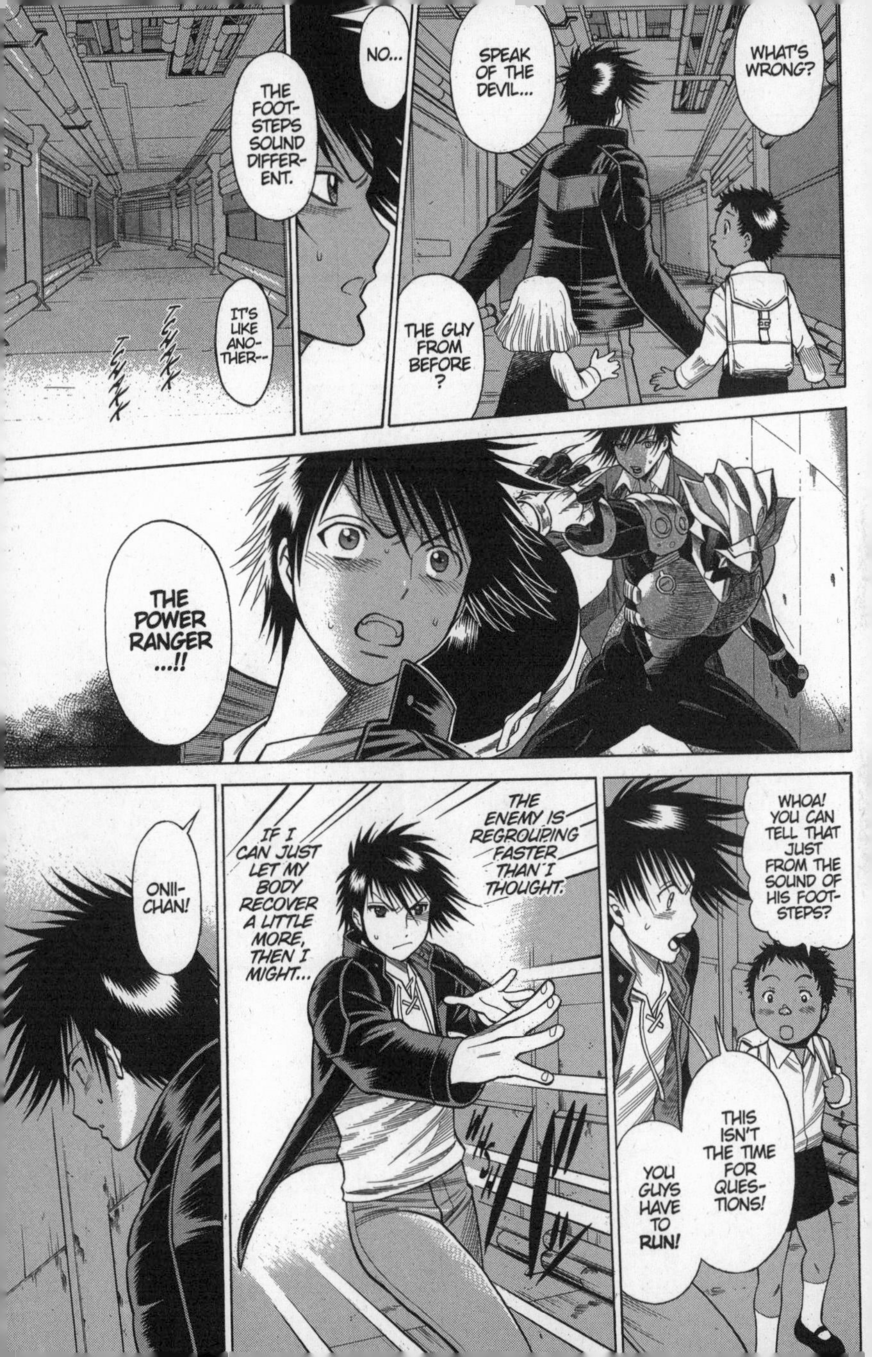
WHAT'S WRONG?
SPEAK OF THE DEVIL...
THE GUY FROM BEFORE?
NO...
THE FOOT-STEPS SOUND DIFFER-ENT.
IT'S LIKE ANO-THER--
TCHAKK
TCHAKK
THE POWER RANGER ...!!
WHOA! YOU CAN TELL THAT JUST FROM THE SOUND OF HIS FOOT-STEPS?
THIS ISN'T THE TIME FOR QUES-TIONS!
YOU GUYS HAVE TO RUN!
THE ENEMY IS REGROUPING FASTER THAN I THOUGHT.
IF I CAN JUST LET MY BODY RECOVER A LITTLE MORE, THEN I MIGHT...
ONII-CHAN!

UP HERE!
TCHAKK
TCHAKK
TCHAKK
KACHAKK
KACHAKK
BEEP
BEEP
BEEP
BEEP
BEE
BEE
BEE
BEE

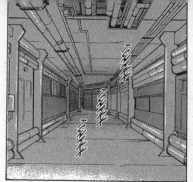

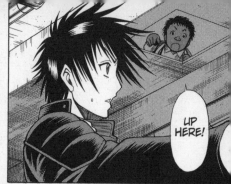

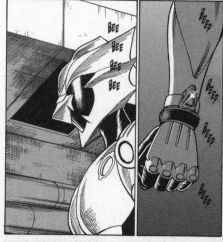

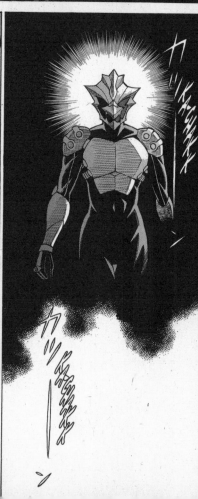

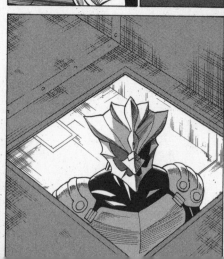

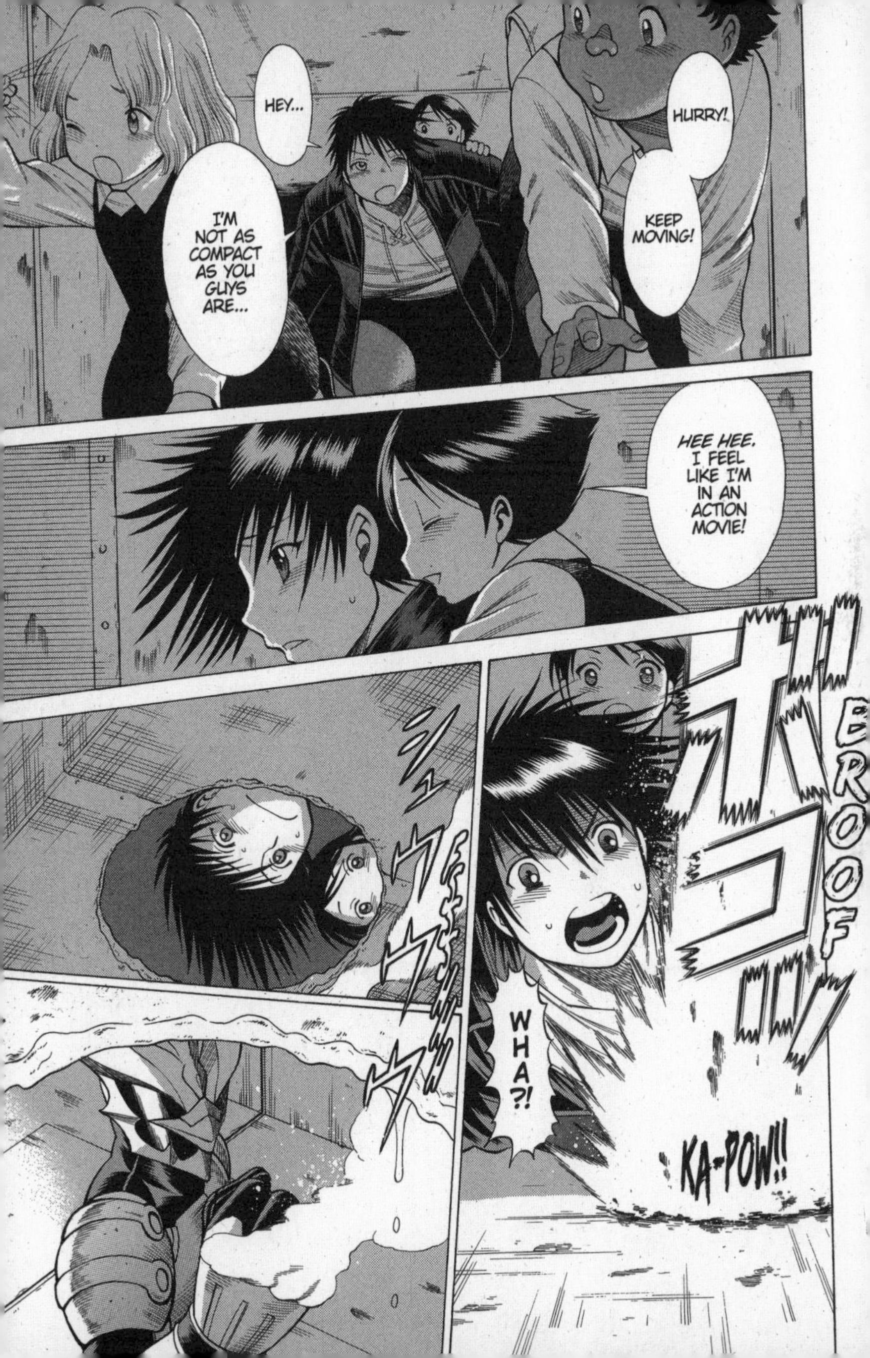
HURRY!
KEEP MOVING!
HEY...
I'M NOT AS COMPACT AS YOU GUYS ARE...
HEE HEE. I FEEL LIKE I'M IN AN ACTION MOVIE!
BROOF
WHA?!
KA-POW!!

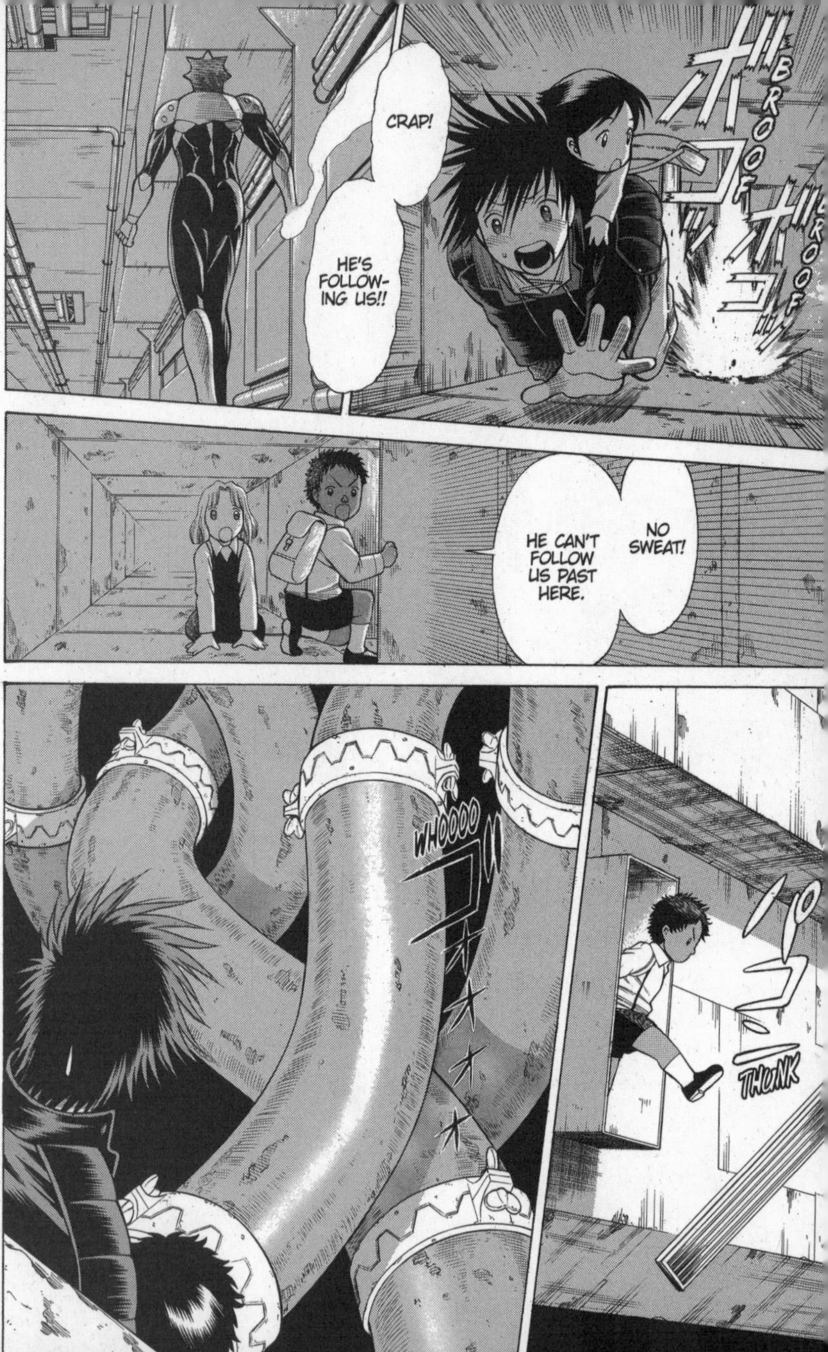
BROOOF
BROOOF
CRAP!
HE'S FOLLOW-ING US!!
NO SWEAT!
HE CAN'T FOLLOW US PAST HERE.
THUNK
WHOOOO

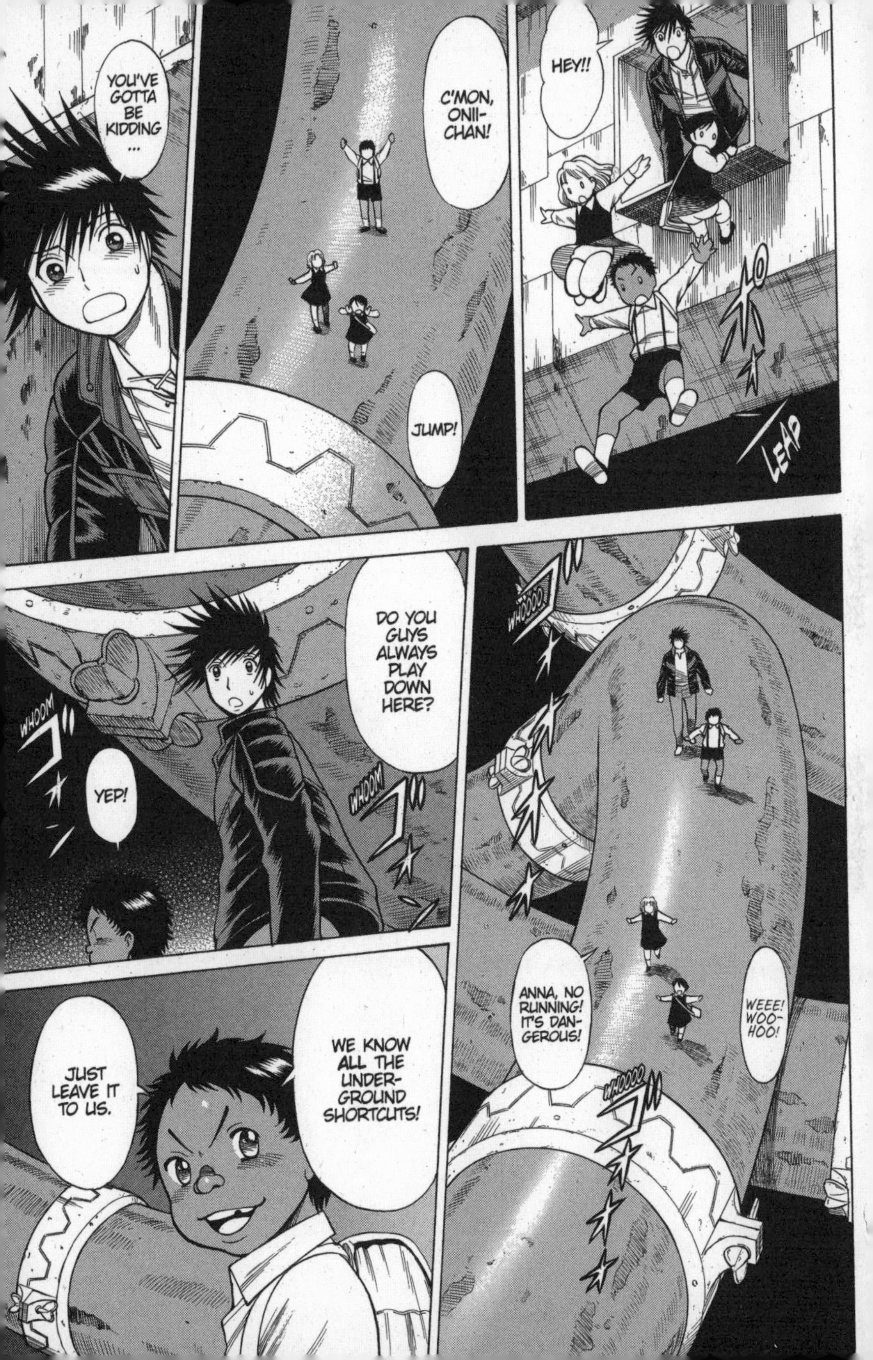
HEY!!
LEAP
C'MON, ONII-CHAN!
JUMP!
YOU'VE GOTTA BE KIDDING ...
WHOOOO
WEEE! WOO-HOO!
ANNA, NO RUNNING! IT'S DAN-GEROUS!
WHOOOO
DO YOU GUYS ALWAYS PLAY DOWN HERE?
WHOOM
WHOOM
YEP!
WE KNOW ALL THE UNDER-GROUND SHORTCUTS!
JUST LEAVE IT TO US.

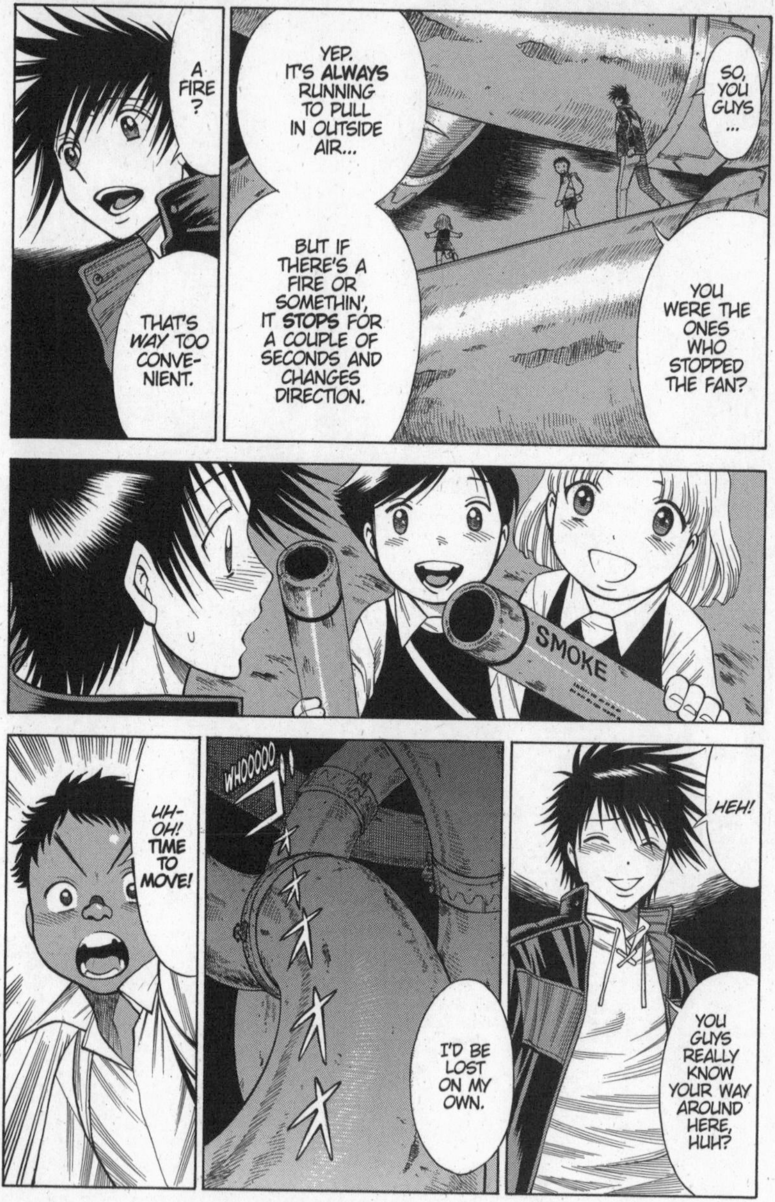

SO, YOU GUYS ...
YOU WERE THE ONES WHO STOPPED THE FAN?
YEP. IT'S **ALWAYS** RUNNING TO PULL IN OUTSIDE AIR...
BUT IF THERE'S A FIRE OR SOMETHIN', IT **STOPS** FOR A COUPLE OF SECONDS AND CHANGES DIRECTION.
A FIRE?
THAT'S *WAY* TOO CONVENIENT.
SMOKE
HEH!
YOU GUYS REALLY KNOW YOUR WAY AROUND HERE, HUH?
I'D BE LOST ON MY OWN.
WHOOOOO
UH-OH! TIME TO MOVE!

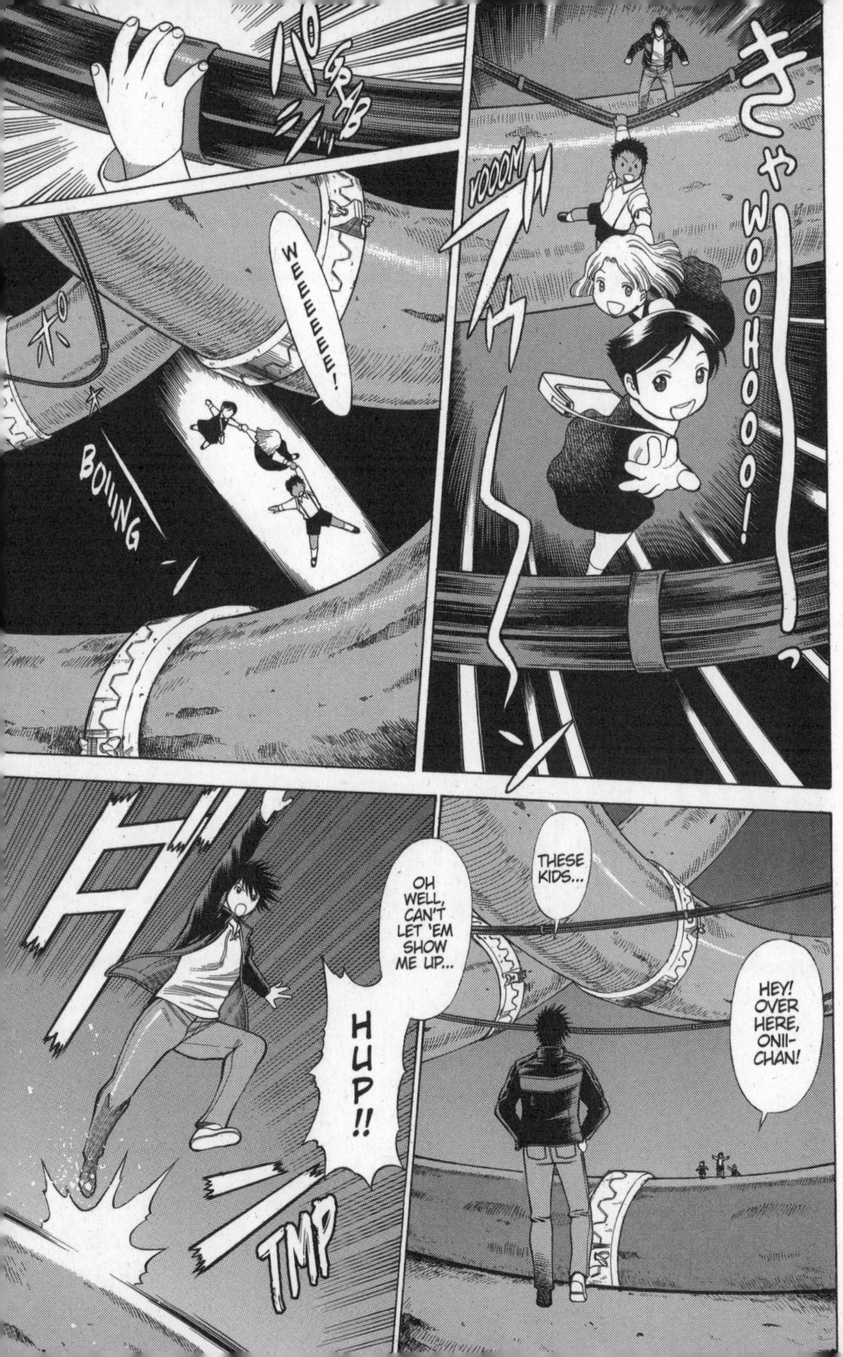
WOOHOOHOOOO!
VOOOM
GRAB
WEEEEEEE!
BOIIING
HEY! OVER HERE, ONII-CHAN!
THESE KIDS...
OH WELL, CAN'T LET 'EM SHOW ME UP...
HUP!!
TMP

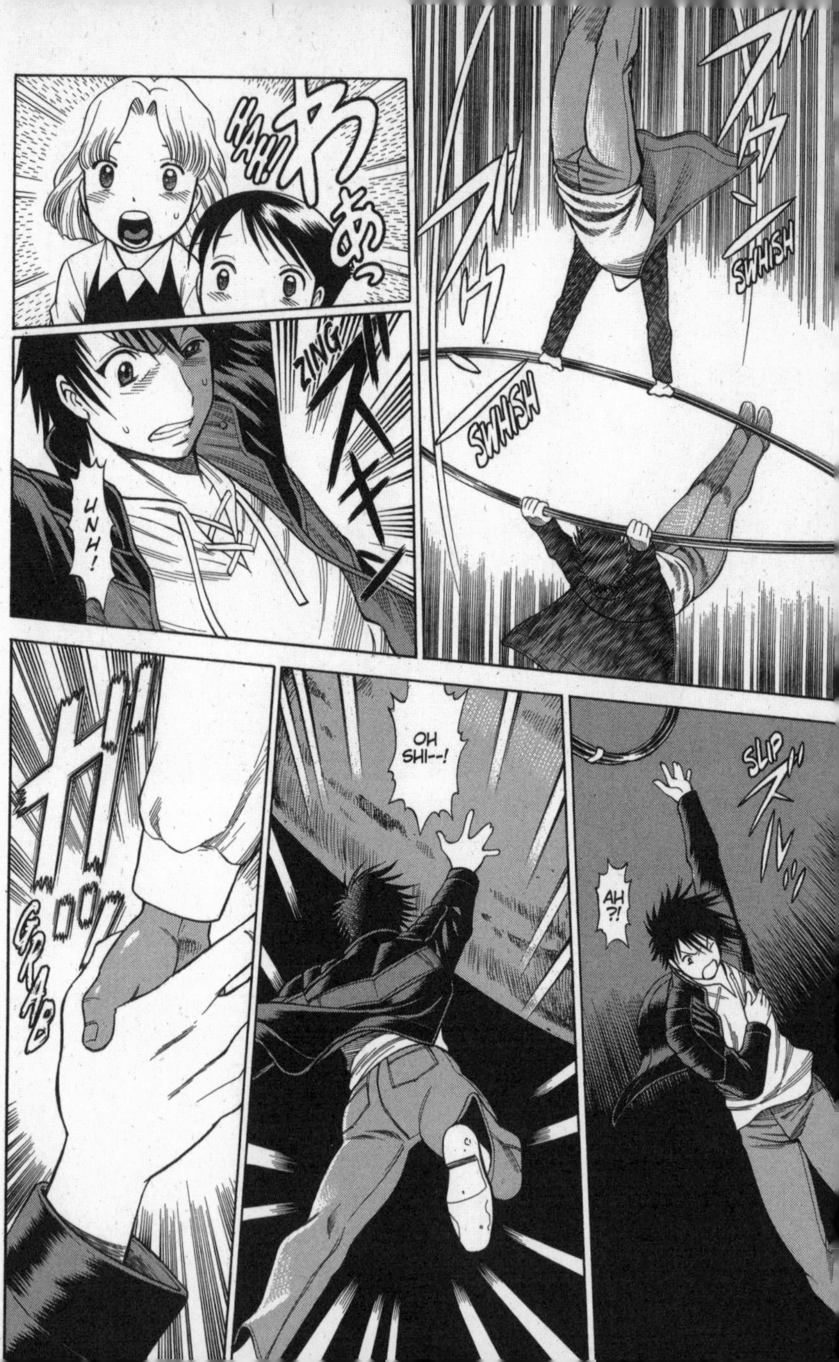
SWHISH
SWHISH
HAH!
わあっ
ZING
UNH!
SLIP
AH?!
OH SHI--!
GRAB

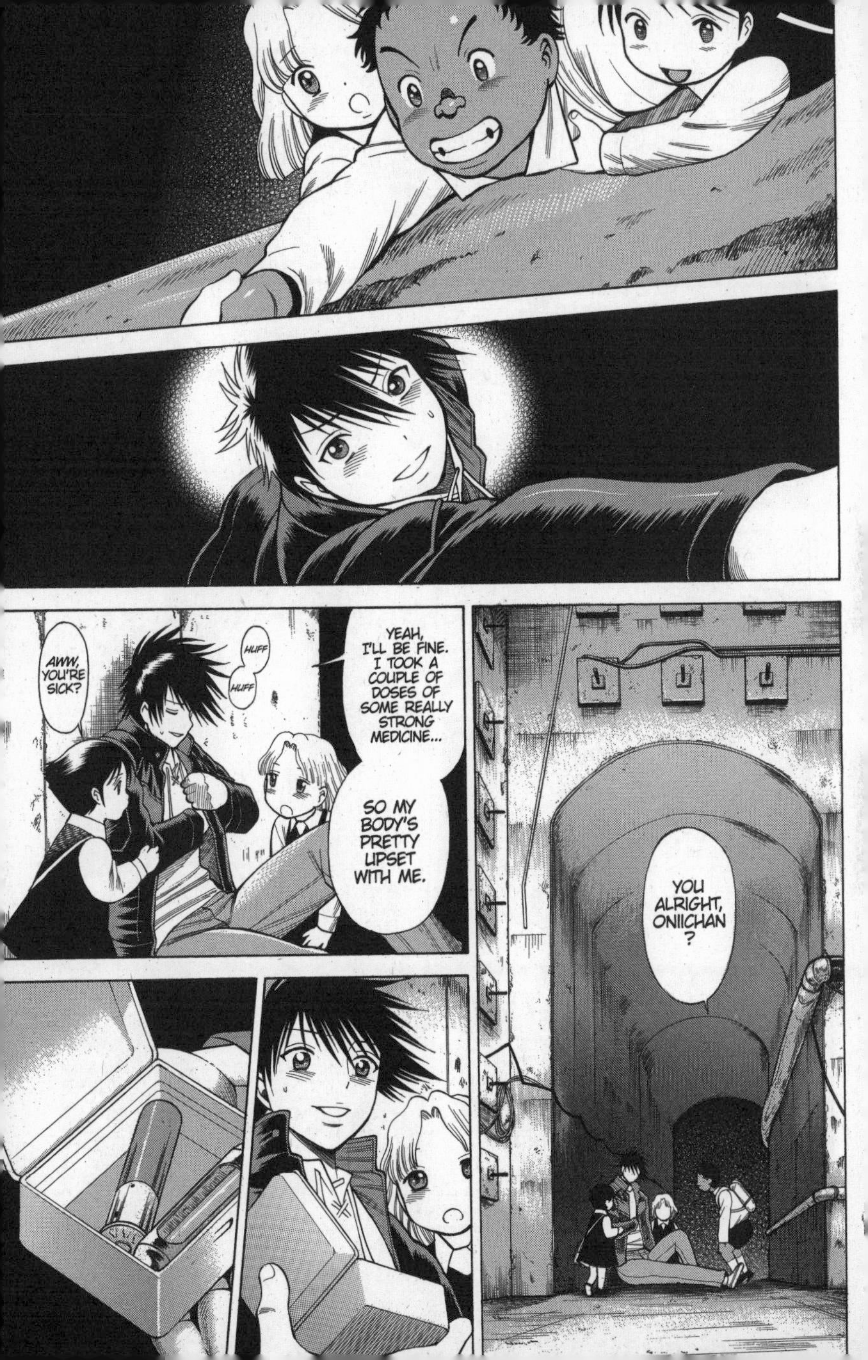
YOU ALRIGHT, ONIICHAN?
YEAH, I'LL BE FINE. I TOOK A COUPLE OF DOSES OF SOME REALLY STRONG MEDICINE...
HUFF
HUFF
SO MY BODY'S PRETTY UPSET WITH ME.
AWW, YOU'RE SICK?

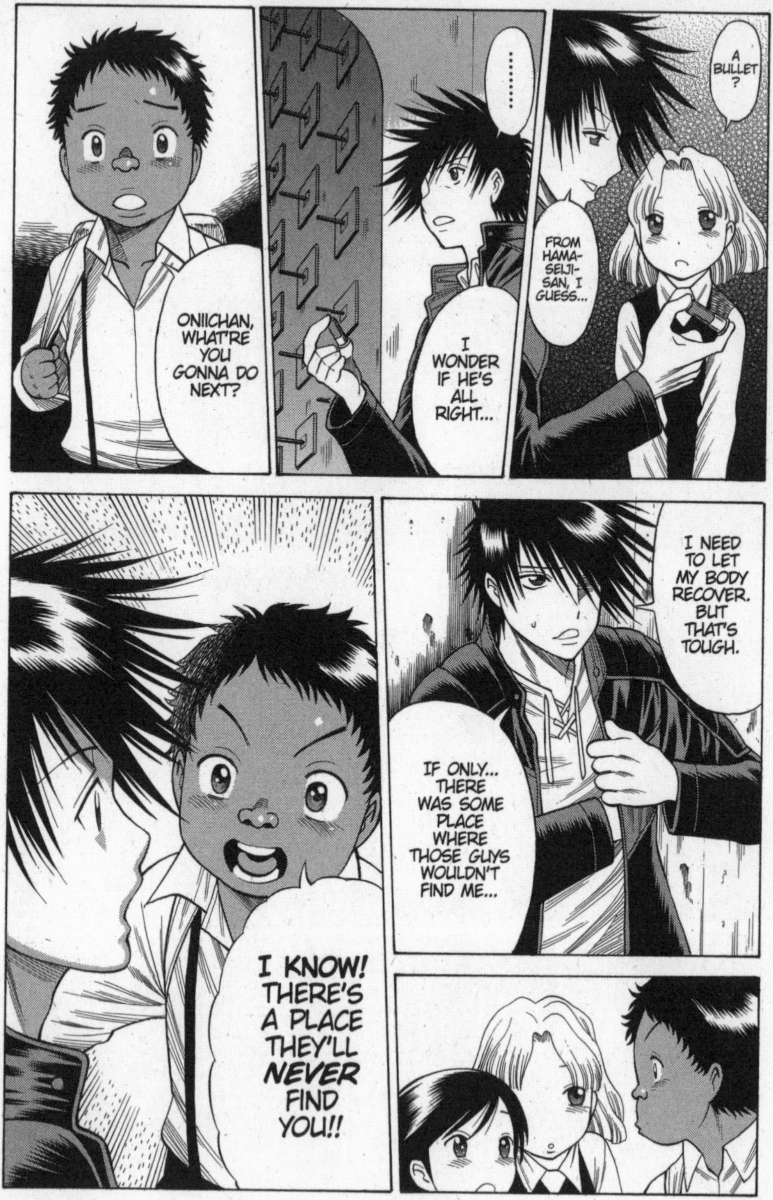
A BULLET?
FROM HAMA-SEIJI-SAN, I GUESS...
......
I WONDER IF HE'S ALL RIGHT...
ONIICHAN, WHAT'RE YOU GONNA DO NEXT?
I NEED TO LET MY BODY RECOVER. BUT THAT'S TOUGH.
IF ONLY... THERE WAS SOME PLACE WHERE THOSE GUYS WOULDN'T FIND ME...
I KNOW! THERE'S A PLACE THEY'LL NEVER FIND YOU!!

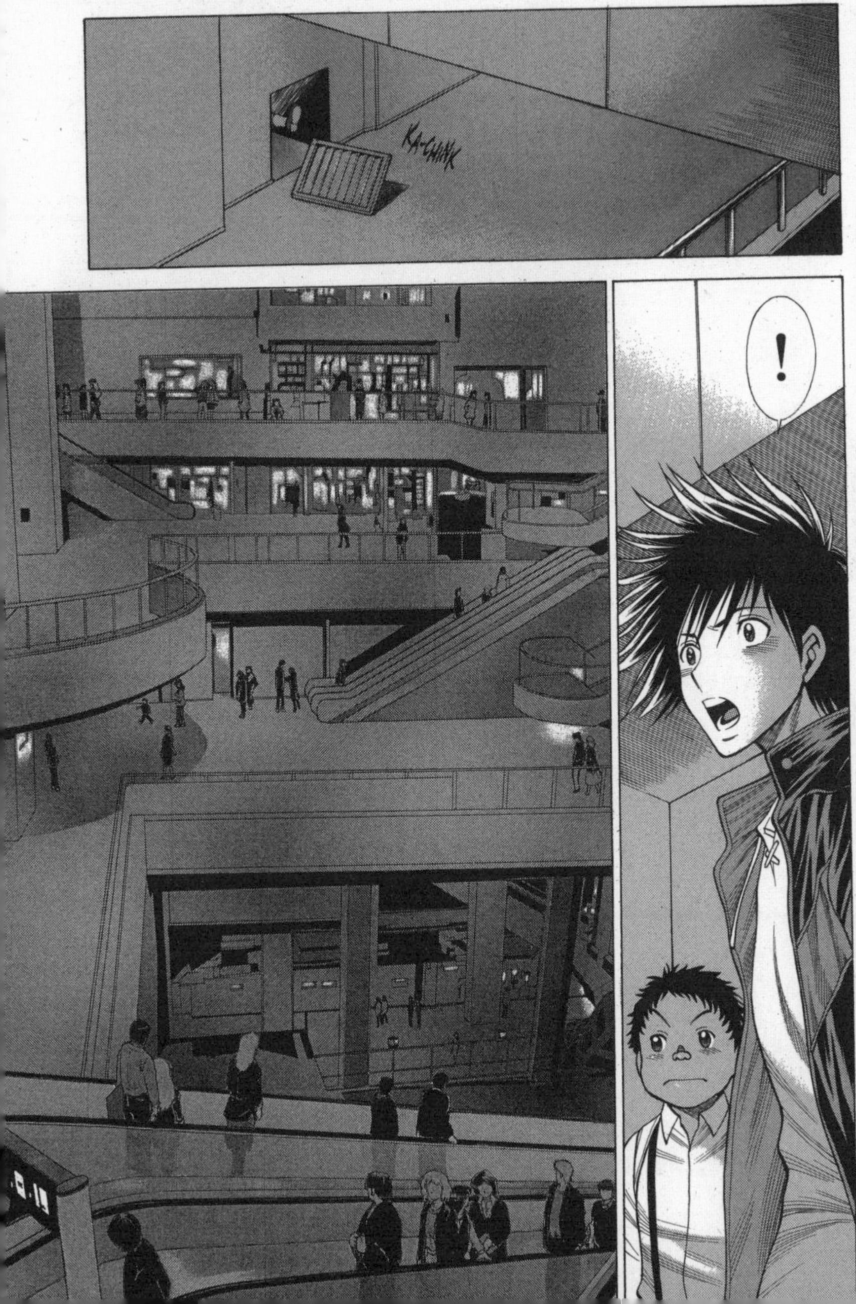
KA-CHINK
!

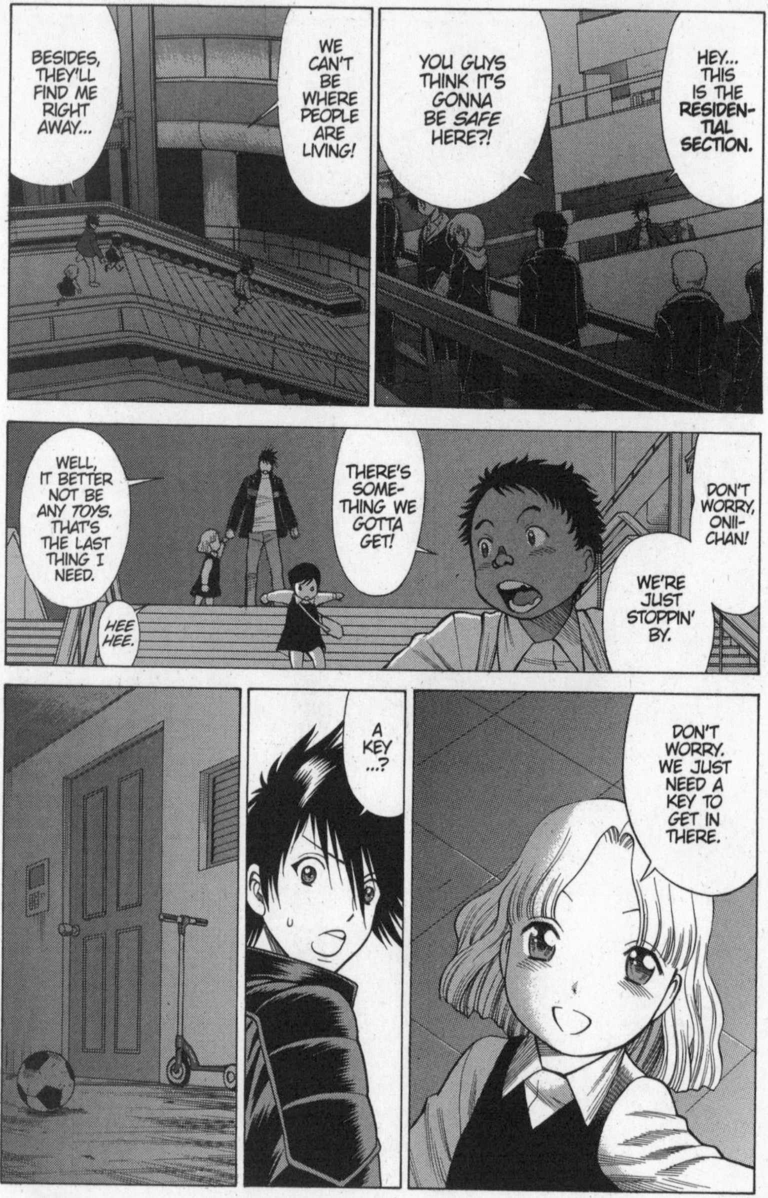
HEY... THIS IS THE RESIDENTIAL SECTION.
YOU GUYS THINK IT'S GONNA BE *SAFE* HERE?!
WE CAN'T BE WHERE PEOPLE ARE LIVING!
BESIDES, THEY'LL FIND ME RIGHT AWAY...
DON'T WORRY, ONII-CHAN!
WE'RE JUST STOPPIN' BY.
THERE'S SOMETHING WE GOTTA GET!
WELL, IT BETTER NOT BE ANY *TOYS*. THAT'S THE LAST THING I NEED.
HEE HEE.
DON'T WORRY. WE JUST NEED A KEY TO GET IN THERE.
A KEY ...?

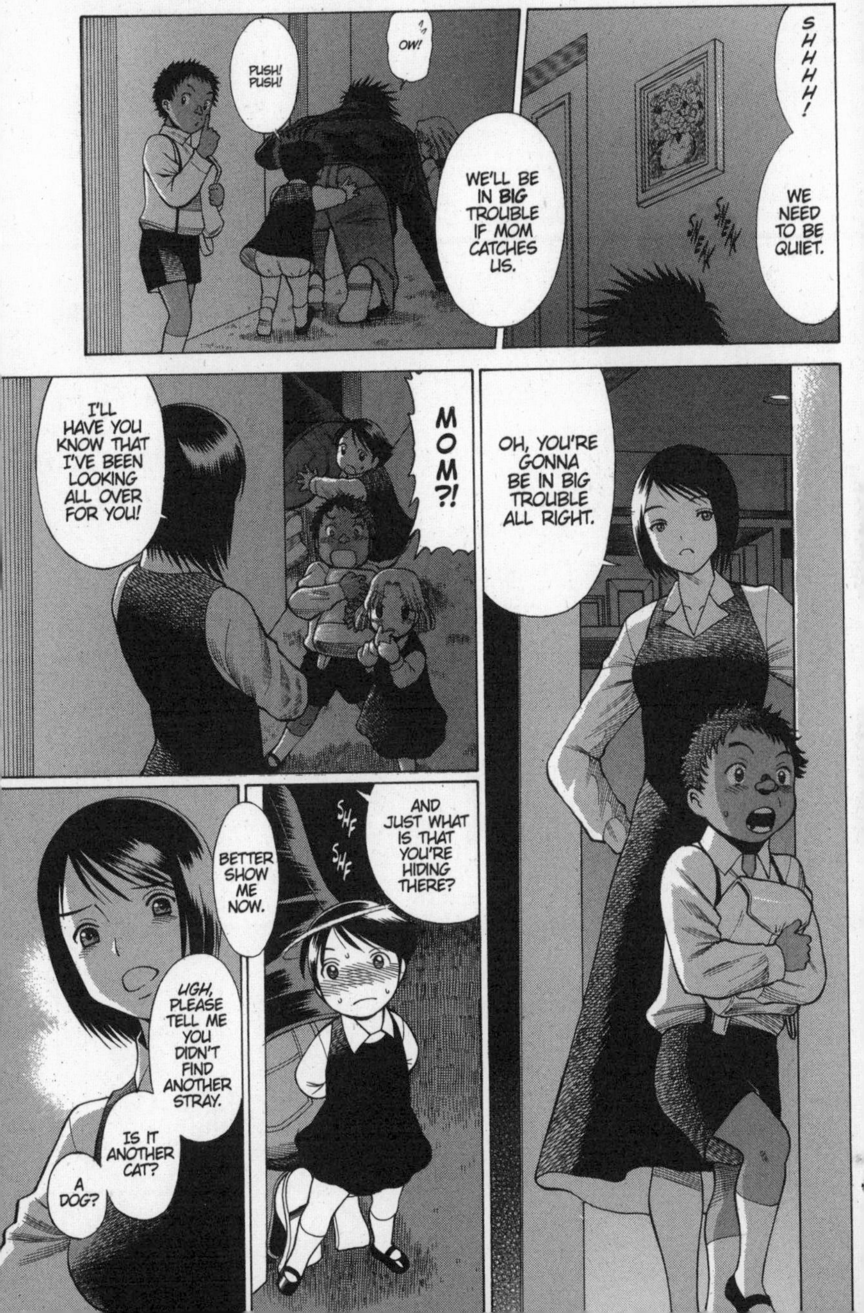
SHHHH!
WE NEED TO BE QUIET.
SHEN SHEN
WE'LL BE IN BIG TROUBLE IF MOM CATCHES US.
OW!
PUSH! PUSH!
OH, YOU'RE GONNA BE IN BIG TROUBLE ALL RIGHT.
MOM?!
I'LL HAVE YOU KNOW THAT I'VE BEEN LOOKING ALL OVER FOR YOU!
AND JUST WHAT IS THAT YOU'RE HIDING THERE?
SHF SHF
BETTER SHOW ME NOW.
UGH, PLEASE TELL ME YOU DIDN'T FIND ANOTHER STRAY.
IS IT ANOTHER CAT?
A DOG?

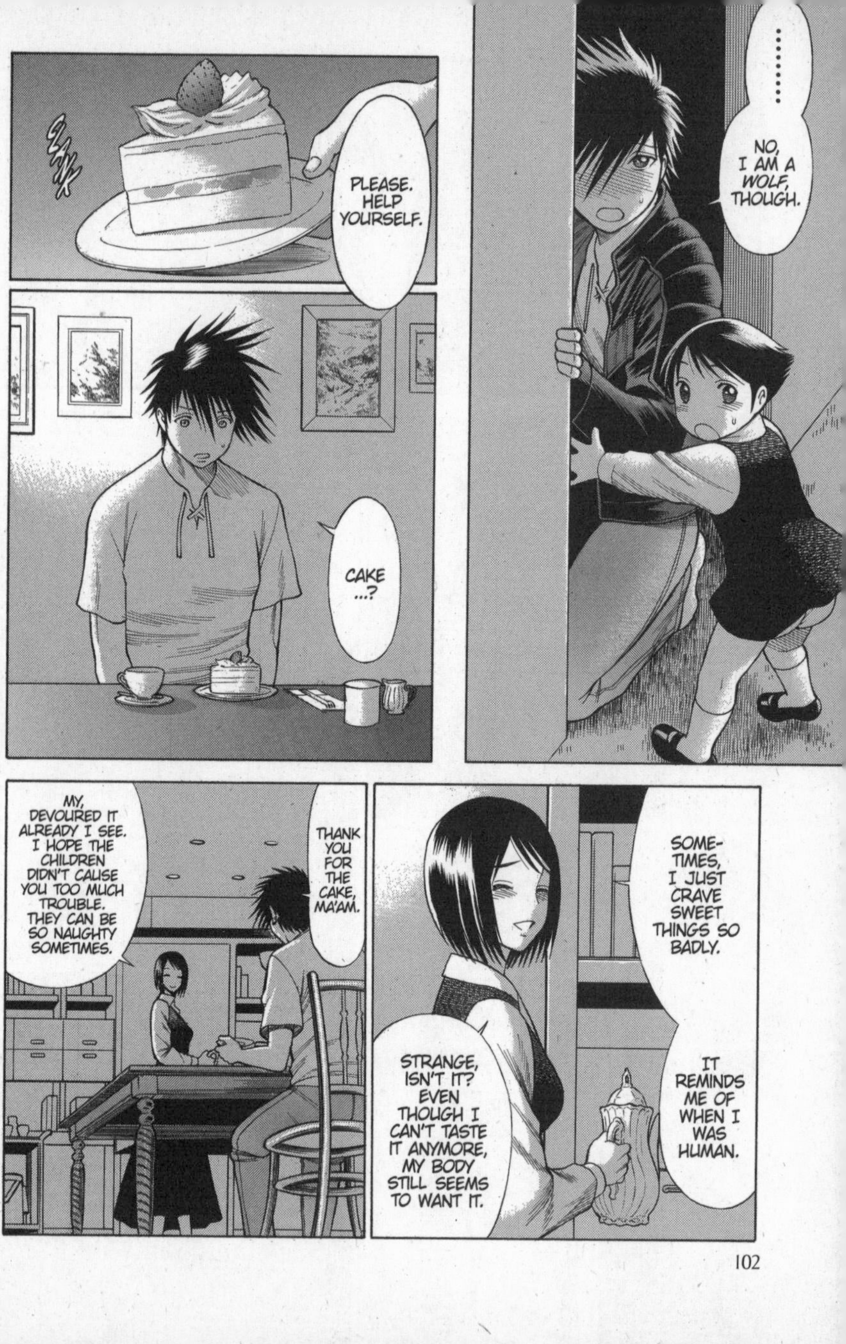
......
NO, I AM A WOLF, THOUGH.
PLEASE. HELP YOURSELF.
CAKE ...?
SOME-TIMES, I JUST CRAVE SWEET THINGS SO BADLY.
IT REMINDS ME OF WHEN I WAS HUMAN.
STRANGE, ISN'T IT? EVEN THOUGH I CAN'T TASTE IT ANYMORE, MY BODY STILL SEEMS TO WANT IT.
THANK YOU FOR THE CAKE, MA'AM.
MY, DEVOURED IT ALREADY I SEE. I HOPE THE CHILDREN DIDN'T CAUSE YOU TOO MUCH TROUBLE. THEY CAN BE SO NAUGHTY SOMETIMES.

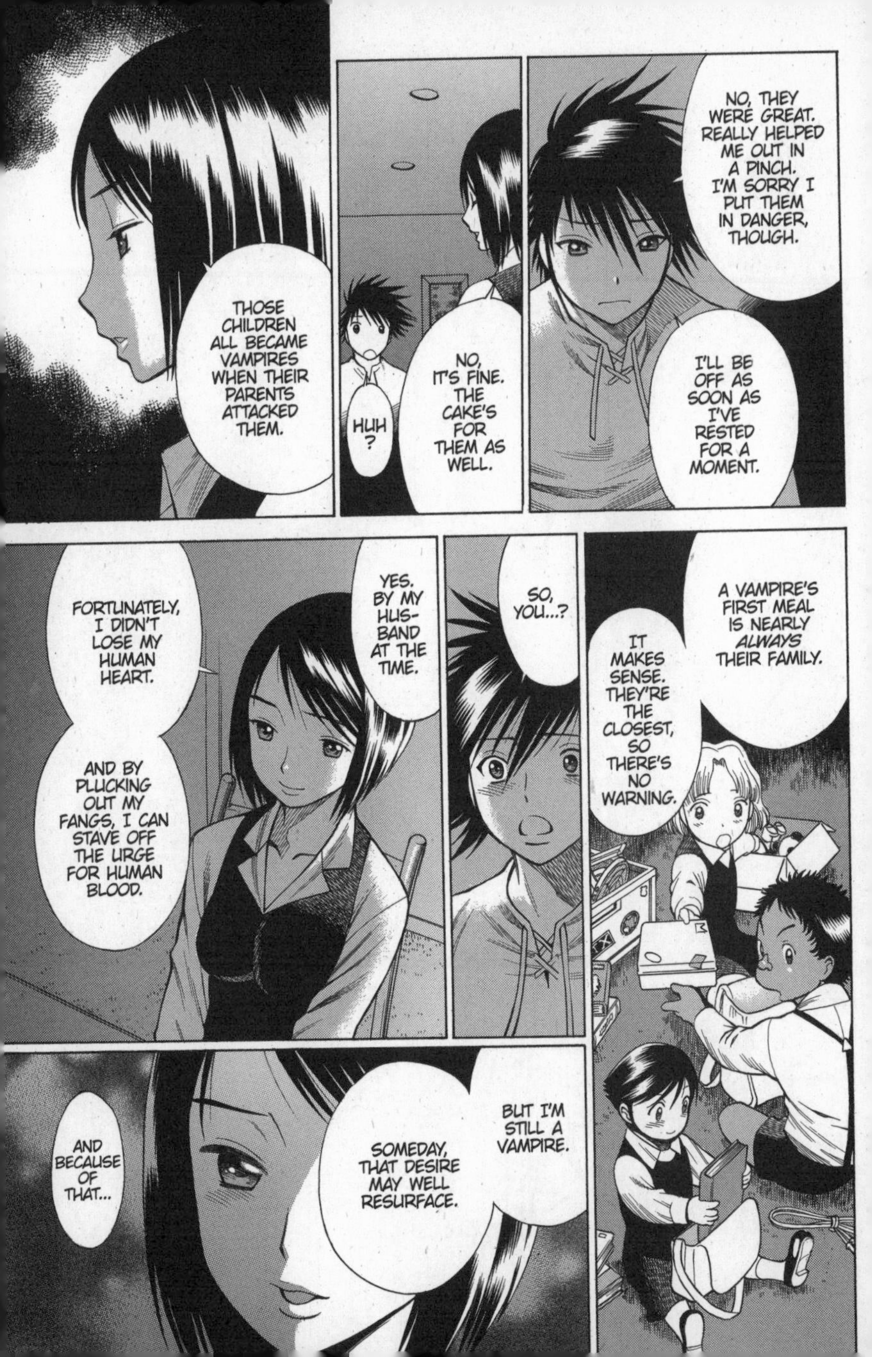
NO, THEY WERE GREAT. REALLY HELPED ME OUT IN A PINCH. I'M SORRY I PUT THEM IN DANGER, THOUGH.
I'LL BE OFF AS SOON AS I'VE RESTED FOR A MOMENT.
NO, IT'S FINE. THE CAKE'S FOR THEM AS WELL.
HUH?
THOSE CHILDREN ALL BECAME VAMPIRES WHEN THEIR PARENTS ATTACKED THEM.
A VAMPIRE'S FIRST MEAL IS NEARLY *ALWAYS* THEIR FAMILY.
IT MAKES SENSE. THEY'RE THE CLOSEST, SO THERE'S NO WARNING.
SO, YOU...?
YES. BY MY HUS-BAND AT THE TIME.
FORTUNATELY, I DIDN'T LOSE MY HUMAN HEART.
AND BY PLUCKING OUT MY FANGS, I CAN STAVE OFF THE URGE FOR HUMAN BLOOD.
BUT I'M STILL A VAMPIRE.
SOMEDAY, THAT DESIRE MAY WELL RESURFACE.
AND BECAUSE OF THAT...

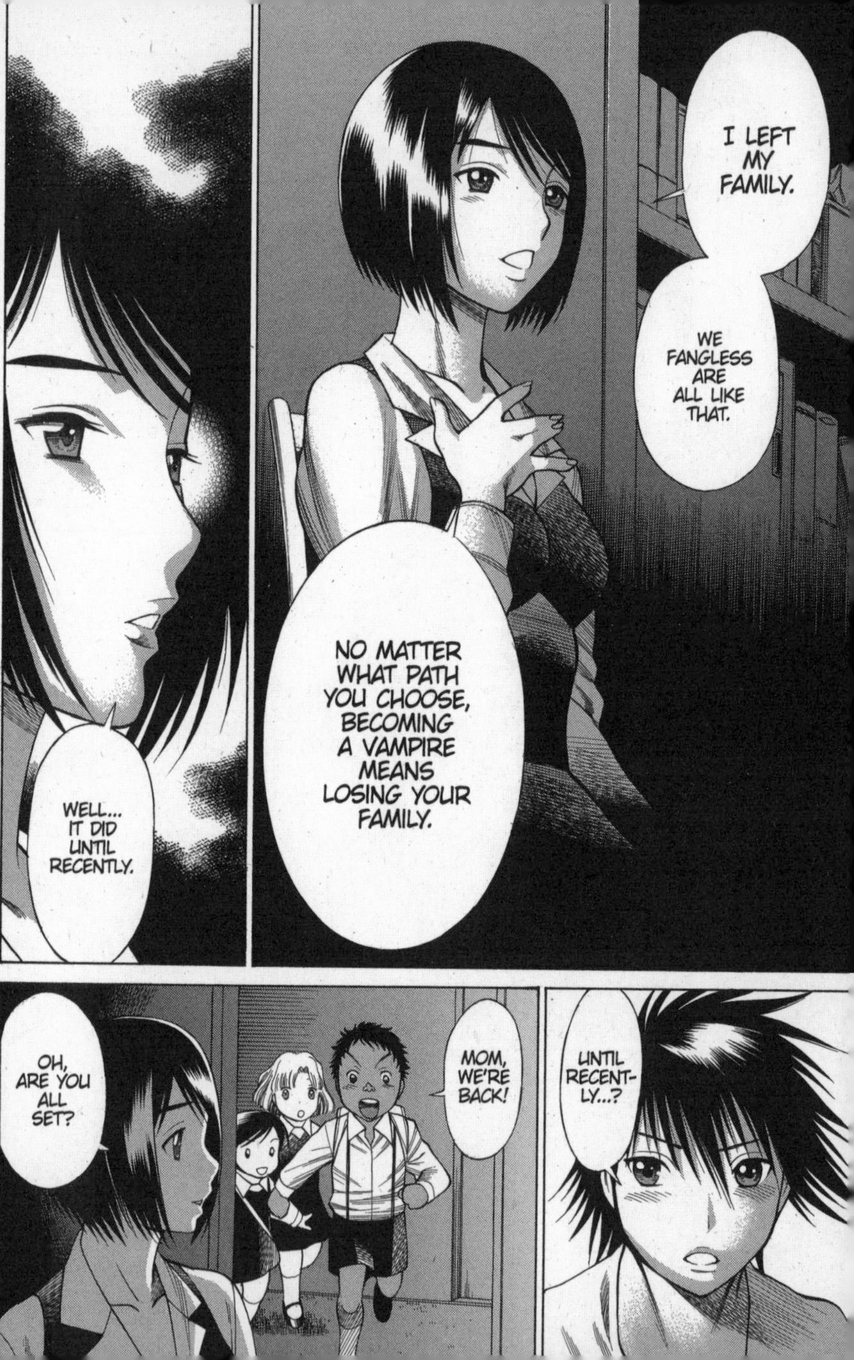
I LEFT MY FAMILY.
WE FANGLESS ARE ALL LIKE THAT.
NO MATTER WHAT PATH YOU CHOOSE, BECOMING A VAMPIRE MEANS LOSING YOUR FAMILY.
WELL... IT DID UNTIL RECENTLY.
UNTIL RECENT-LY...?
MOM, WE'RE BACK!
OH, ARE YOU ALL SET?

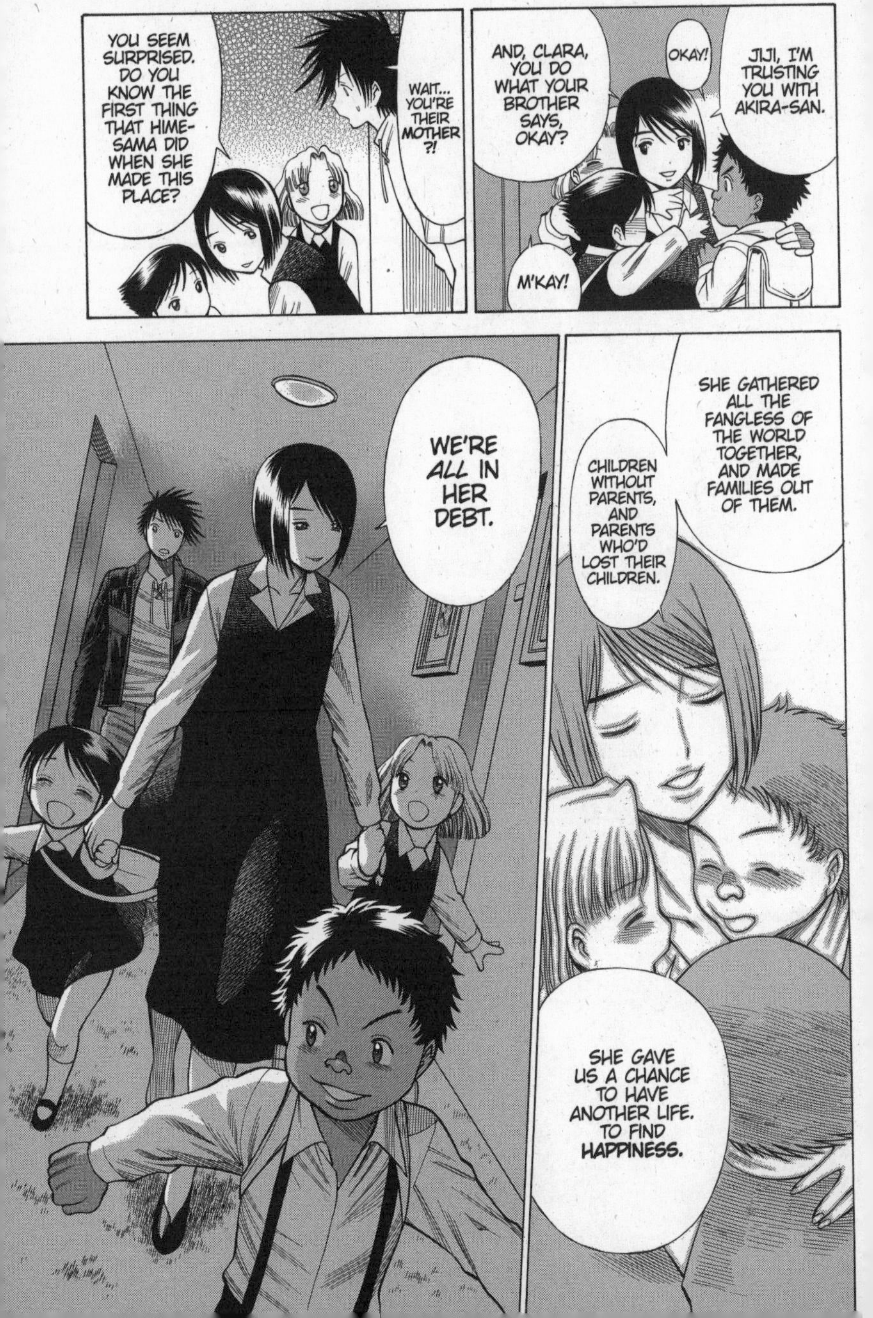
JIJI, I'M TRUSTING YOU WITH AKIRA-SAN.
OKAY!
AND, CLARA, YOU DO WHAT YOUR BROTHER SAYS, OKAY?
M'KAY!
WAIT... YOU'RE THEIR MOTHER?!
YOU SEEM SURPRISED. DO YOU KNOW THE FIRST THING THAT HIME-SAMA DID WHEN SHE MADE THIS PLACE?
SHE GATHERED ALL THE FANGLESS OF THE WORLD TOGETHER, AND MADE FAMILIES OUT OF THEM.
CHILDREN WITHOUT PARENTS, AND PARENTS WHO'D LOST THEIR CHILDREN.
SHE GAVE US A CHANCE TO HAVE ANOTHER LIFE. TO FIND **HAPPINESS.**
WE'RE *ALL* IN HER DEBT.

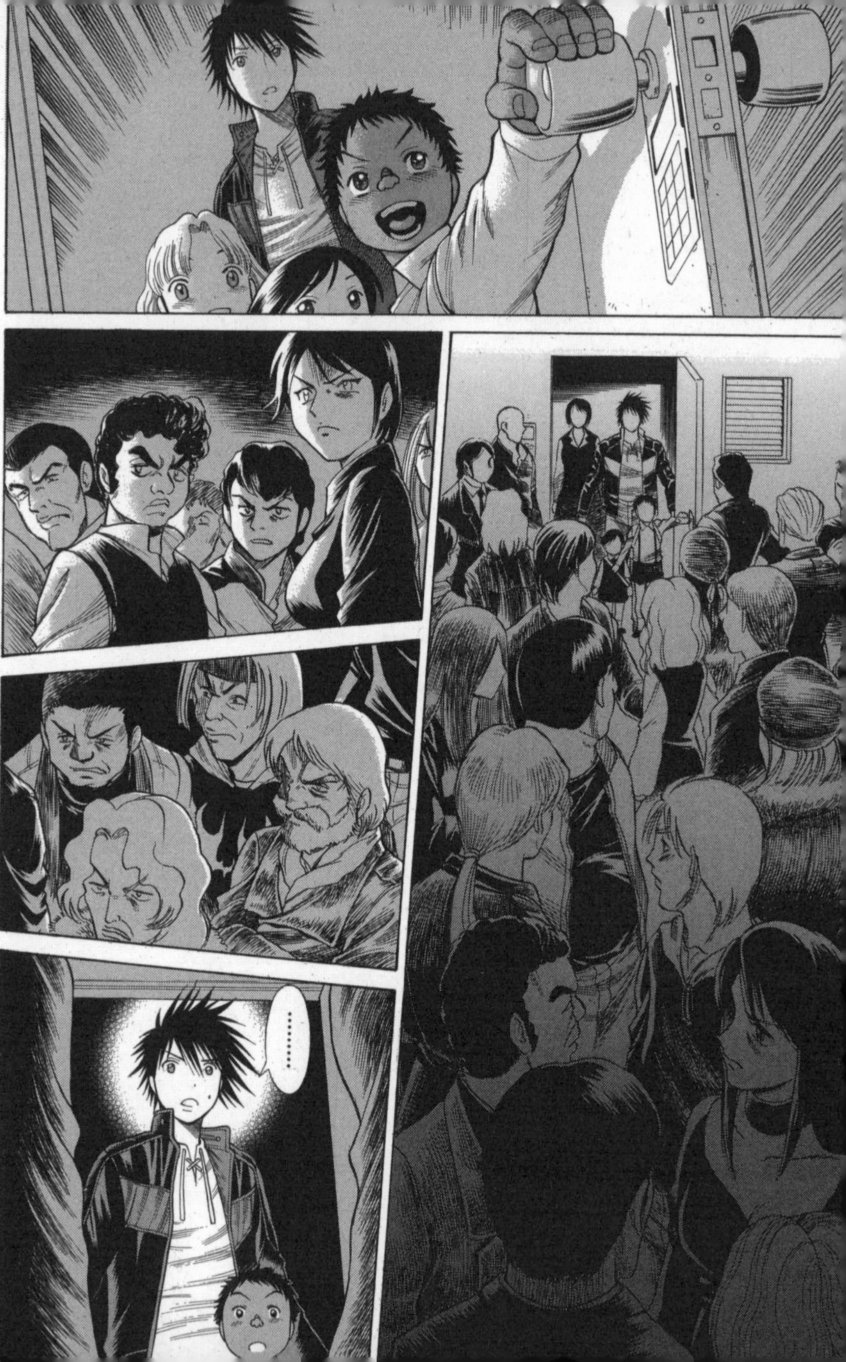
……

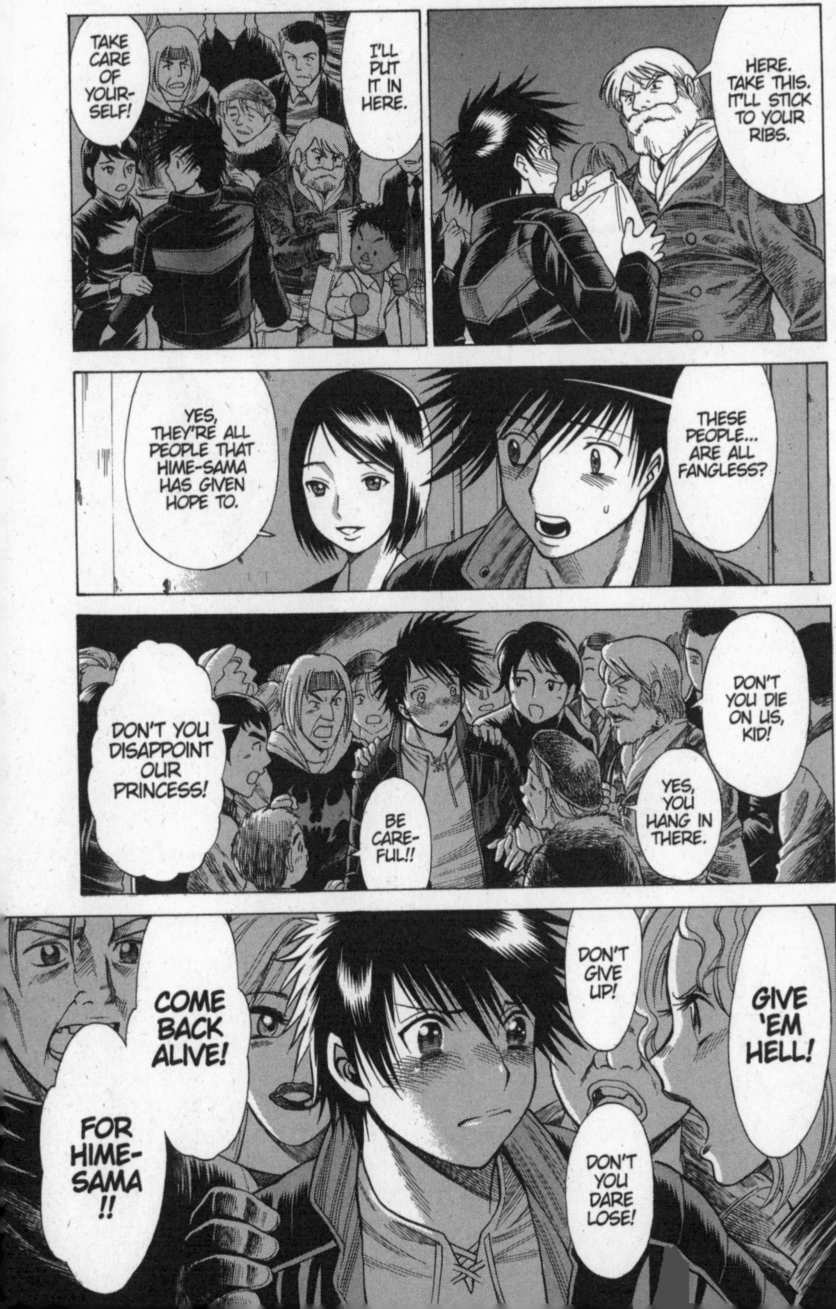
HERE. TAKE THIS. IT'LL STICK TO YOUR RIBS.
I'LL PUT IT IN HERE.
TAKE CARE OF YOURSELF!
THESE PEOPLE... ARE ALL FANGLESS?
YES, THEY'RE ALL PEOPLE THAT HIME-SAMA HAS GIVEN HOPE TO.
DON'T YOU DIE ON US, KID!
YES, YOU HANG IN THERE.
BE CAREFUL!!
DON'T YOU DISAPPOINT OUR PRINCESS!
GIVE 'EM HELL!
DON'T GIVE UP!
DON'T YOU DARE LOSE!
COME BACK ALIVE!
FOR HIME-SAMA!!

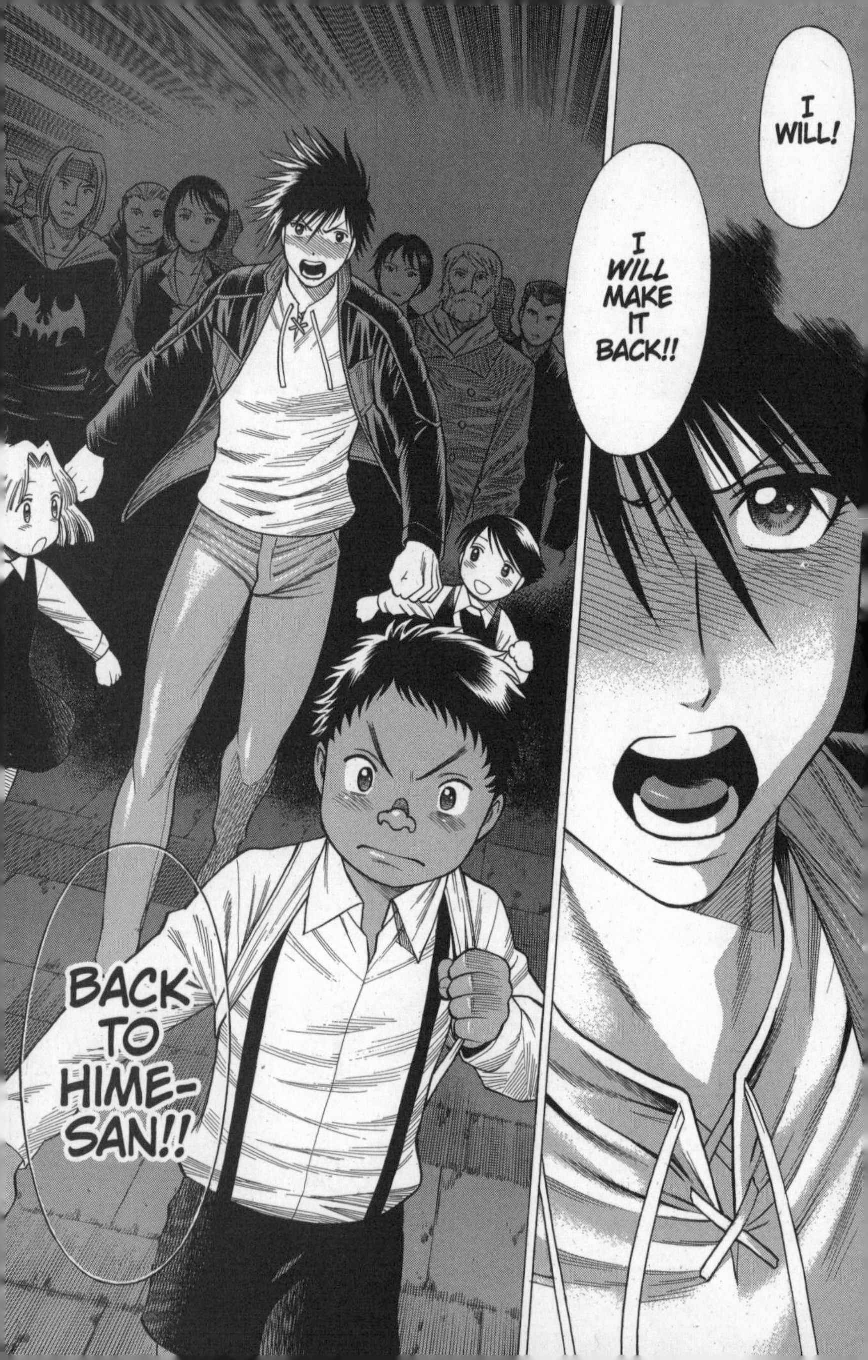
I WILL!
I WILL MAKE IT BACK!!
BACK TO HIME-SAN!!

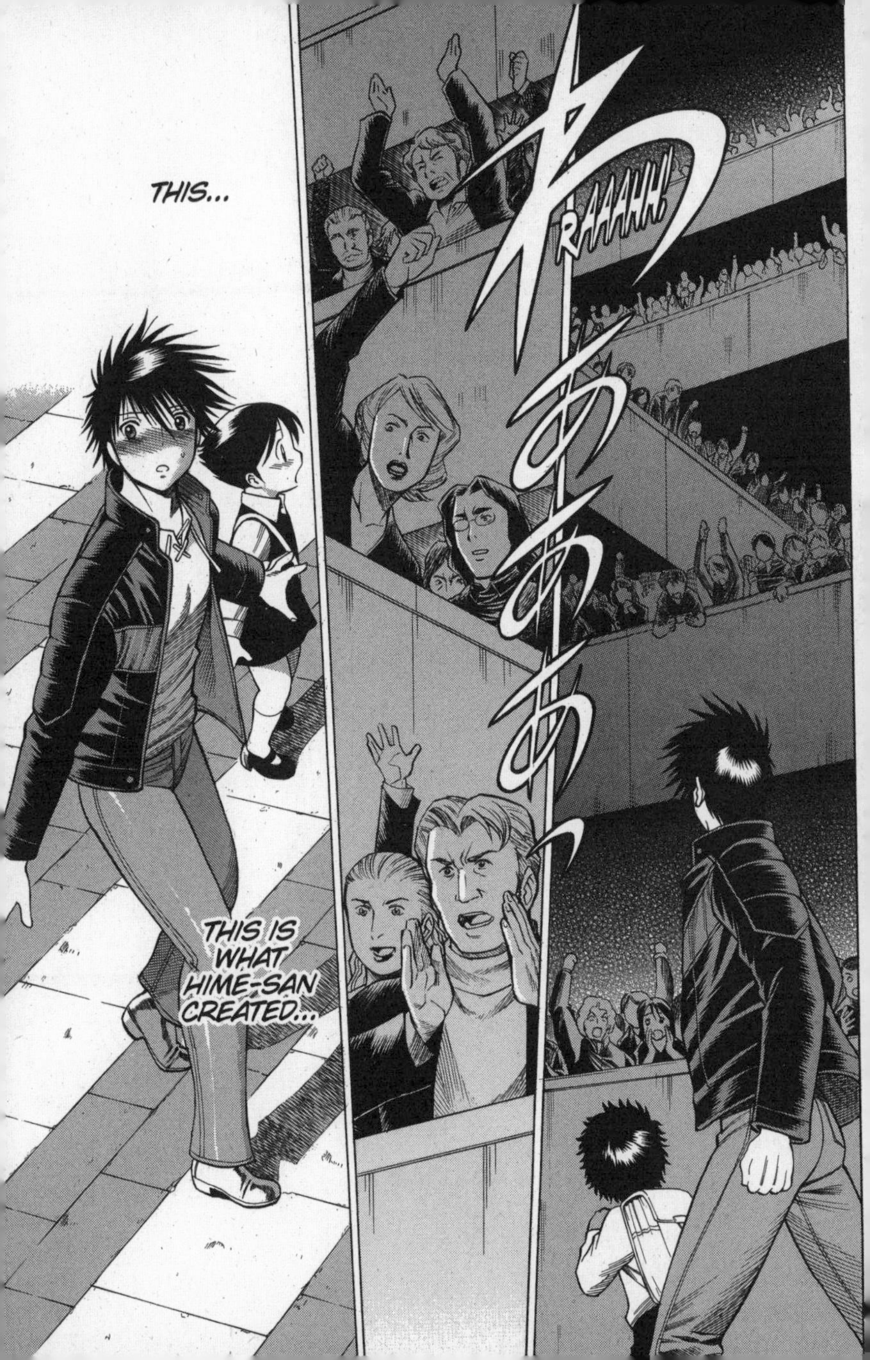
RAAAHH!
THIS...
THIS IS WHAT HIME-SAN CREATED...

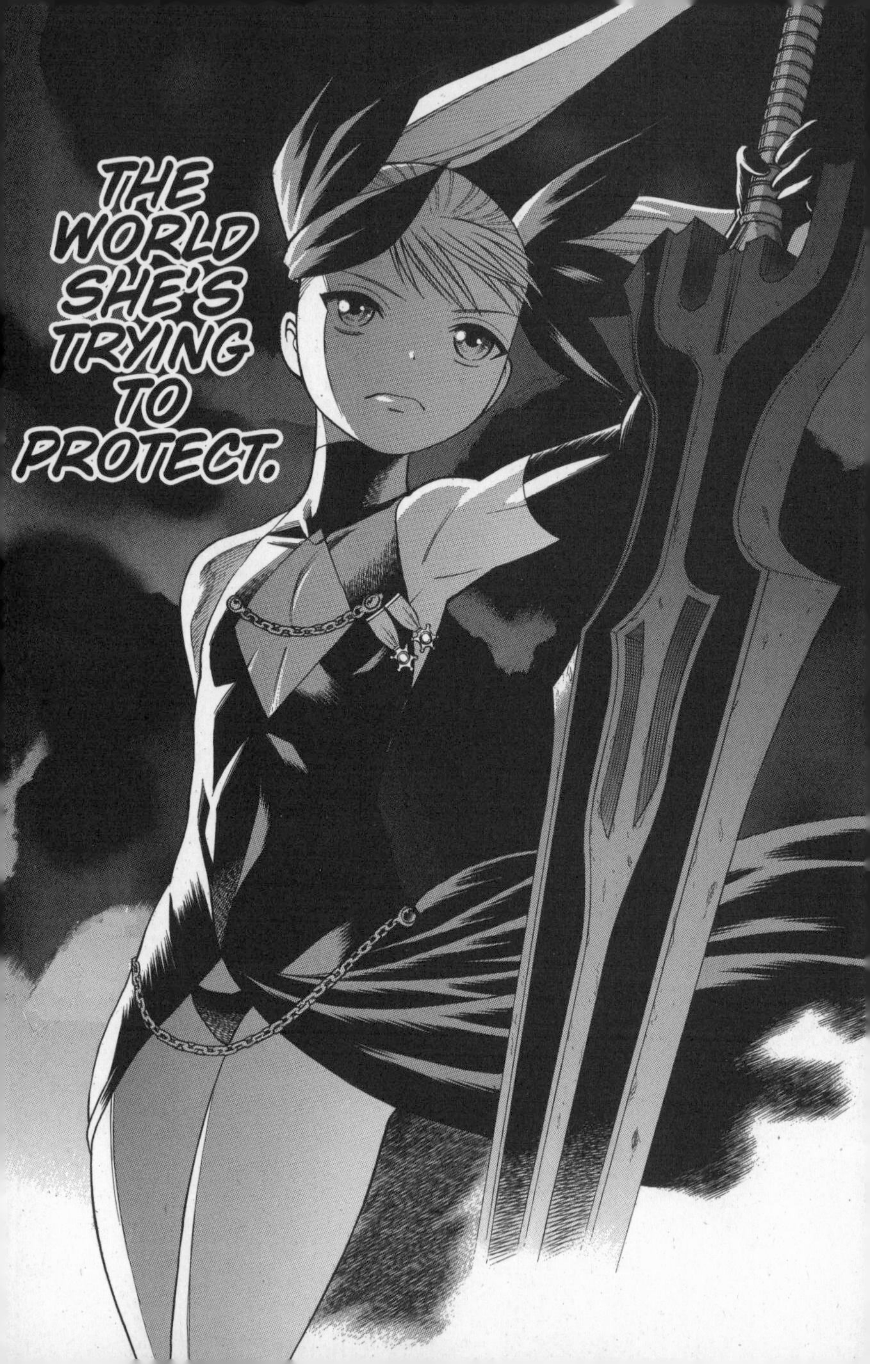
THE WORLD SHE'S TRYING TO PROTECT.

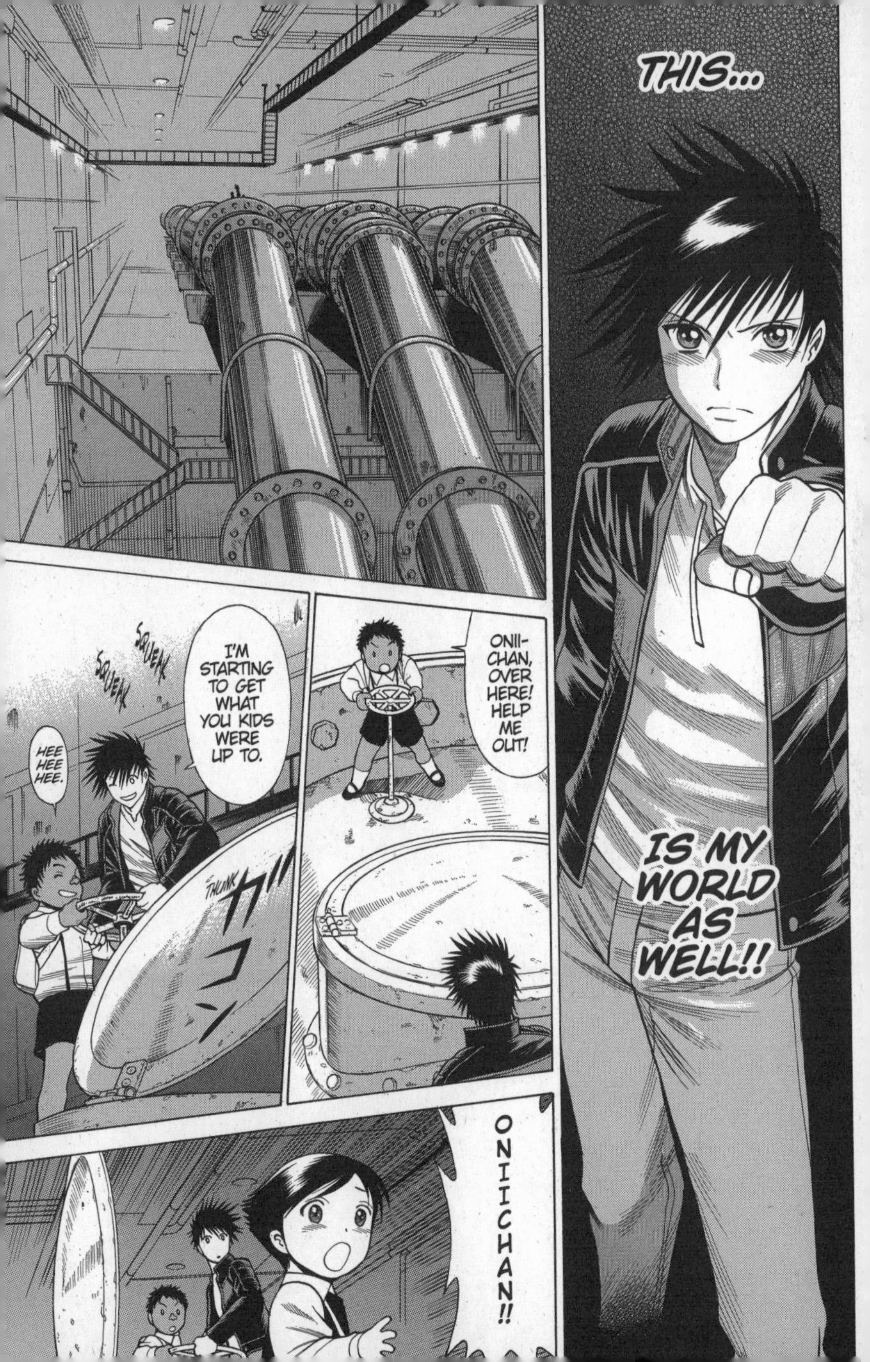
THIS...
IS MY WORLD AS WELL!!
ONII-CHAN, OVER HERE! HELP ME OUT!
I'M STARTING TO GET WHAT YOU KIDS WERE UP TO.
SQUEAK SQUEAK
HEE HEE HEE.
THUNK
ONIICHAN!!

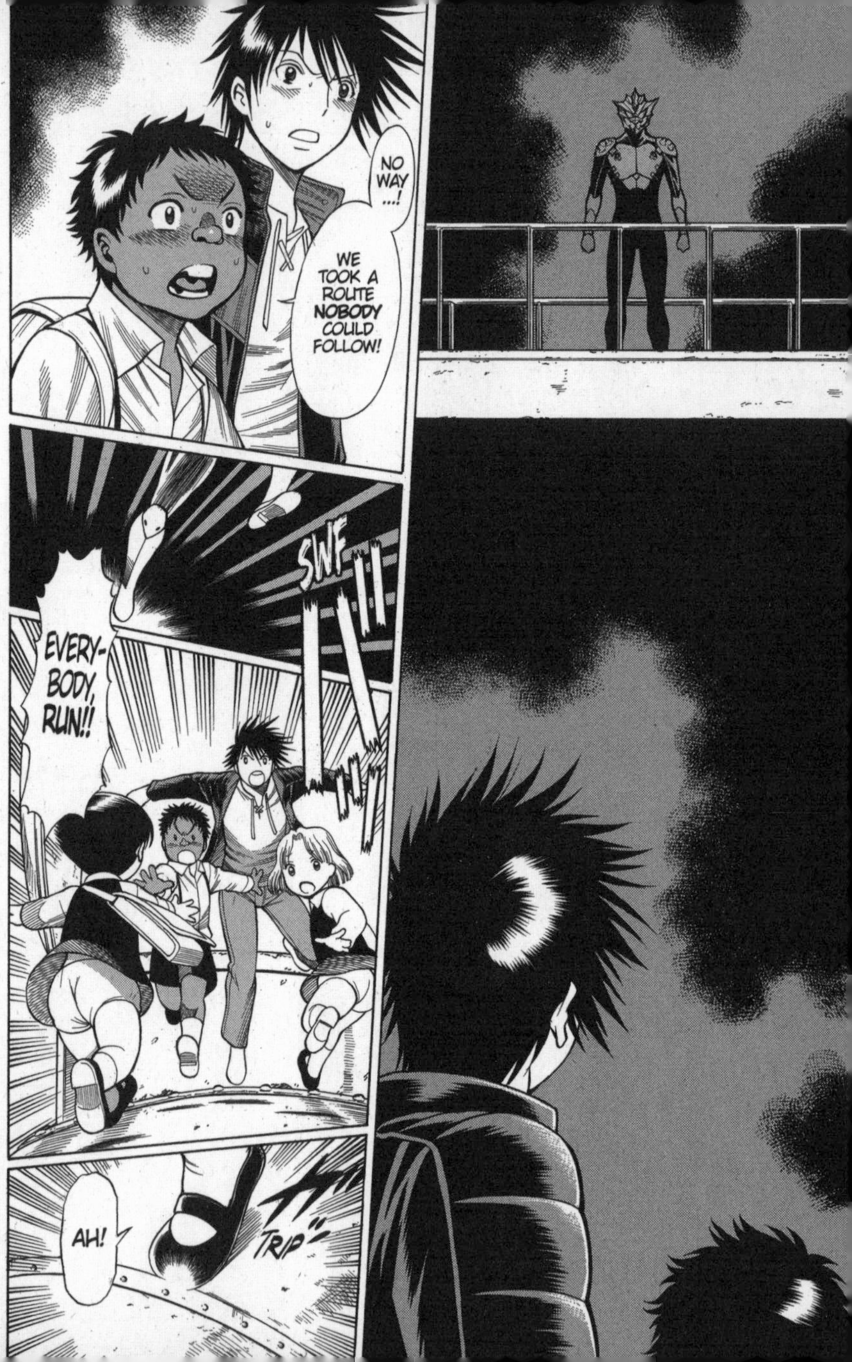
NO WAY ...!
WE TOOK A ROUTE NOBODY COULD FOLLOW!
SWF
EVERY-BODY, RUN!!
AH!
TRIP

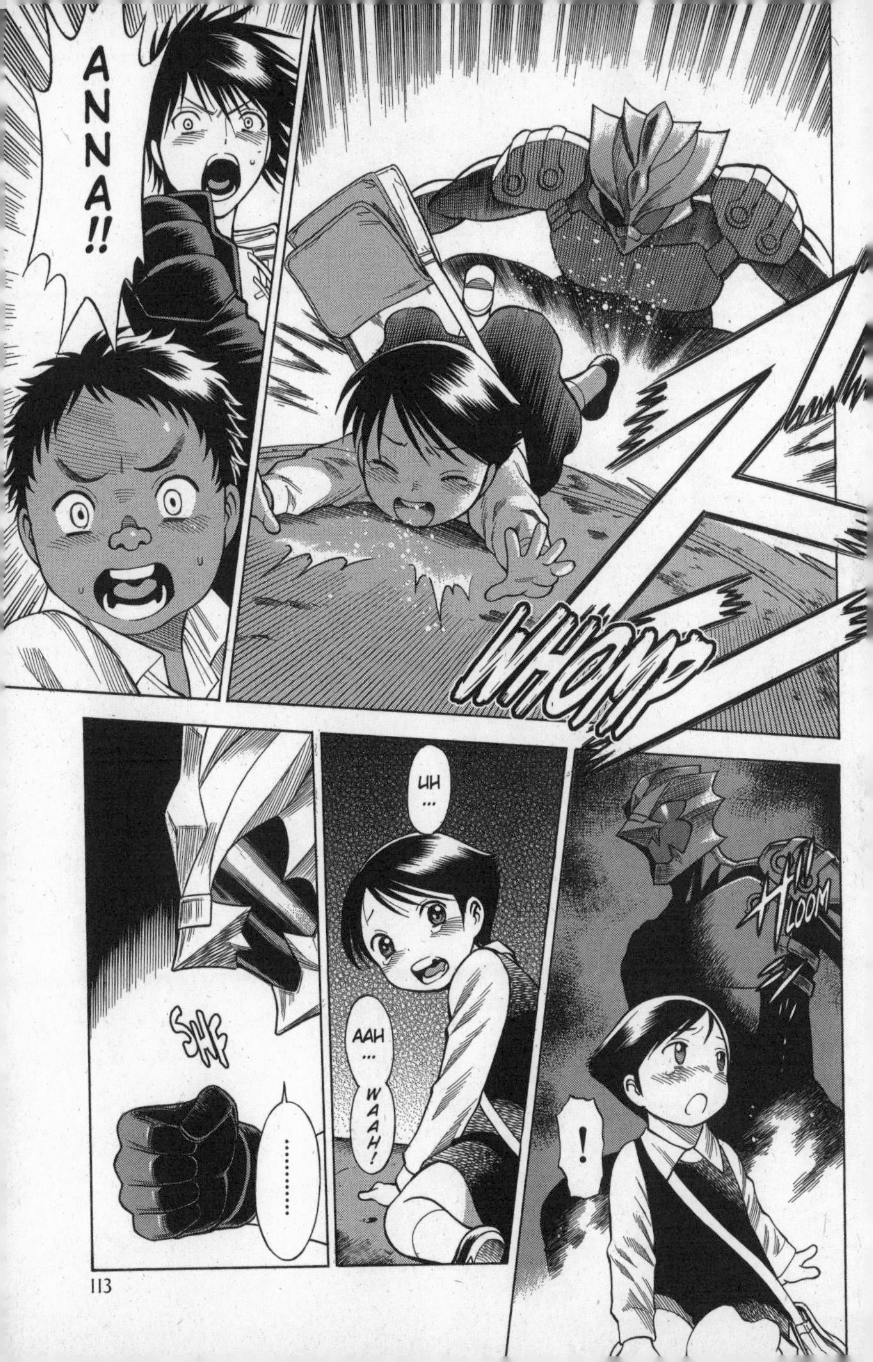

WHOMP
ANNA!!
HLOOM
!
UH ...
AAH ...
WAAH!
SHF
....

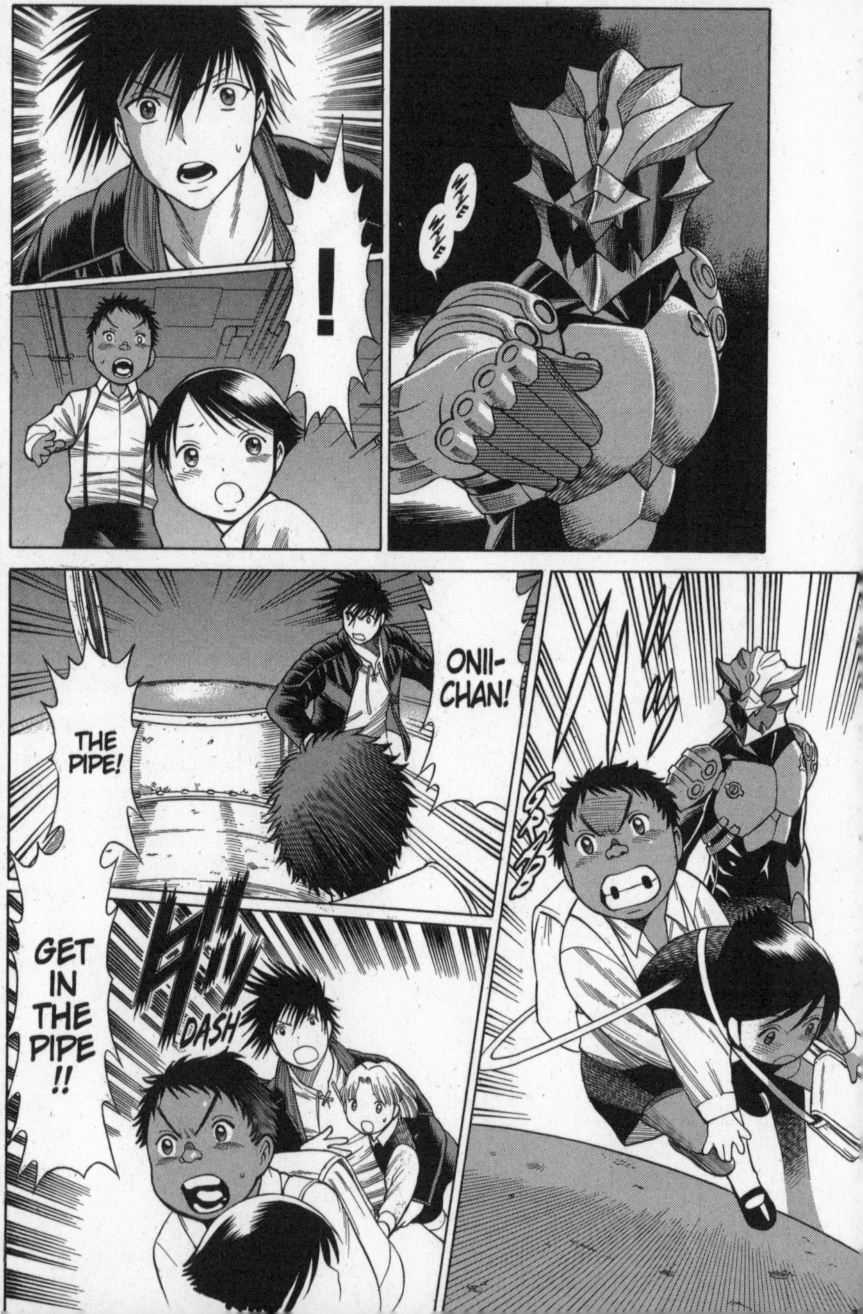
WANE
WANE
!
GRAB
ONII-CHAN!
THE PIPE!
DASH
GET IN THE PIPE!!

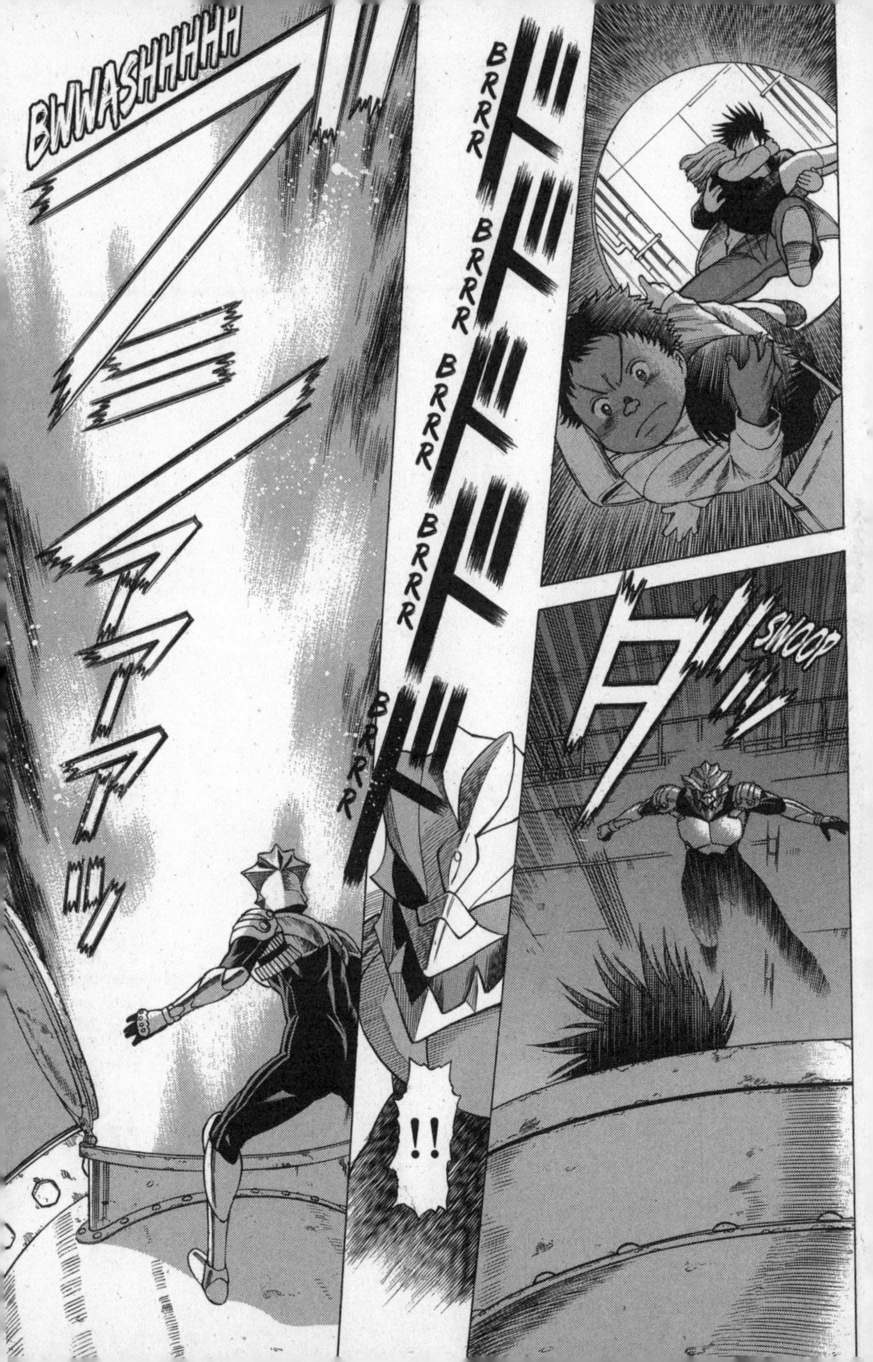
SWOOP
BRRRR
BRRRR
BRRRR
BRRRR
BRRR
!!
BWWASHHHHH

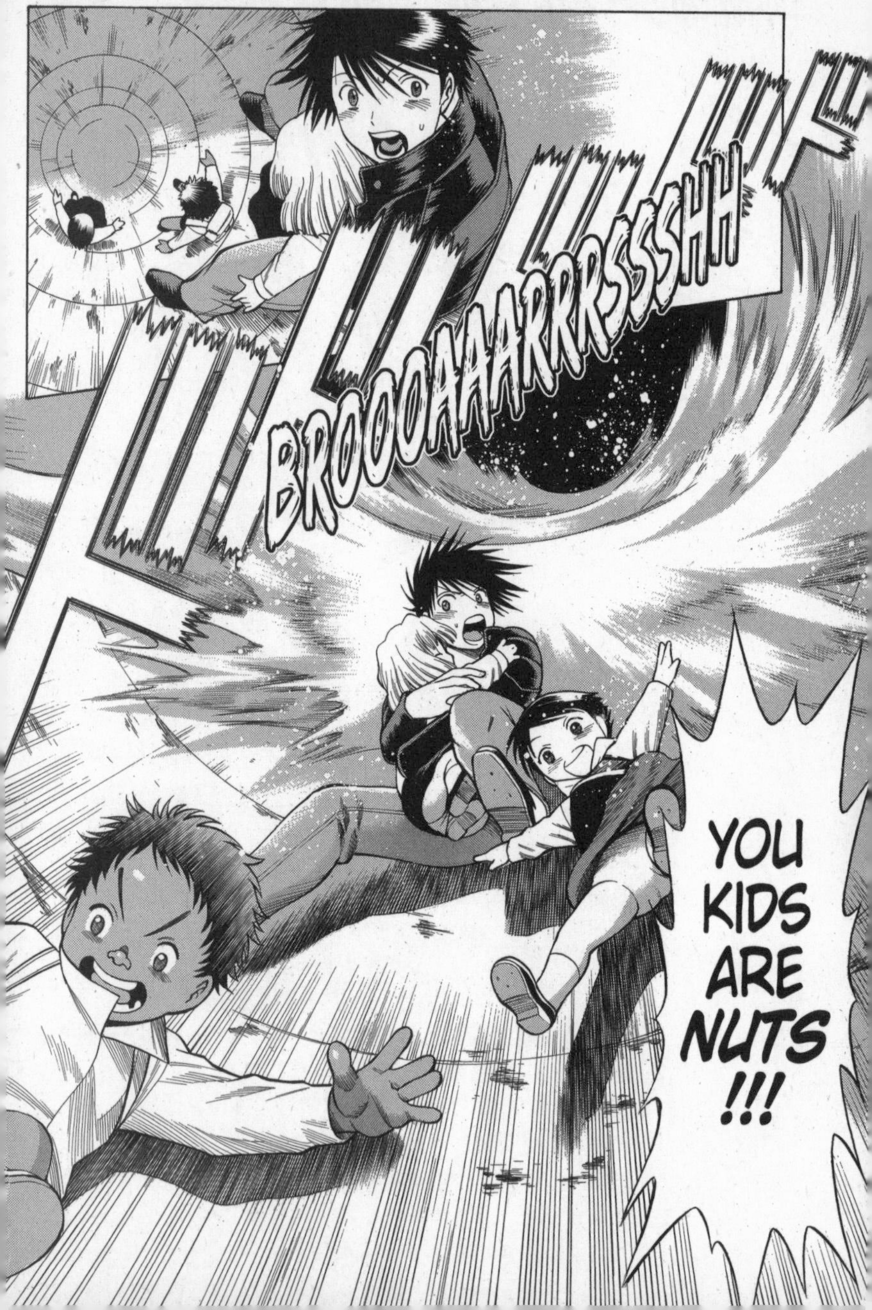
BROOOAAARRRSSSHH
YOU KIDS ARE NUTS !!!

Chapter 29: A Single Frozen Way

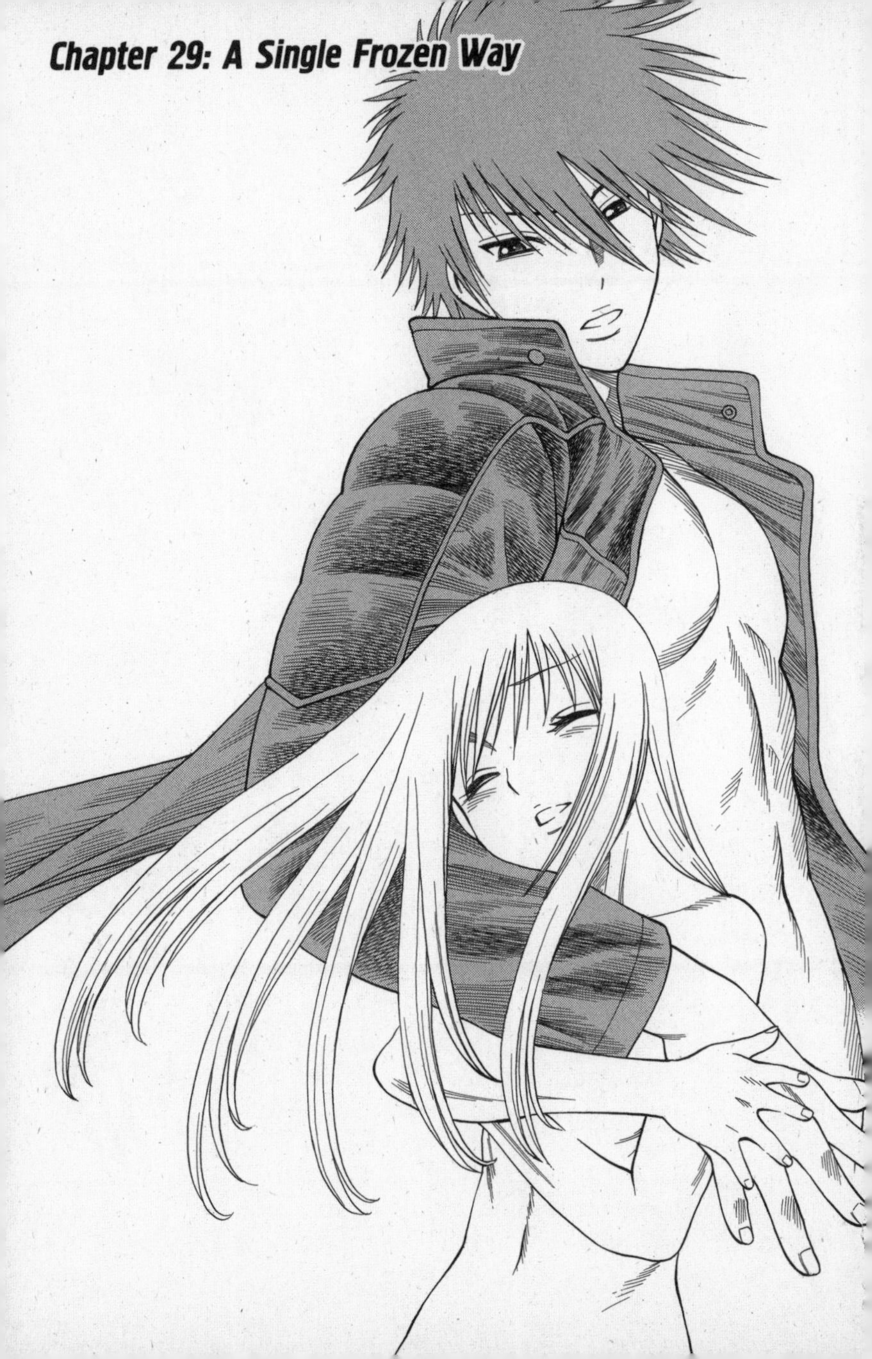

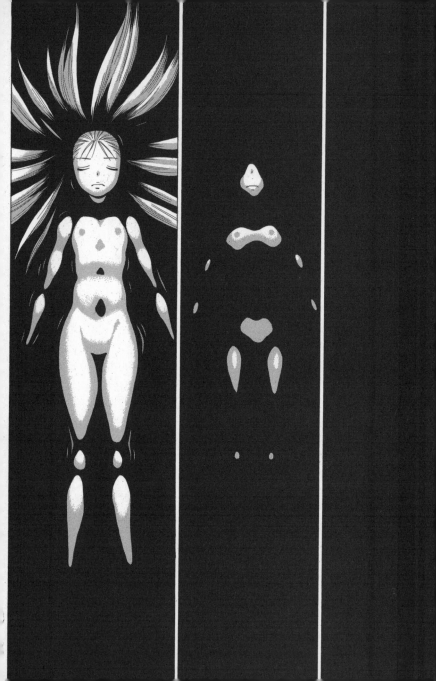

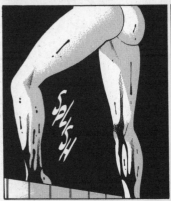

SPLASH

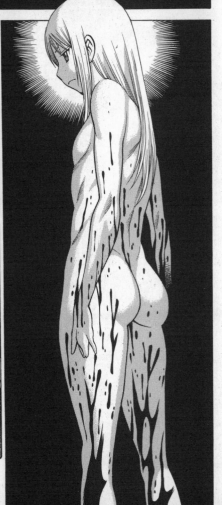

YOUR TOWEL, HIME-SAMA.

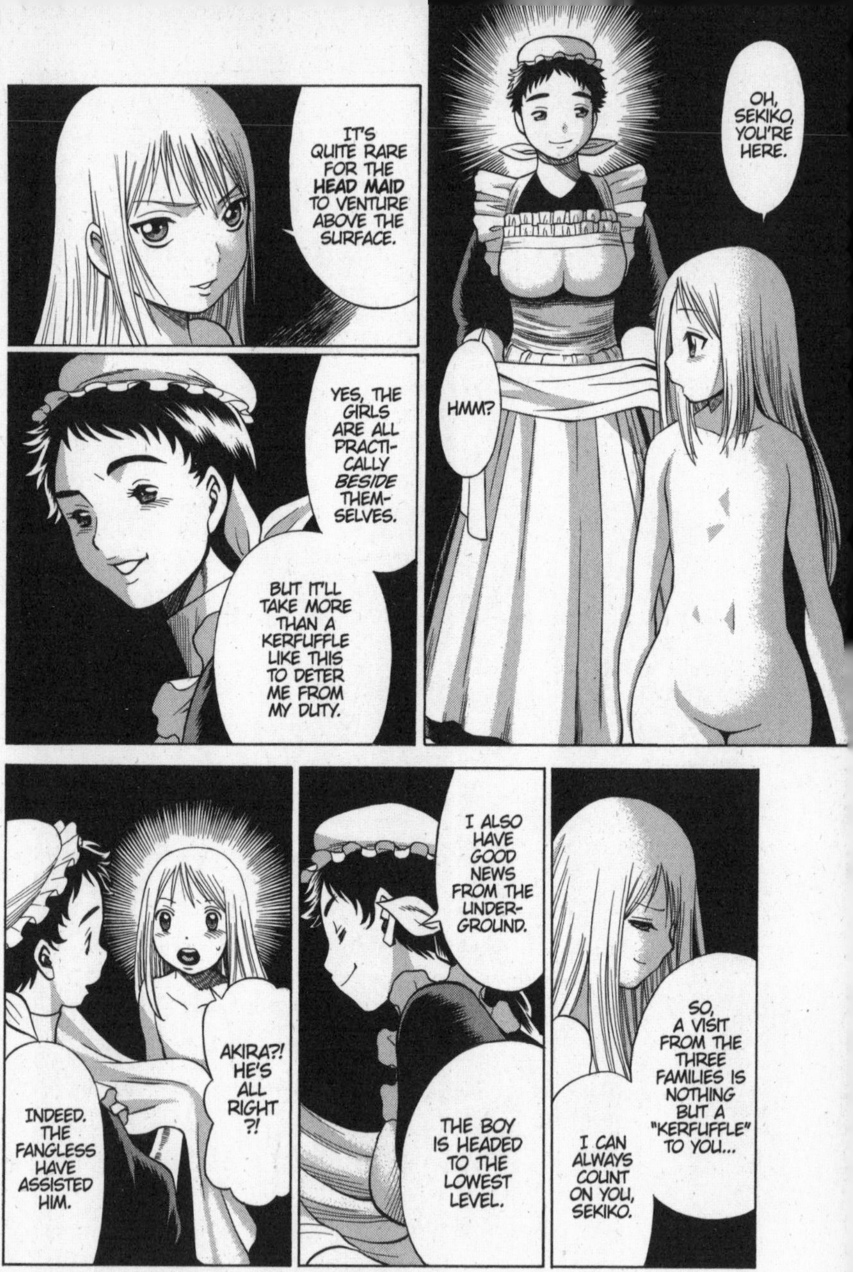
OH, SEKIKO, YOU'RE HERE.
HMM?
IT'S QUITE RARE FOR THE HEAD MAID TO VENTURE ABOVE THE SURFACE.
YES, THE GIRLS ARE ALL PRACTI-CALLY *BESIDE* THEM-SELVES.
BUT IT'LL TAKE MORE THAN A KERFUFFLE LIKE THIS TO DETER ME FROM MY DUTY.
SO, A VISIT FROM THE THREE FAMILIES IS NOTHING BUT A "KERFUFFLE" TO YOU...
I CAN ALWAYS COUNT ON YOU, SEKIKO.
I ALSO HAVE GOOD NEWS FROM THE UNDER-GROUND.
THE BOY IS HEADED TO THE LOWEST LEVEL.
AKIRA?! HE'S ALL RIGHT ?!
INDEED. THE FANGLESS HAVE ASSISTED HIM.

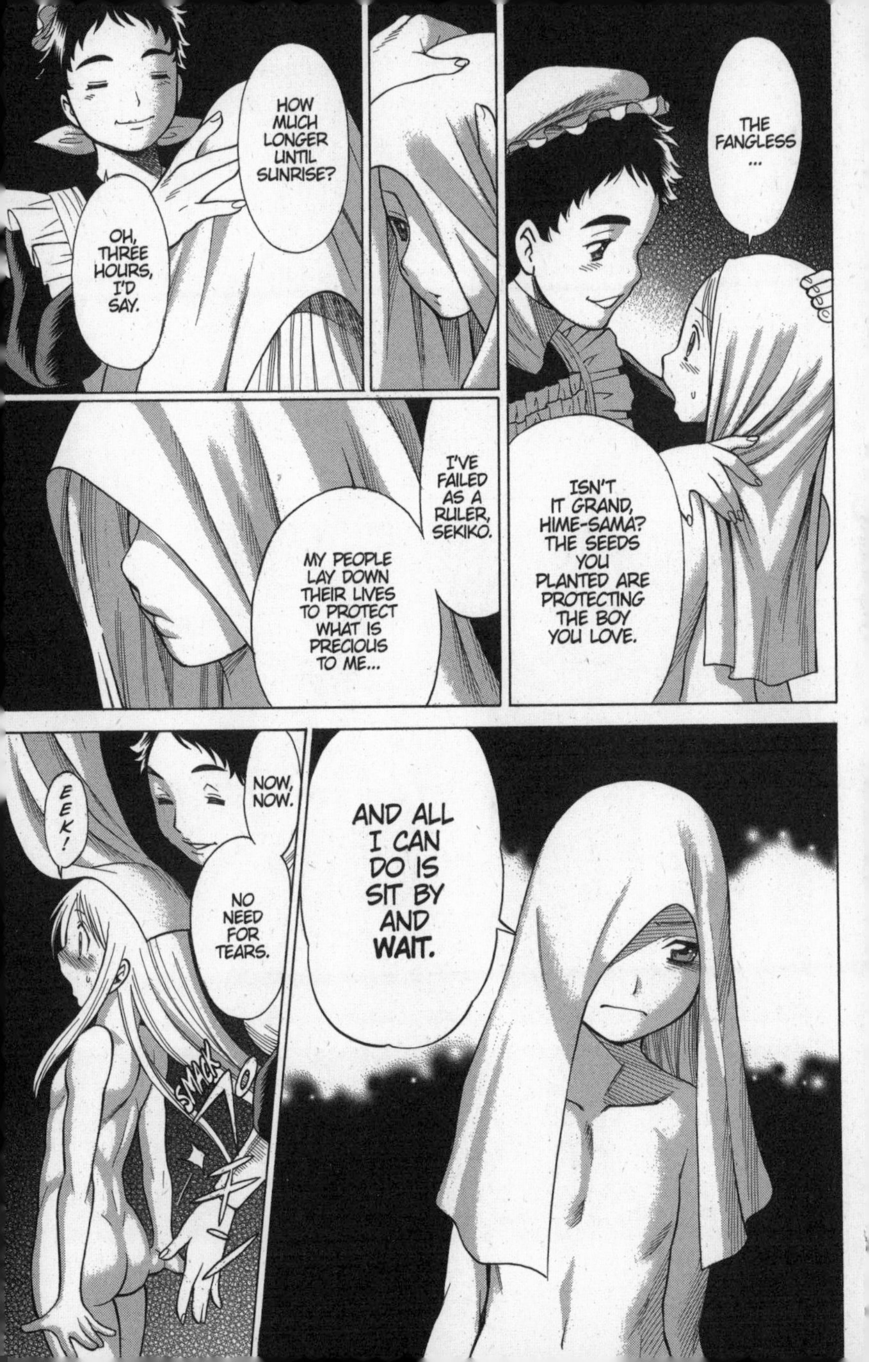
THE FANGLESS ...
HOW MUCH LONGER UNTIL SUNRISE?
OH, THREE HOURS, I'D SAY.
ISN'T IT GRAND, HIME-SAMA? THE SEEDS YOU PLANTED ARE PROTECTING THE BOY YOU LOVE.
I'VE FAILED AS A RULER, SEKIKO.
MY PEOPLE LAY DOWN THEIR LIVES TO PROTECT WHAT IS PRECIOUS TO ME...
AND ALL I CAN DO IS SIT BY AND WAIT.
NOW, NOW.
EEK!
NO NEED FOR TEARS.
SMACK

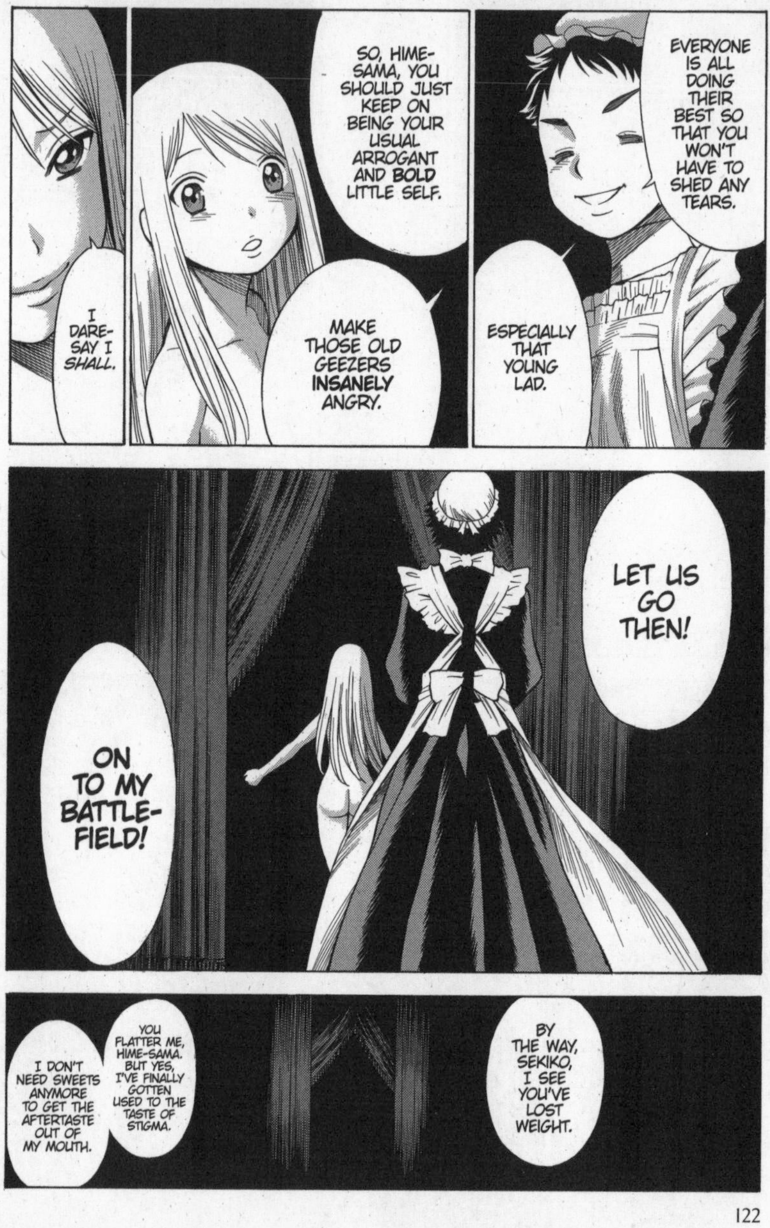
EVERYONE IS ALL DOING THEIR BEST SO THAT YOU WON'T HAVE TO SHED ANY TEARS.
ESPECIALLY THAT YOUNG LAD.
SO, HIME-SAMA, YOU SHOULD JUST KEEP ON BEING YOUR USUAL ARROGANT AND BOLD LITTLE SELF.
MAKE THOSE OLD GEEZERS INSANELY ANGRY.
I DARESAY I SHALL.
LET US GO THEN!
ON TO MY BATTLEFIELD!
BY THE WAY, SEKIKO, I SEE YOU'VE LOST WEIGHT.
YOU FLATTER ME, HIME-SAMA. BUT YES, I'VE FINALLY GOTTEN USED TO THE TASTE OF STIGMA.
I DON'T NEED SWEETS ANYMORE TO GET THE AFTERTASTE OUT OF MY MOUTH.

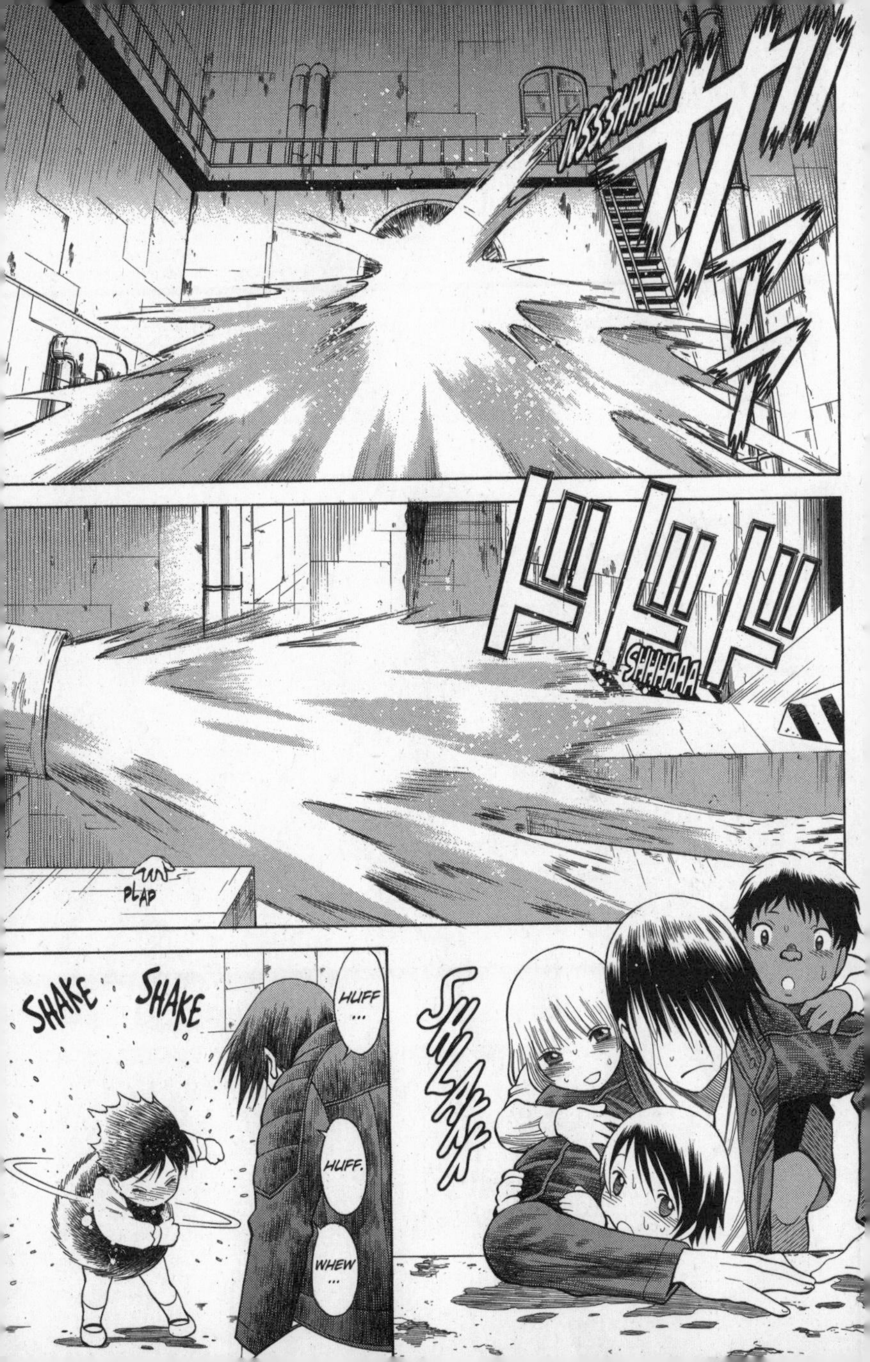
WSSSHHHH
SHHHAAA
PLAP
HUFF ...
SHAKE
SHAKE
HUFF.
WHEW ...

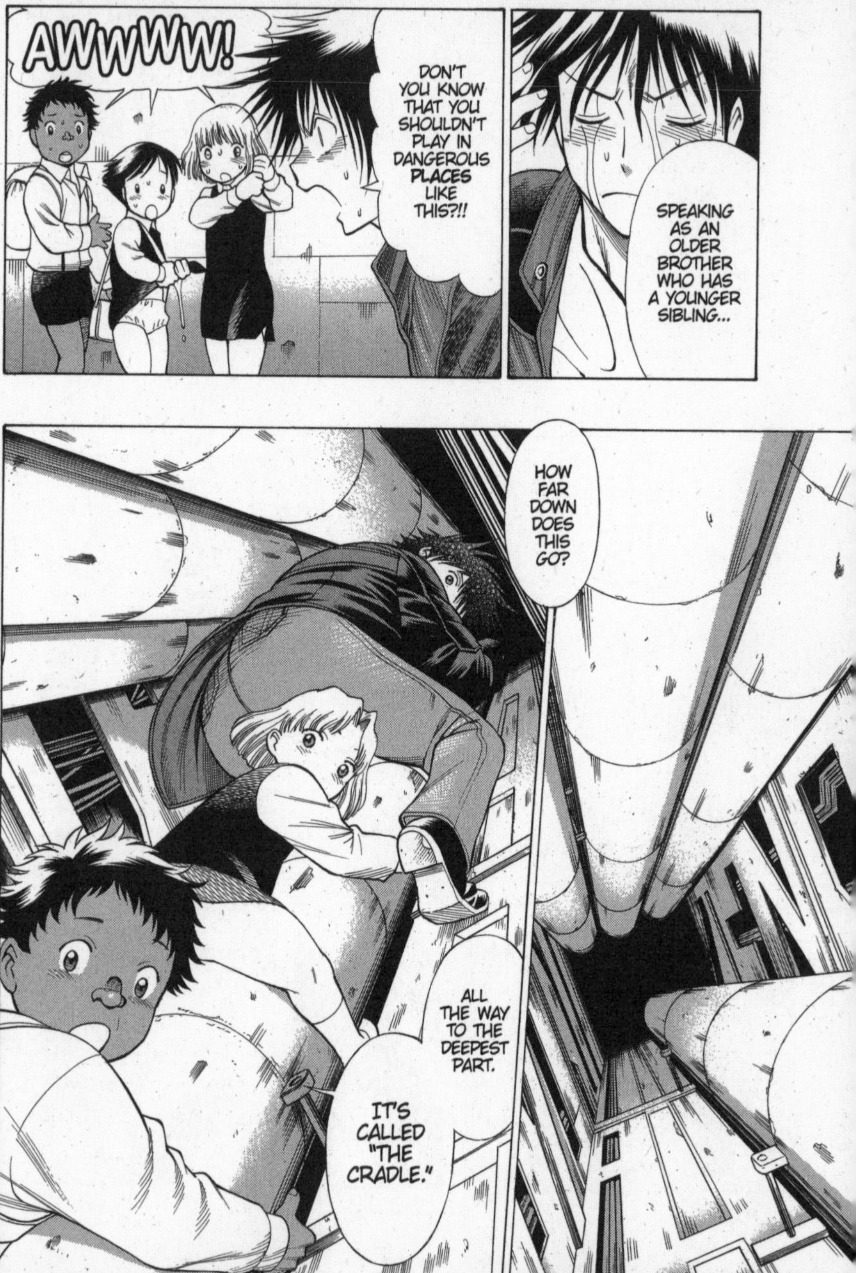
SPEAKING AS AN OLDER BROTHER WHO HAS A YOUNGER SIBLING...
DON'T YOU KNOW THAT YOU SHOULDN'T PLAY IN DANGEROUS PLACES LIKE THIS?!!
AWWWWW!
HOW FAR DOWN DOES THIS GO?
ALL THE WAY TO THE DEEPEST PART.
IT'S CALLED "THE CRADLE."

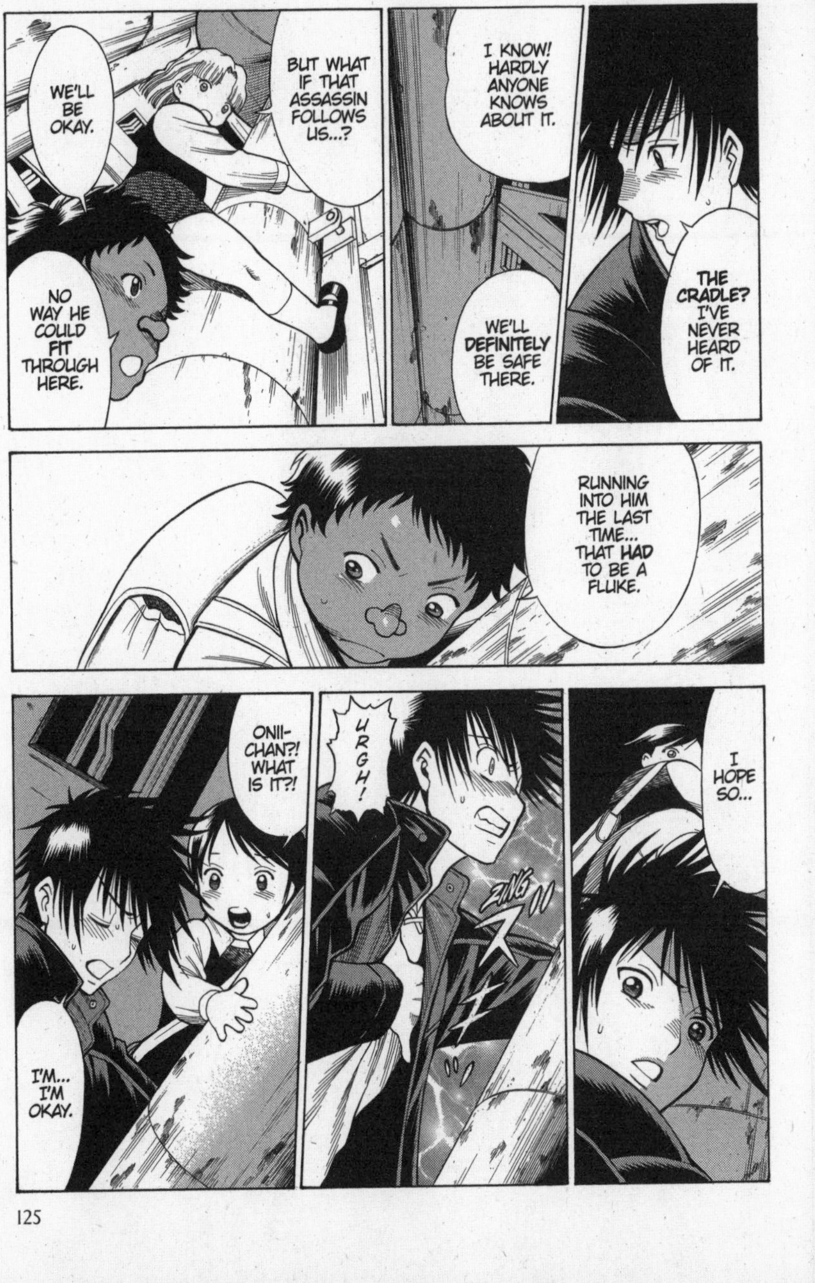
THE CRADLE? I'VE NEVER HEARD OF IT.
I KNOW! HARDLY ANYONE KNOWS ABOUT IT.
WE'LL DEFINITELY BE SAFE THERE.
BUT WHAT IF THAT ASSASSIN FOLLOWS US...?
WE'LL BE OKAY.
NO WAY HE COULD FIT THROUGH HERE.
RUNNING INTO HIM THE LAST TIME... THAT HAD TO BE A FLUKE.
I HOPE SO...
URGH!
ZING
ONII-CHAN?! WHAT IS IT?!
I'M... I'M OKAY.

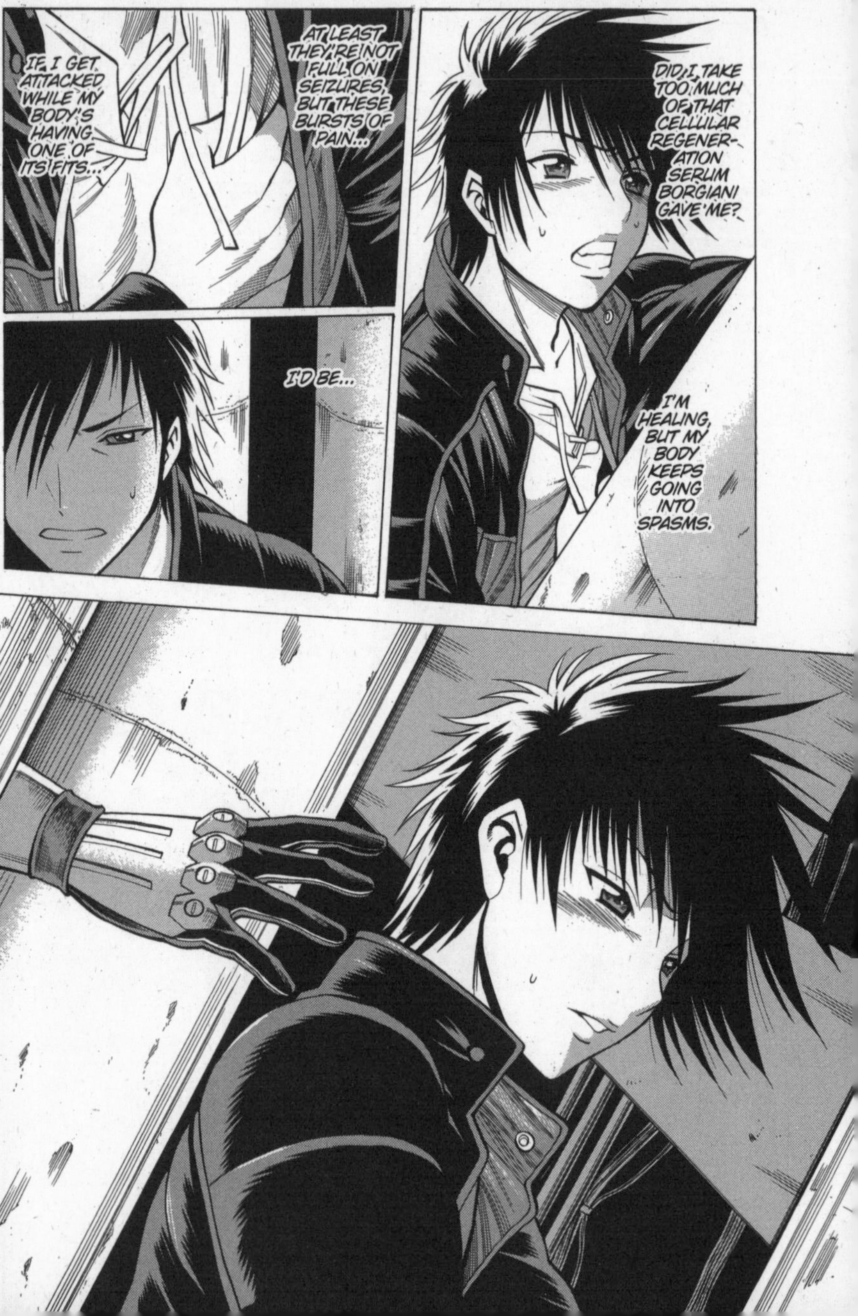
DID I TAKE TOO MUCH OF THAT CELLULAR REGENER-ATION SERUM BORGIANI GAVE ME?
I'M HEALING, BUT MY BODY KEEPS GOING INTO SPASMS.
AT LEAST THEY'RE NOT FULL ON SEIZURES, BUT THESE BURSTS OF PAIN...
IF I GET ATTACKED WHILE MY BODY'S HAVING ONE OF ITS FITS...
I'D BE...

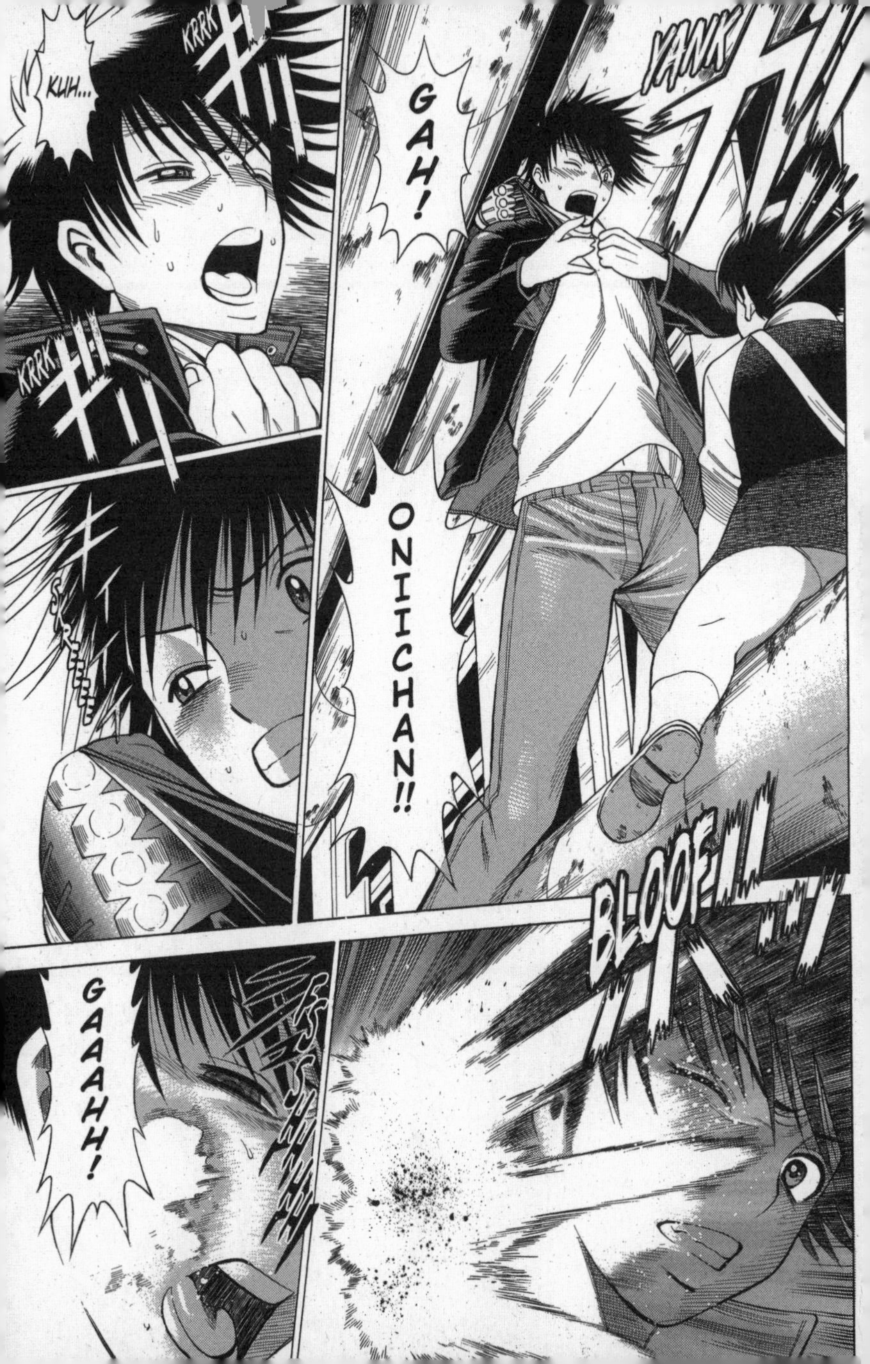
YANK
GAH!
ONIICHAN!!
KRRK
KUH...
KRRK
SKREEEE
BLOOF!!
GAAAHH!

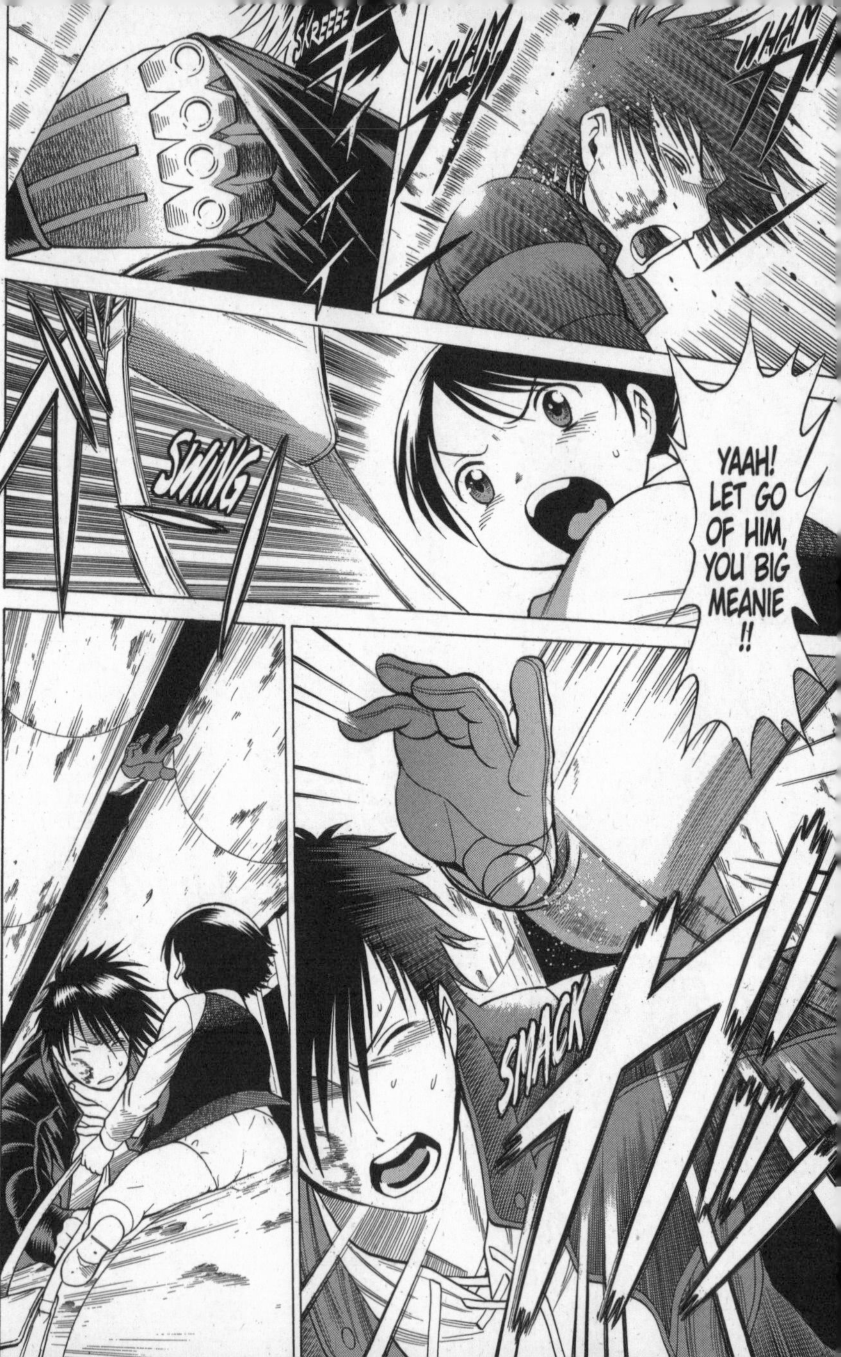
WHAM
WHAM
SKREEEE
YAAH! LET GO OF HIM, YOU BIG MEANIE !!
SWING
SMACK

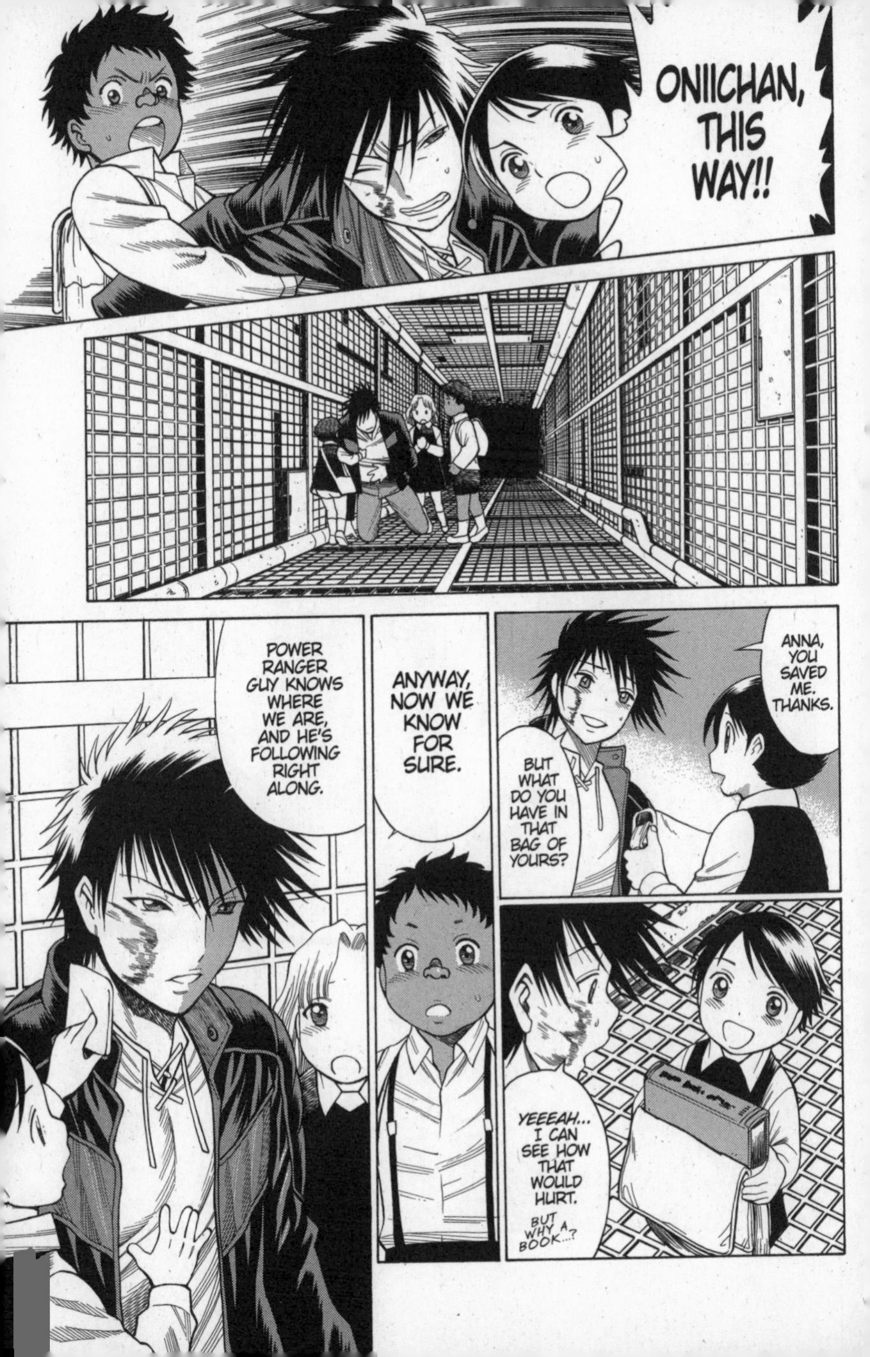
ONIICHAN, THIS WAY!!
ANNA, YOU SAVED ME. THANKS.
BUT WHAT DO YOU HAVE IN THAT BAG OF YOURS?
YEEEAH... I CAN SEE HOW THAT WOULD HURT.
BUT WHY A BOOK...?
ANYWAY, NOW WE KNOW FOR SURE.
POWER RANGER GUY KNOWS WHERE WE ARE, AND HE'S FOLLOWING RIGHT ALONG.

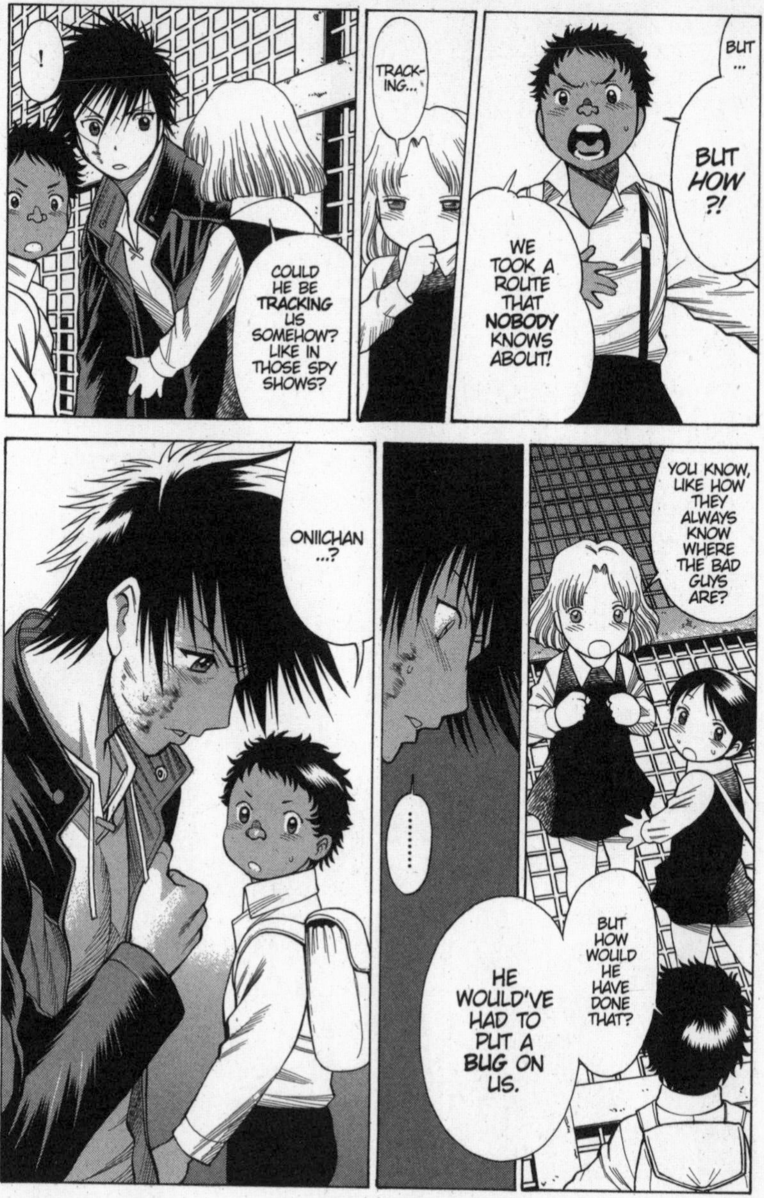
BUT ...
BUT HOW ?!
WE TOOK A ROUTE THAT NOBODY KNOWS ABOUT!
TRACKING...
!
COULD HE BE TRACKING US SOMEHOW? LIKE IN THOSE SPY SHOWS?
YOU KNOW, LIKE HOW THEY ALWAYS KNOW WHERE THE BAD GUYS ARE?
BUT HOW WOULD HE HAVE DONE THAT?
HE WOULD'VE HAD TO PUT A BUG ON US.
......
ONIICHAN ...?

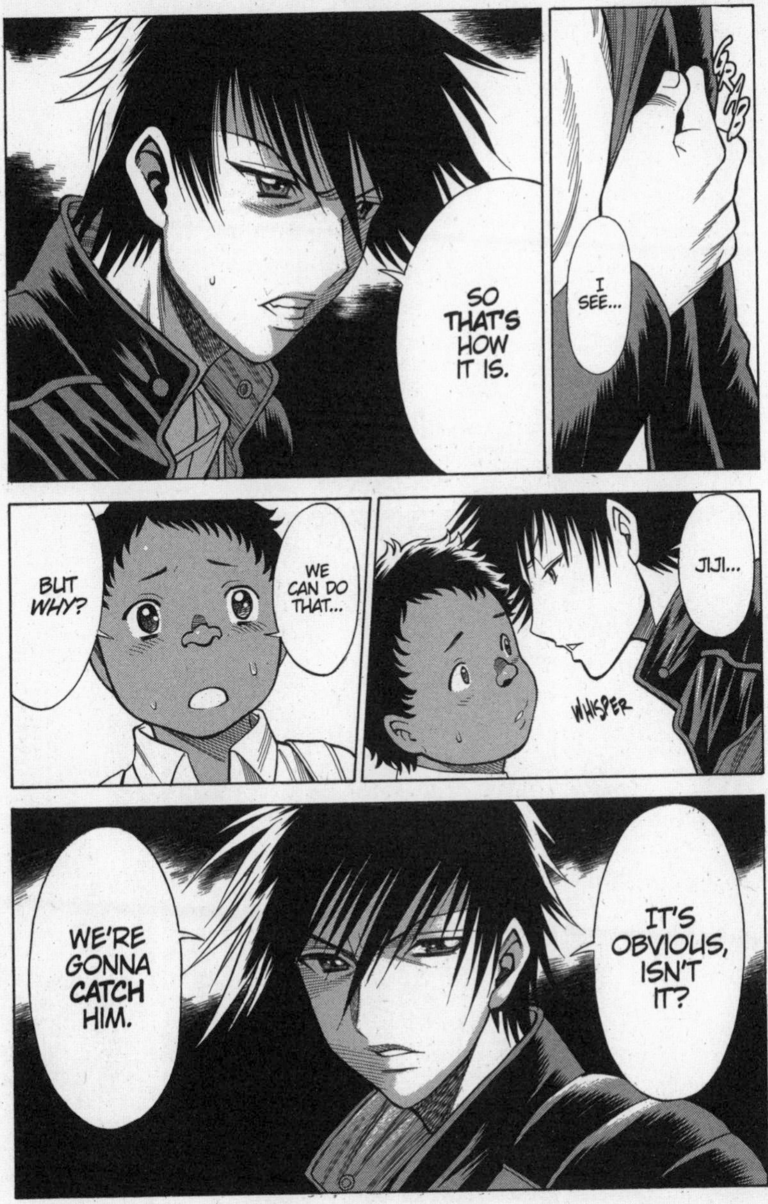
GRAB
I SEE...
SO THAT'S HOW IT IS.
JIJI...
WHISPER
WE CAN DO THAT...
BUT WHY?
IT'S OBVIOUS, ISN'T IT?
WE'RE GONNA CATCH HIM.

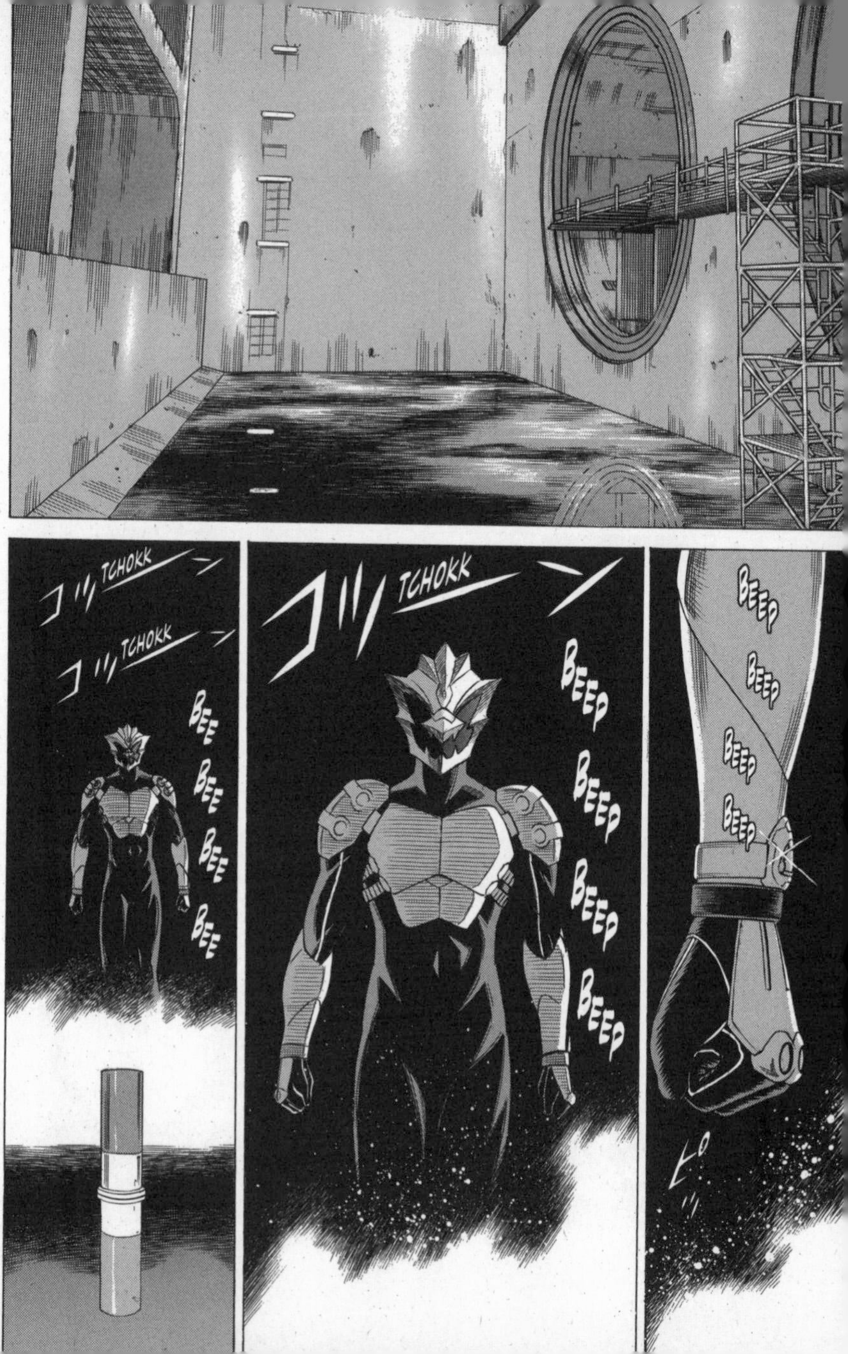
BEEP
BEEP
BEEP
BEEP
TCHOKK
BEEP
BEEP
BEEP
BEEP
BEEP
TCHOKK
TCHOKK
BEE
BEE
BEE
BEE

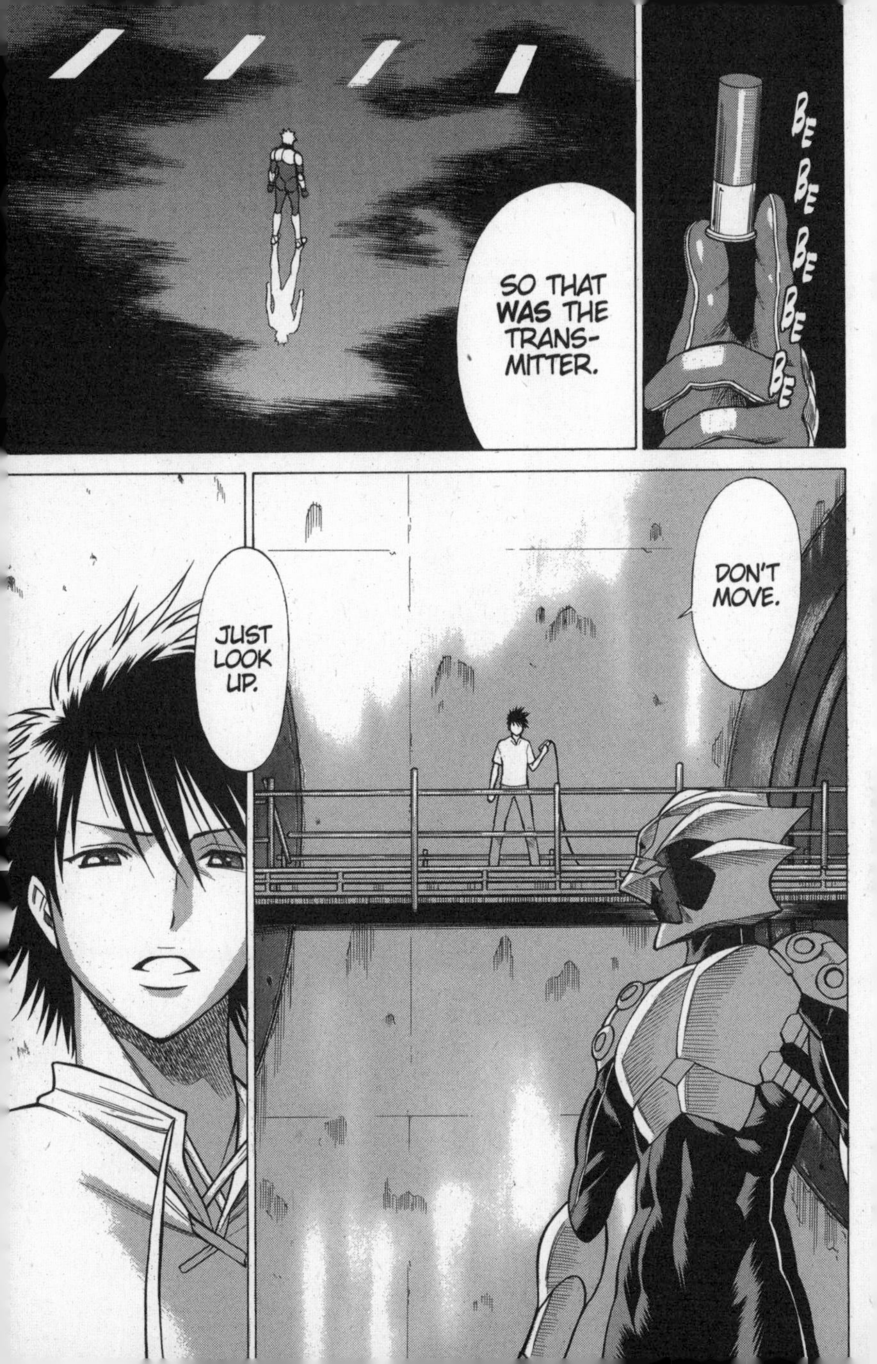
BE BE BE BE BE BE
SO THAT WAS THE TRANS-MITTER.
DON'T MOVE.
JUST LOOK UP.

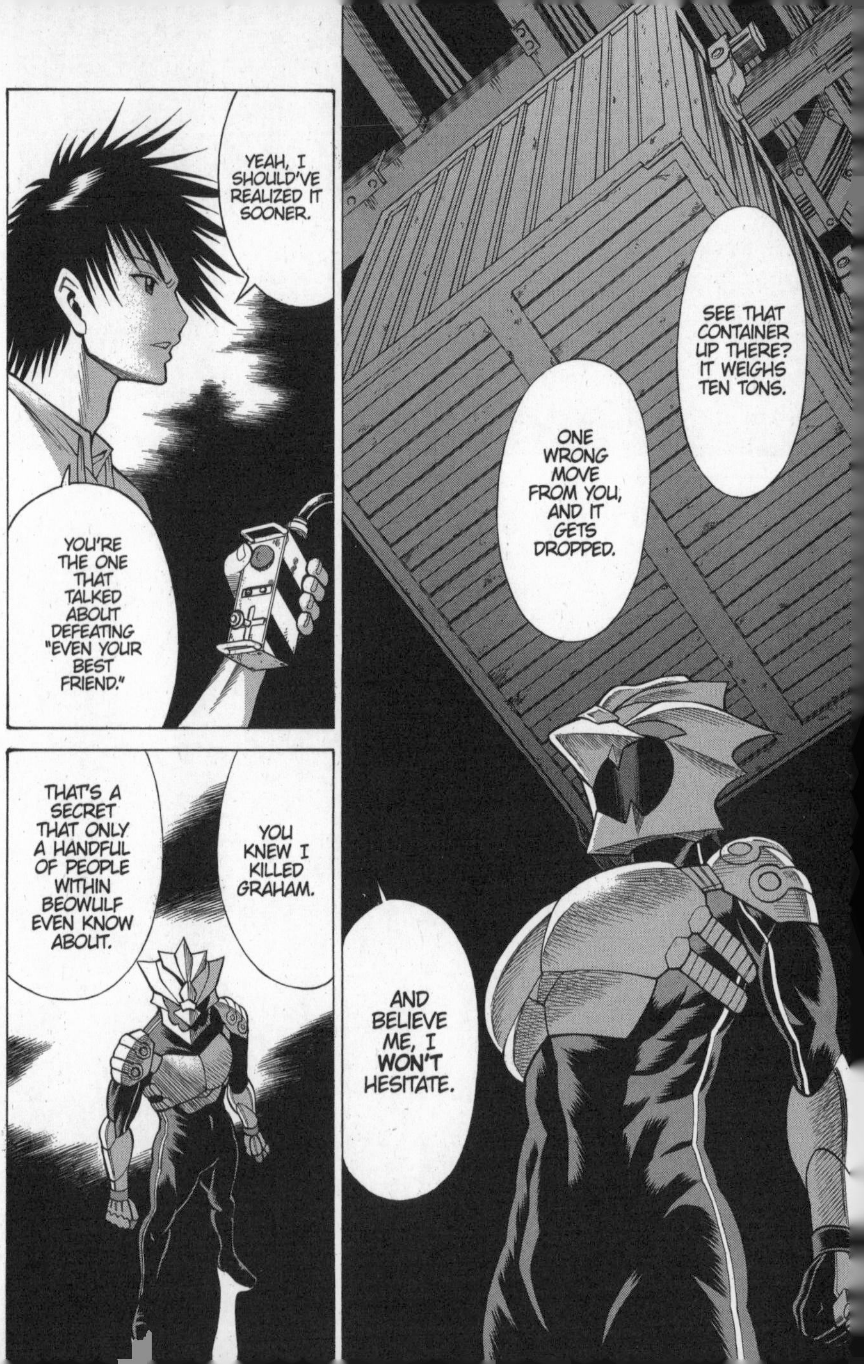
SEE THAT CONTAINER UP THERE? IT WEIGHS TEN TONS.
ONE WRONG MOVE FROM YOU, AND IT GETS DROPPED.
AND BELIEVE ME, I WON'T HESITATE.
YEAH, I SHOULD'VE REALIZED IT SOONER.
YOU'RE THE ONE THAT TALKED ABOUT DEFEATING "EVEN YOUR BEST FRIEND."
YOU KNEW I KILLED GRAHAM.
THAT'S A SECRET THAT ONLY A HANDFUL OF PEOPLE WITHIN BEOWULF EVEN KNOW ABOUT.

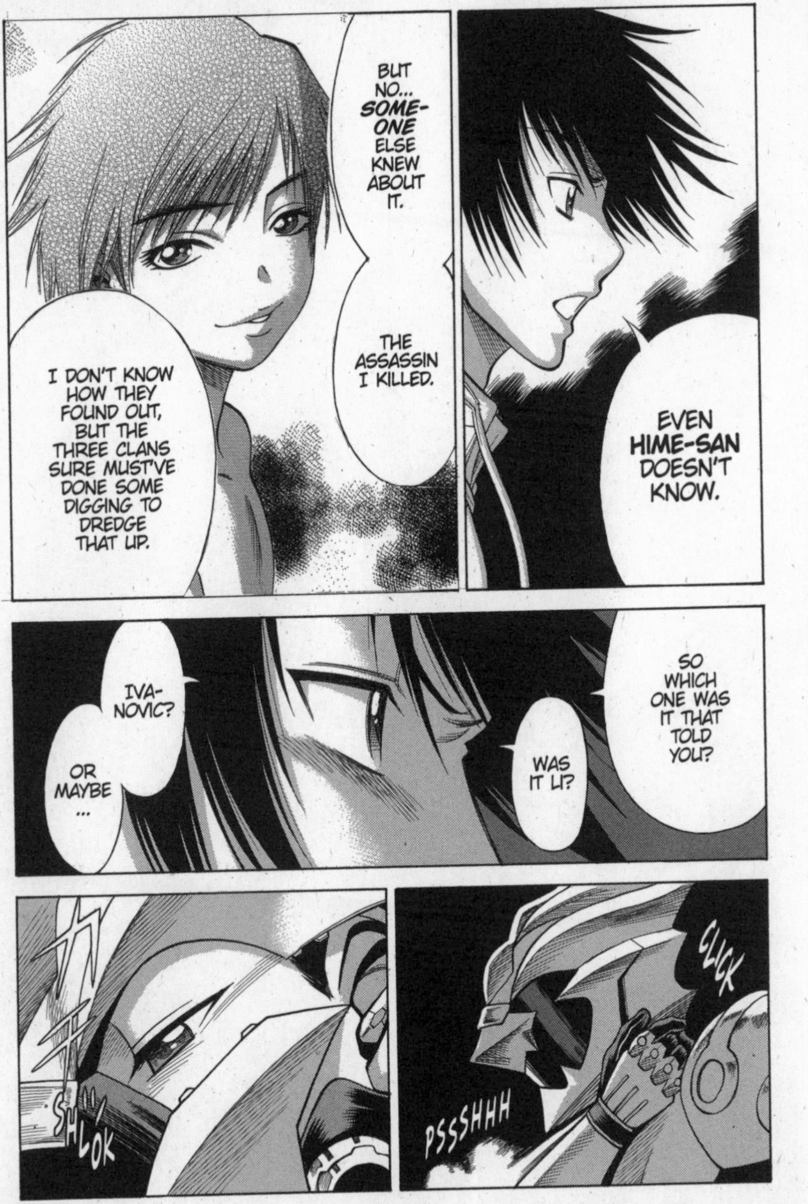
EVEN HIME-SAN DOESN'T KNOW.
BUT NO... *SOME-ONE* ELSE KNEW ABOUT IT.
THE ASSASSIN I KILLED.
I DON'T KNOW HOW THEY FOUND OUT, BUT THE THREE CLANS SURE MUST'VE DONE SOME DIGGING TO DREDGE THAT UP.
SO WHICH ONE WAS IT THAT TOLD YOU?
WAS IT LI?
IVA-NOVIC?
OR MAYBE ...
CLICK
PSSSHHH
SHLOK

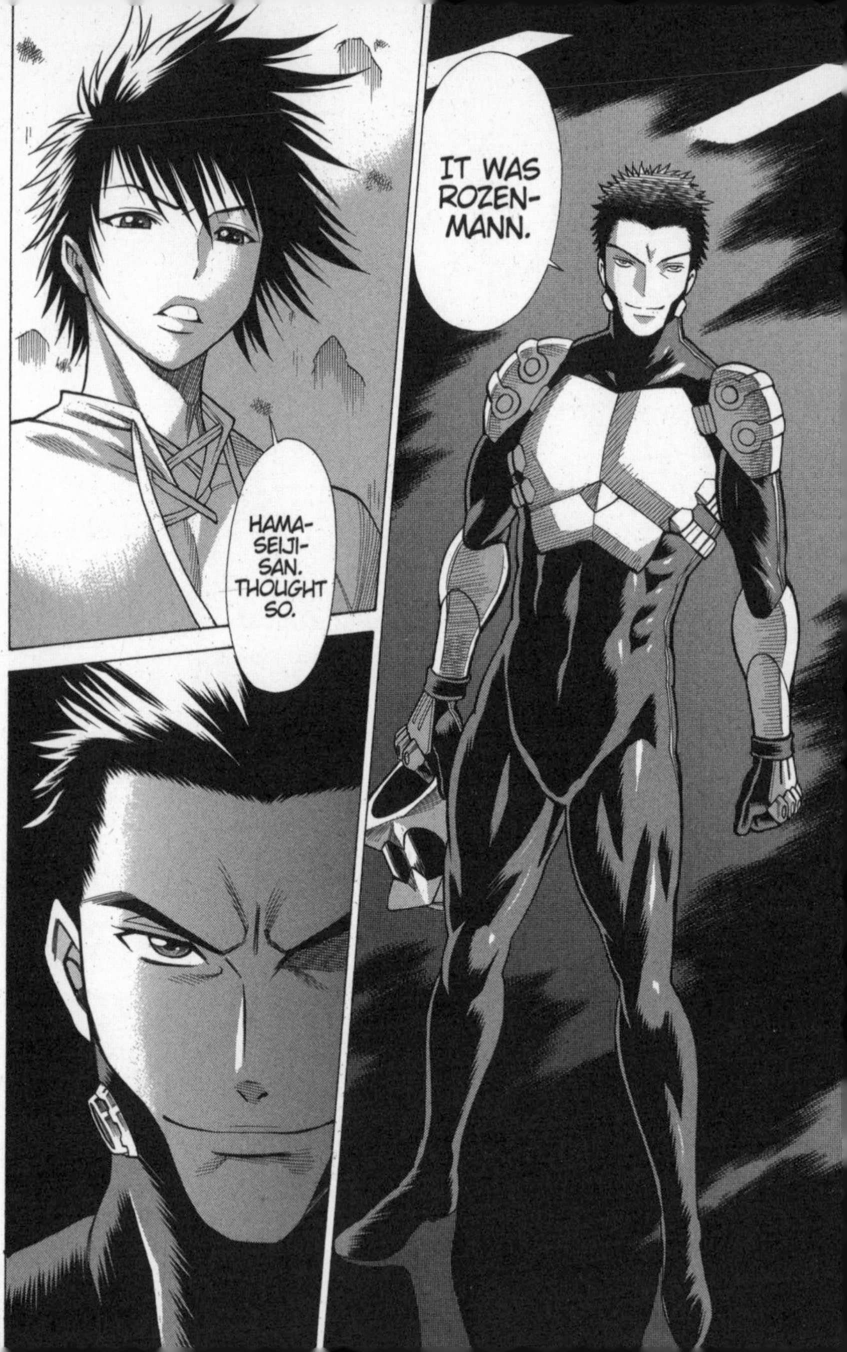
IT WAS ROZEN-MANN.
HAMA-SEIJI-SAN. THOUGHT SO.

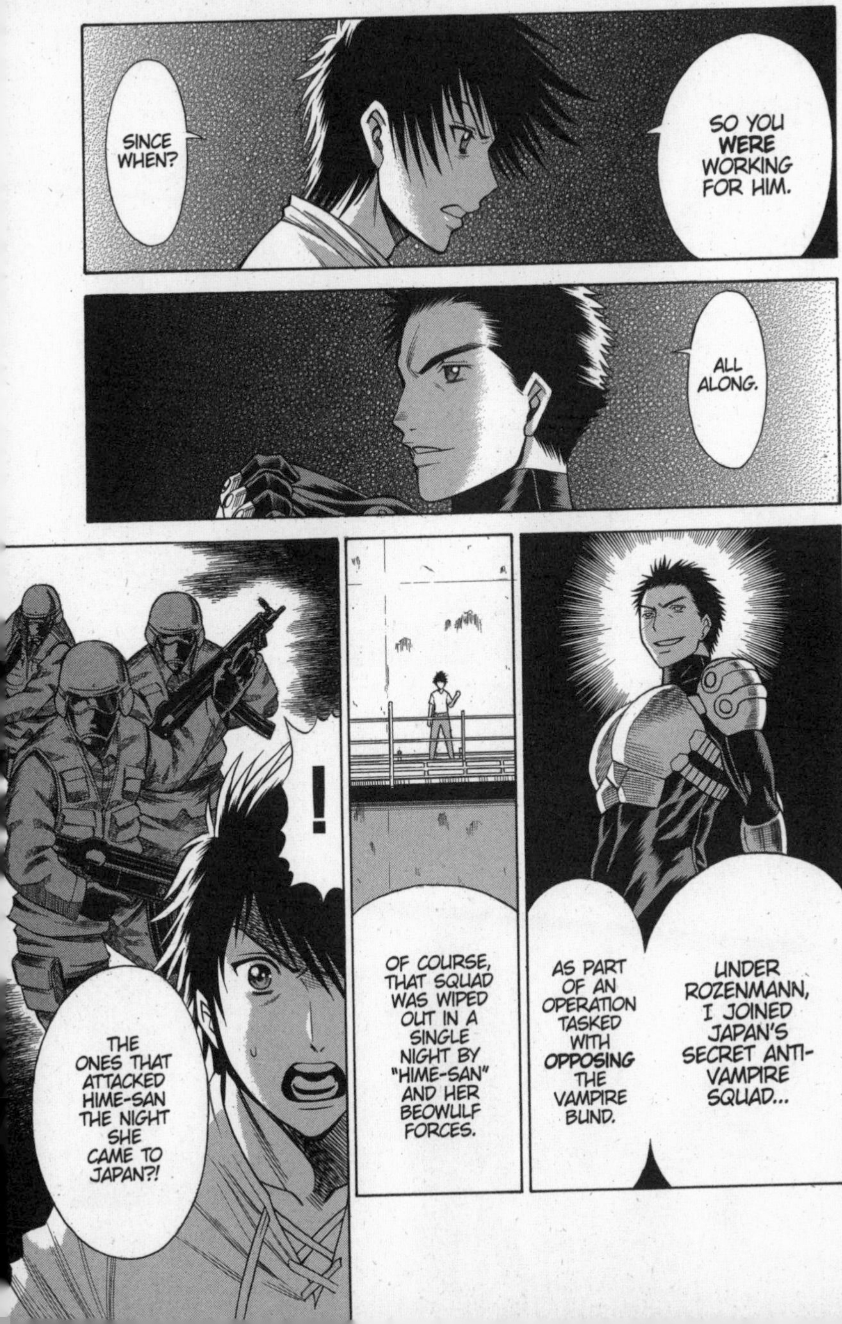
SO YOU WERE WORKING FOR HIM.
SINCE WHEN?
ALL ALONG.
UNDER ROZENMANN, I JOINED JAPAN'S SECRET ANTI-VAMPIRE SQUAD...
AS PART OF AN OPERATION TASKED WITH **OPPOSING** THE VAMPIRE BUND.
OF COURSE, THAT SQUAD WAS WIPED OUT IN A SINGLE NIGHT BY "HIME-SAN" AND HER BEOWULF FORCES.
!
THE ONES THAT ATTACKED HIME-SAN THE NIGHT SHE CAME TO JAPAN?!

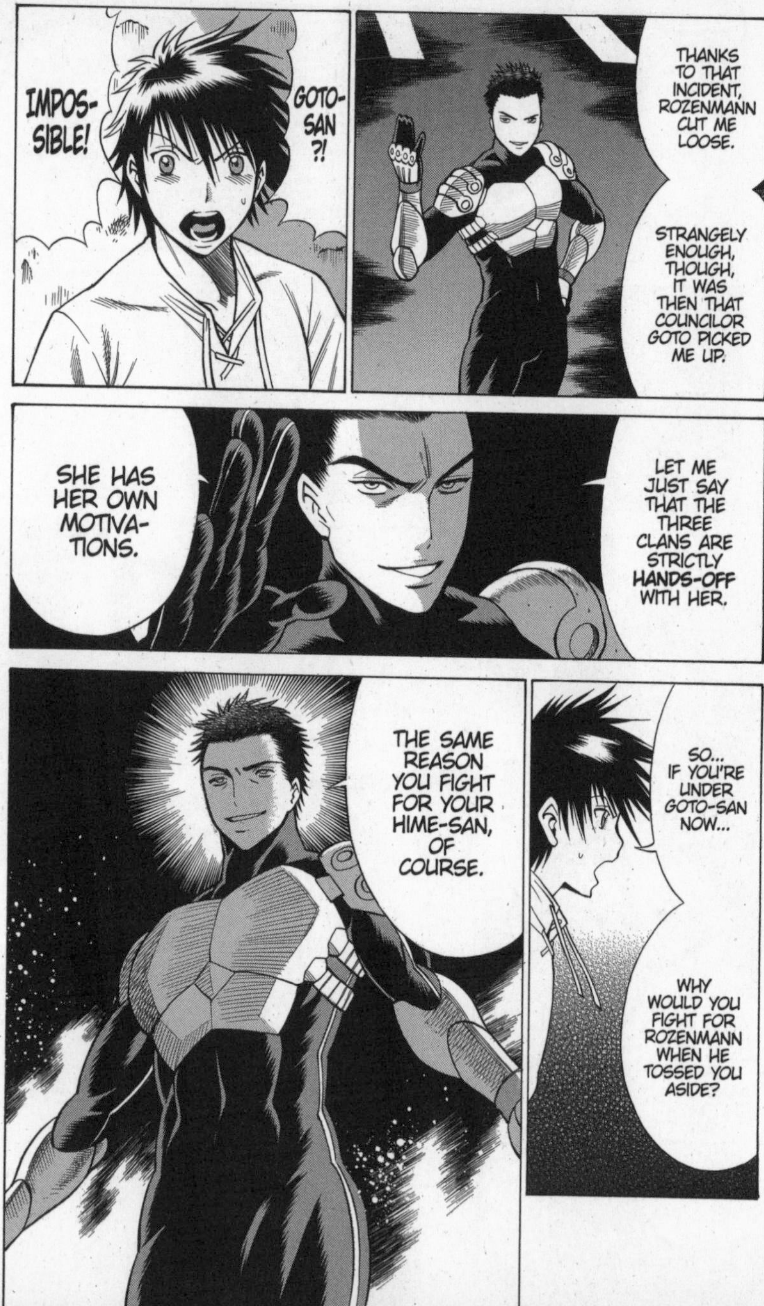
THANKS TO THAT INCIDENT, ROZENMANN CUT ME LOOSE.
STRANGELY ENOUGH, THOUGH, IT WAS THEN THAT COUNCILOR GOTO PICKED ME UP.
GOTO-SAN?!
IMPOSSIBLE!
LET ME JUST SAY THAT THE THREE CLANS ARE STRICTLY **HANDS-OFF** WITH HER.
SHE HAS HER OWN MOTIVATIONS.
SO... IF YOU'RE UNDER GOTO-SAN NOW...
WHY WOULD YOU FIGHT FOR ROZENMANN WHEN HE TOSSED YOU ASIDE?
THE SAME REASON YOU FIGHT FOR YOUR HIME-SAN, OF COURSE.

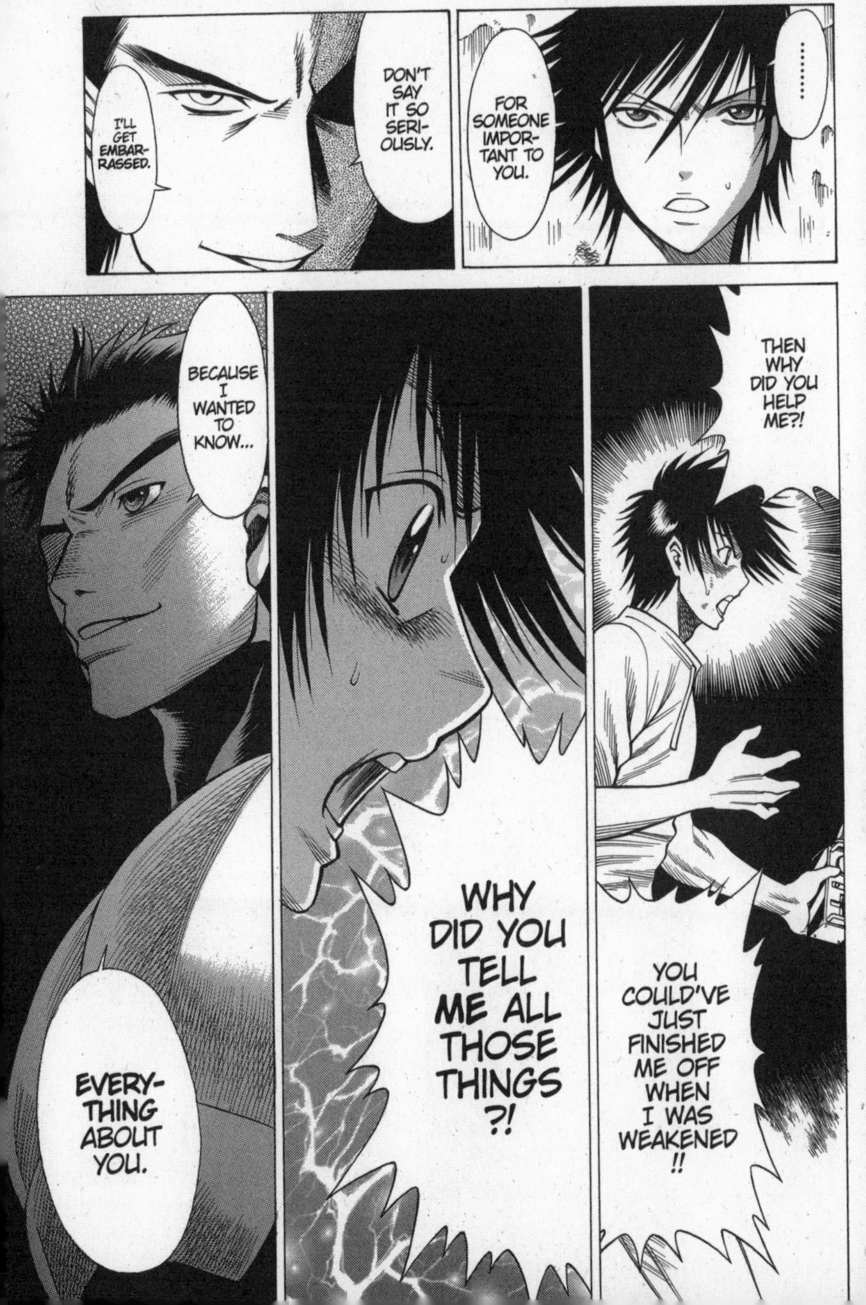
......
FOR SOMEONE IMPORTANT TO YOU.
DON'T SAY IT SO SERIOUSLY.
I'LL GET EMBARRASSED.
THEN WHY DID YOU HELP ME?!
YOU COULD'VE JUST FINISHED ME OFF WHEN I WAS WEAKENED!!
WHY DID YOU TELL ME ALL THOSE THINGS?!
BECAUSE I WANTED TO KNOW...
EVERYTHING ABOUT YOU.

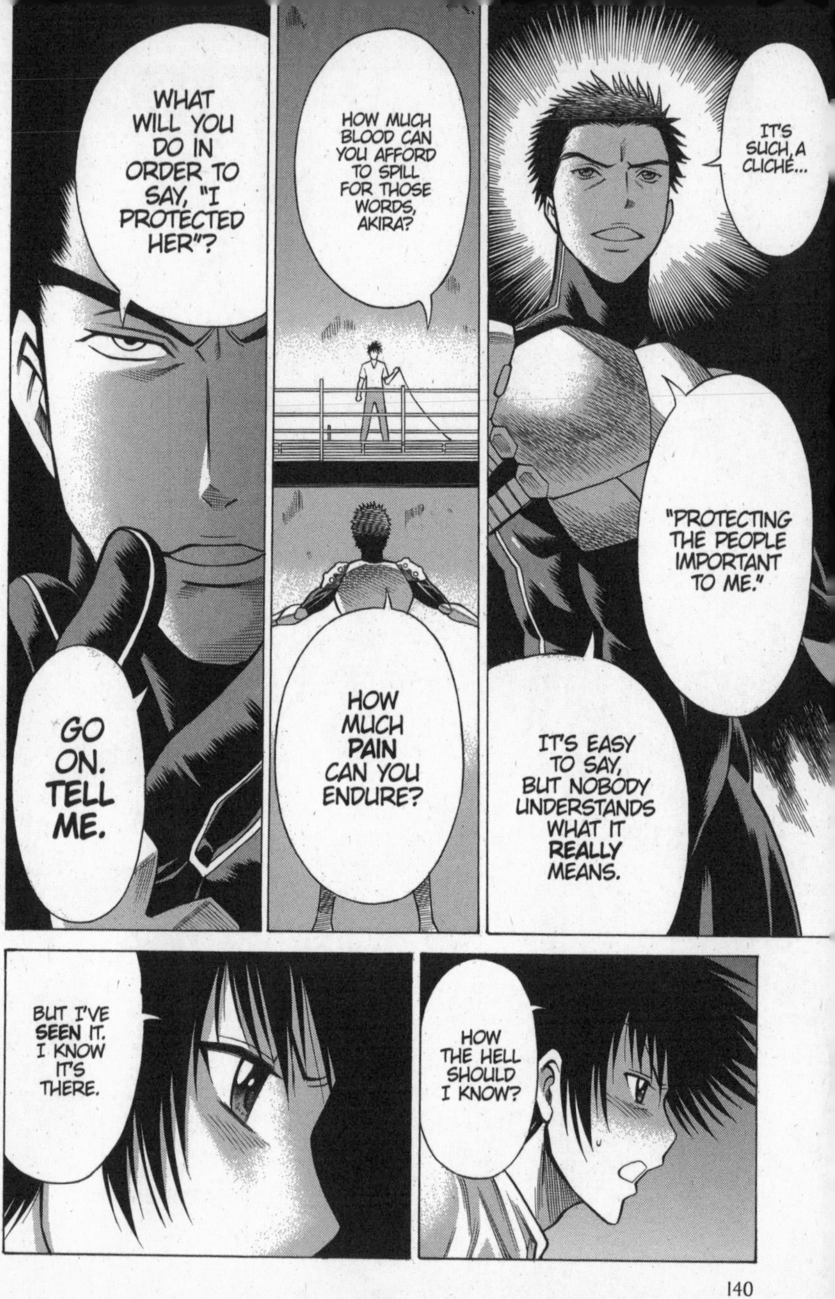
IT'S SUCH A CLICHÉ...
"PROTECTING THE PEOPLE IMPORTANT TO ME."
IT'S EASY TO SAY, BUT NOBODY UNDERSTANDS WHAT IT REALLY MEANS.
HOW MUCH BLOOD CAN YOU AFFORD TO SPILL FOR THOSE WORDS, AKIRA?
HOW MUCH PAIN CAN YOU ENDURE?
WHAT WILL YOU DO IN ORDER TO SAY, "I PROTECTED HER"?
GO ON. TELL ME.
HOW THE HELL SHOULD I KNOW?
BUT I'VE SEEN IT. I KNOW IT'S THERE.

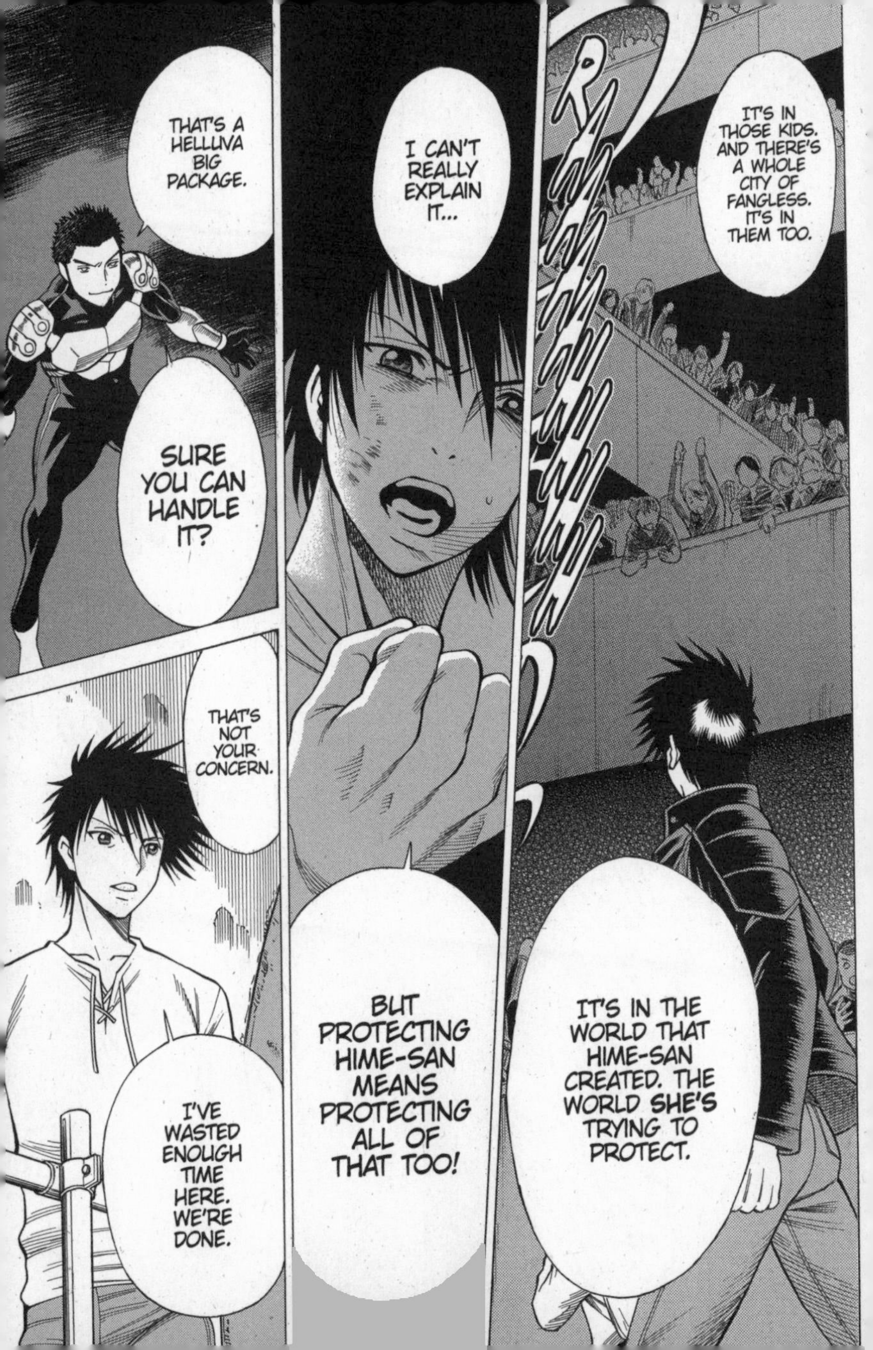
IT'S IN THOSE KIDS. AND THERE'S A WHOLE CITY OF FANGLESS. IT'S IN THEM TOO.
IT'S IN THE WORLD THAT HIME-SAN CREATED. THE WORLD SHE'S TRYING TO PROTECT.
I CAN'T REALLY EXPLAIN IT...
BUT PROTECTING HIME-SAN MEANS PROTECTING ALL OF THAT TOO!
THAT'S A HELLUVA BIG PACKAGE.
SURE YOU CAN HANDLE IT?
THAT'S NOT YOUR CONCERN.
I'VE WASTED ENOUGH TIME HERE. WE'RE DONE.

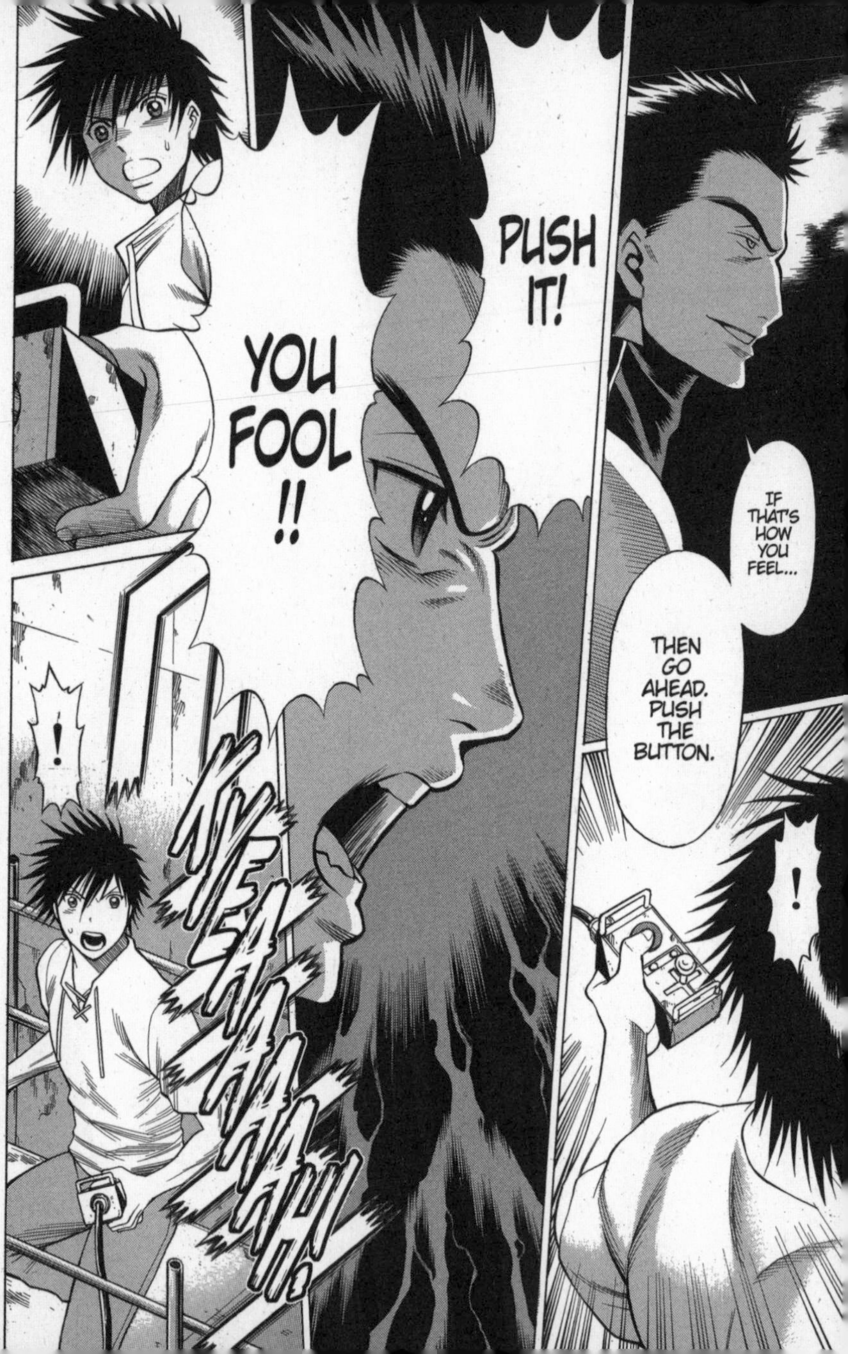
IF THAT'S HOW YOU FEEL...
THEN GO AHEAD. PUSH THE BUTTON.
!
PUSH IT!
YOU FOOL !!
!

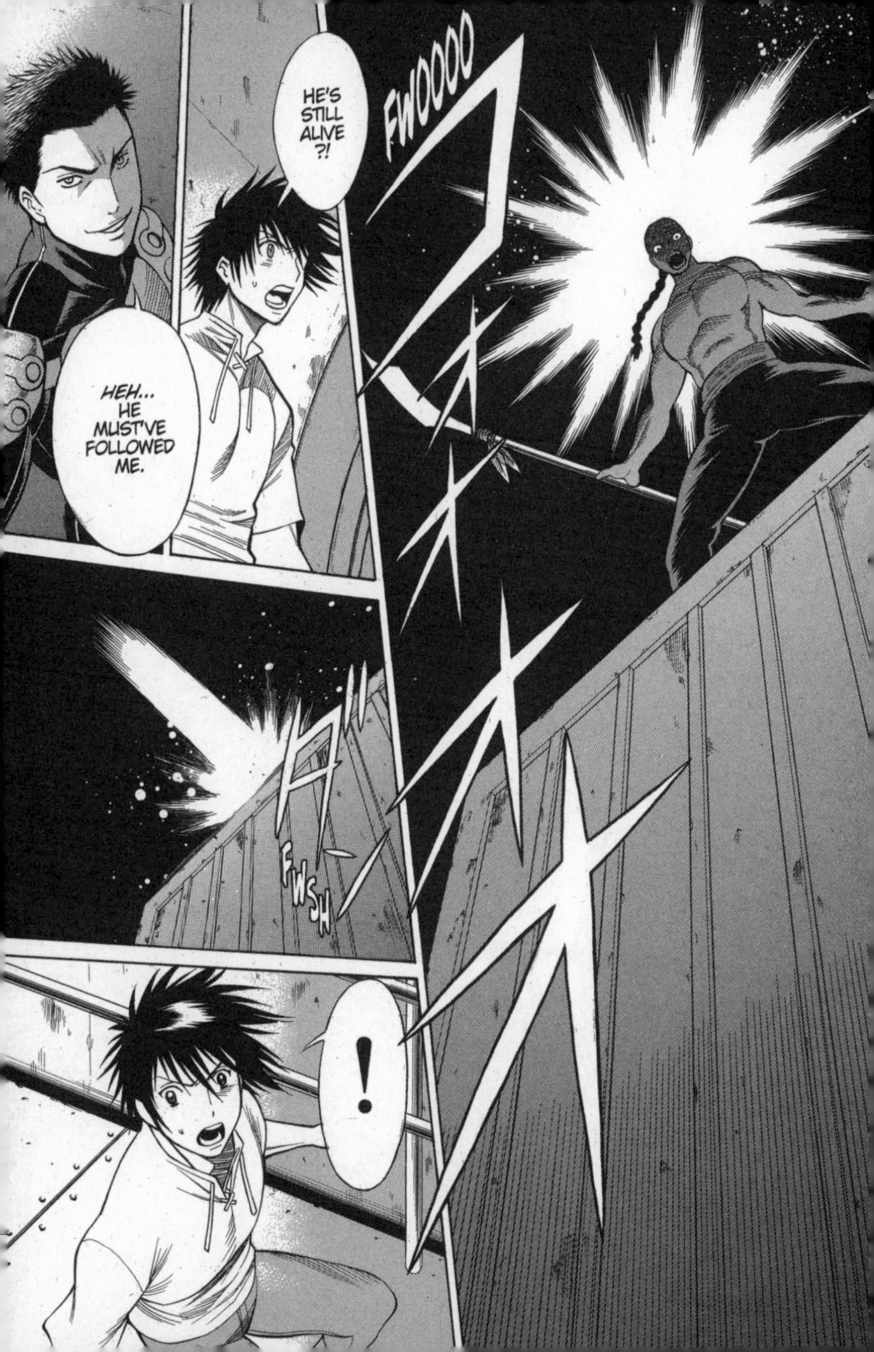
FWOOOO
HE'S STILL ALIVE ?!
HEH... HE MUST'VE FOLLOWED ME.
FWSH
!

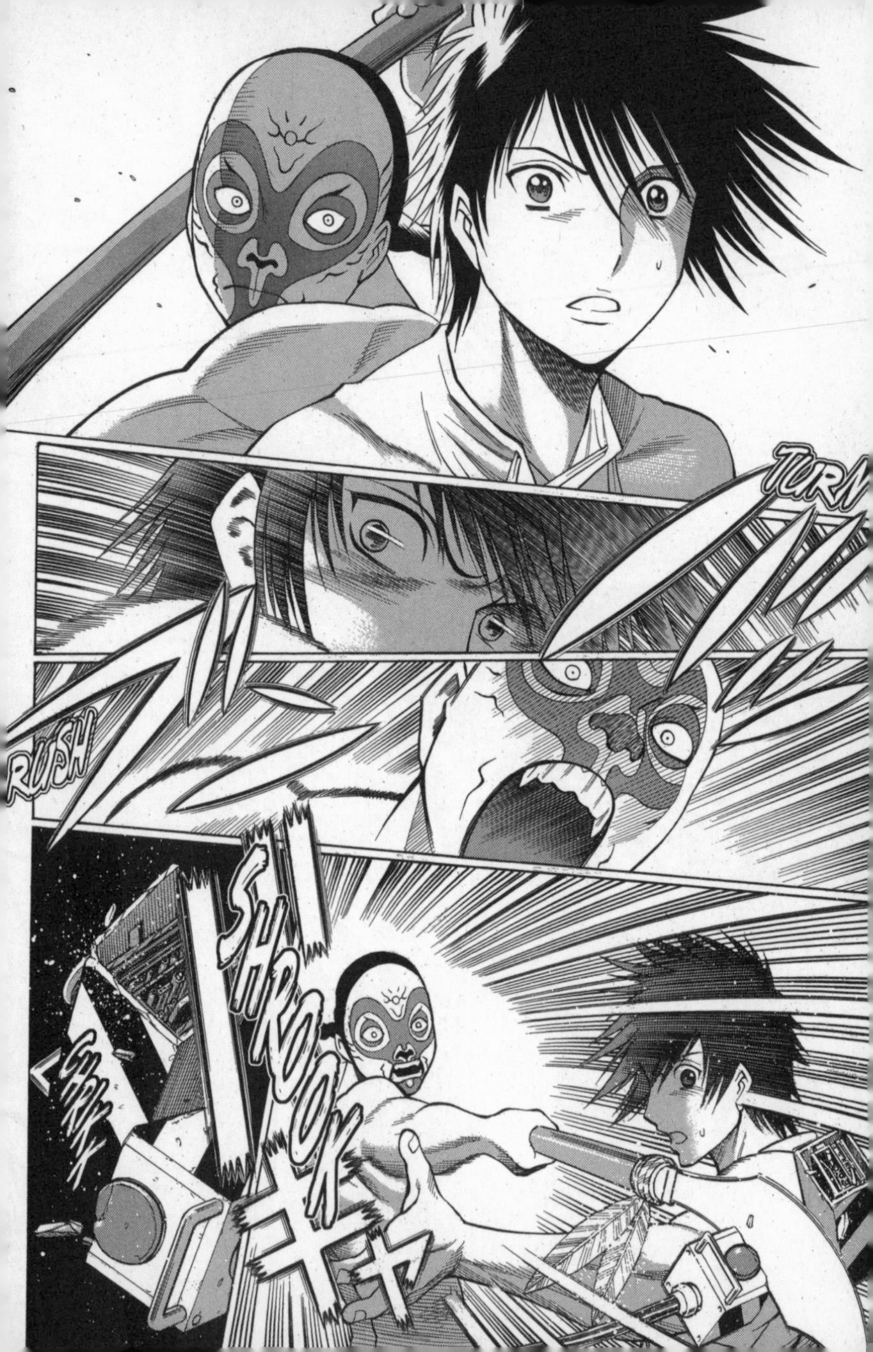
TURN
RUSH
SHROOOK
GYRK

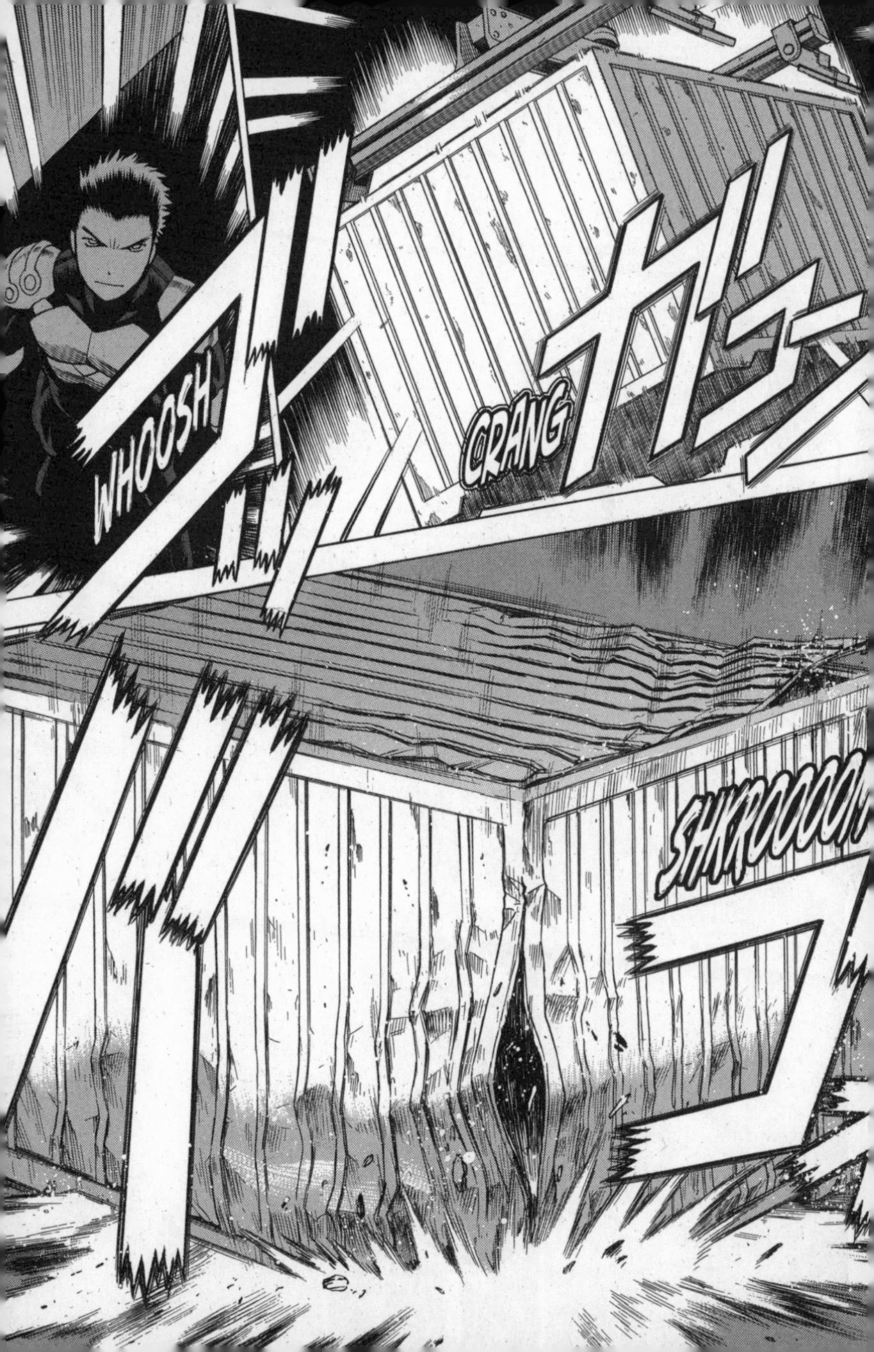
CRANG
WHOOSH
SHKROOOO

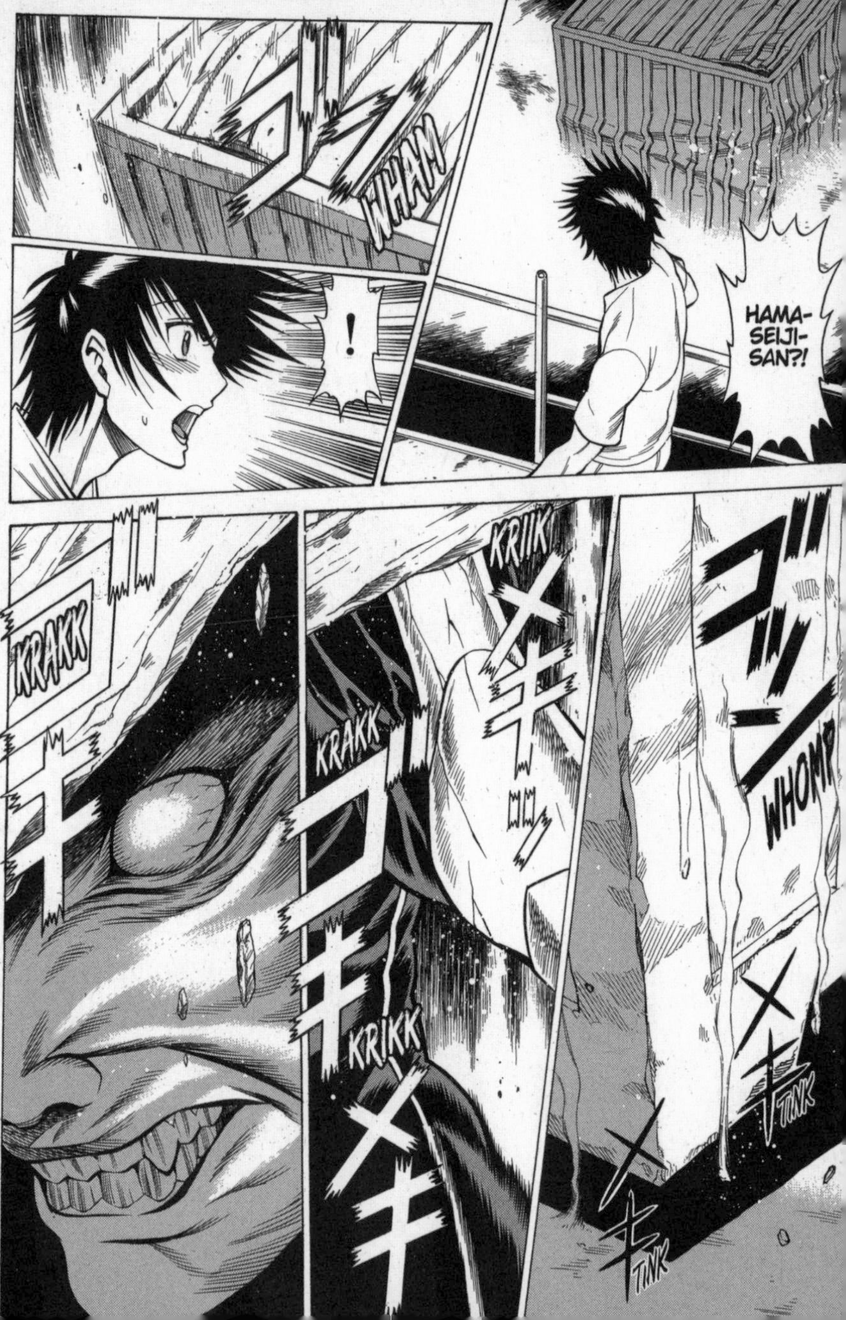
HAMA-SEIJI-SAN?!
WHAM
!
WHOMP
TINK
TINK
KRIIK
KRAKK
KRIKK
KRAKK

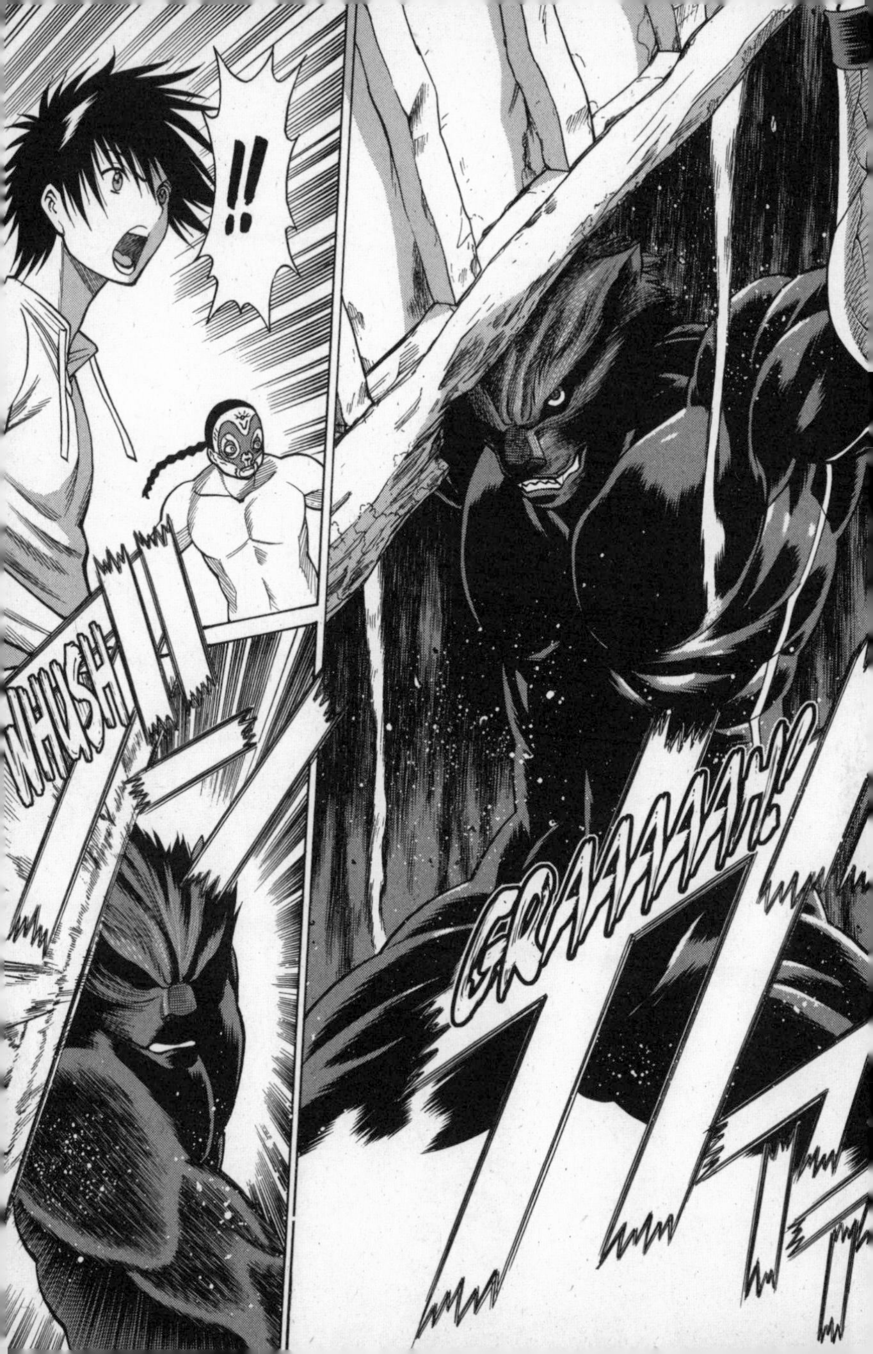
GRAAAAAH!
!!
WHUSH!!

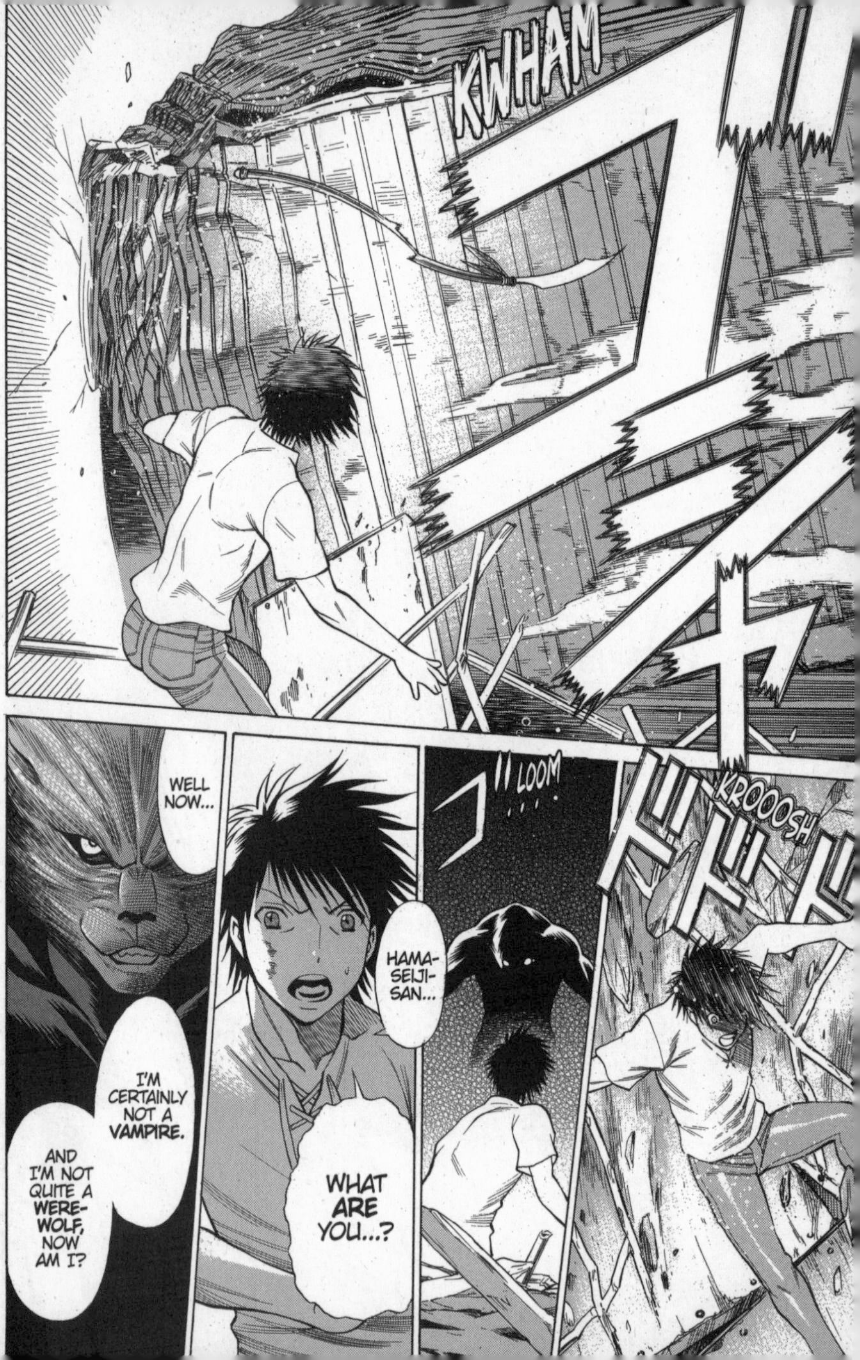
KWHAM
KROOOSH
LOOM
HAMA-SEIJI-SAN...
WHAT ARE YOU...?
WELL NOW...
I'M CERTAINLY NOT A VAMPIRE.
AND I'M NOT QUITE A WERE-WOLF, NOW AM I?

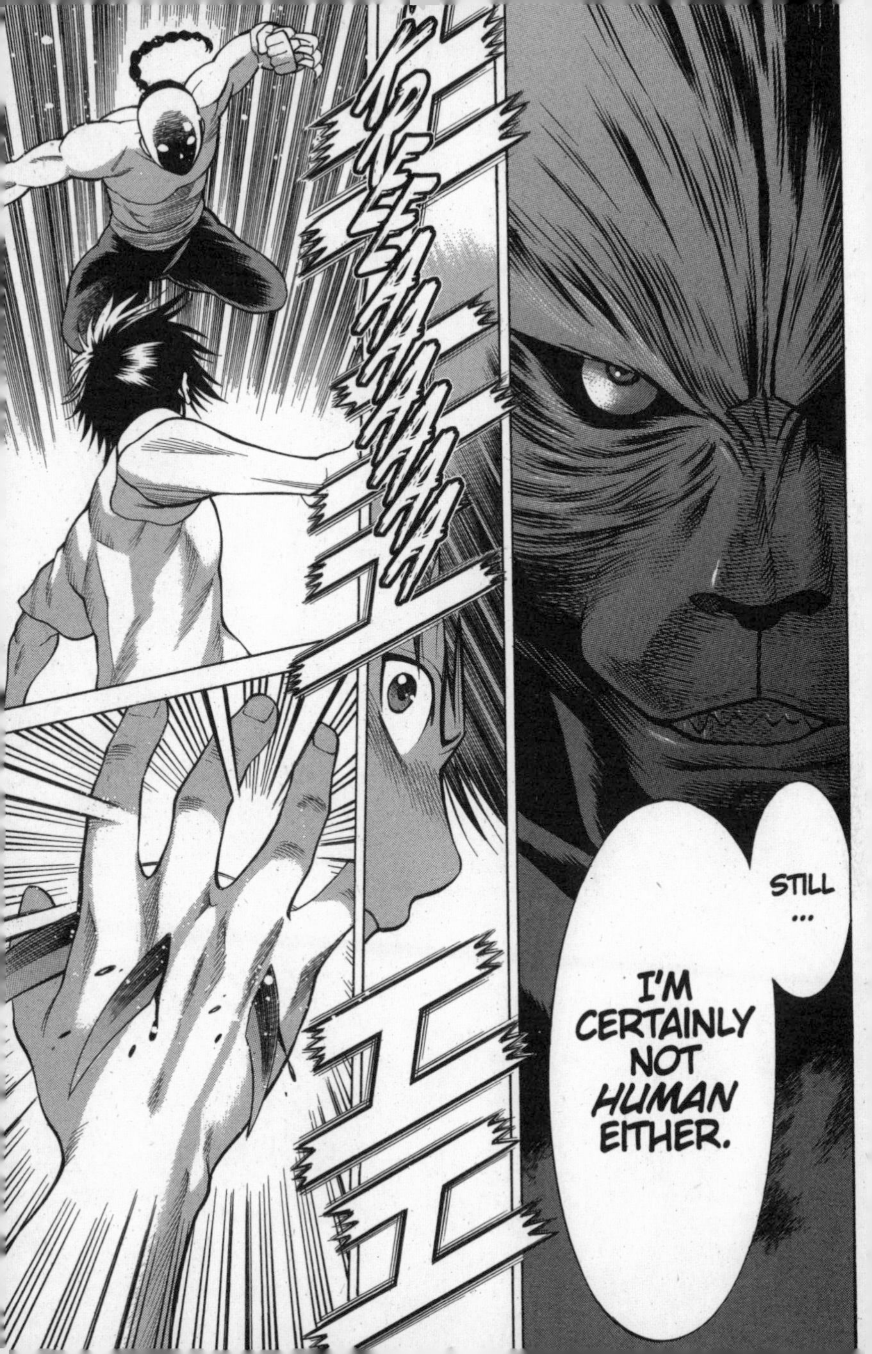
STILL ... I'M CERTAINLY NOT HUMAN EITHER.

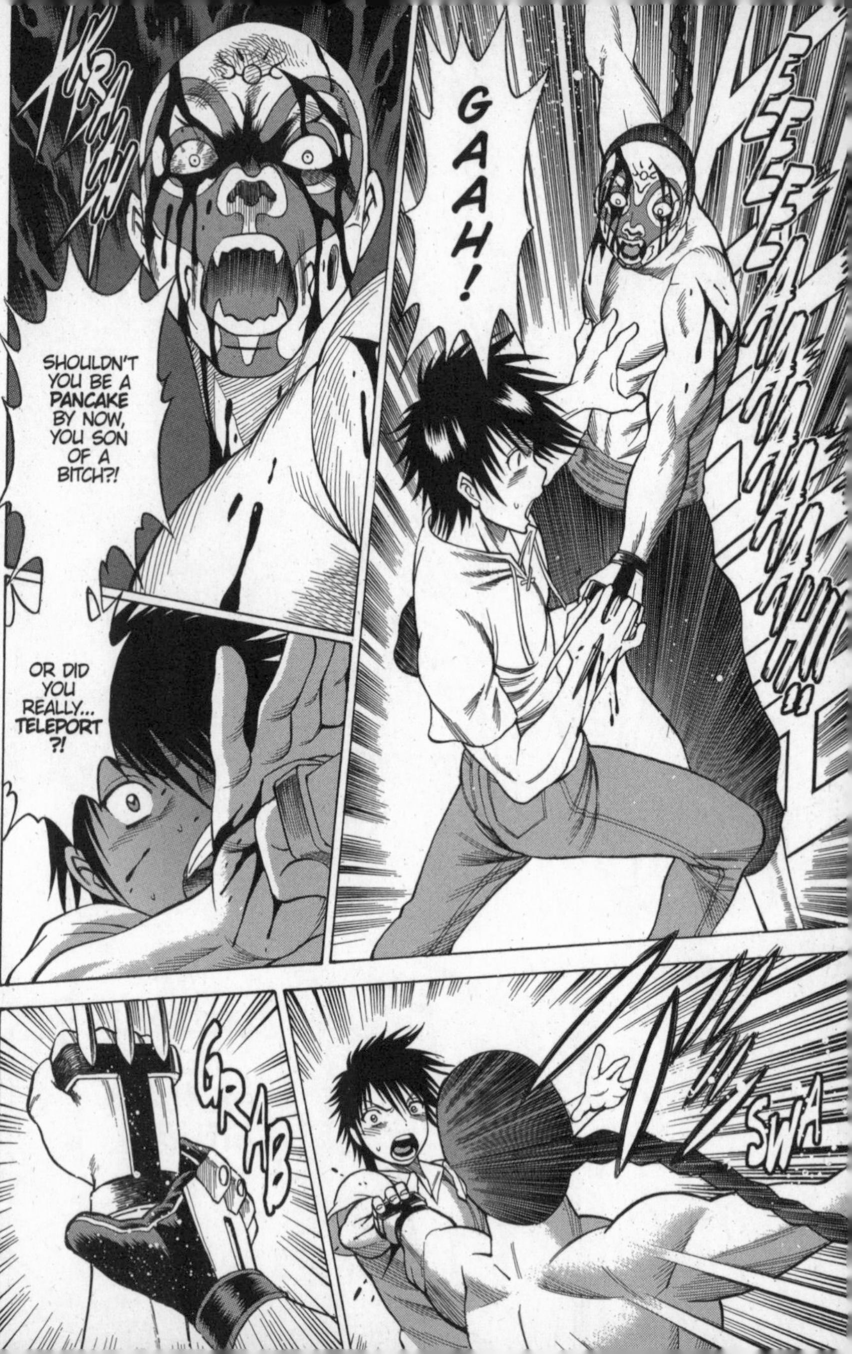
GAAH!
SHOULDN'T YOU BE A PANCAKE BY NOW, YOU SON OF A BITCH?!
OR DID YOU REALLY... TELEPORT ?!
SWA
GRAB

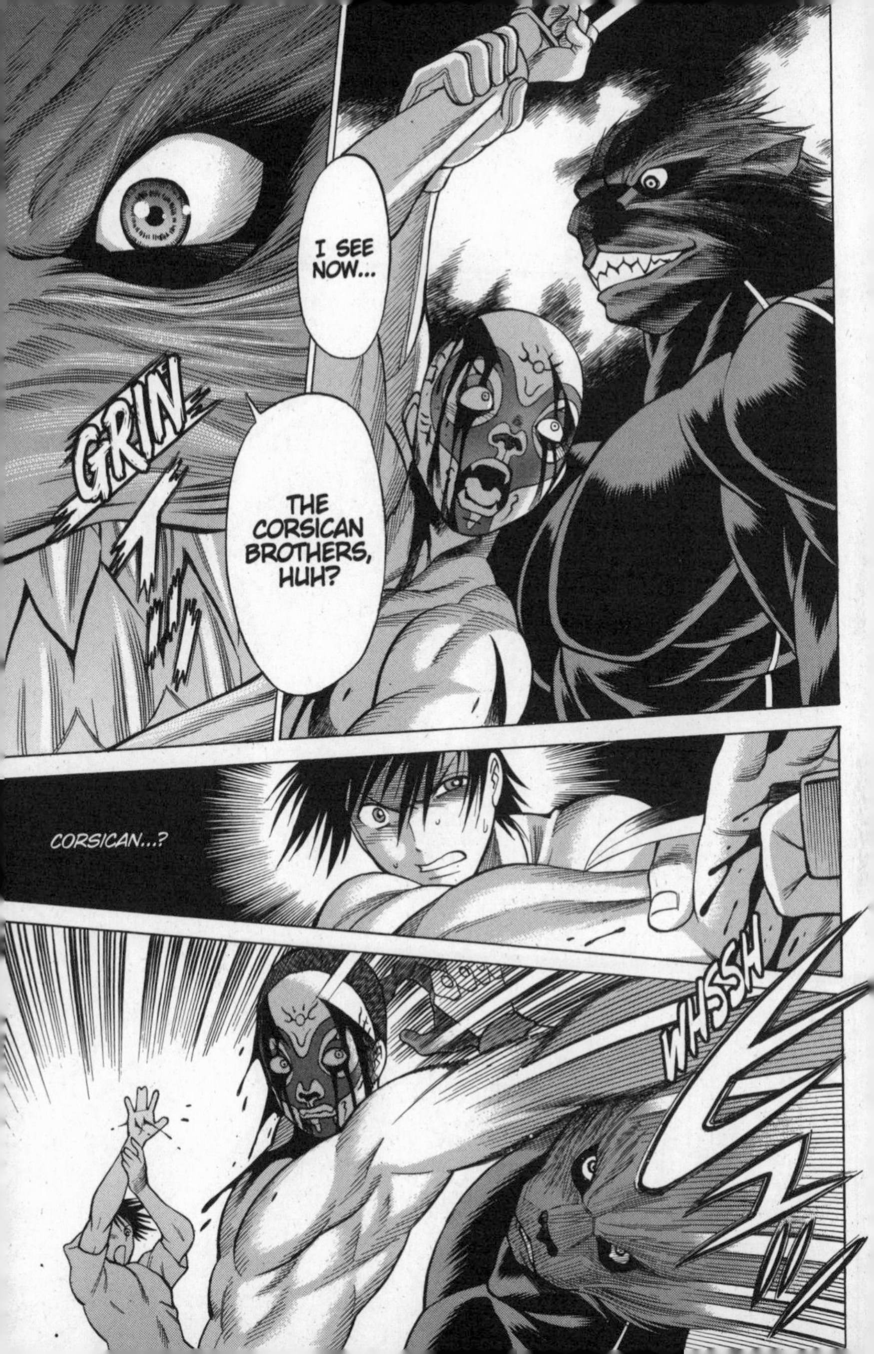
I SEE NOW...
THE CORSICAN BROTHERS, HUH?
GRIN
CORSICAN...?
WHSSH

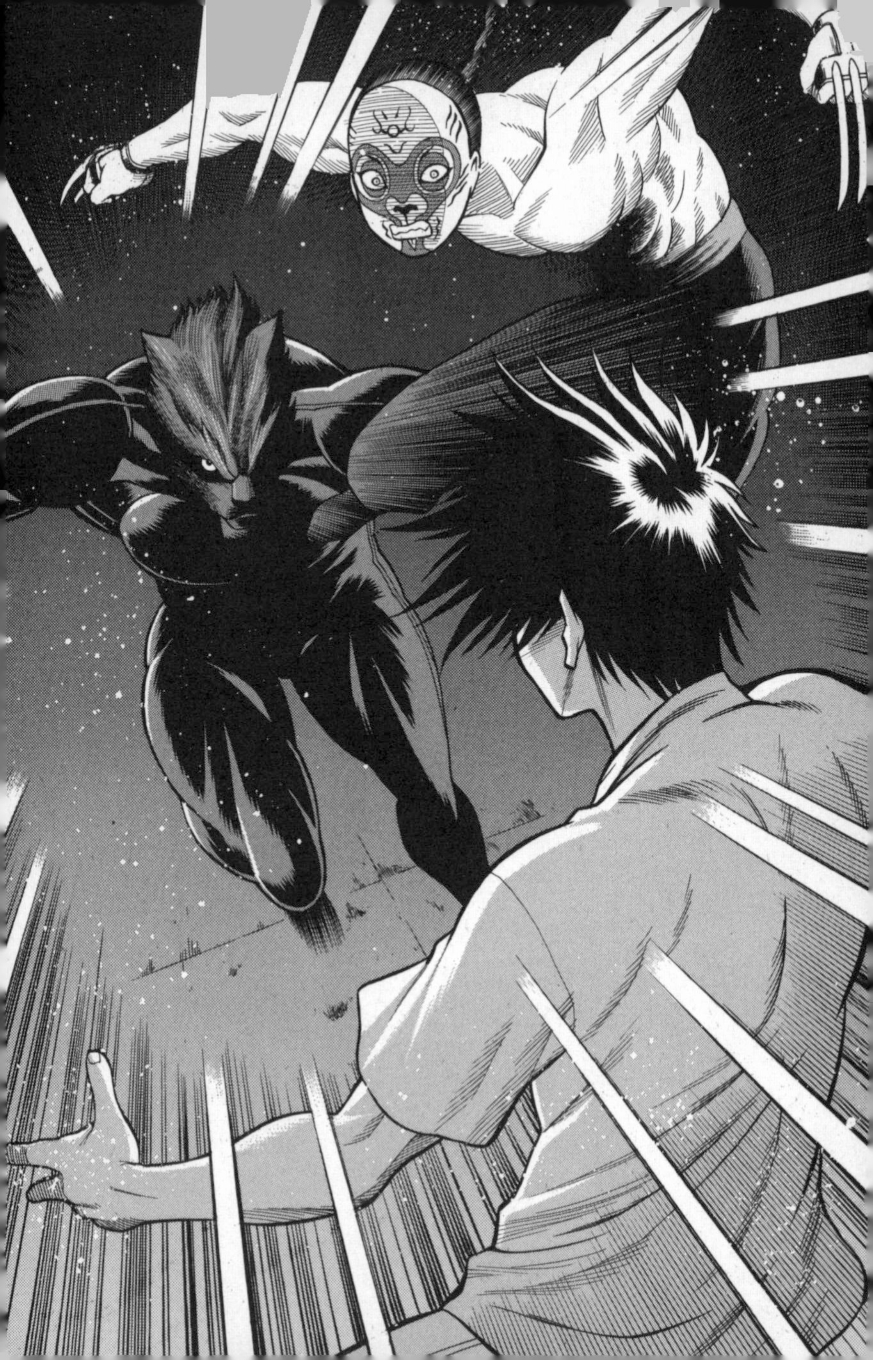

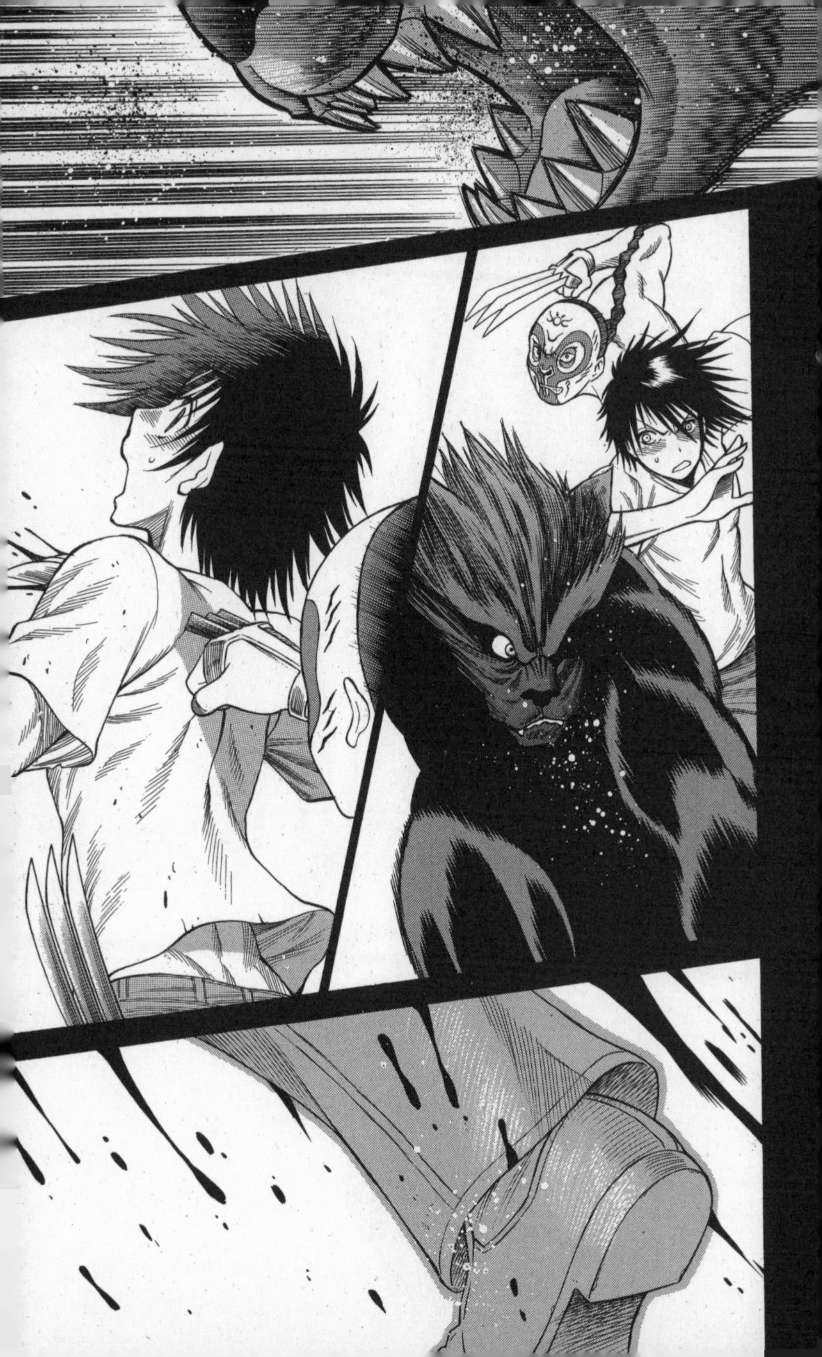

Chapter 30: The Cradle Will Rock

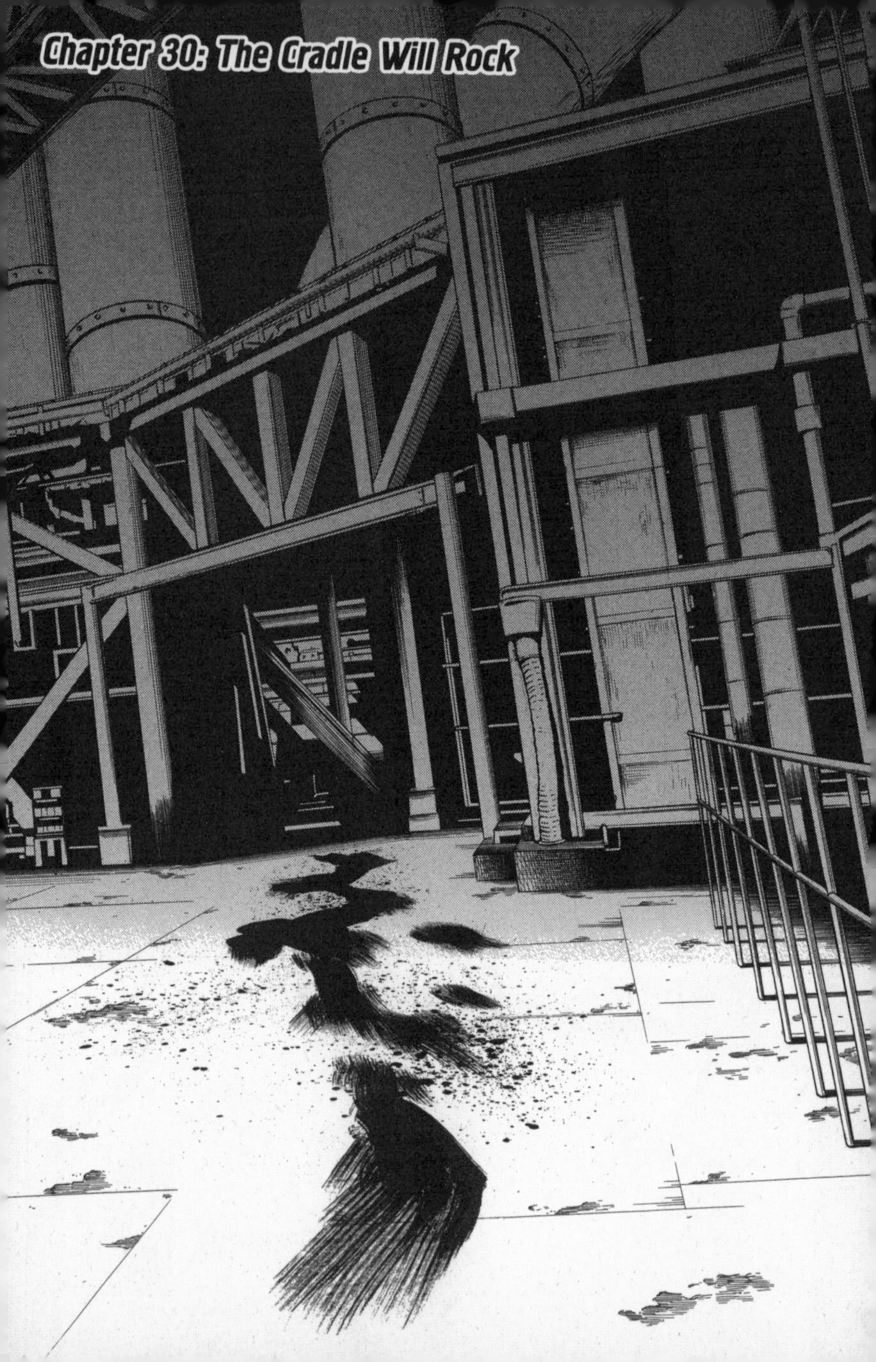

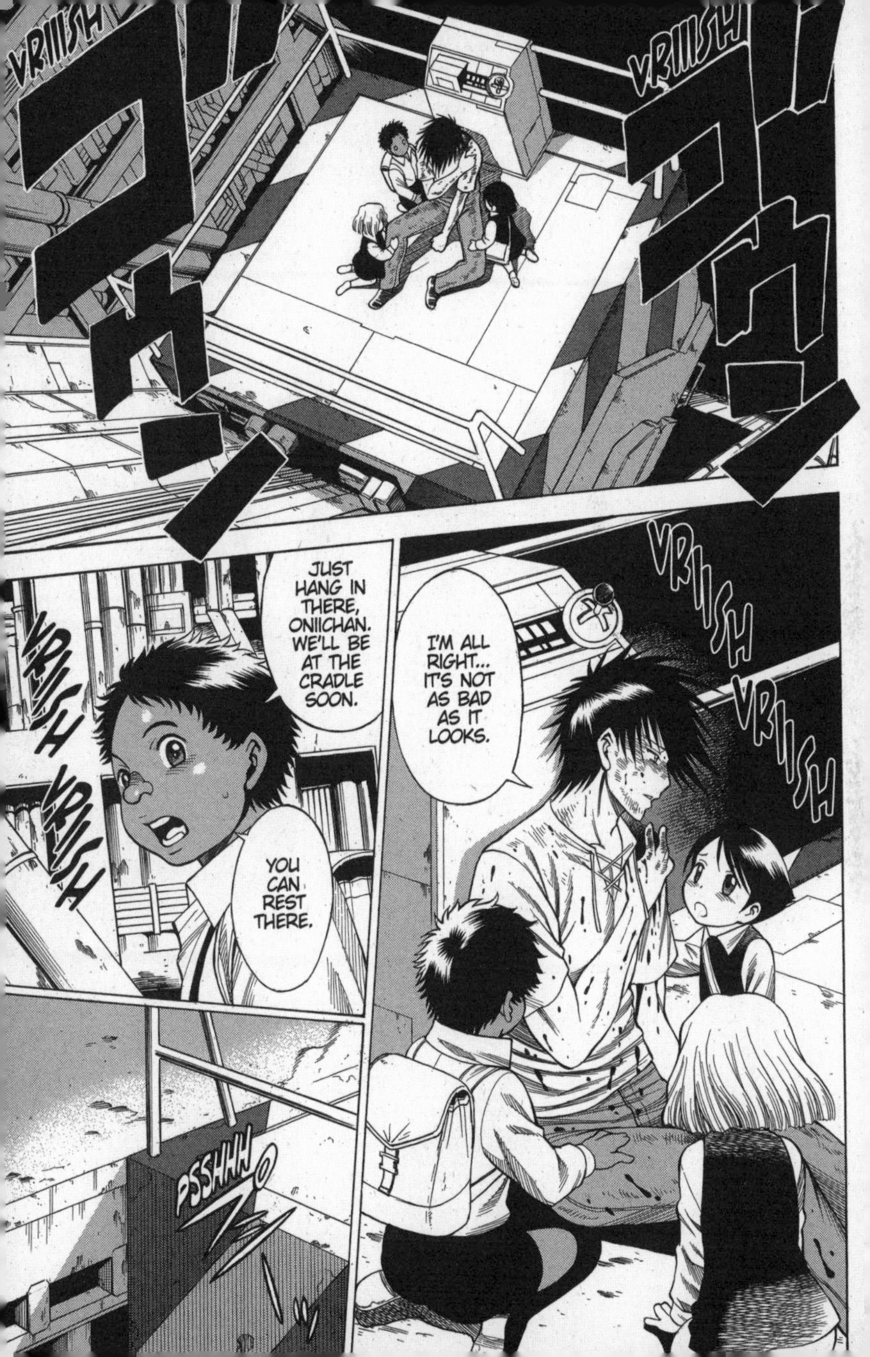
VRIIISH
VRIIISH
VRIISH
VRIISH
I'M ALL RIGHT... IT'S NOT AS BAD AS IT LOOKS.
PSSHHH
JUST HANG IN THERE, ONIICHAN. WE'LL BE AT THE CRADLE SOON.
YOU CAN REST THERE.
VRIISH
VRIISH

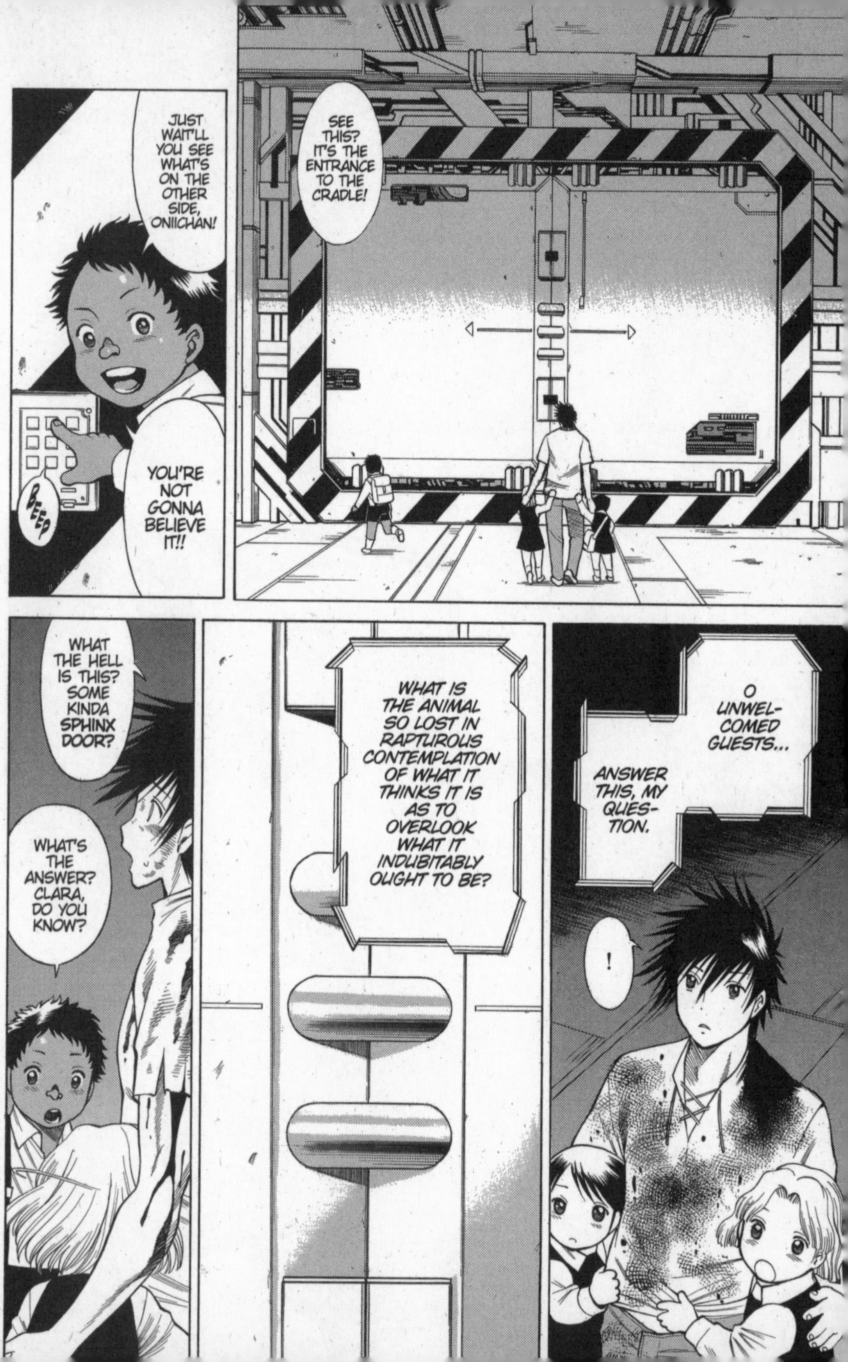
SEE THIS? IT'S THE ENTRANCE TO THE CRADLE!
JUST WAIT'LL YOU SEE WHAT'S ON THE OTHER SIDE, ONIICHAN!
YOU'RE NOT GONNA BELIEVE IT!!
BEEP
O UNWEL-COMED GUESTS...
ANSWER THIS, MY QUES-TION.
!
WHAT IS THE ANIMAL SO LOST IN RAPTUROUS CONTEMPLATION OF WHAT IT THINKS IT IS AS TO OVERLOOK WHAT IT INDUBITABLY OUGHT TO BE?
WHAT THE HELL IS THIS? SOME KINDA SPHINX DOOR?
WHAT'S THE ANSWER? CLARA, DO YOU KNOW?

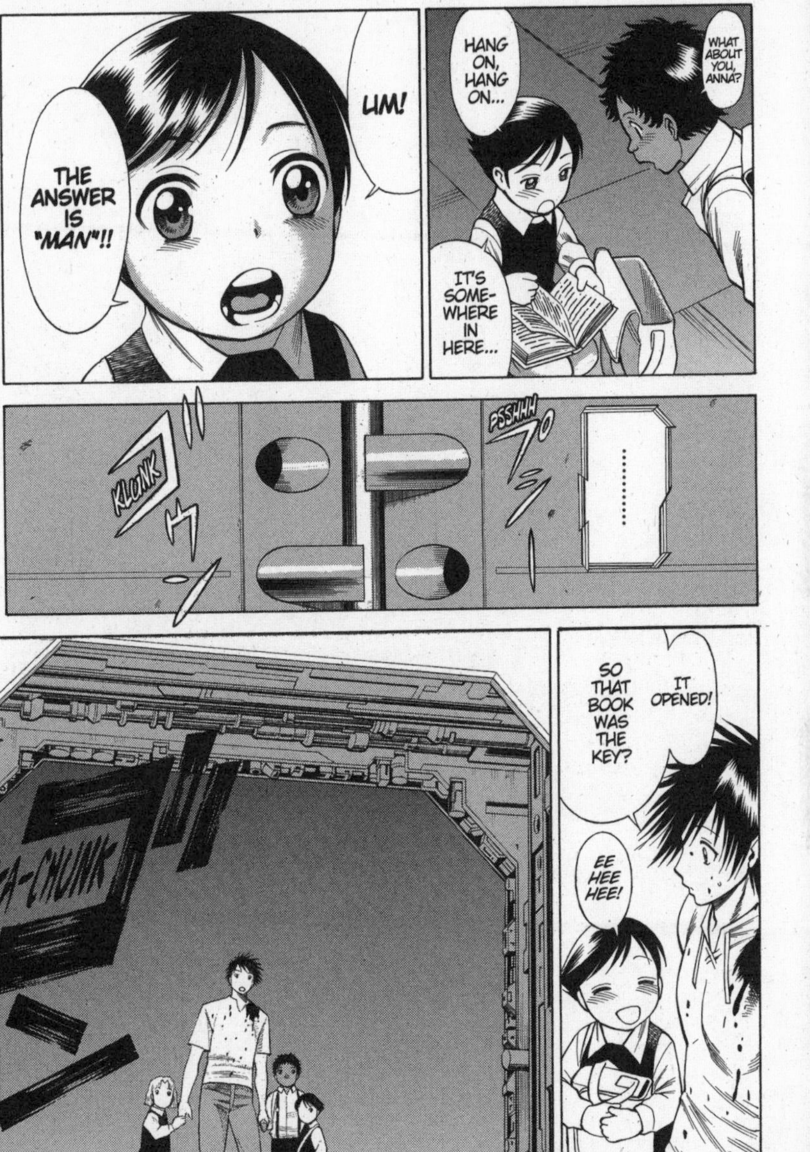
WHAT ABOUT YOU, ANNA?
HANG ON, HANG ON...
IT'S SOME-WHERE IN HERE...
UM!
THE ANSWER IS "MAN"!!
......
PSSHHH
KLONK
IT OPENED!
SO THAT BOOK WAS THE KEY?
EE HEE HEE!
KA-CHUNK

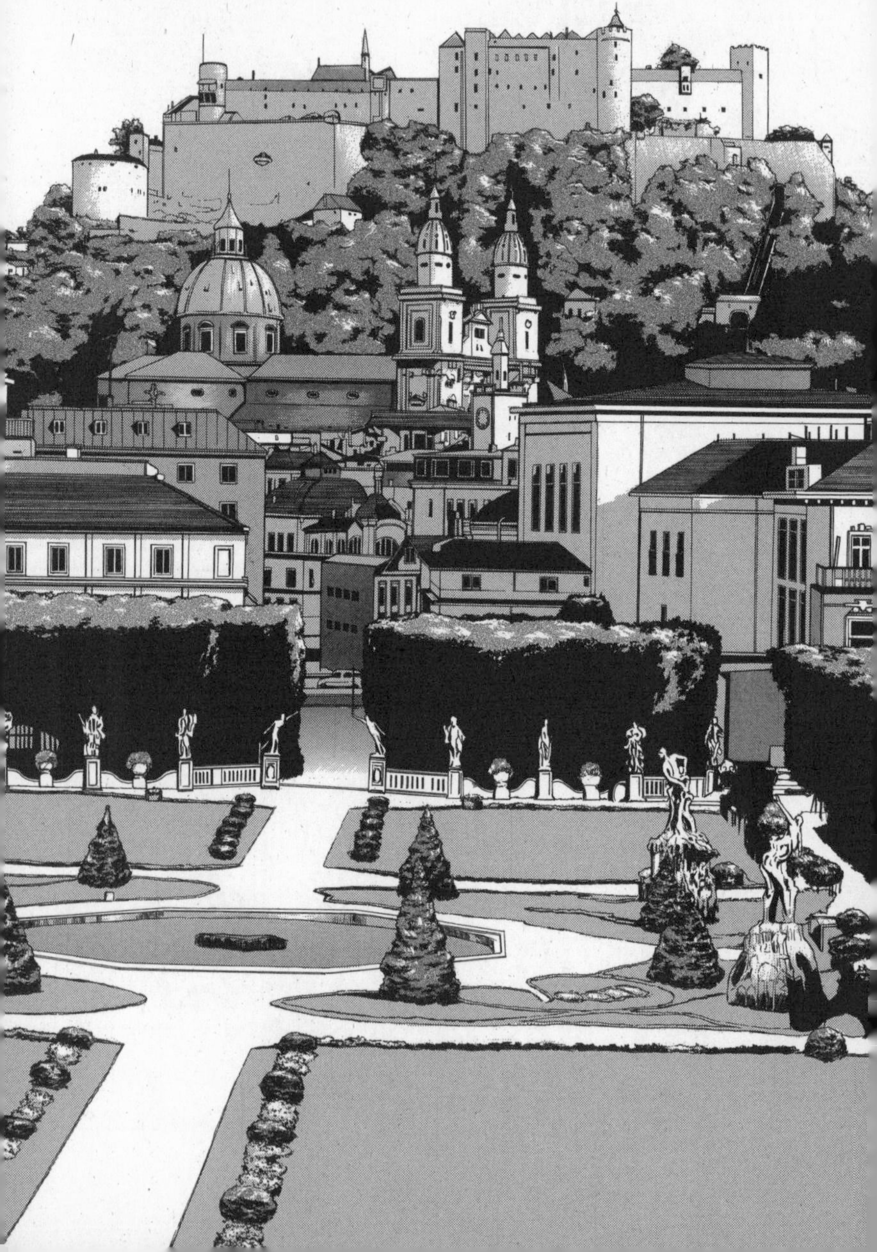

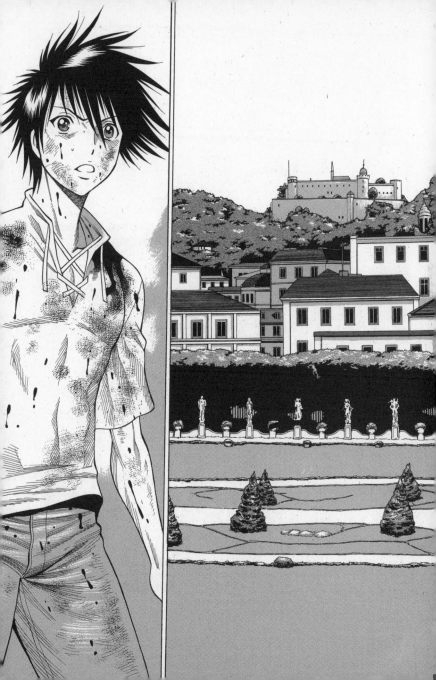

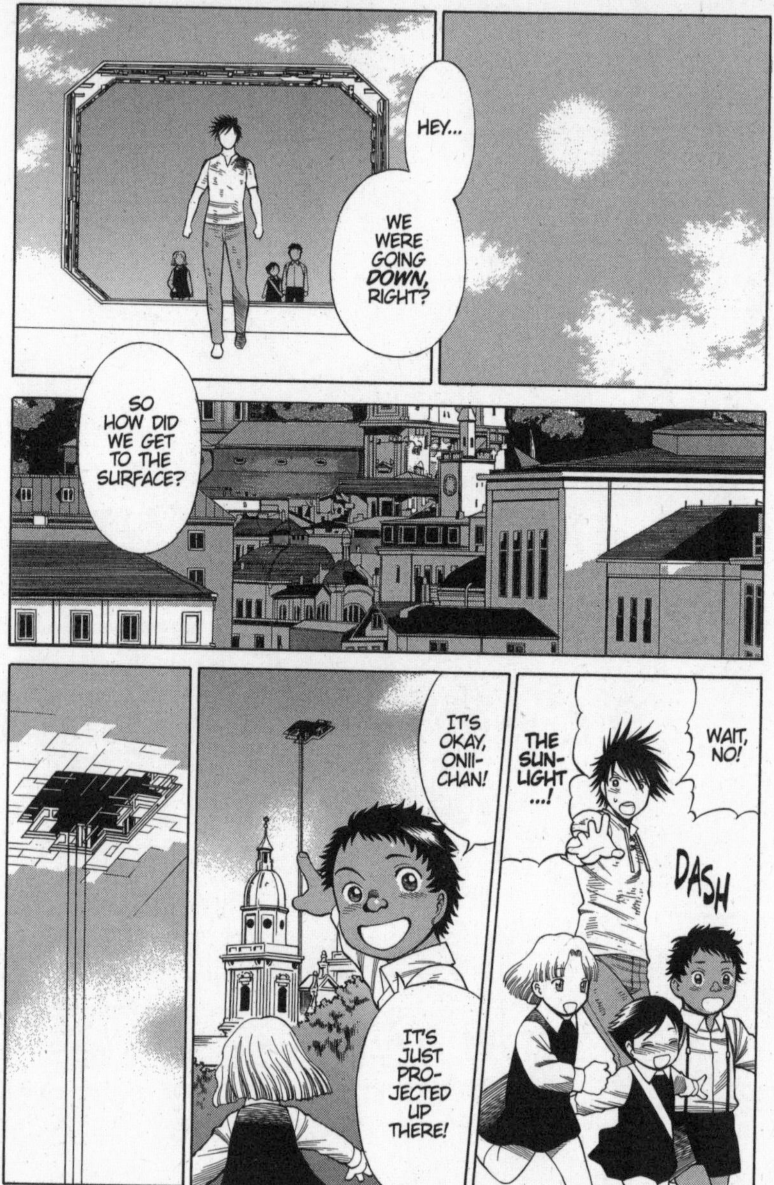
HEY...
WE WERE GOING DOWN, RIGHT?
SO HOW DID WE GET TO THE SURFACE?
WAIT, NO!
THE SUN-LIGHT ...!
DASH
IT'S OKAY, ONII-CHAN!
IT'S JUST PRO-JECTED UP THERE!

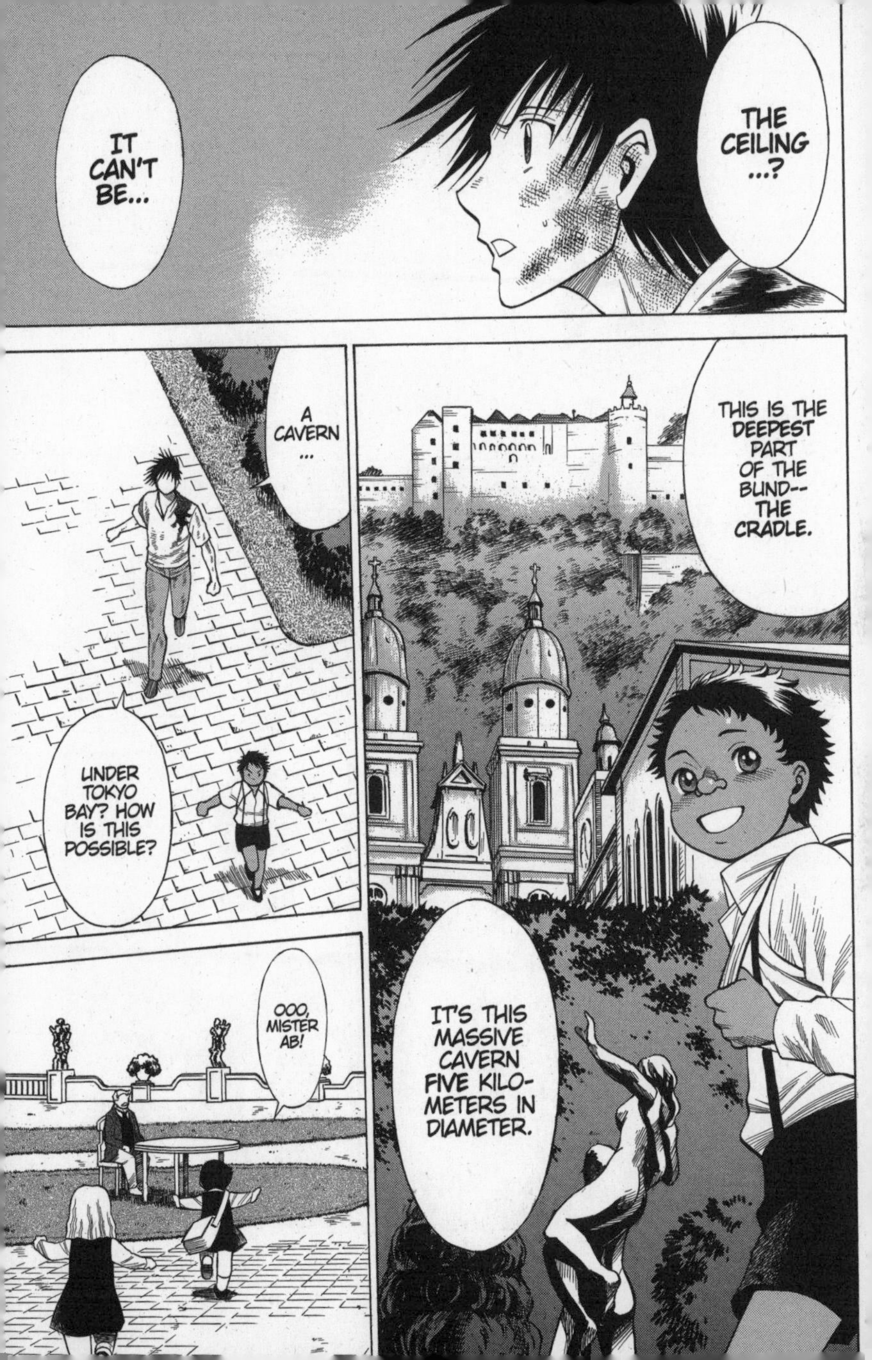
THE CEILING ...?
IT CAN'T BE...
THIS IS THE DEEPEST PART OF THE BUND-- THE CRADLE.
IT'S THIS MASSIVE CAVERN FIVE KILO-METERS IN DIAMETER.
A CAVERN ...
UNDER TOKYO BAY? HOW IS THIS POSSIBLE?
OOO, MISTER AB!

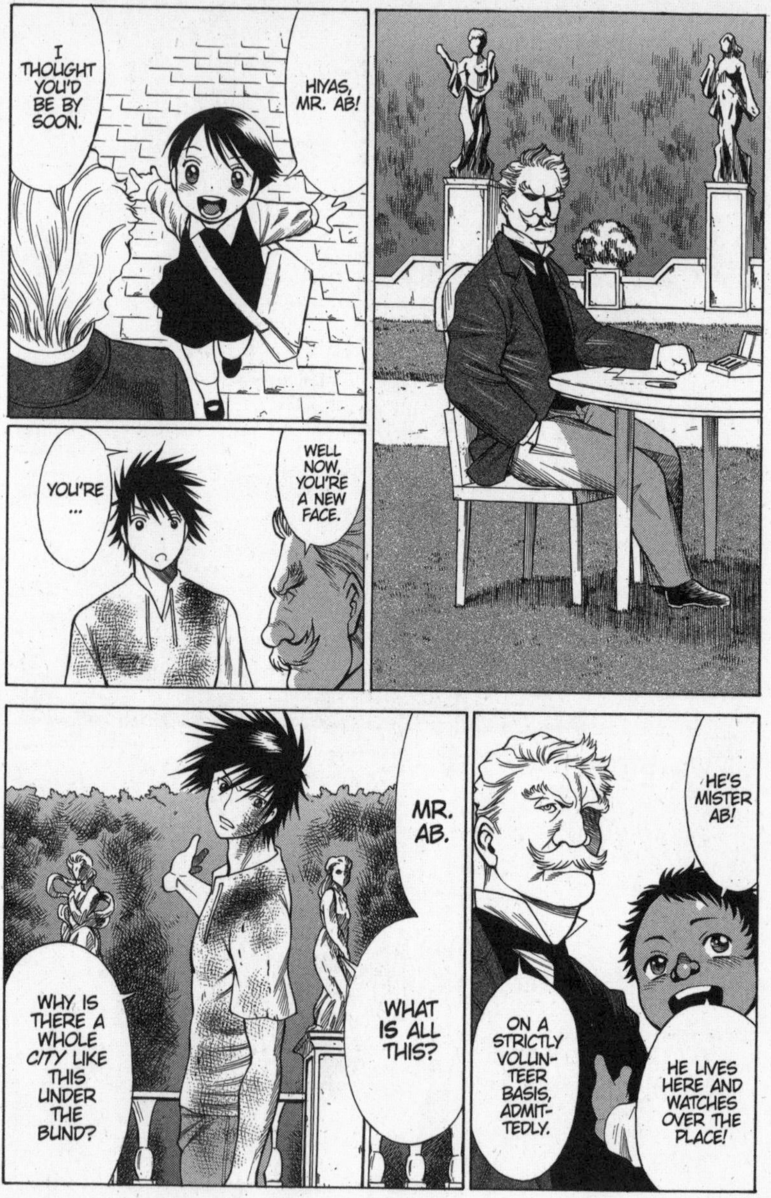
HIYAS, MR. AB!
I THOUGHT YOU'D BE BY SOON.
WELL NOW, YOU'RE A NEW FACE.
YOU'RE ...
HE'S MISTER AB!
HE LIVES HERE AND WATCHES OVER THE PLACE!
ON A STRICTLY VOLUN-TEER BASIS, ADMIT-TEDLY.
MR. AB.
WHAT IS ALL THIS?
WHY IS THERE A WHOLE CITY LIKE THIS UNDER THE BUND?

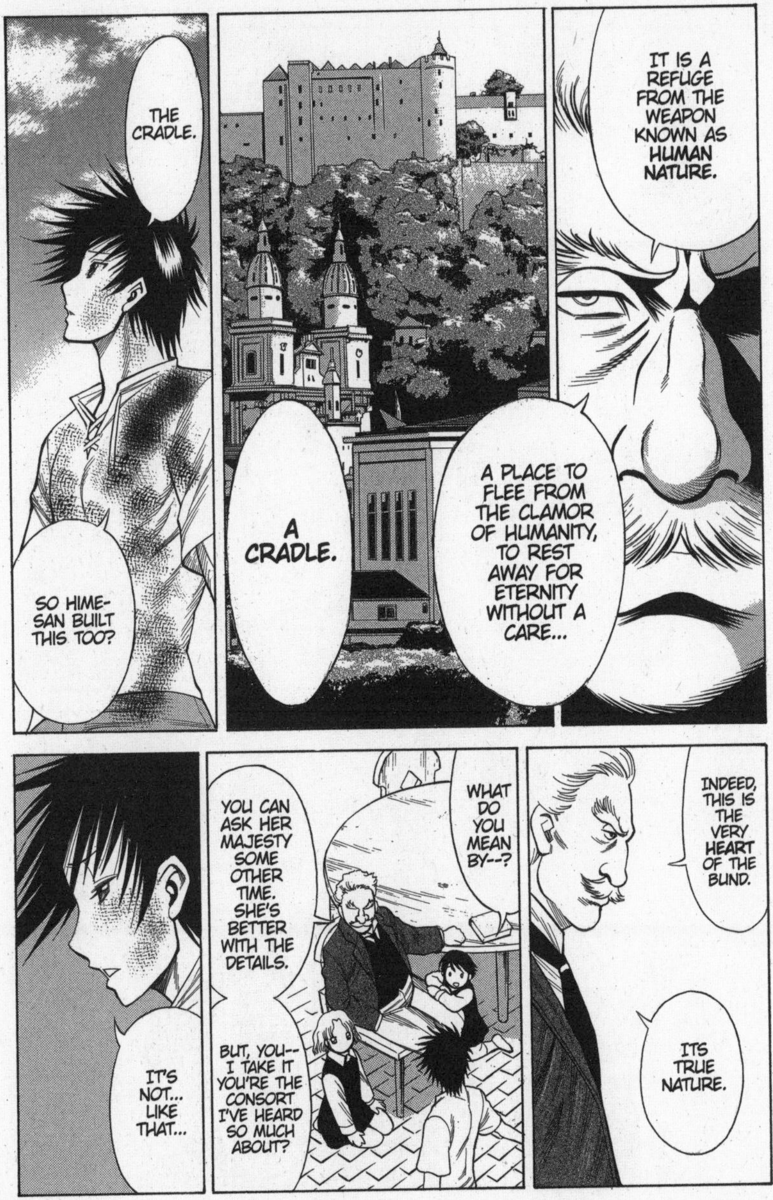
IT IS A REFUGE FROM THE WEAPON KNOWN AS HUMAN NATURE.
A PLACE TO FLEE FROM THE CLAMOR OF HUMANITY, TO REST AWAY FOR ETERNITY WITHOUT A CARE...
A CRADLE.
THE CRADLE.
SO HIME-SAN BUILT THIS TOO?
INDEED, THIS IS THE VERY HEART OF THE BUND.
ITS TRUE NATURE.
WHAT DO YOU MEAN BY--?
YOU CAN ASK HER MAJESTY SOME OTHER TIME. SHE'S BETTER WITH THE DETAILS.
BUT, YOU-- I TAKE IT YOU'RE THE CONSORT I'VE HEARD SO MUCH ABOUT?
IT'S NOT... LIKE THAT...

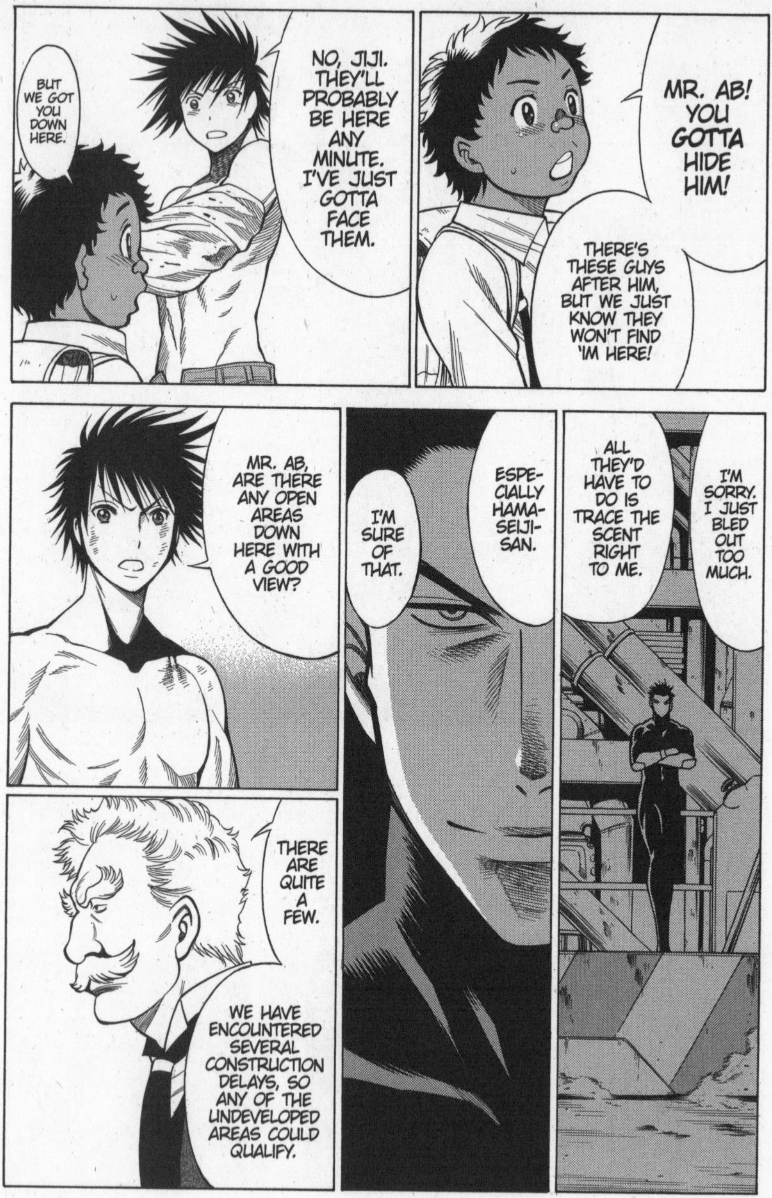
MR. AB! YOU GOTTA HIDE HIM!
THERE'S THESE GUYS AFTER HIM, BUT WE JUST KNOW THEY WON'T FIND 'IM HERE!
NO, JIJI. THEY'LL PROBABLY BE HERE ANY MINUTE. I'VE JUST GOTTA FACE THEM.
BUT WE GOT YOU DOWN HERE.
I'M SORRY. I JUST BLED OUT TOO MUCH.
ALL THEY'D HAVE TO DO IS TRACE THE SCENT RIGHT TO ME.
ESPE-CIALLY HAMA-SEIJI-SAN.
I'M SURE OF THAT.
MR. AB, ARE THERE ANY OPEN AREAS DOWN HERE WITH A GOOD VIEW?
THERE ARE QUITE A FEW.
WE HAVE ENCOUNTERED SEVERAL CONSTRUCTION DELAYS, SO ANY OF THE UNDEVELOPED AREAS COULD QUALIFY.

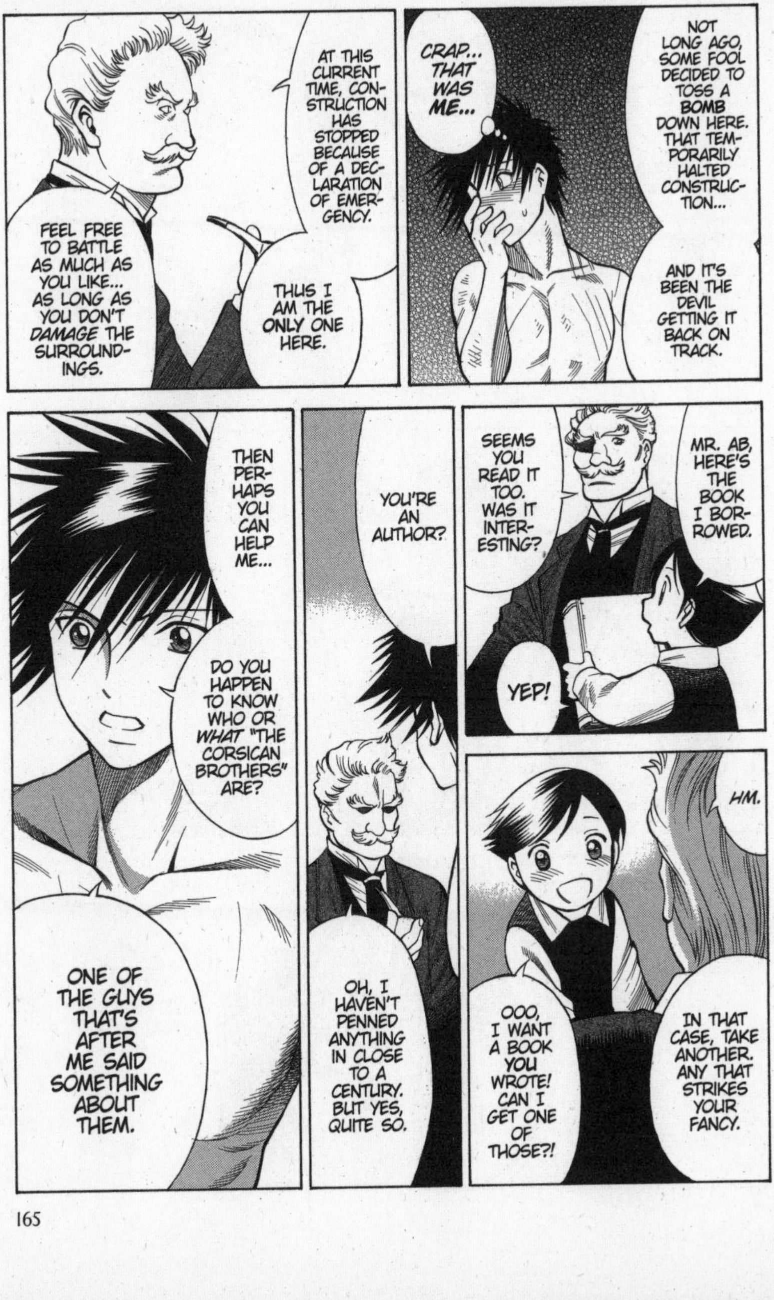
NOT LONG AGO, SOME FOOL DECIDED TO TOSS A **BOMB** DOWN HERE. THAT TEMPORARILY HALTED CONSTRUCTION...
CRAP... THAT WAS ME...
AND IT'S BEEN THE DEVIL GETTING IT BACK ON TRACK.
AT THIS CURRENT TIME, CONSTRUCTION HAS STOPPED BECAUSE OF A DECLARATION OF EMERGENCY.
THUS I AM THE ONLY ONE HERE.
FEEL FREE TO BATTLE AS MUCH AS YOU LIKE... AS LONG AS YOU DON'T *DAMAGE* THE SURROUNDINGS.
MR. AB, HERE'S THE BOOK I BORROWED.
SEEMS YOU READ IT TOO. WAS IT INTERESTING?
YEP!
HM.
IN THAT CASE, TAKE ANOTHER. ANY THAT STRIKES YOUR FANCY.
OOO, I WANT A BOOK **YOU** WROTE! CAN I GET ONE OF THOSE?!
YOU'RE AN AUTHOR?
OH, I HAVEN'T PENNED ANYTHING IN CLOSE TO A CENTURY. BUT YES, QUITE SO.
THEN PERHAPS YOU CAN HELP ME...
DO YOU HAPPEN TO KNOW WHO OR *WHAT* "THE CORSICAN BROTHERS" ARE?
ONE OF THE GUYS THAT'S AFTER ME SAID SOMETHING ABOUT THEM.

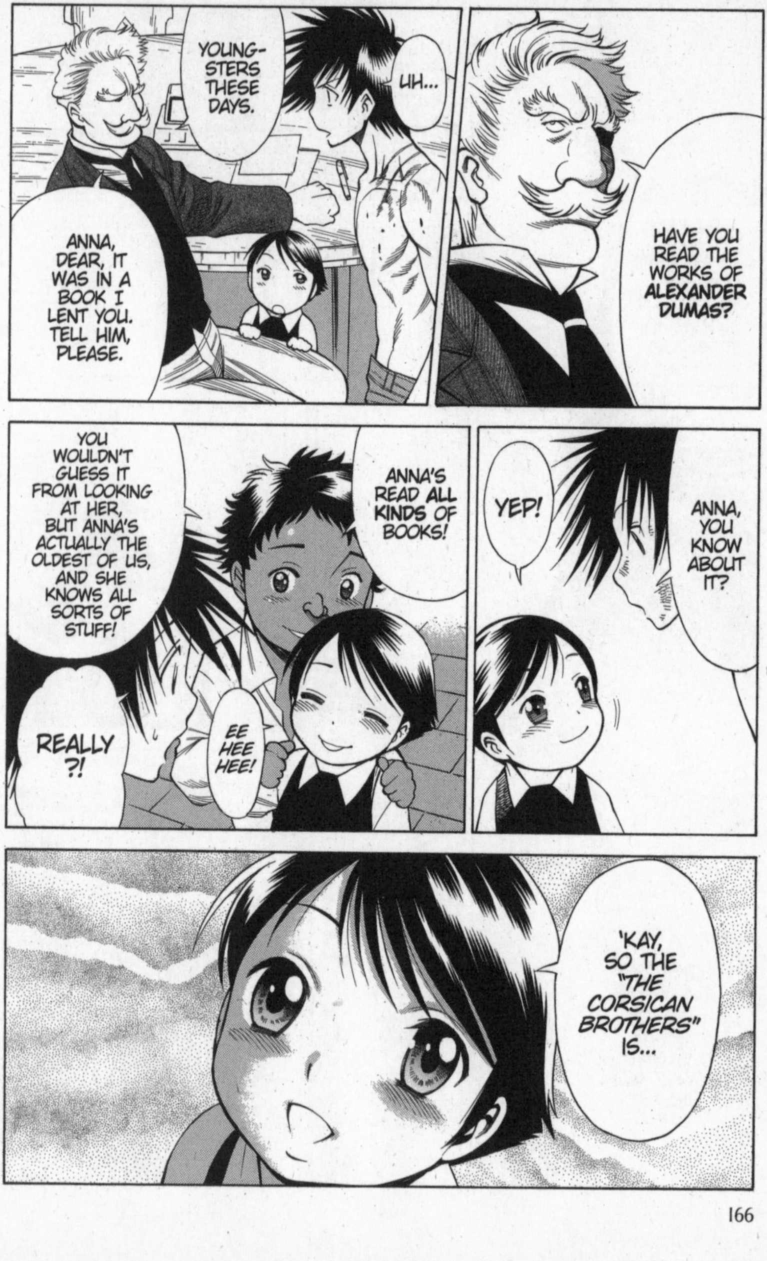
HAVE YOU READ THE WORKS OF ALEXANDER DUMAS?
UH...
YOUNG-STERS THESE DAYS.
ANNA, DEAR, IT WAS IN A BOOK I LENT YOU. TELL HIM, PLEASE.
ANNA, YOU KNOW ABOUT IT?
YEP!
ANNA'S READ ALL KINDS OF BOOKS!
YOU WOULDN'T GUESS IT FROM LOOKING AT HER, BUT ANNA'S ACTUALLY THE OLDEST OF US, AND SHE KNOWS ALL SORTS OF STUFF!
EE HEE HEE!
REALLY ?!
'KAY, SO THE "THE CORSICAN BROTHERS" IS...

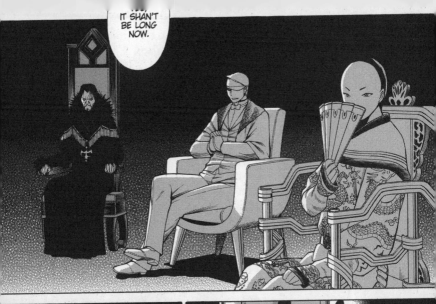

IT SHAN'T BE LONG NOW.

ONCE THE SUN RISES...

WHOEVER FIRST PASSES THROUGH THOSE DOORS SHALL BE THE VICTOR.

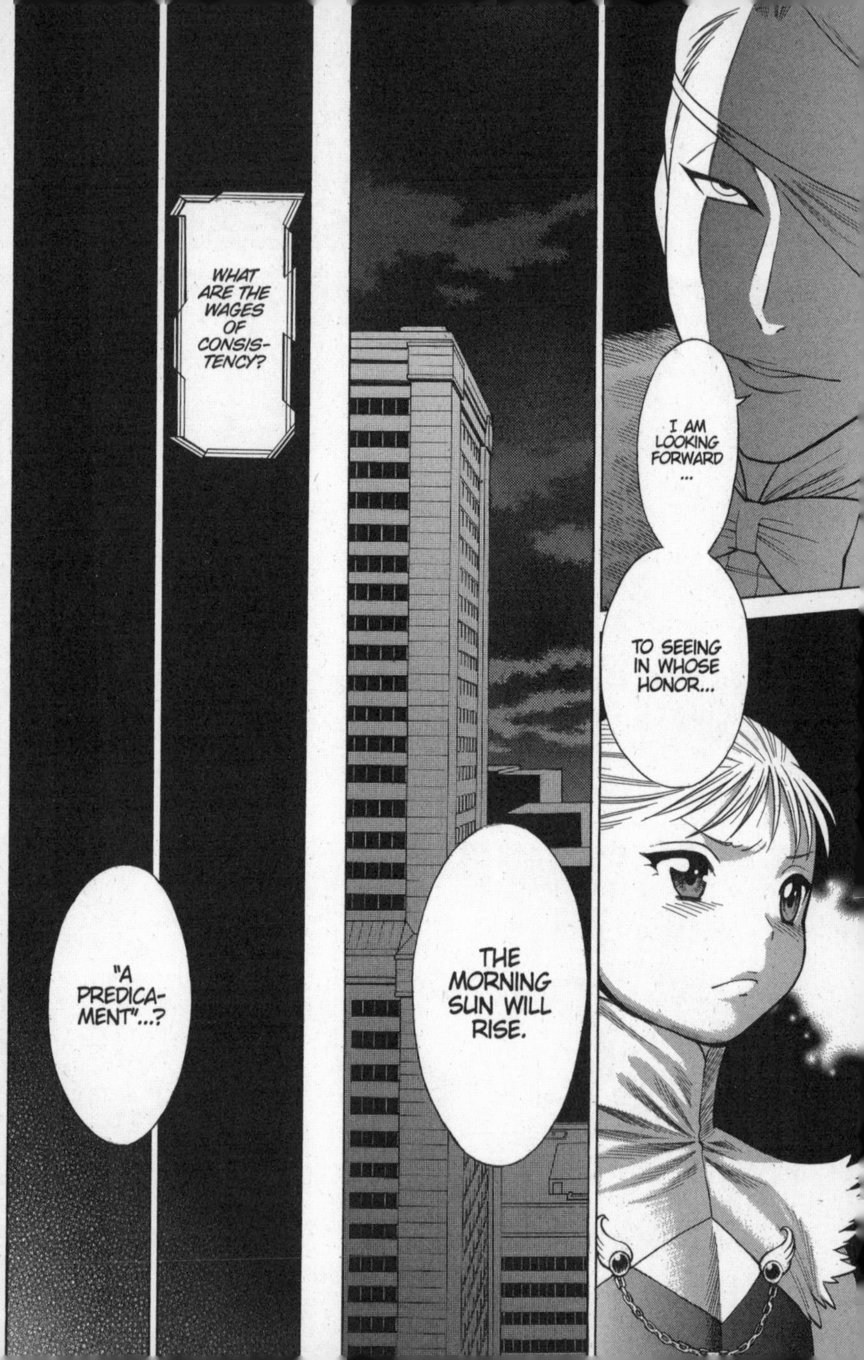
I AM LOOKING FORWARD ...
TO SEEING IN WHOSE HONOR...
THE MORNING SUN WILL RISE.
WHAT ARE THE WAGES OF CONSIS-TENCY?
"A PREDICA-MENT"...?

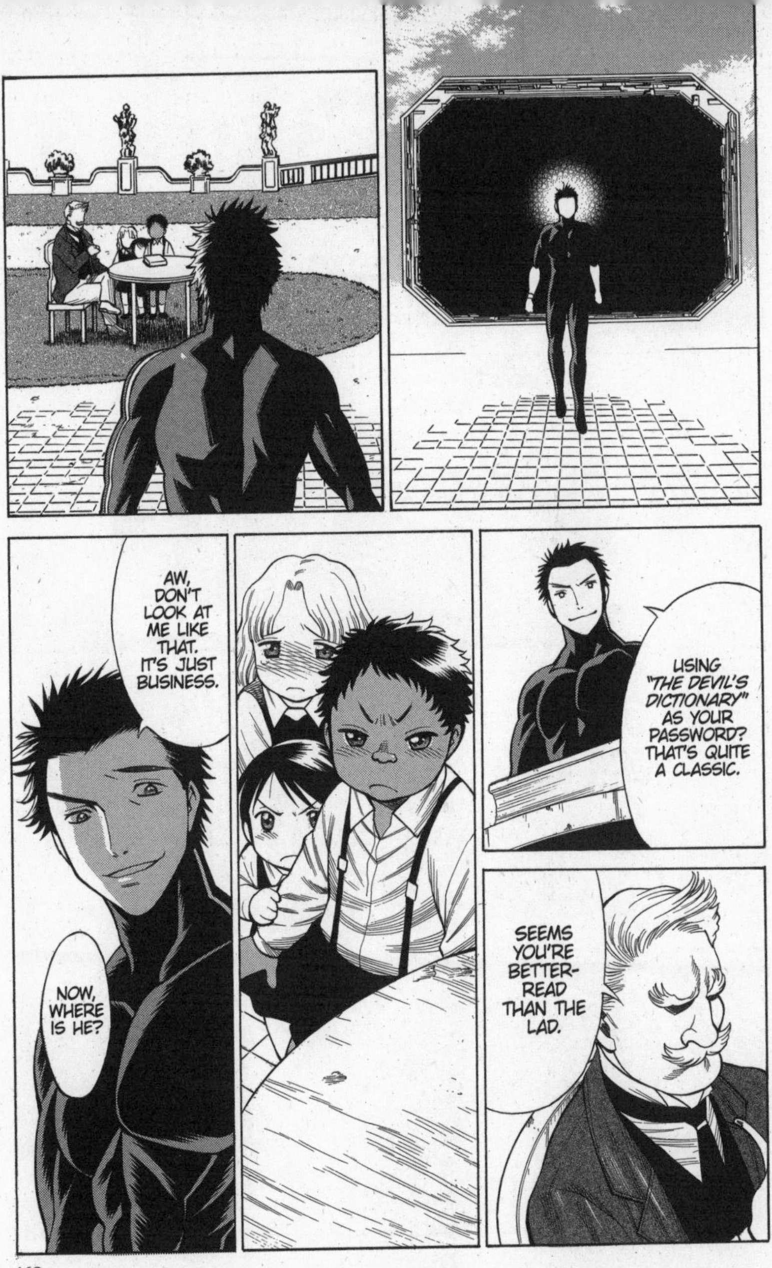
USING "THE DEVIL'S DICTIONARY" AS YOUR PASSWORD? THAT'S QUITE A CLASSIC.
SEEMS YOU'RE BETTER-READ THAN THE LAD.
AW, DON'T LOOK AT ME LIKE THAT. IT'S JUST BUSINESS.
NOW, WHERE IS HE?

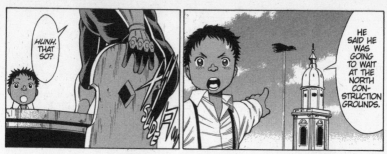

HE SAID HE WAS GOING TO WAIT AT THE NORTH CON-STRUCTION GROUNDS.
HUNH. THAT SO?
SLIDE
WHAT, AREN'T YOU GOING?!
KREAK
I'VE GOT A LITTLE TIME YET.
I'LL LET THEM TAKE A CRACK AT HIM FIRST.
RUSTLE
RUSTLE
RUSTLE
KRAAAAAAH

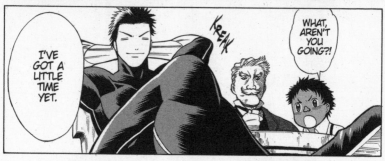

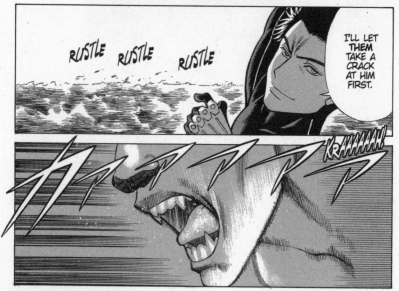

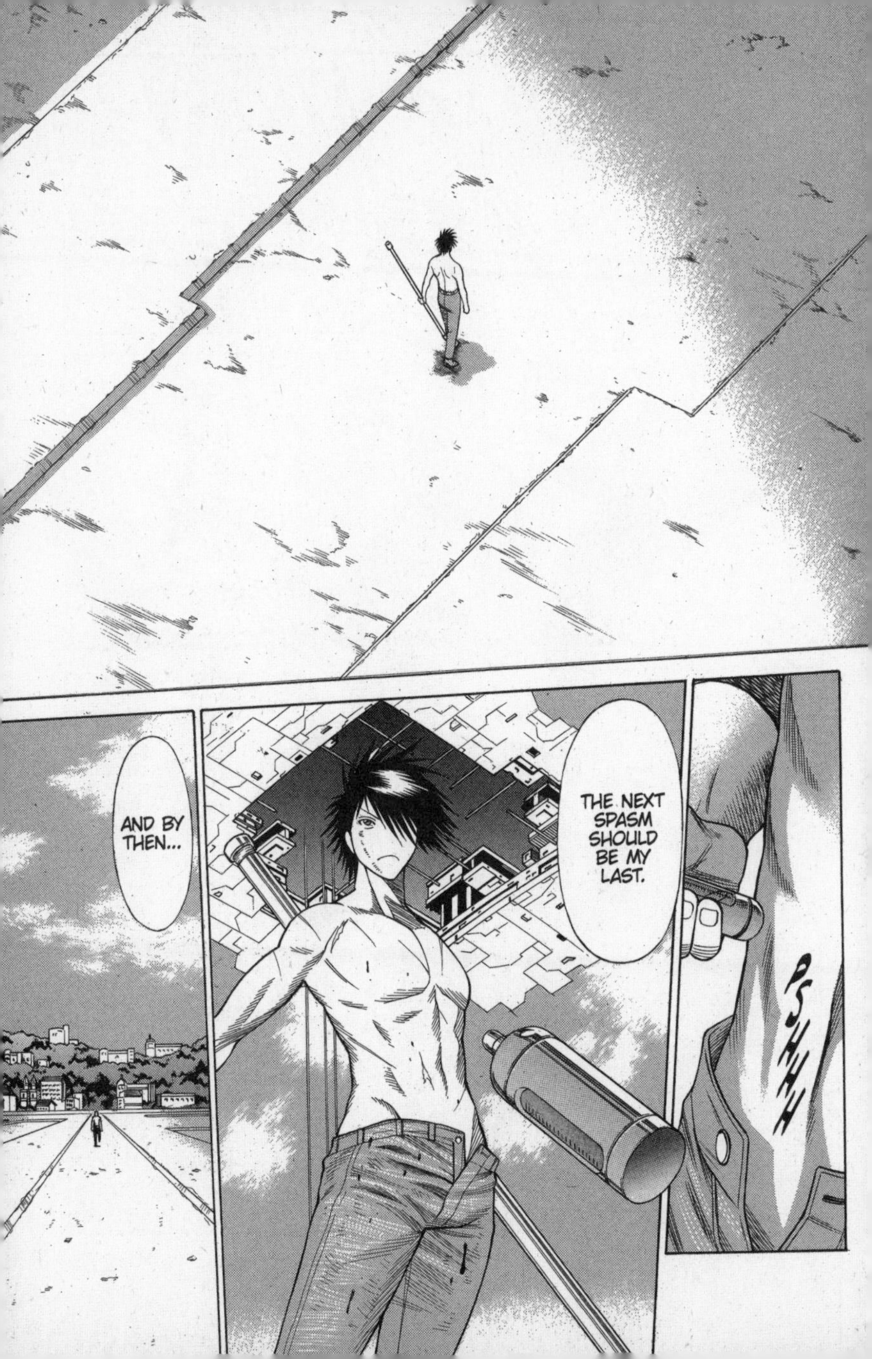
PSHHHH
THE NEXT SPASM SHOULD BE MY LAST.
AND BY THEN...

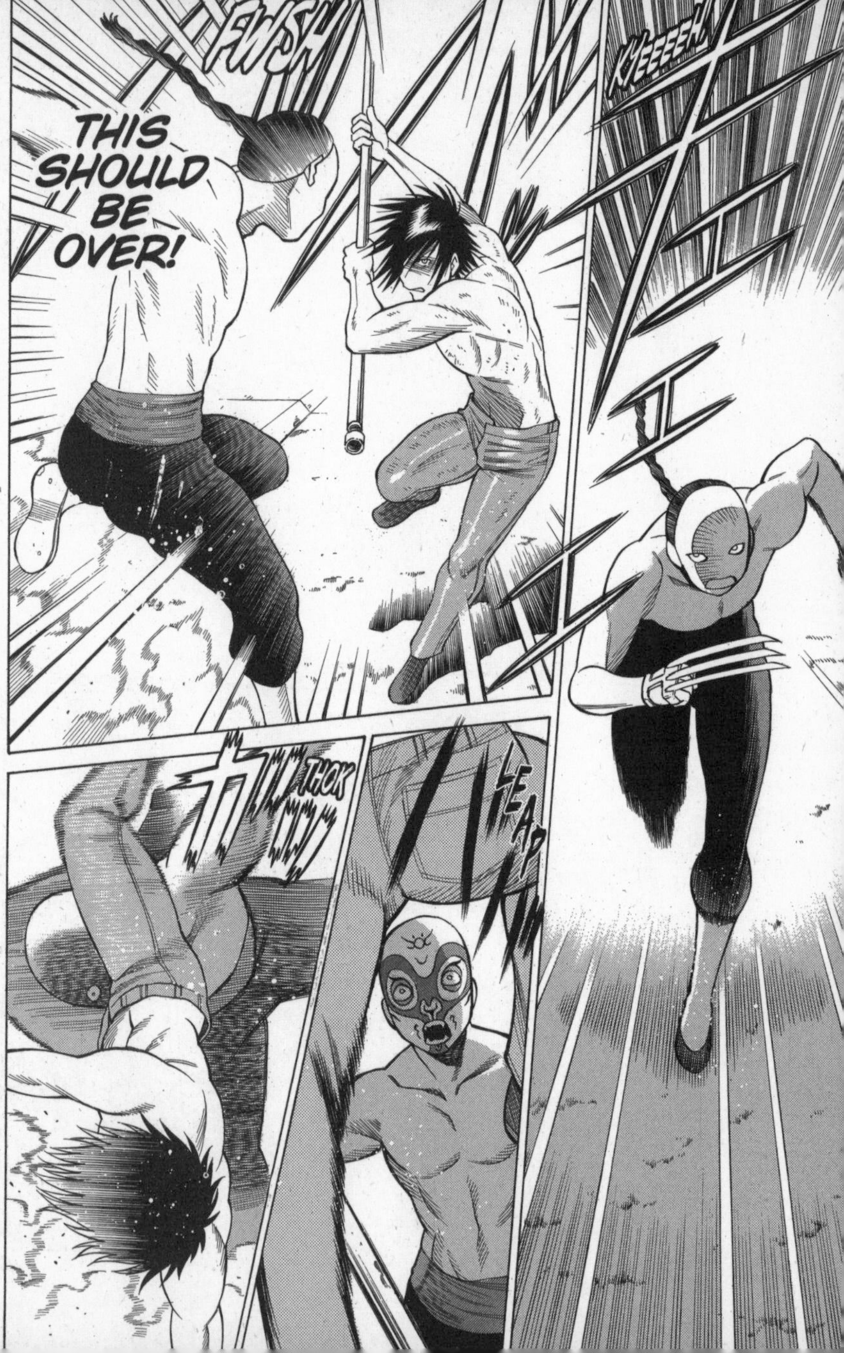
KYEEEEEH
FWISH
THIS SHOULD BE OVER!
LEAP
THOK

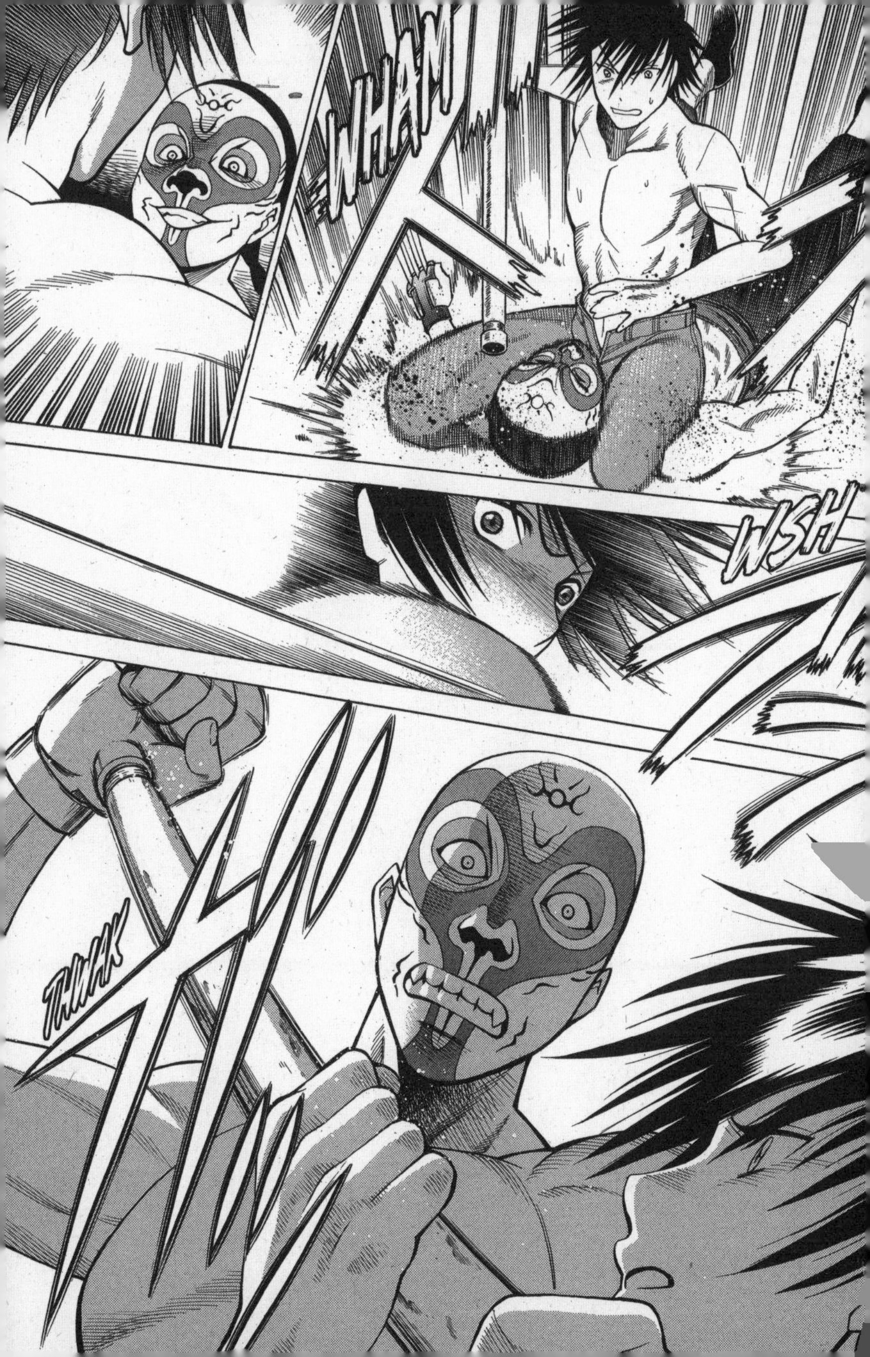
WHAM
WSH
THWAK

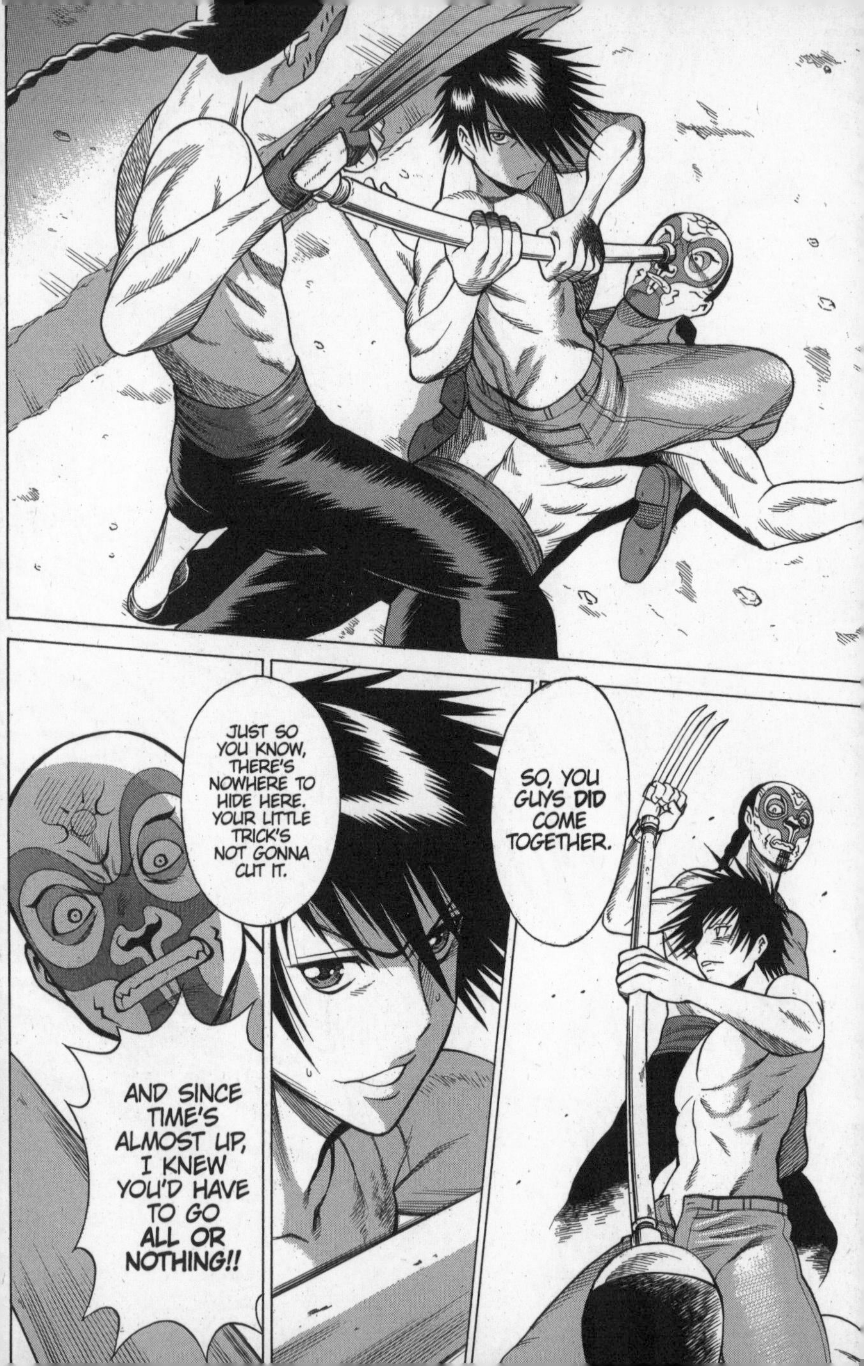
SO, YOU GUYS DID COME TOGETHER.
JUST SO YOU KNOW, THERE'S NOWHERE TO HIDE HERE. YOUR LITTLE TRICK'S NOT GONNA CUT IT.
AND SINCE TIME'S ALMOST UP, I KNEW YOU'D HAVE TO GO ALL OR NOTHING!!

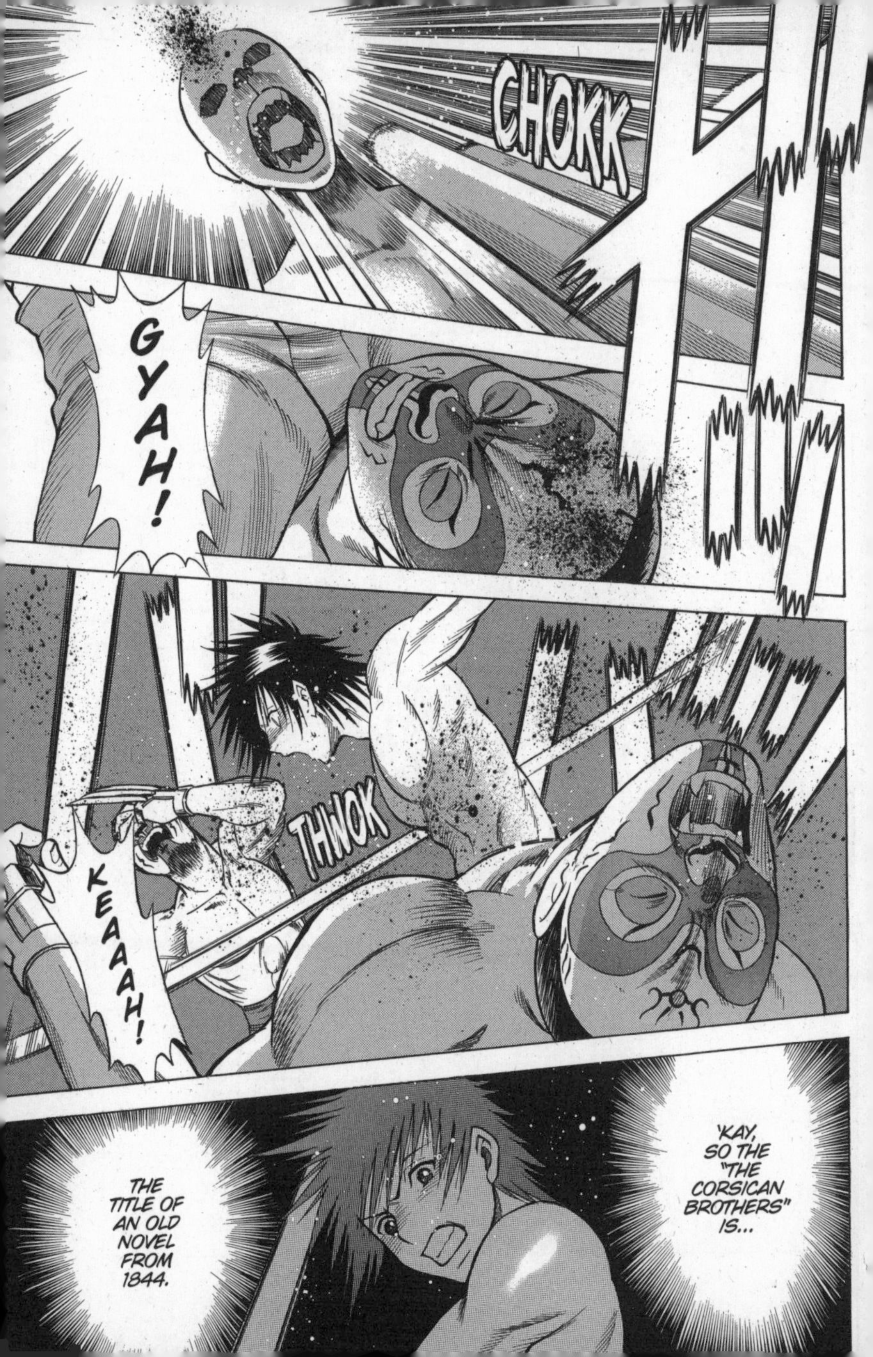
CHOKK
GYAH!
THWOK
KEAAAH!
'KAY, SO THE "THE CORSICAN BROTHERS" IS...
THE TITLE OF AN OLD NOVEL FROM 1844.

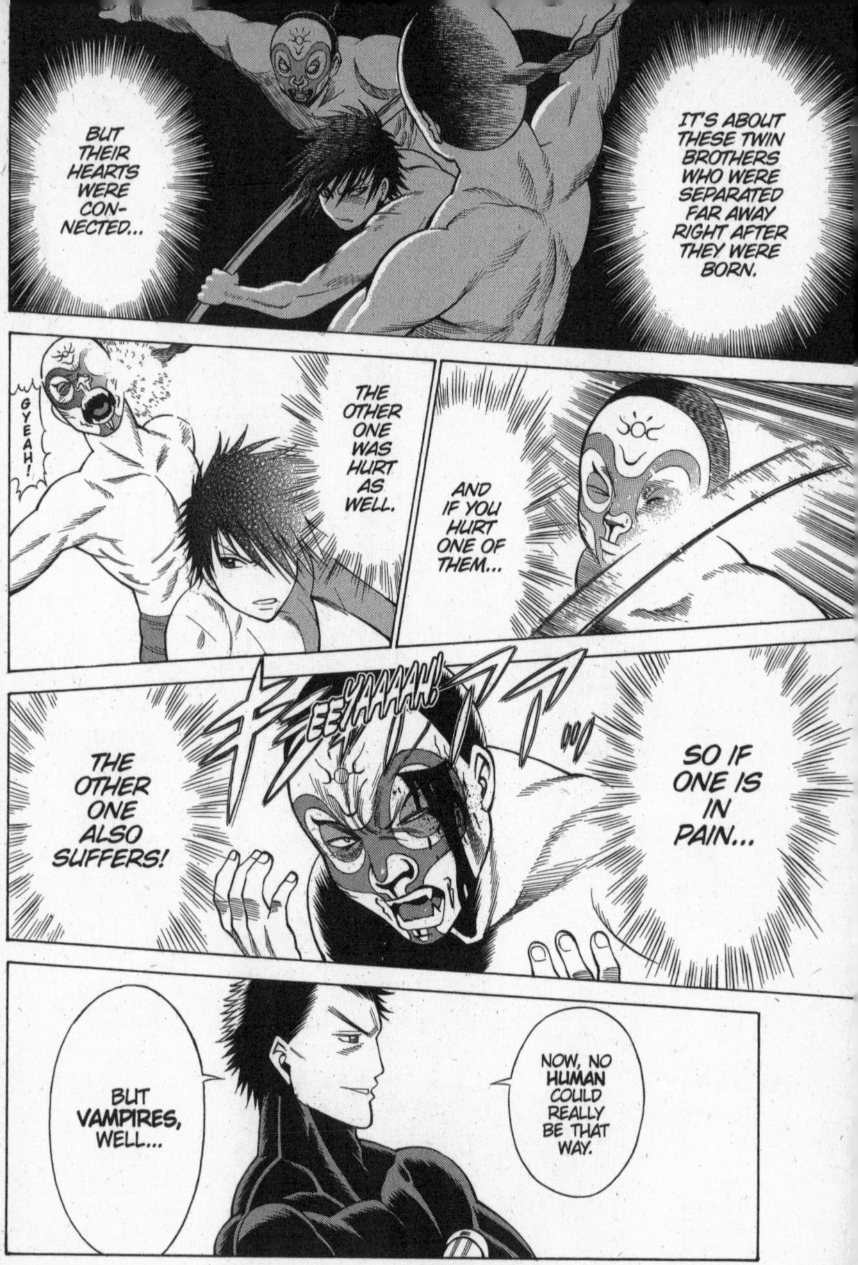
IT'S ABOUT THESE TWIN BROTHERS WHO WERE SEPARATED FAR AWAY RIGHT AFTER THEY WERE BORN.
BUT THEIR HEARTS WERE CONNECTED...
AND IF YOU HURT ONE OF THEM...
THE OTHER ONE WAS HURT AS WELL.
GYEAH!
SO IF ONE IS IN PAIN...
EEYAAAAH!
THE OTHER ONE ALSO SUFFERS!
NOW, NO HUMAN COULD REALLY BE THAT WAY.
BUT VAMPIRES, WELL...

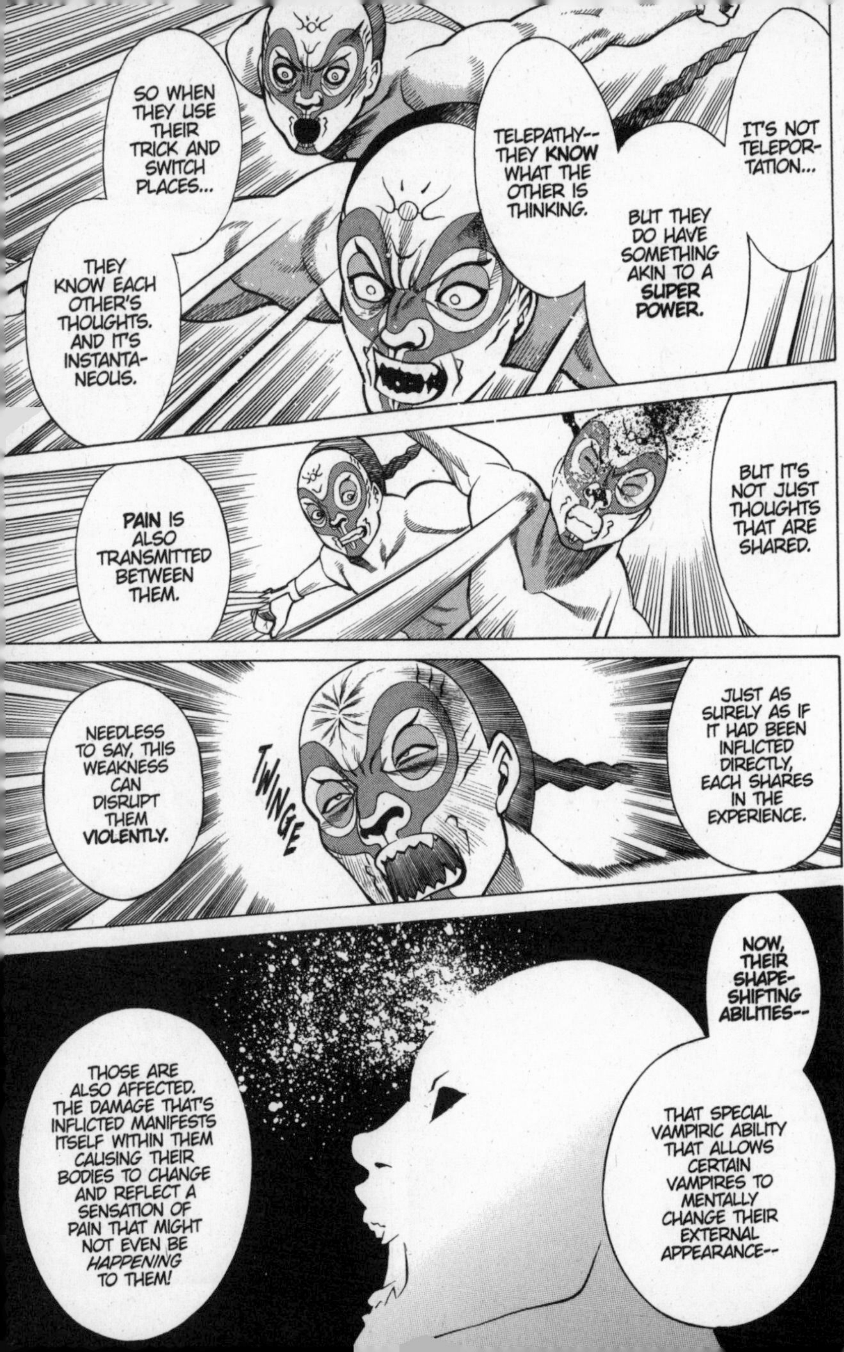
IT'S NOT TELEPORTATION...
BUT THEY DO HAVE SOMETHING AKIN TO A SUPER POWER.
TELEPATHY-- THEY KNOW WHAT THE OTHER IS THINKING.
SO WHEN THEY USE THEIR TRICK AND SWITCH PLACES...
THEY KNOW EACH OTHER'S THOUGHTS. AND IT'S INSTANTANEOUS.
BUT IT'S NOT JUST THOUGHTS THAT ARE SHARED.
PAIN IS ALSO TRANSMITTED BETWEEN THEM.
JUST AS SURELY AS IF IT HAD BEEN INFLICTED DIRECTLY, EACH SHARES IN THE EXPERIENCE.
TWINGE
NEEDLESS TO SAY, THIS WEAKNESS CAN DISRUPT THEM VIOLENTLY.
NOW, THEIR SHAPE-SHIFTING ABILITIES--
THAT SPECIAL VAMPIRIC ABILITY THAT ALLOWS CERTAIN VAMPIRES TO MENTALLY CHANGE THEIR EXTERNAL APPEARANCE--
THOSE ARE ALSO AFFECTED. THE DAMAGE THAT'S INFLICTED MANIFESTS ITSELF WITHIN THEM CAUSING THEIR BODIES TO CHANGE AND REFLECT A SENSATION OF PAIN THAT MIGHT NOT EVEN BE HAPPENING TO THEM!

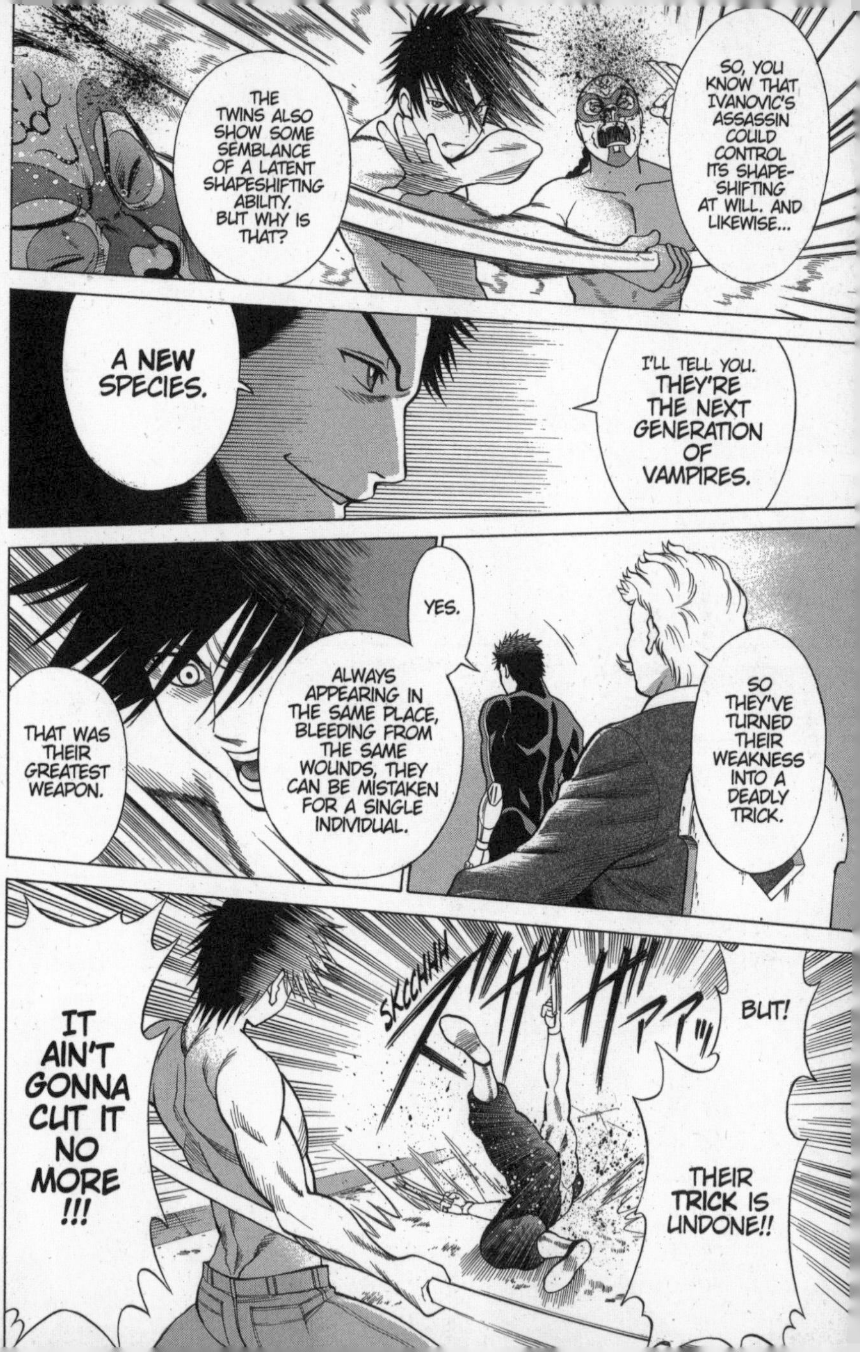
SO, YOU KNOW THAT IVANOVIC'S ASSASSIN COULD CONTROL ITS SHAPE-SHIFTING AT WILL. AND LIKEWISE...
THE TWINS ALSO SHOW SOME SEMBLANCE OF A LATENT SHAPESHIFTING ABILITY. BUT WHY IS THAT?
I'LL TELL YOU. THEY'RE THE NEXT GENERATION OF VAMPIRES.
A NEW SPECIES.
SO THEY'VE TURNED THEIR WEAKNESS INTO A DEADLY TRICK.
YES.
ALWAYS APPEARING IN THE SAME PLACE, BLEEDING FROM THE SAME WOUNDS, THEY CAN BE MISTAKEN FOR A SINGLE INDIVIDUAL.
THAT WAS THEIR GREATEST WEAPON.
BUT!
SKCCHHH
THEIR TRICK IS UNDONE!!
IT AIN'T GONNA CUT IT NO MORE!!!

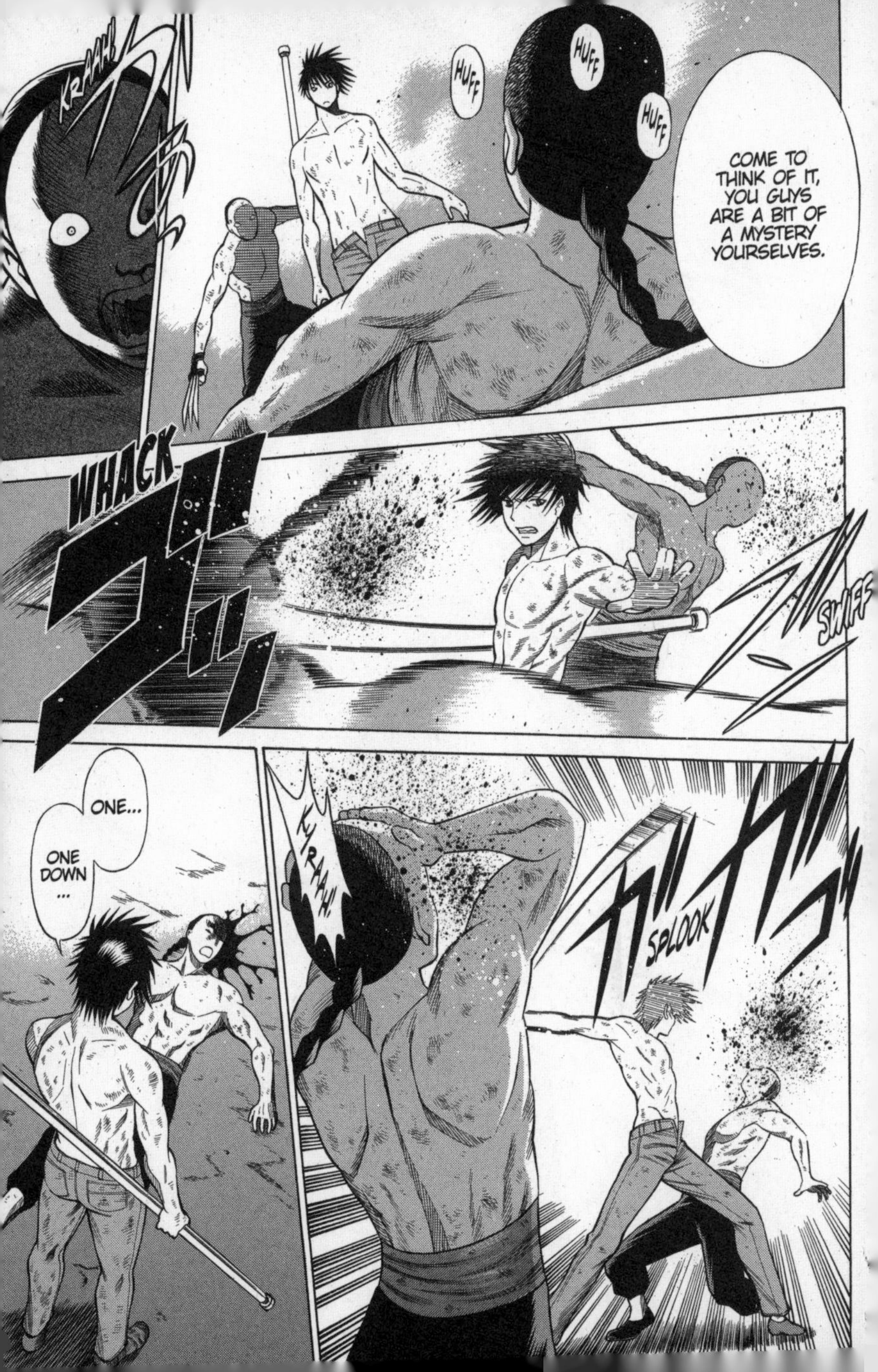
HUFF
HUFF
COME TO THINK OF IT, YOU GUYS ARE A BIT OF A MYSTERY YOURSELVES.
HUFF
KRAAH!
SWIFF
WHACK
SPLOOK
KYRAAH!
ONE...
ONE DOWN ...

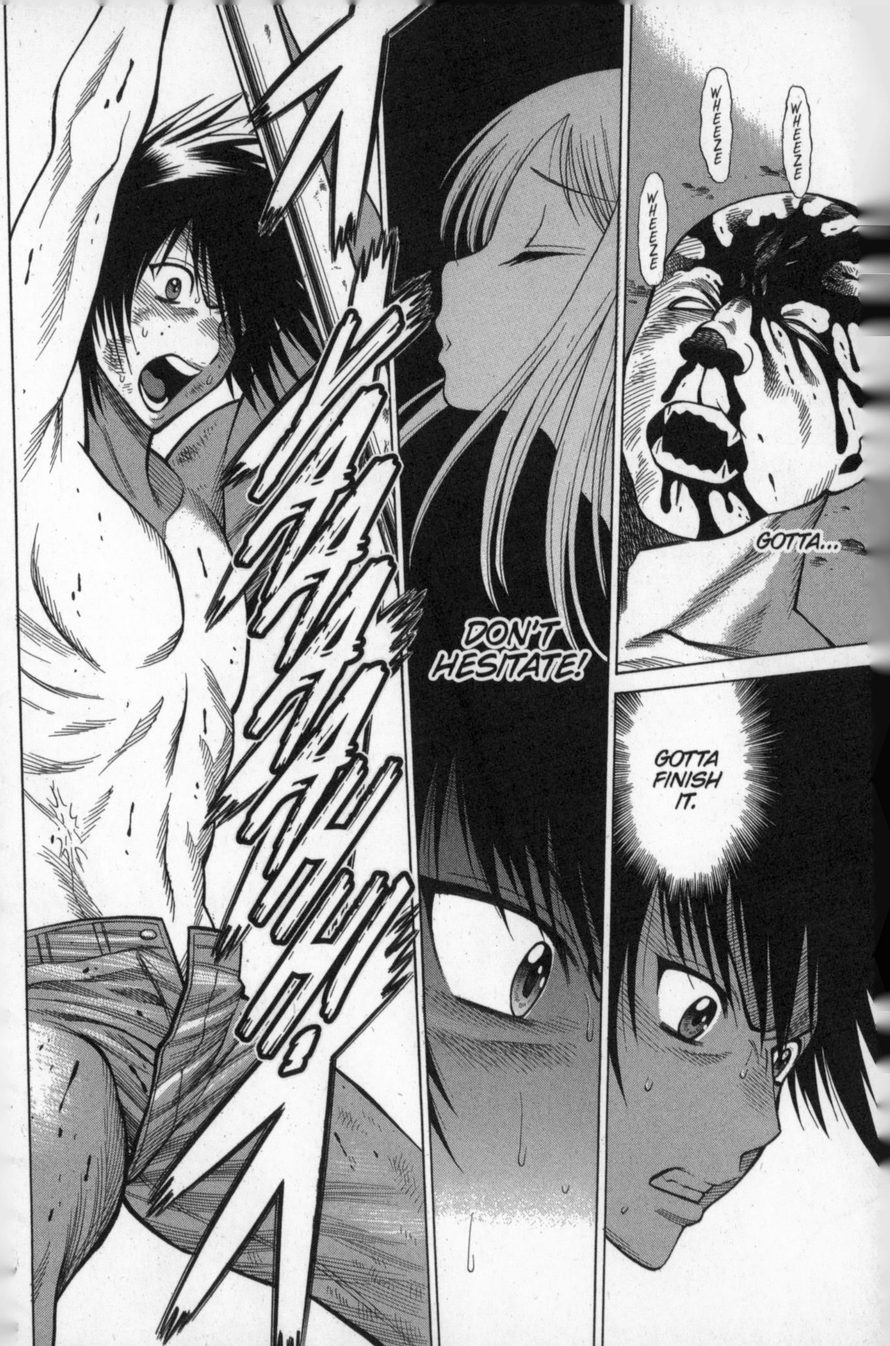
WHEEZE
WHEEZE
WHEEZE
GOTTA...
GOTTA FINISH IT.
DON'T HESITATE!

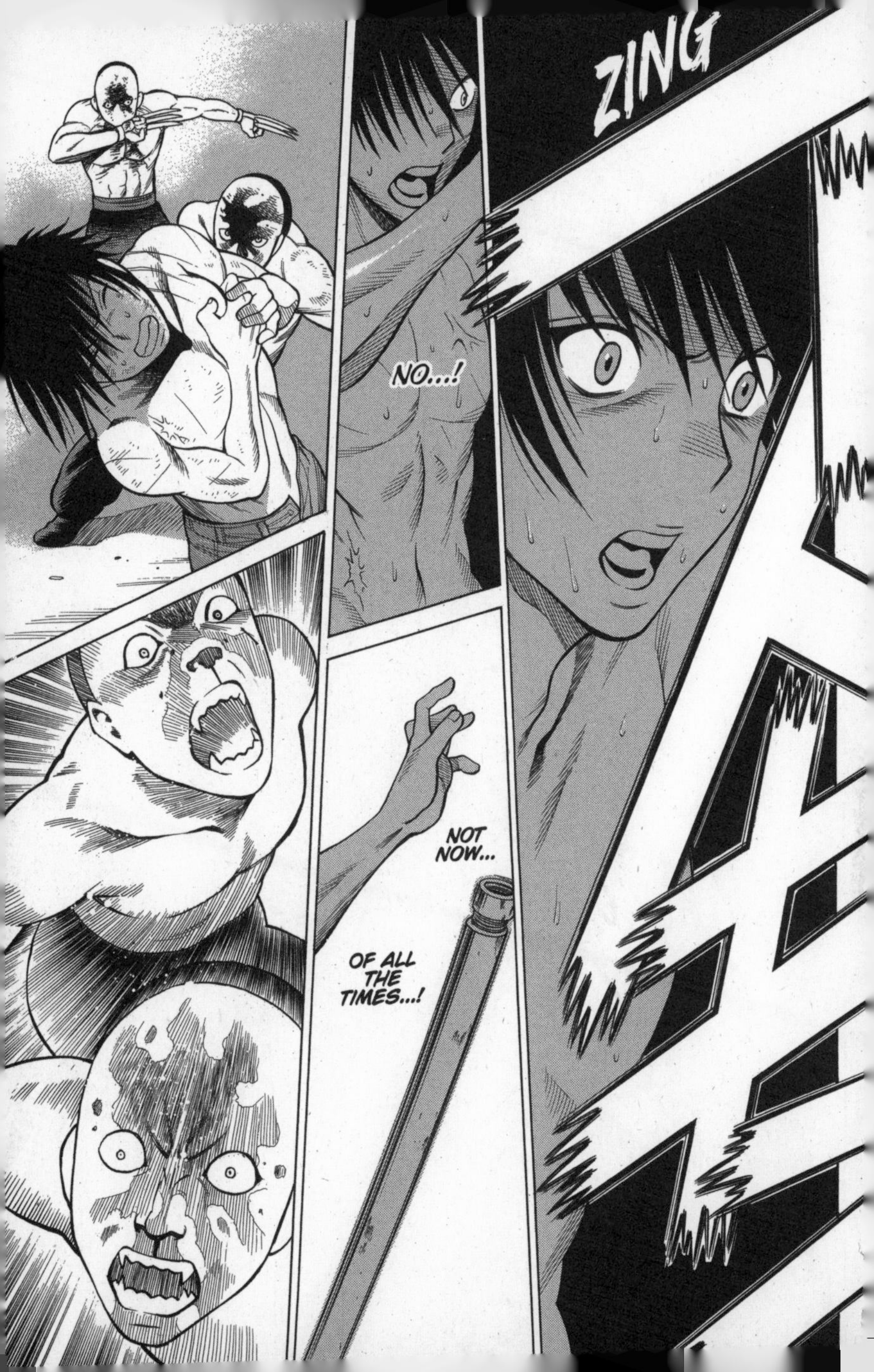
ZING
NO...!
NOT NOW...
OF ALL THE TIMES...!

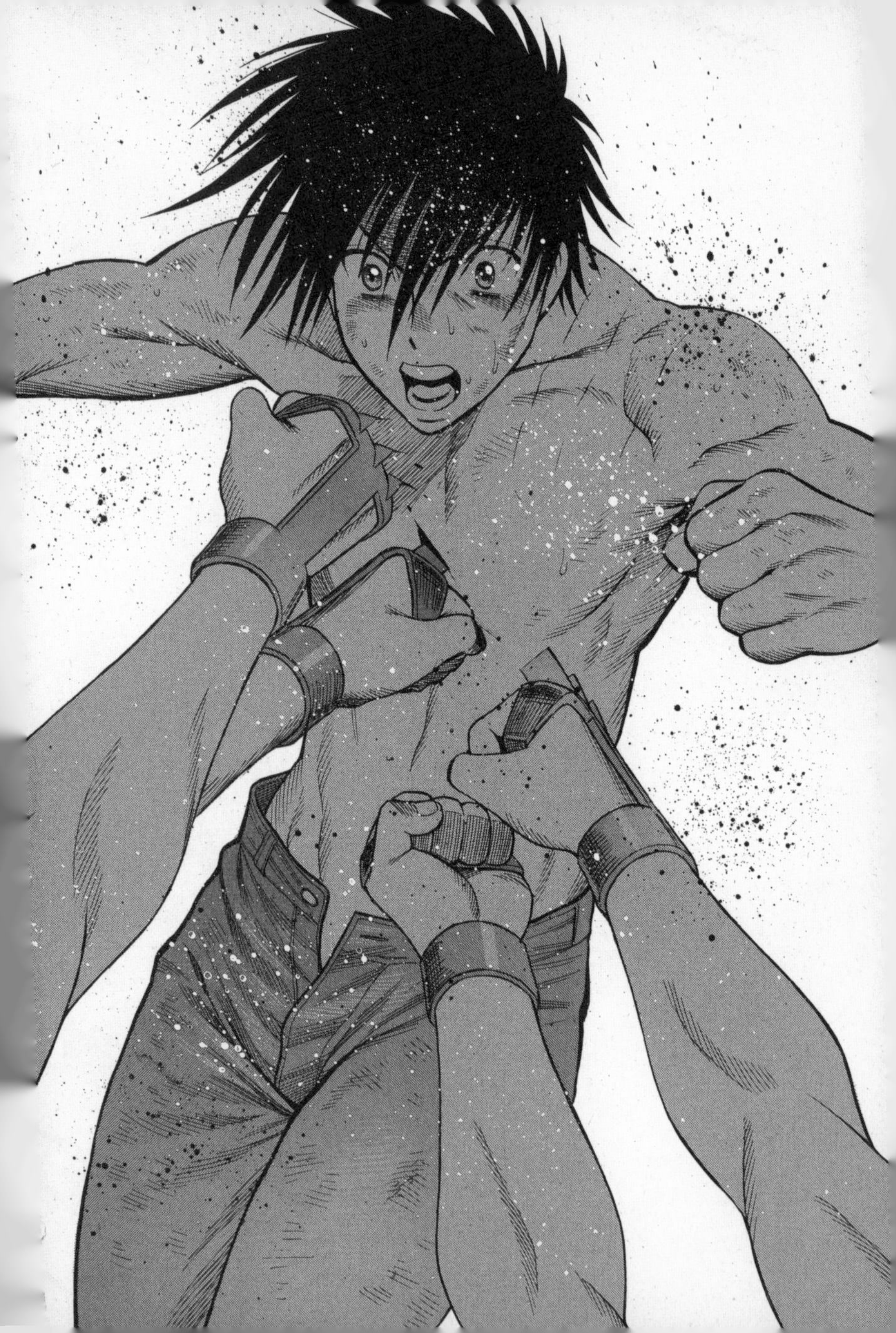

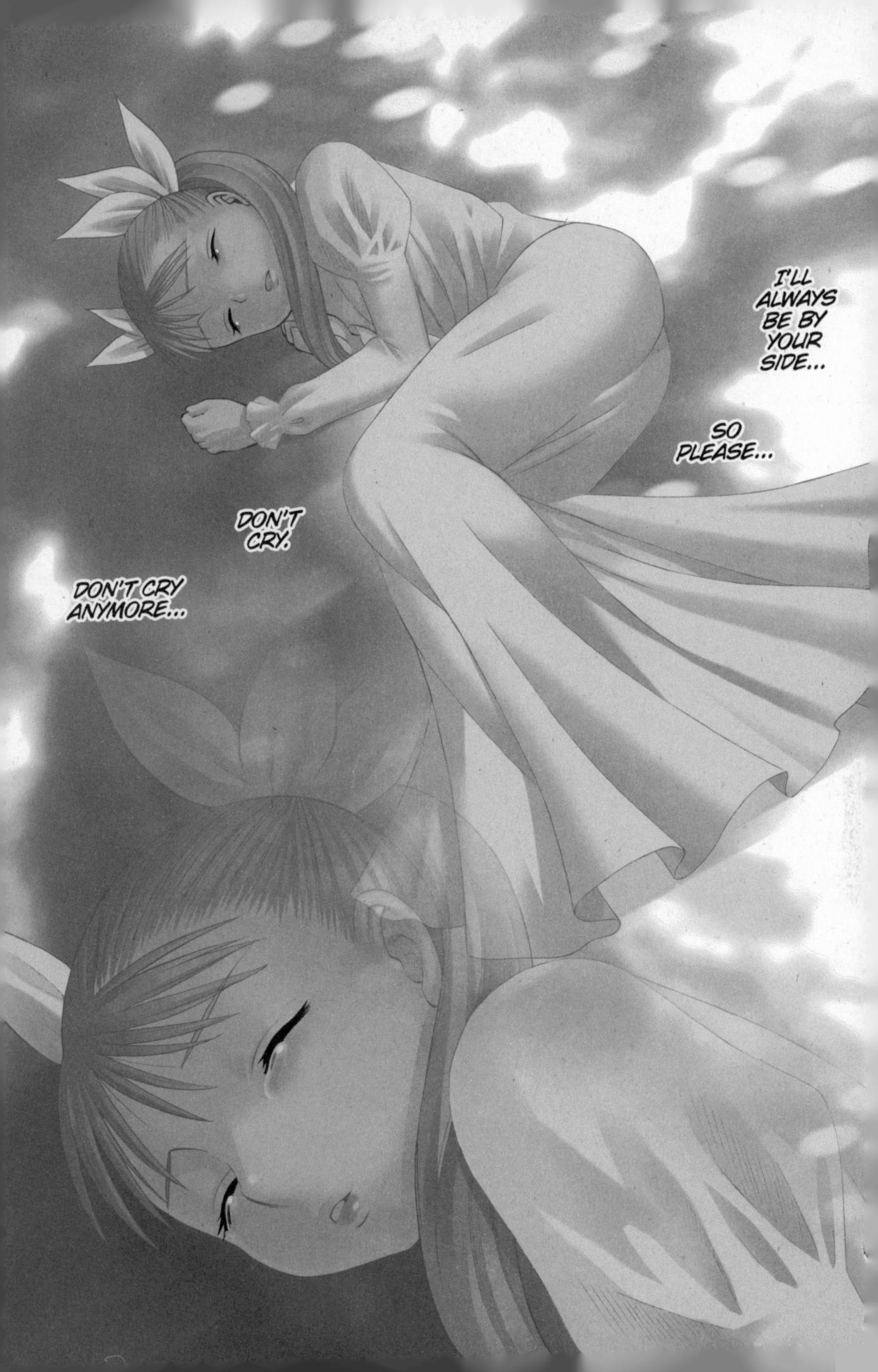
I'LL ALWAYS BE BY YOUR SIDE...
SO PLEASE...
DON'T CRY.
DON'T CRY ANYMORE...

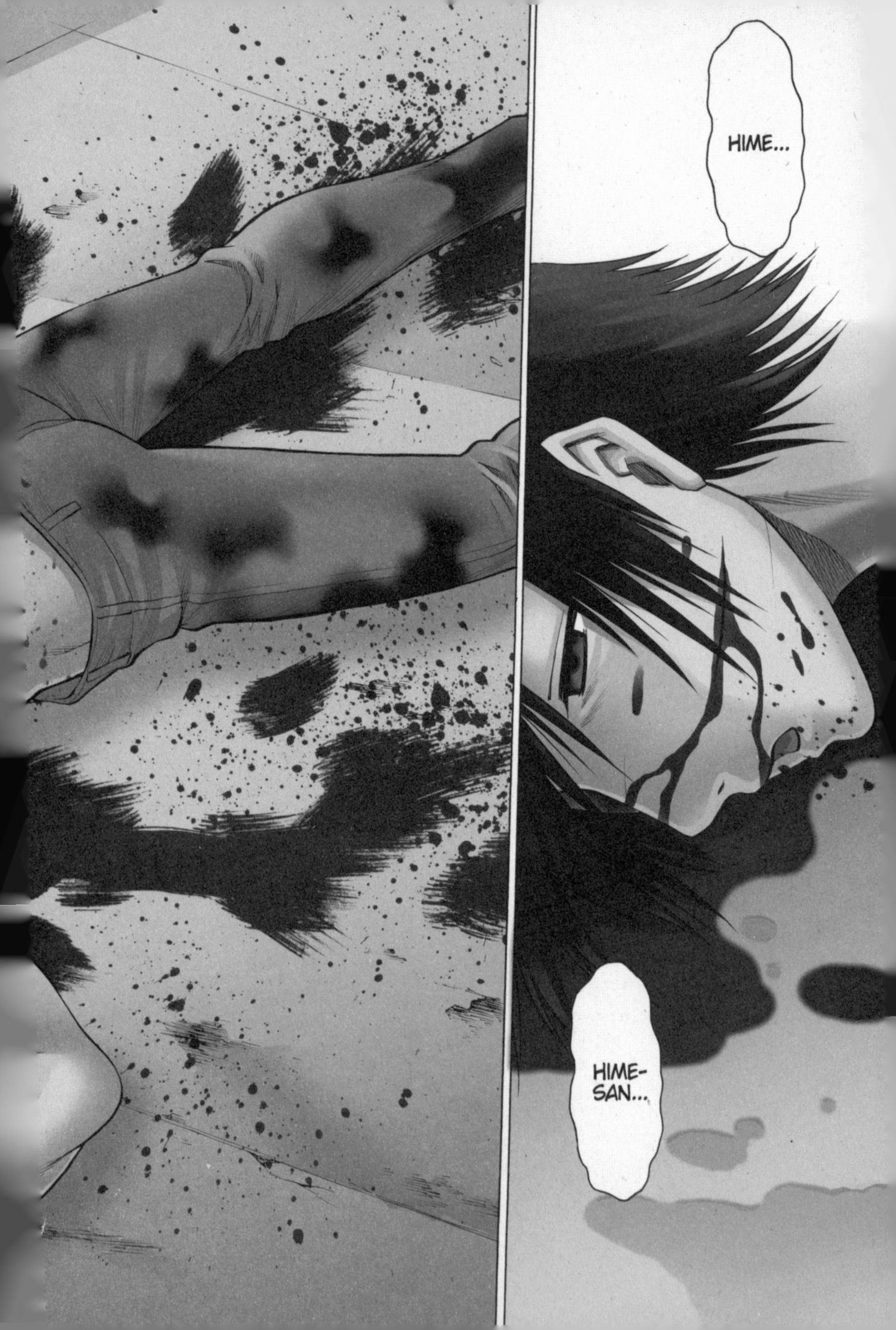
HIME...
HIME-SAN...

Chapter 31: A Man of Determination

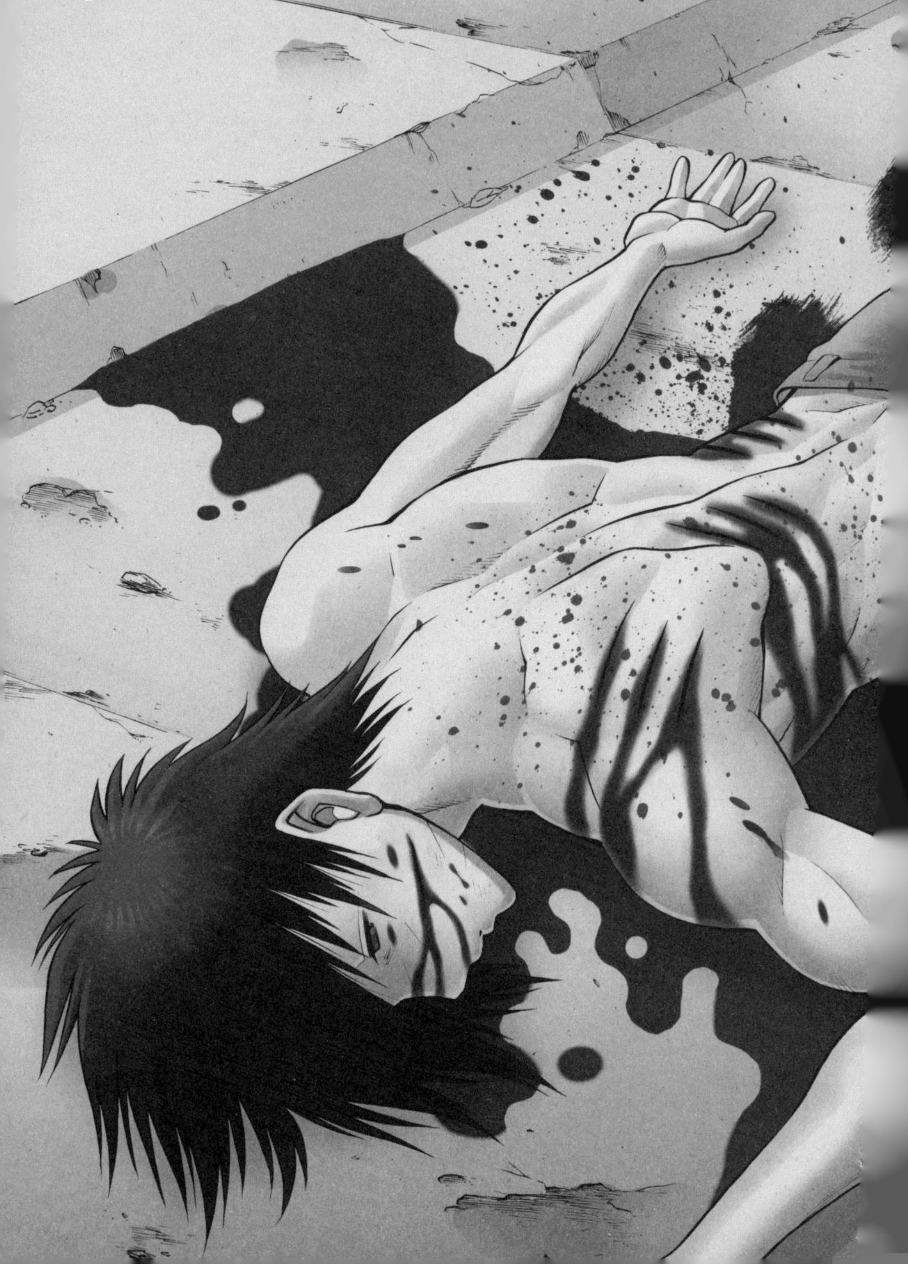

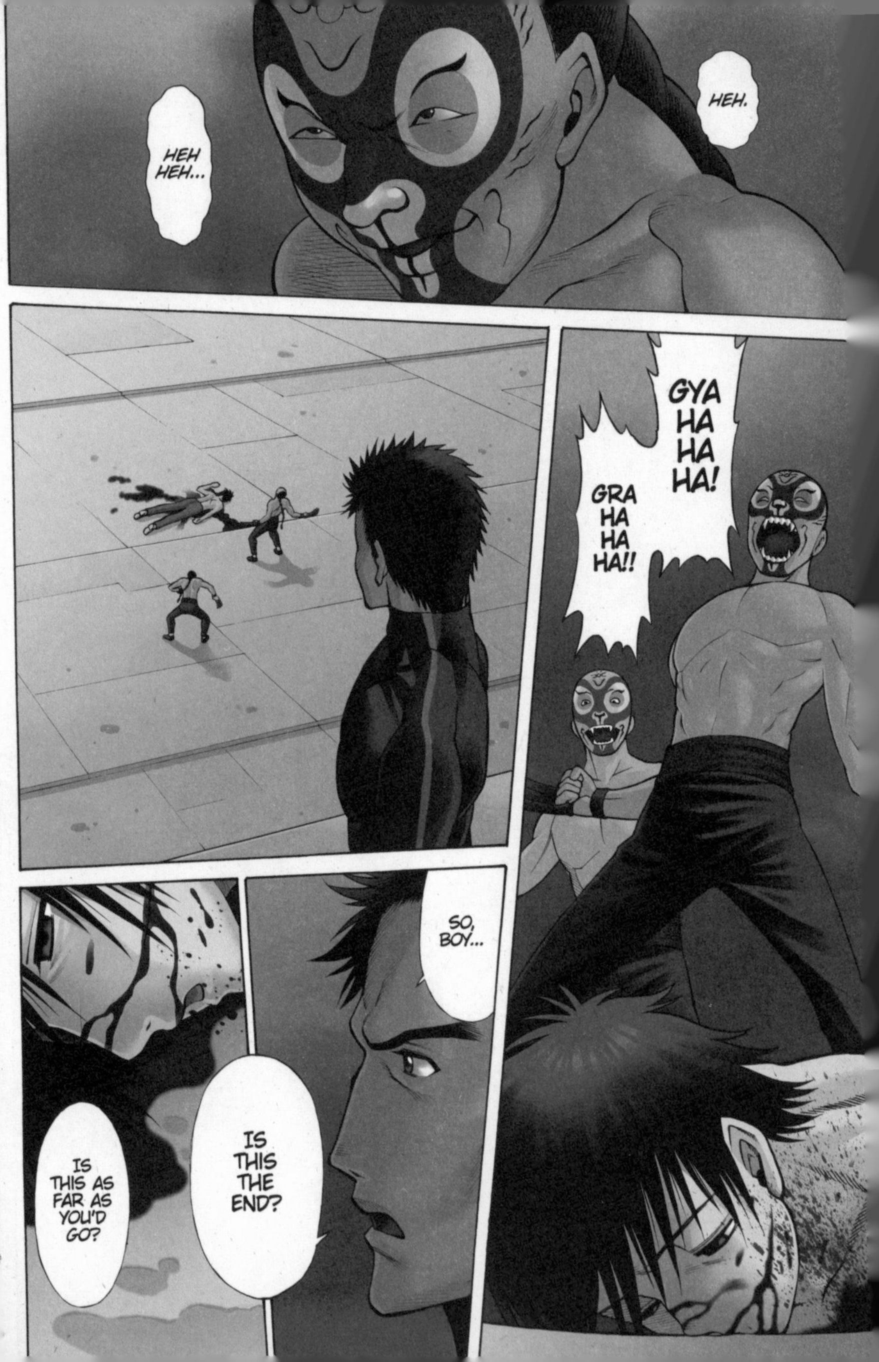
HEH.
HEH HEH...
GYA HA HA HA HA!
GRA HA HA HA HA!!
SO, BOY...
IS THIS THE END?
IS THIS AS FAR AS YOU'D GO?

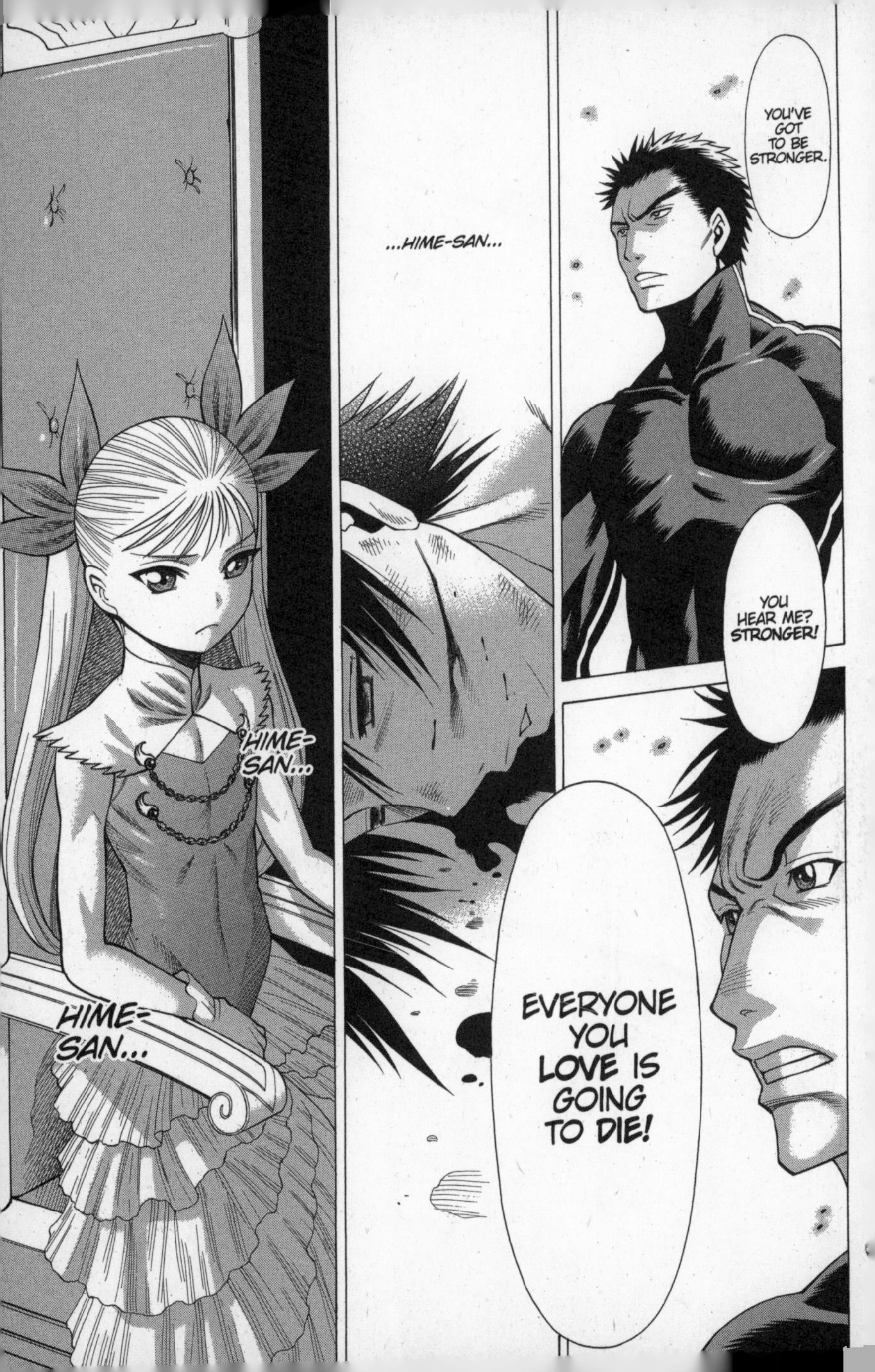
YOU'VE GOT TO BE STRONGER.
YOU HEAR ME? STRONGER!
EVERYONE YOU LOVE IS GOING TO DIE!
...HIME-SAN...
HIME-SAN...
HIME-SAN...

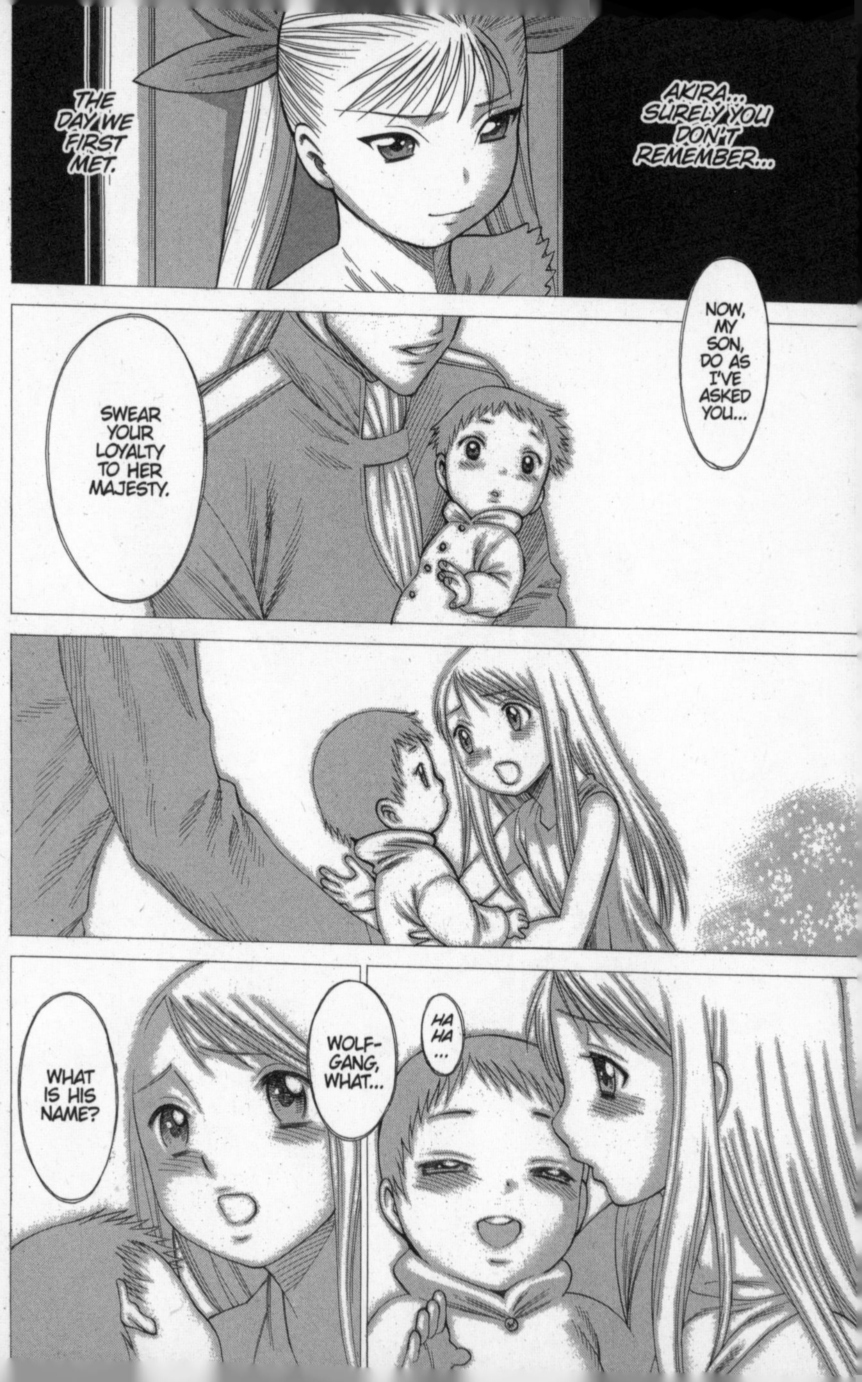
AKIRA... SURELY YOU DON'T REMEMBER...
THE DAY WE FIRST MET.
NOW, MY SON, DO AS I'VE ASKED YOU...
SWEAR YOUR LOYALTY TO HER MAJESTY.
HA HA ...
WOLF-GANG, WHAT...
WHAT IS HIS NAME?

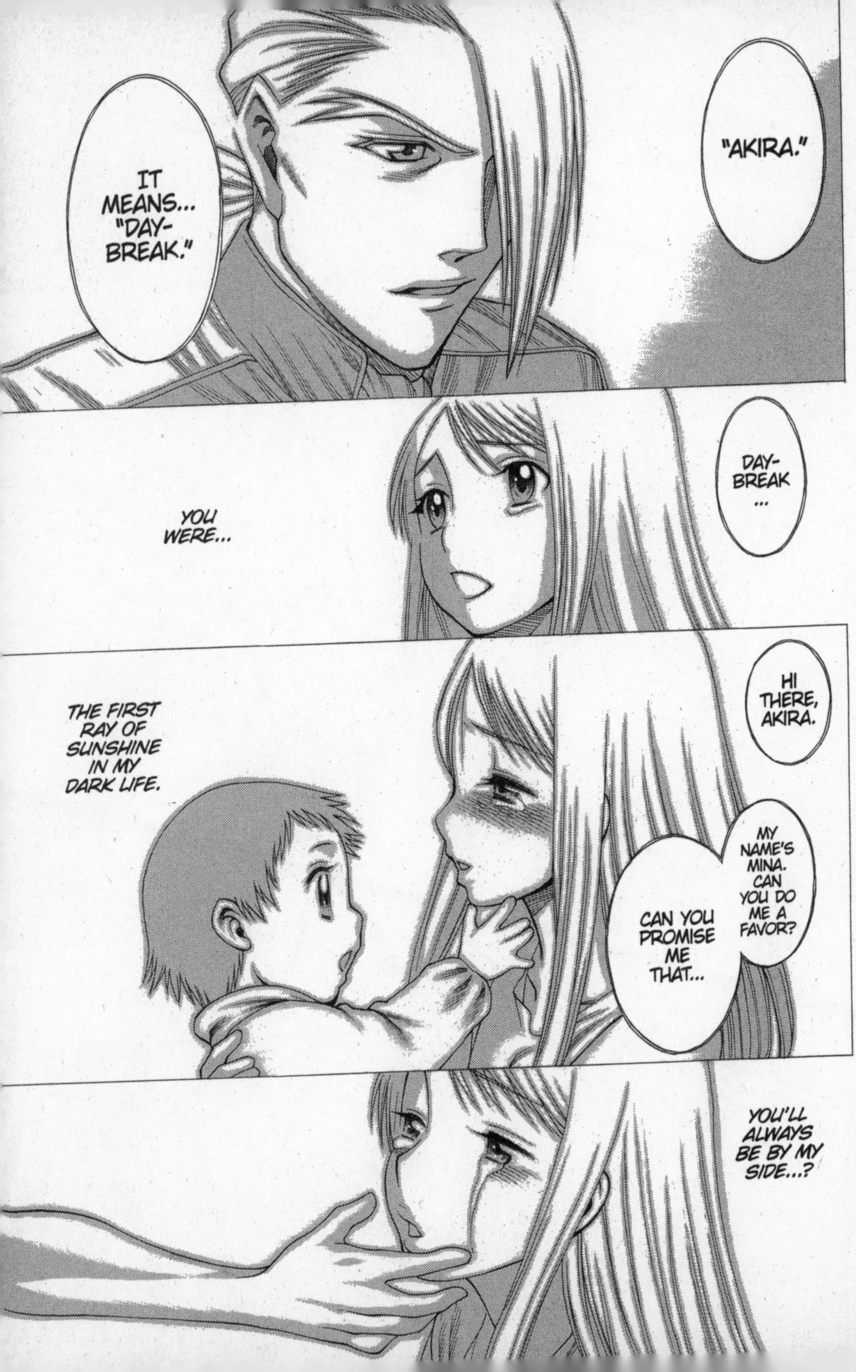
"AKIRA."
IT MEANS... "DAY-BREAK."
DAY-BREAK...
YOU WERE...
HI THERE, AKIRA.
THE FIRST RAY OF SUNSHINE IN MY DARK LIFE.
MY NAME'S MINA. CAN YOU DO ME A FAVOR?
CAN YOU PROMISE ME THAT...
YOU'LL ALWAYS BE BY MY SIDE...?

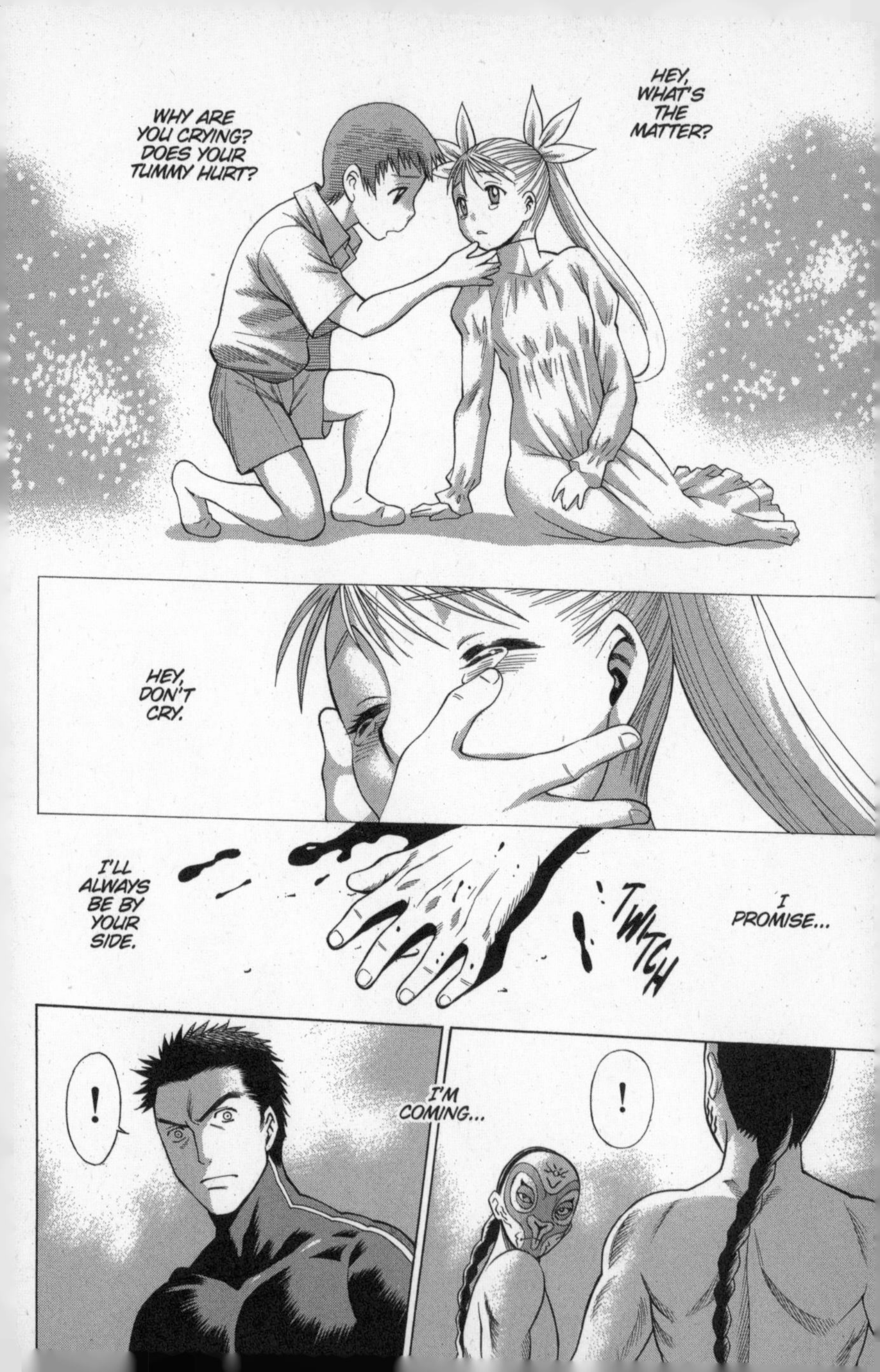
HEY, WHAT'S THE MATTER?
WHY ARE YOU CRYING? DOES YOUR TUMMY HURT?
HEY, DON'T CRY.
I PROMISE...
TWITCH
I'LL ALWAYS BE BY YOUR SIDE.
!
I'M COMING...
!

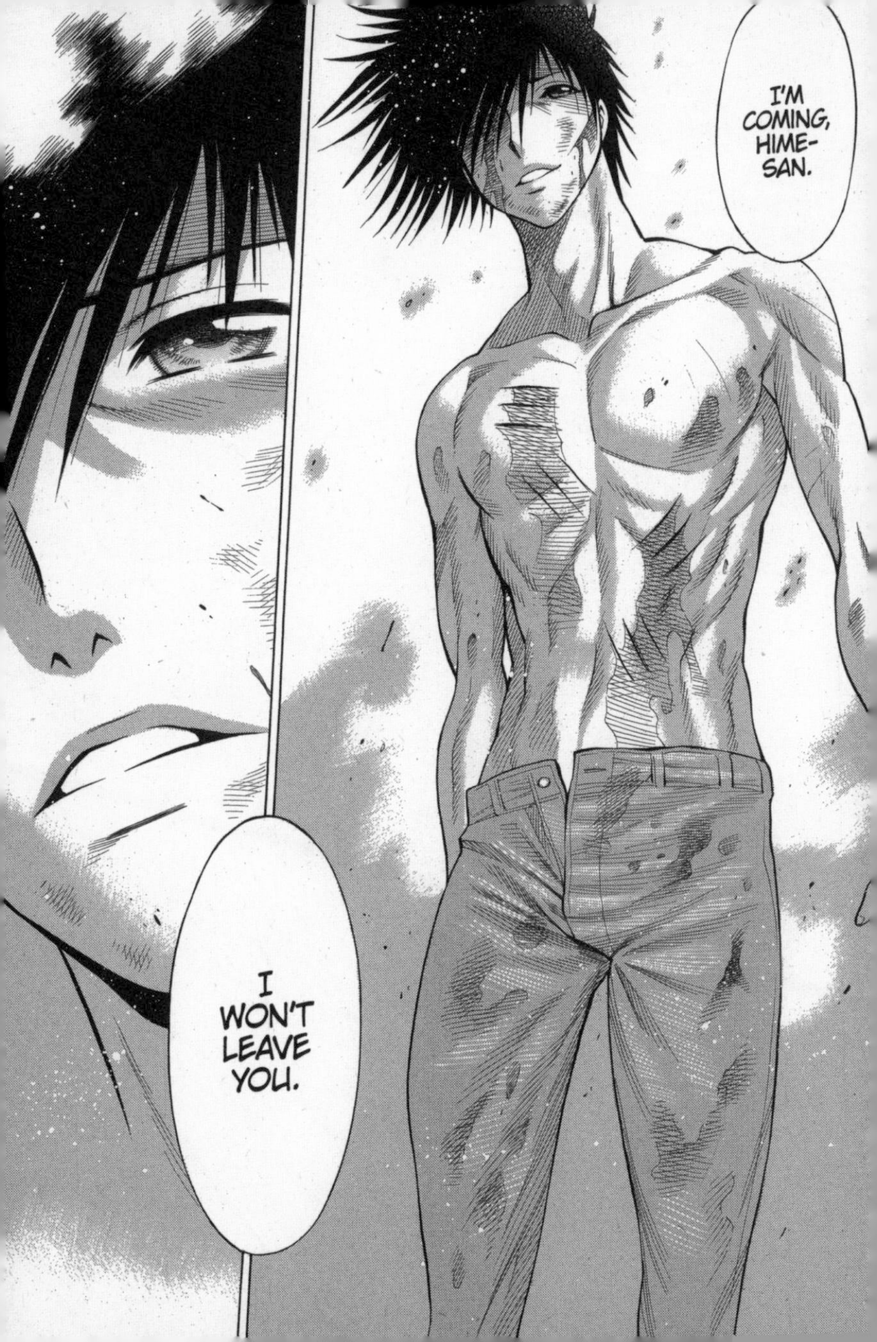
I'M COMING, HIME-SAN.
I WON'T LEAVE YOU.

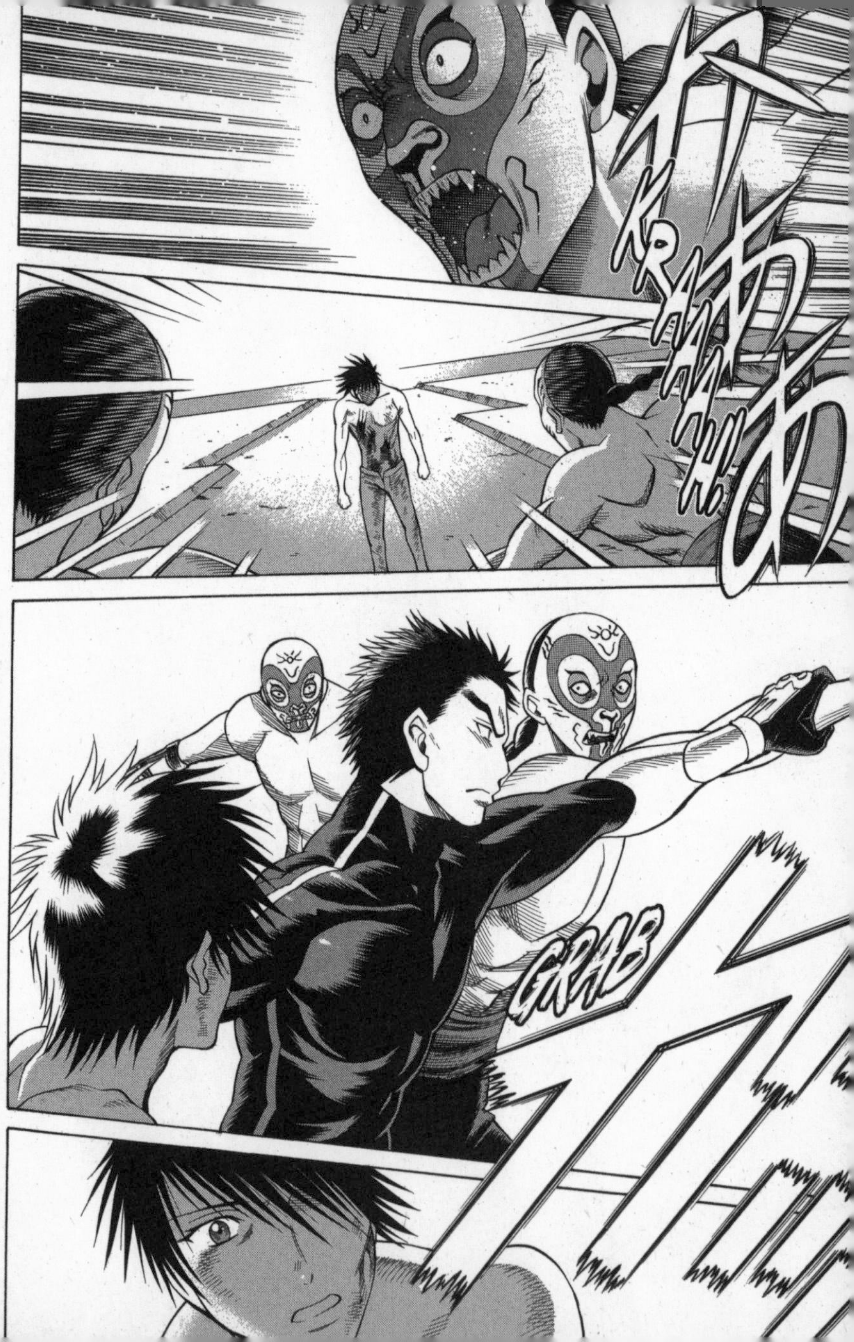
KRAAAHH!!
GRAB

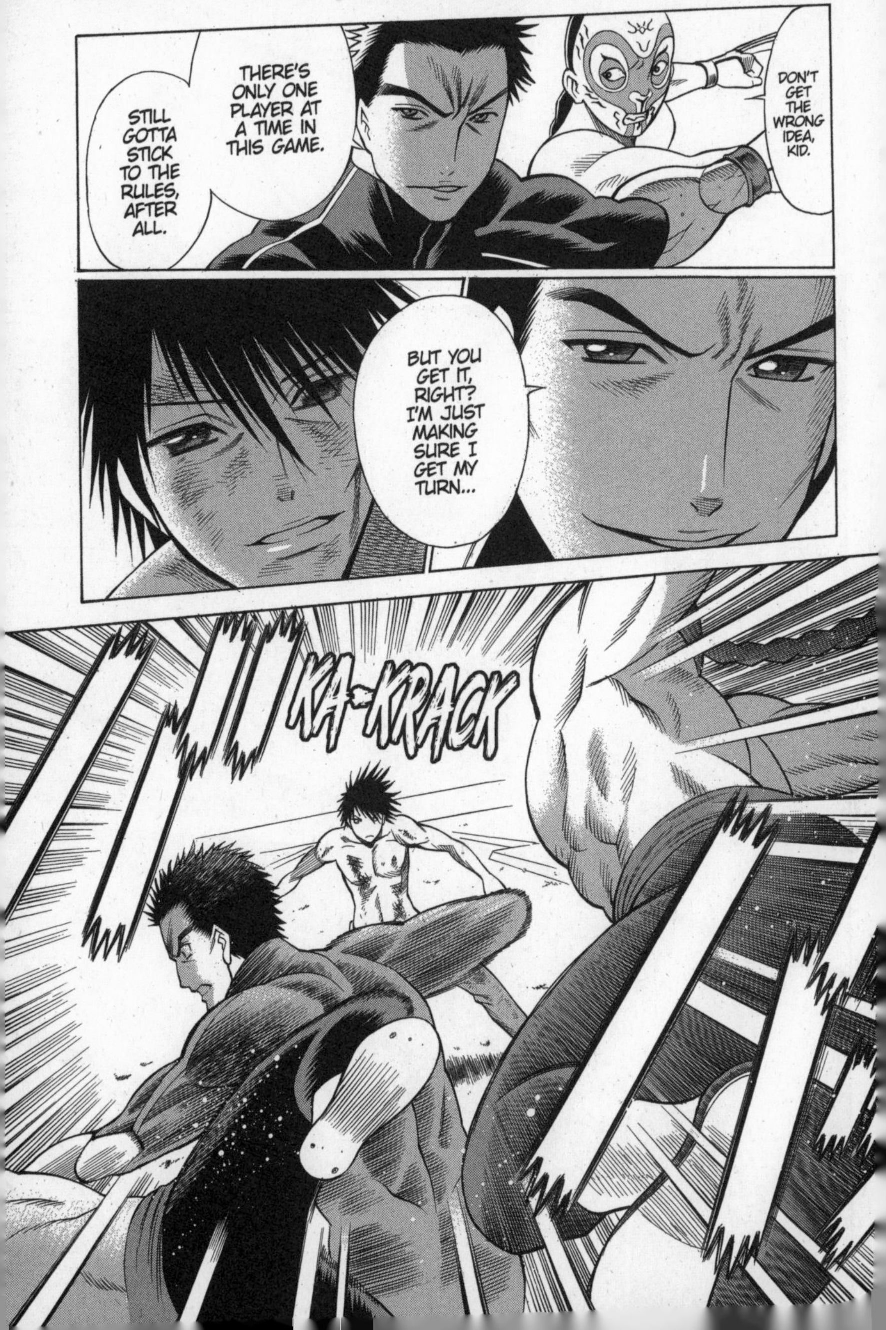
DON'T GET THE WRONG IDEA, KID.
THERE'S ONLY ONE PLAYER AT A TIME IN THIS GAME.
STILL GOTTA STICK TO THE RULES, AFTER ALL.
BUT YOU GET IT, RIGHT? I'M JUST MAKING SURE I GET MY TURN...
KA-KRACK

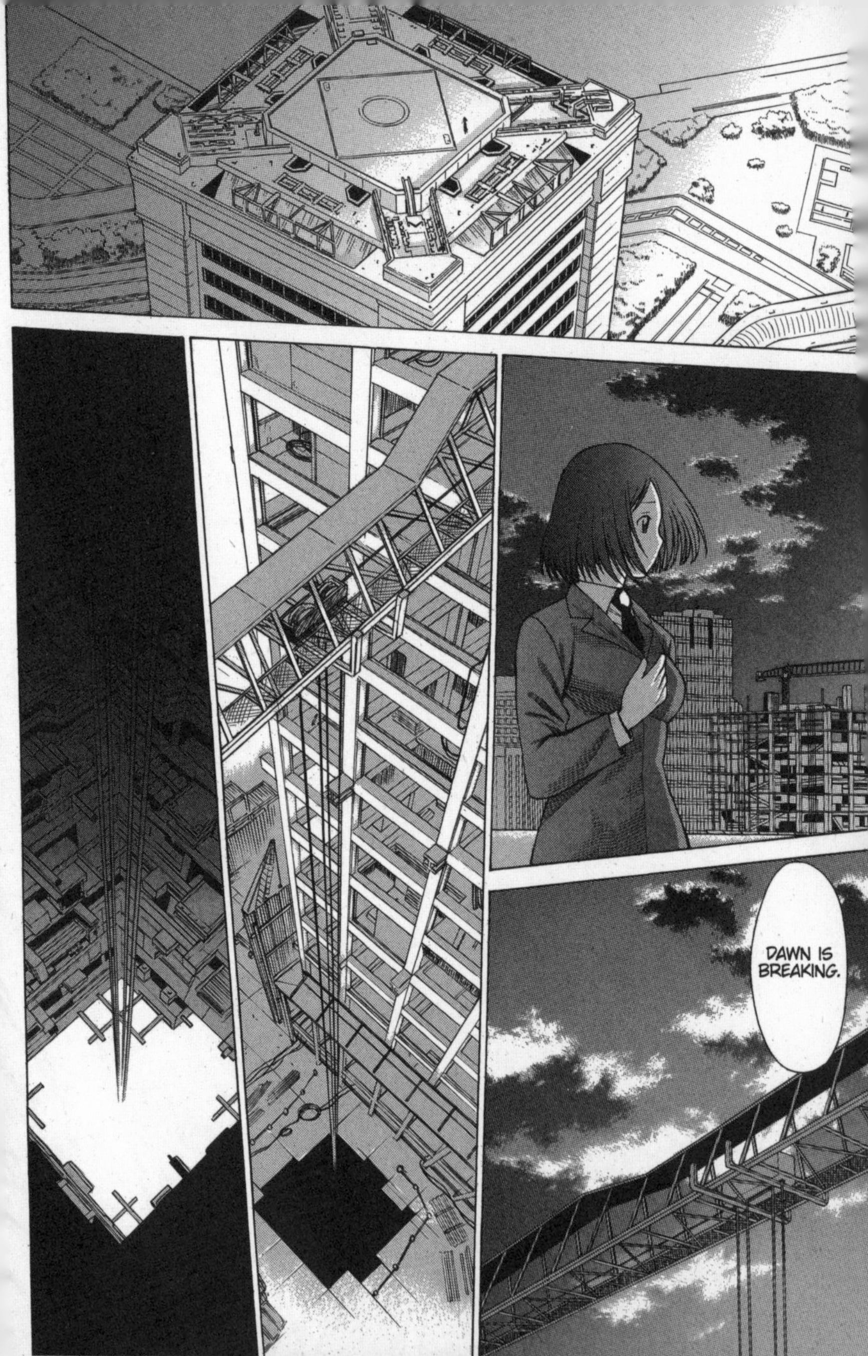
DAWN IS BREAKING.

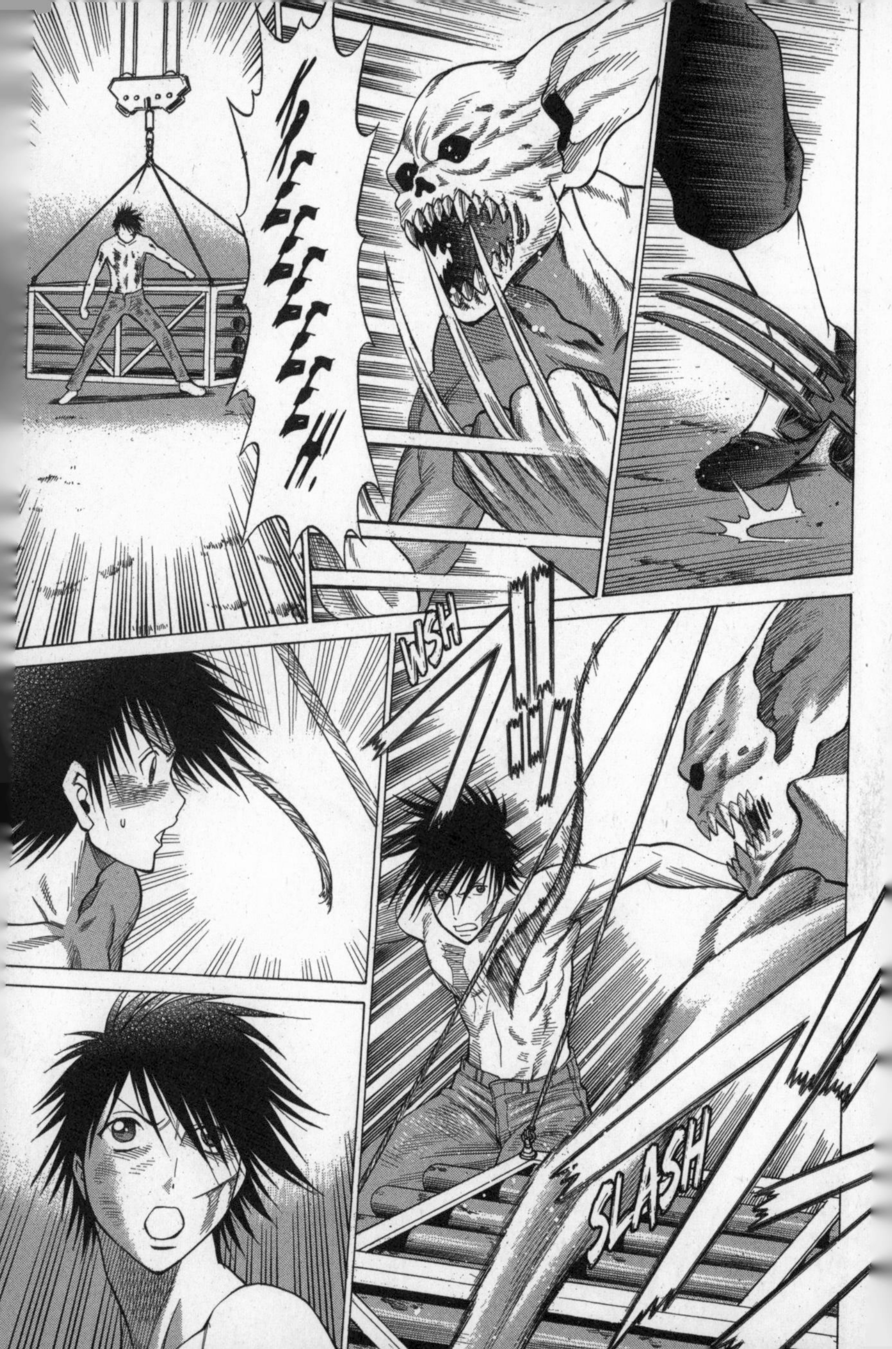
KRGEEEEEEEEEH!
WSH
SLASH

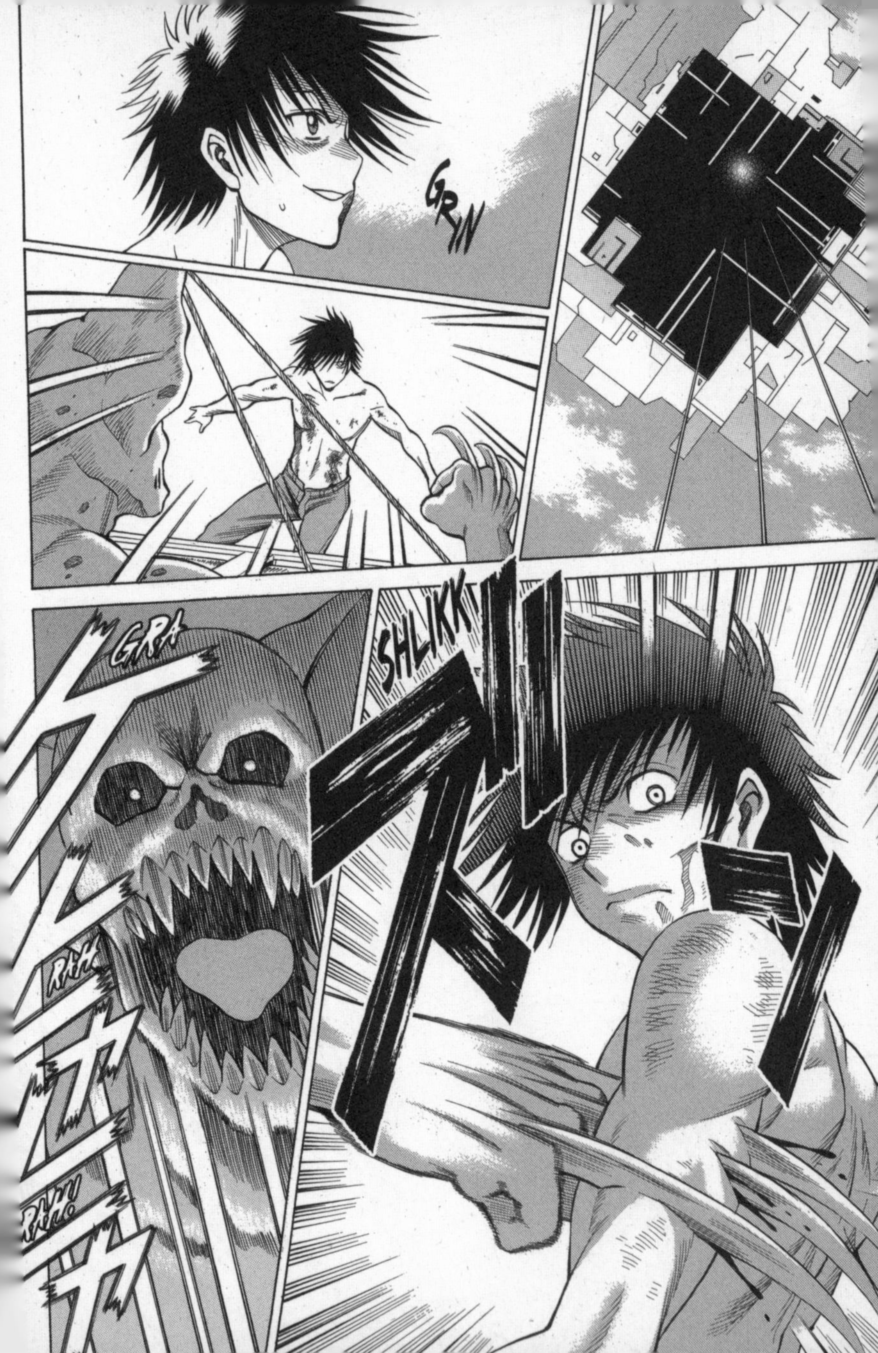
GRIN
SHLIKK
GRA
RAH

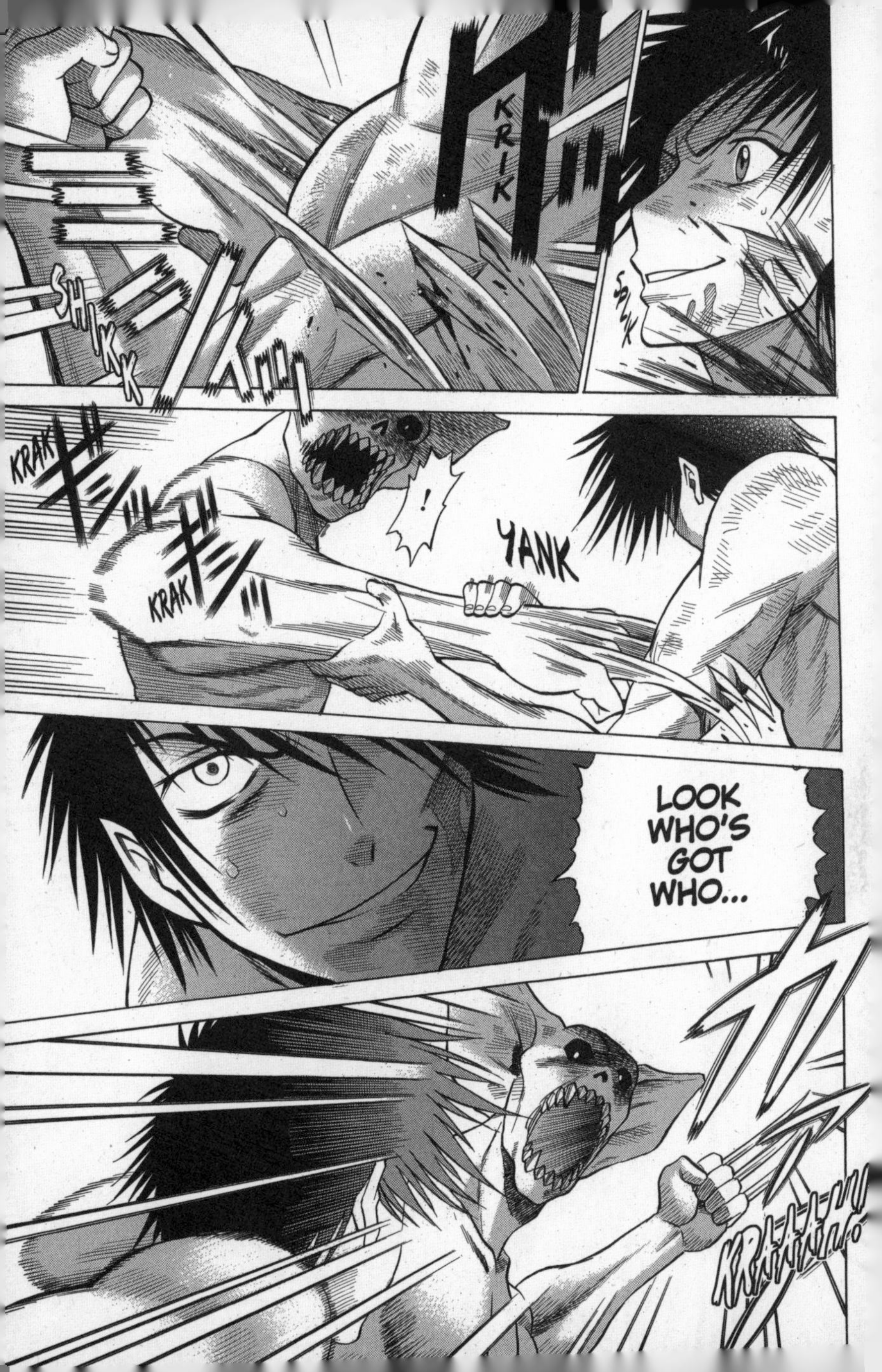
SPLUK
KRIK
SHIKKK
YANK
!
KRAK
KRAK
LOOK WHO'S GOT WHO...

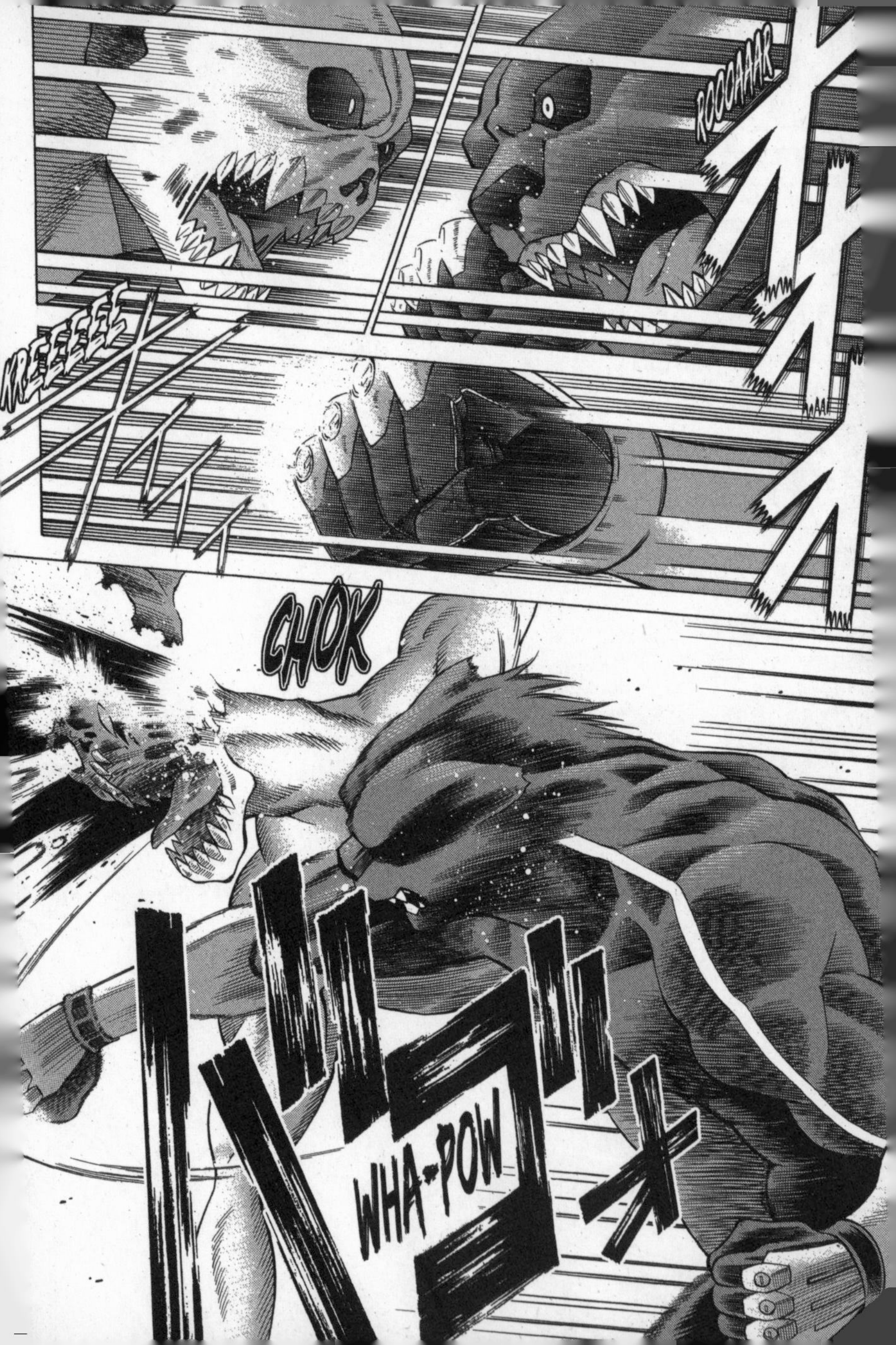
ROOAAAR
KREEEEEE
CHOK
WHA-POW

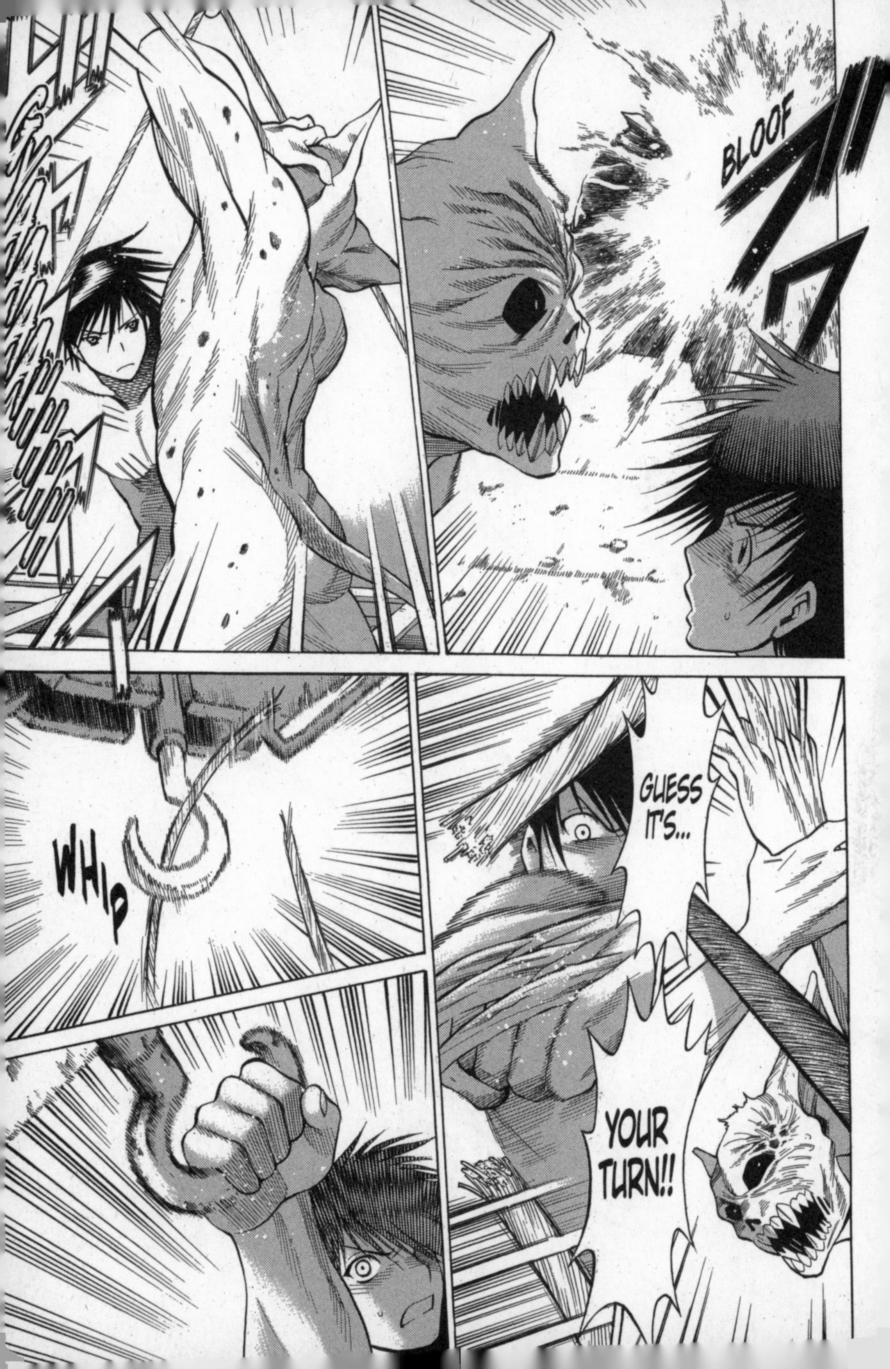
BLOOF
GUESS IT'S...
YOUR TURN!!
WHIP

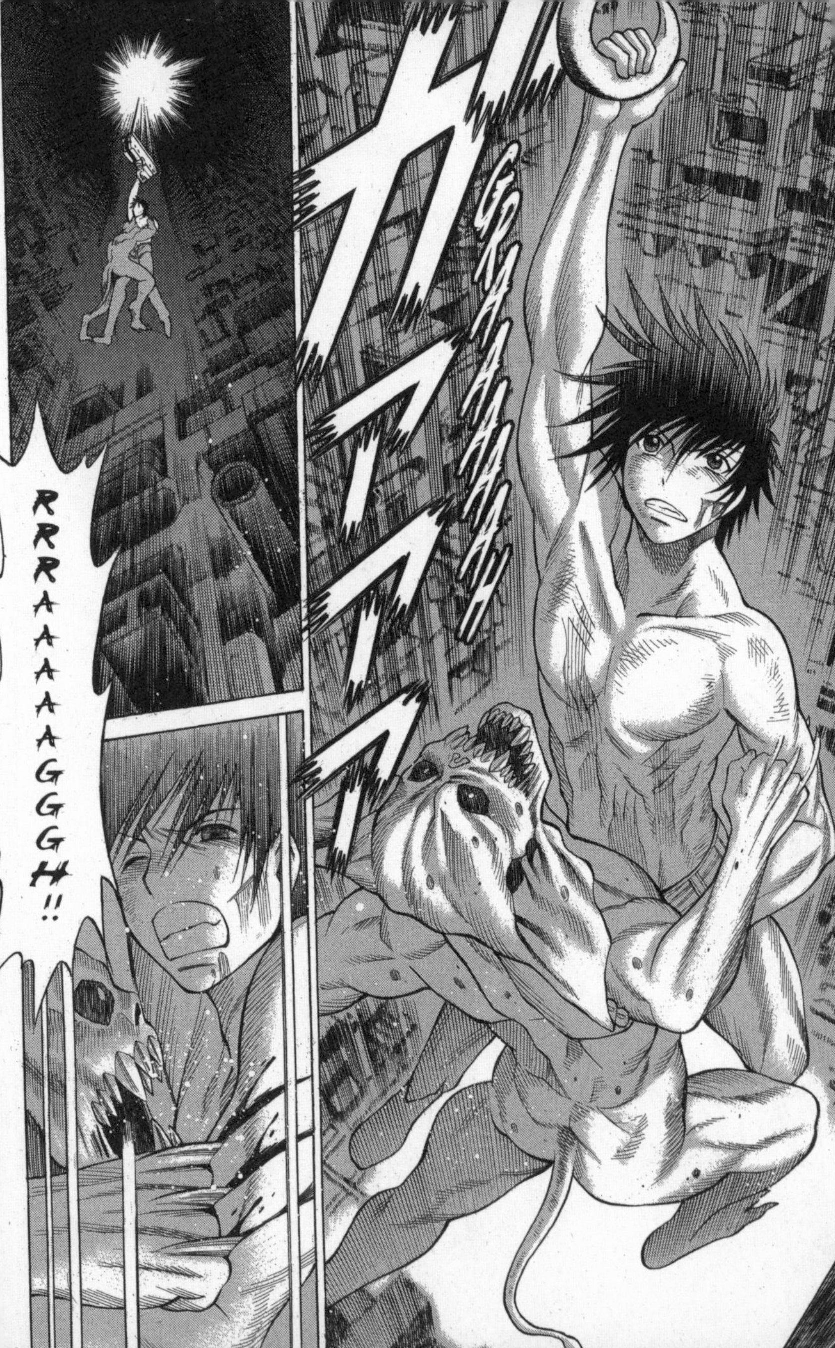
GRAAAAAAH
RRRAAAAAAAGGGGH!!

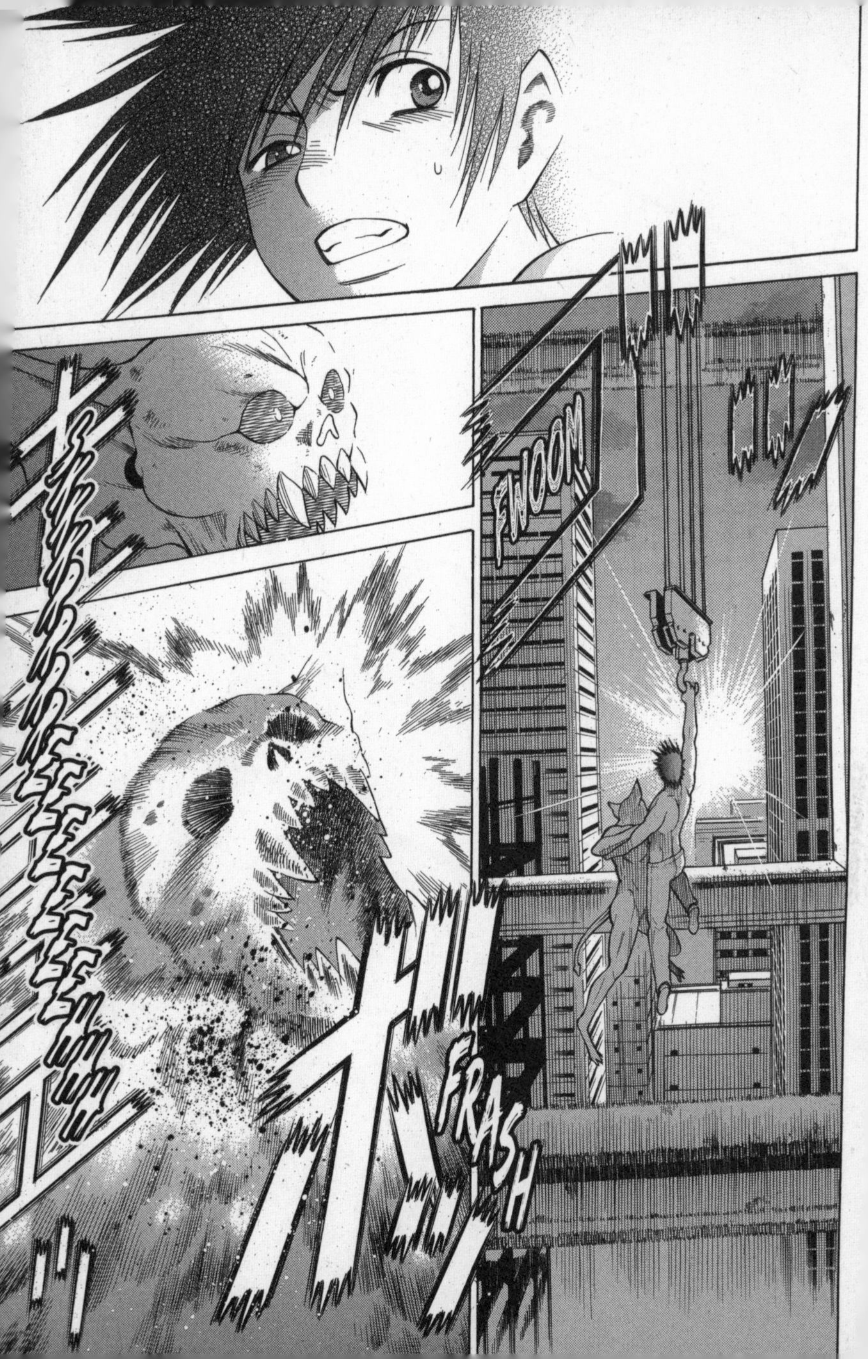
FWOOM
FRASH

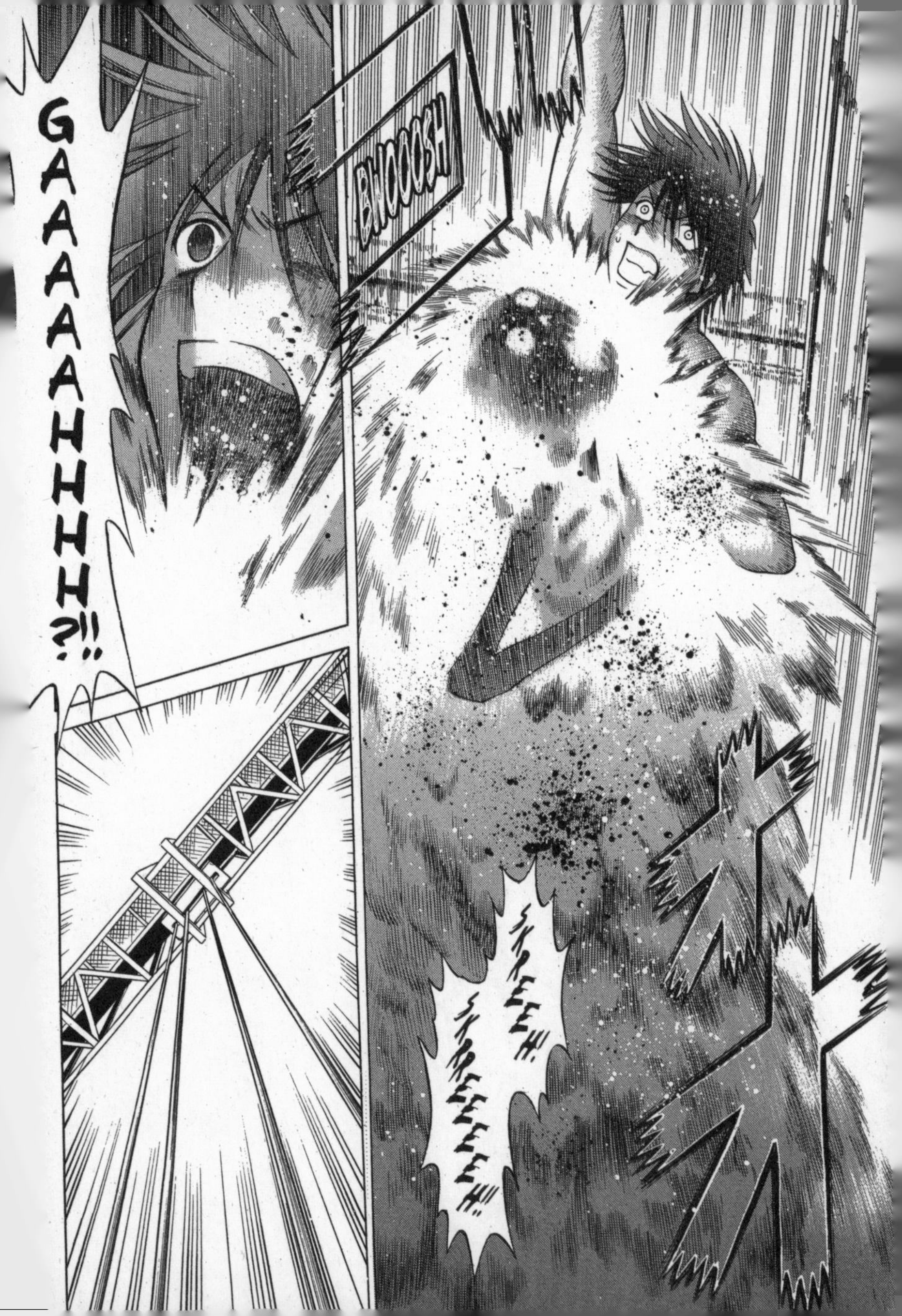
BHOOOSH
SKREEEH!
SKRREEEEEEH!!
GAAAAAHHHH?!!

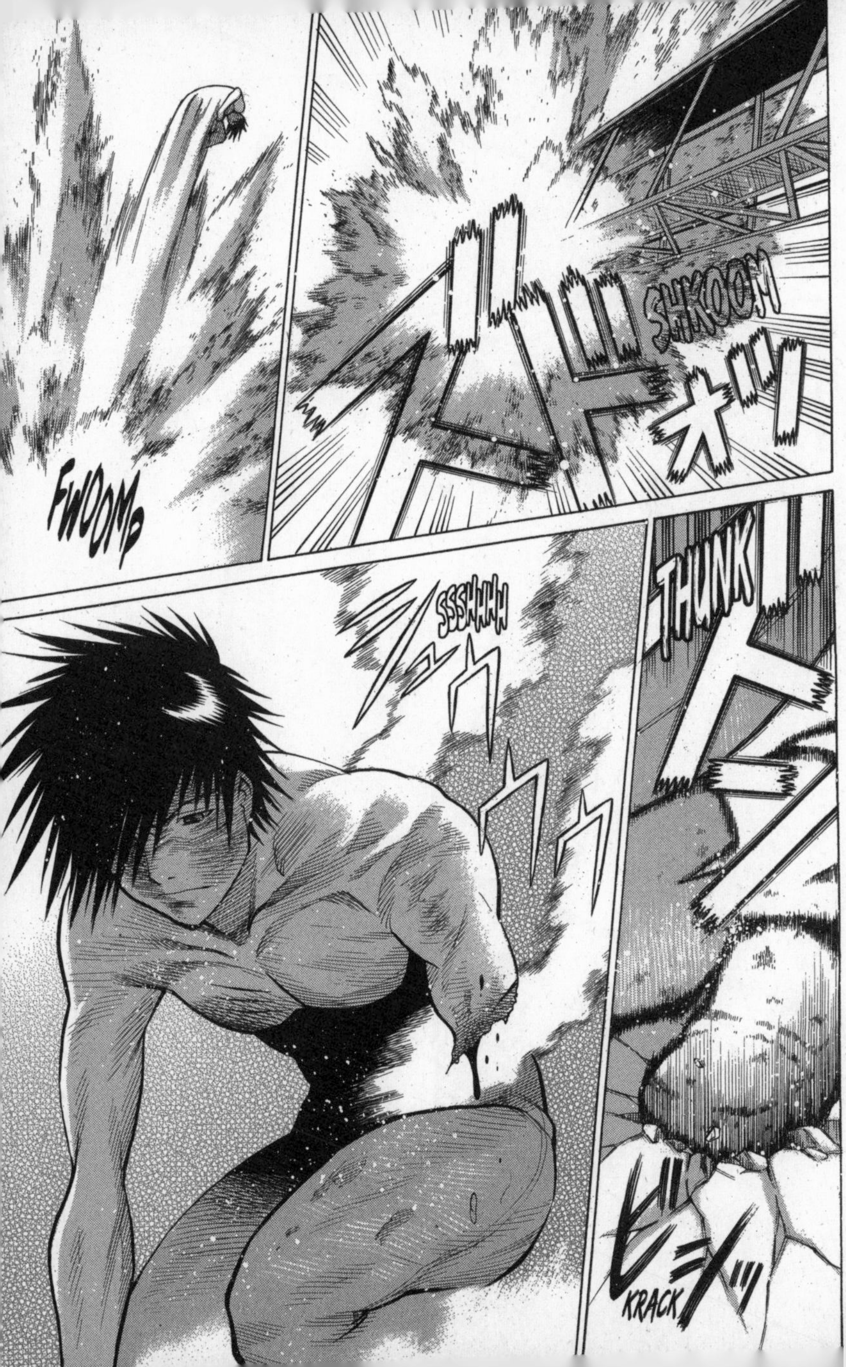
SHKOOM
FWOOMP
THUNK
KRACK
SSSHHHH

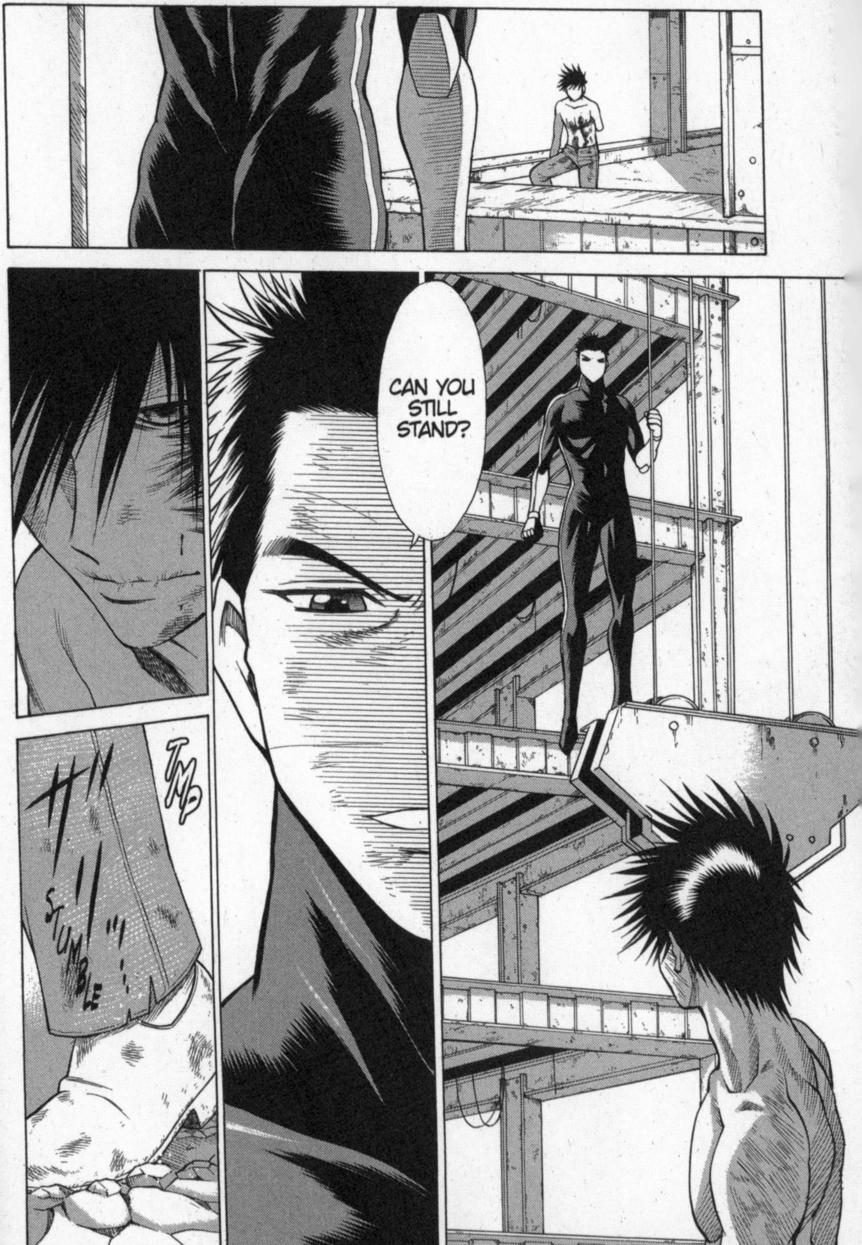
CAN YOU STILL STAND?
TMP
STUMBLE

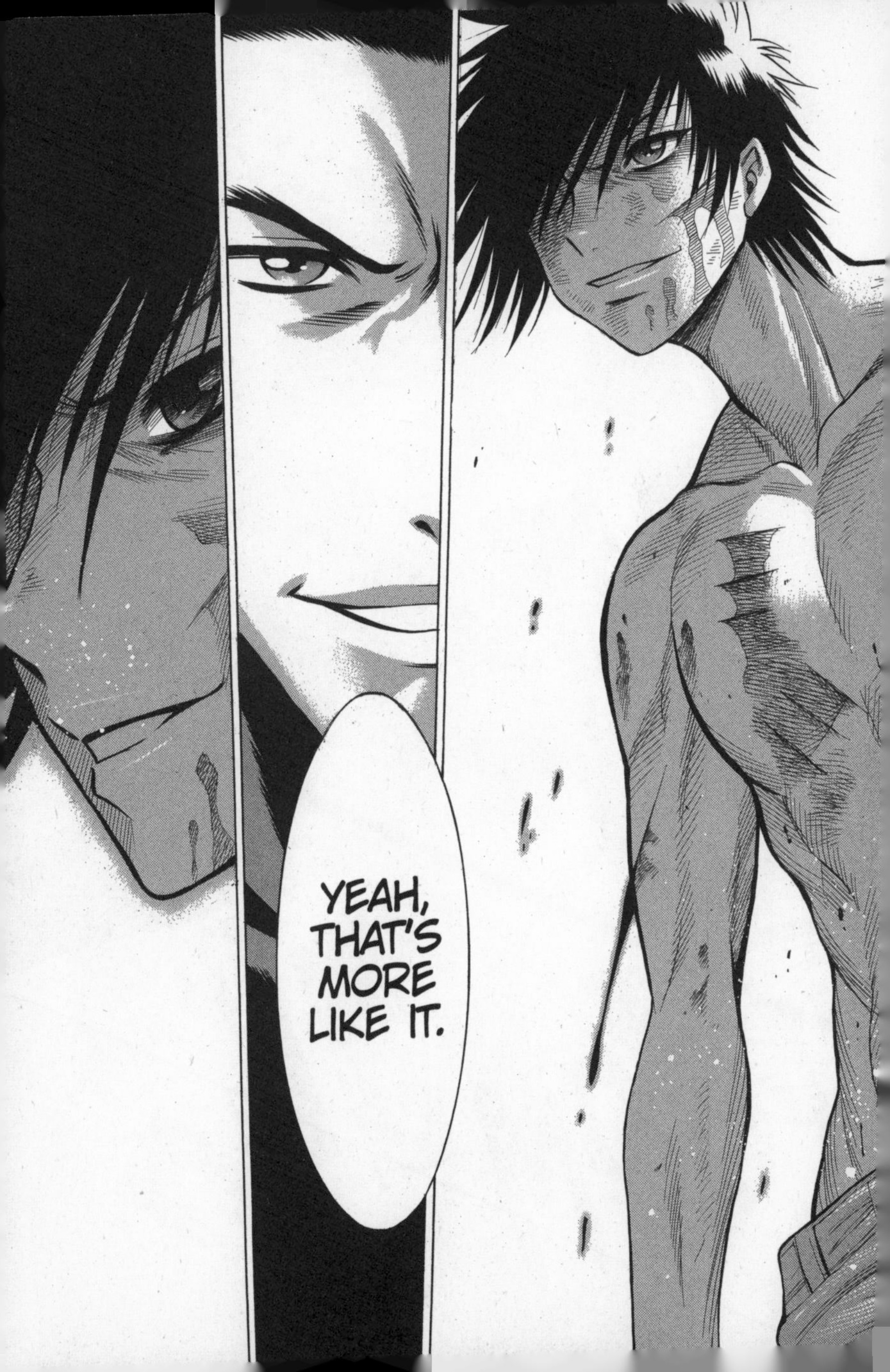
YEAH, THAT'S MORE LIKE IT.

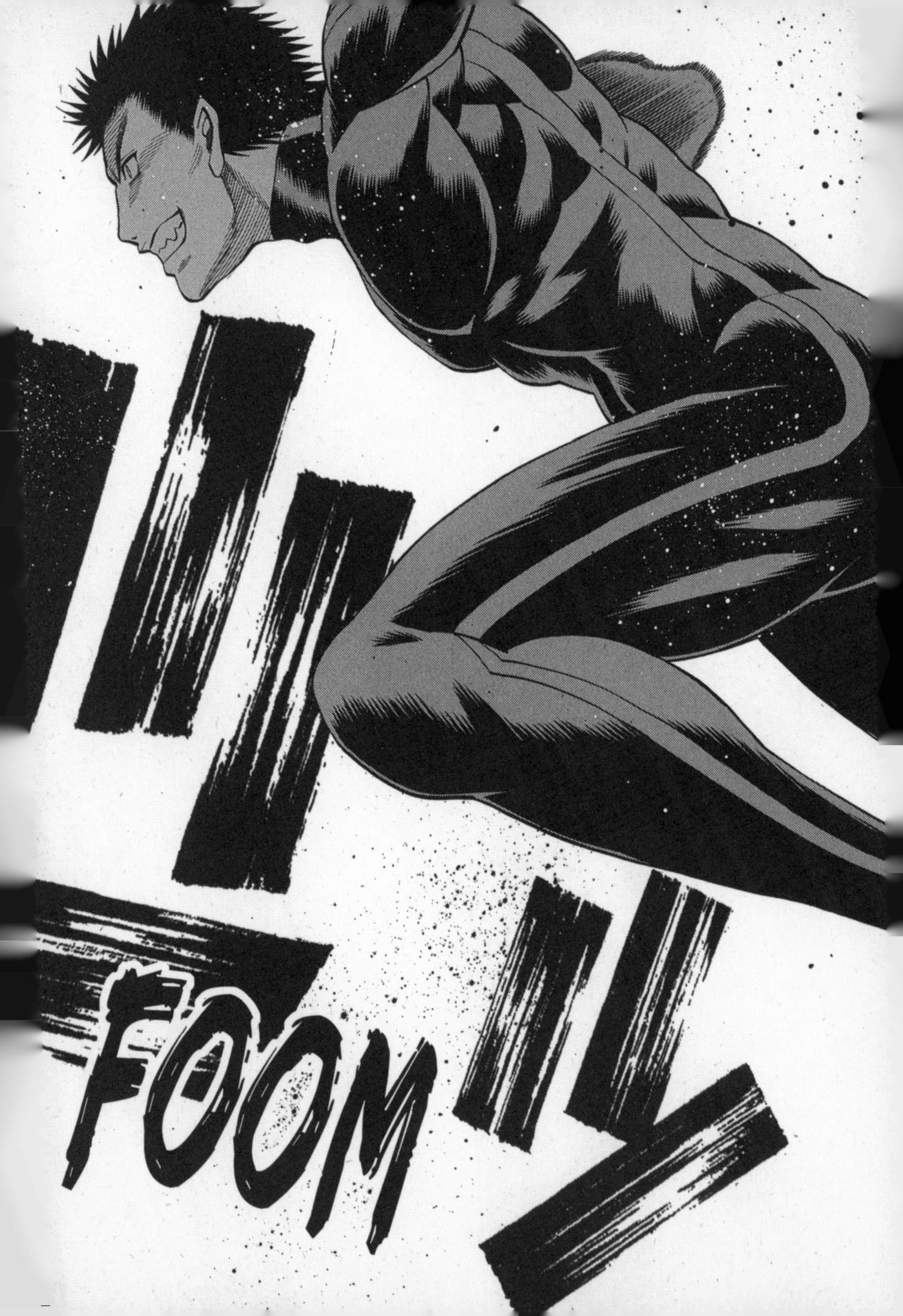
FOOM

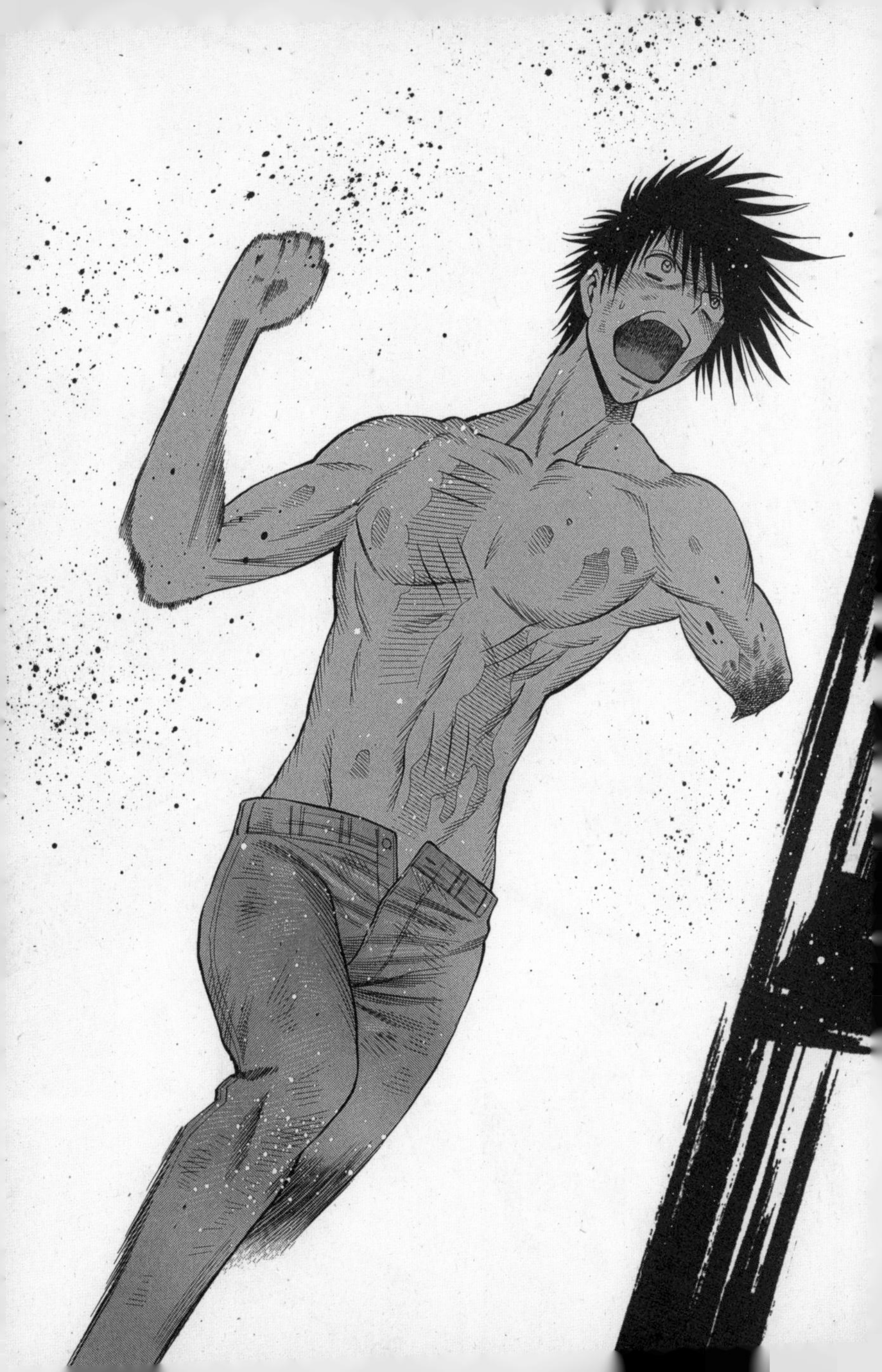

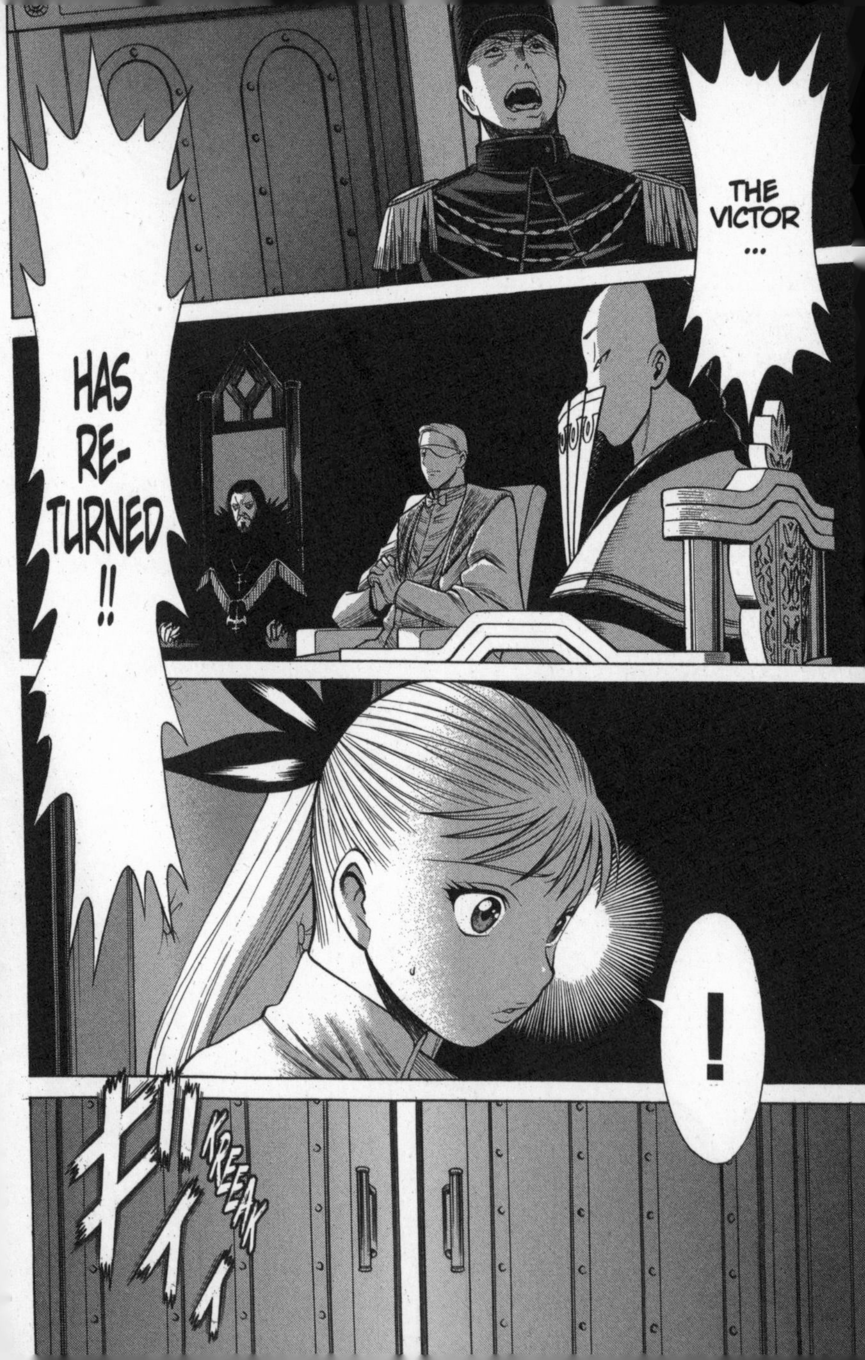
THE VICTOR ...
HAS RE-TURNED !!
!
KREEAK

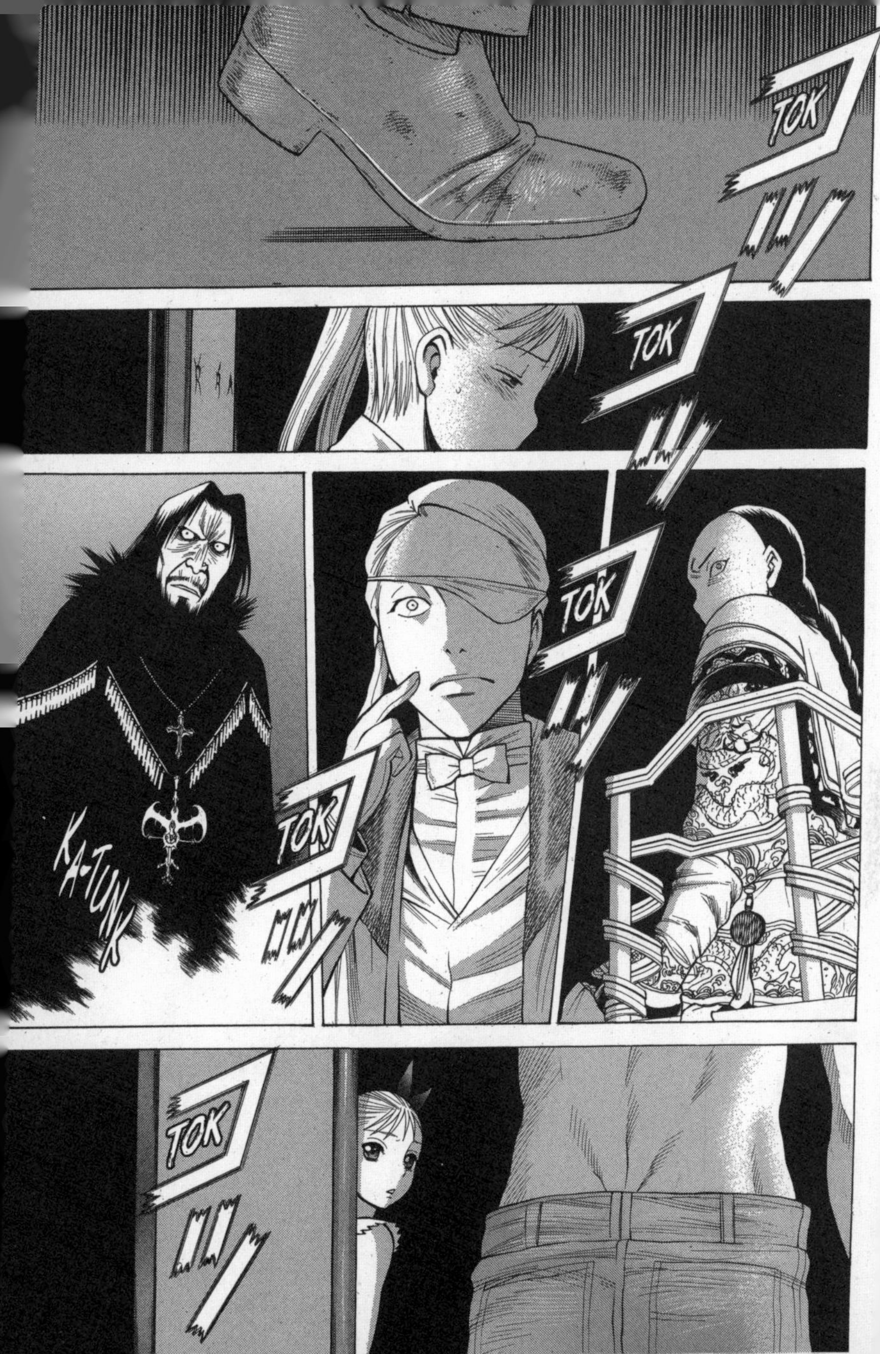
TOK
TOK
TOK
TOK
KA-TUNK
TOK

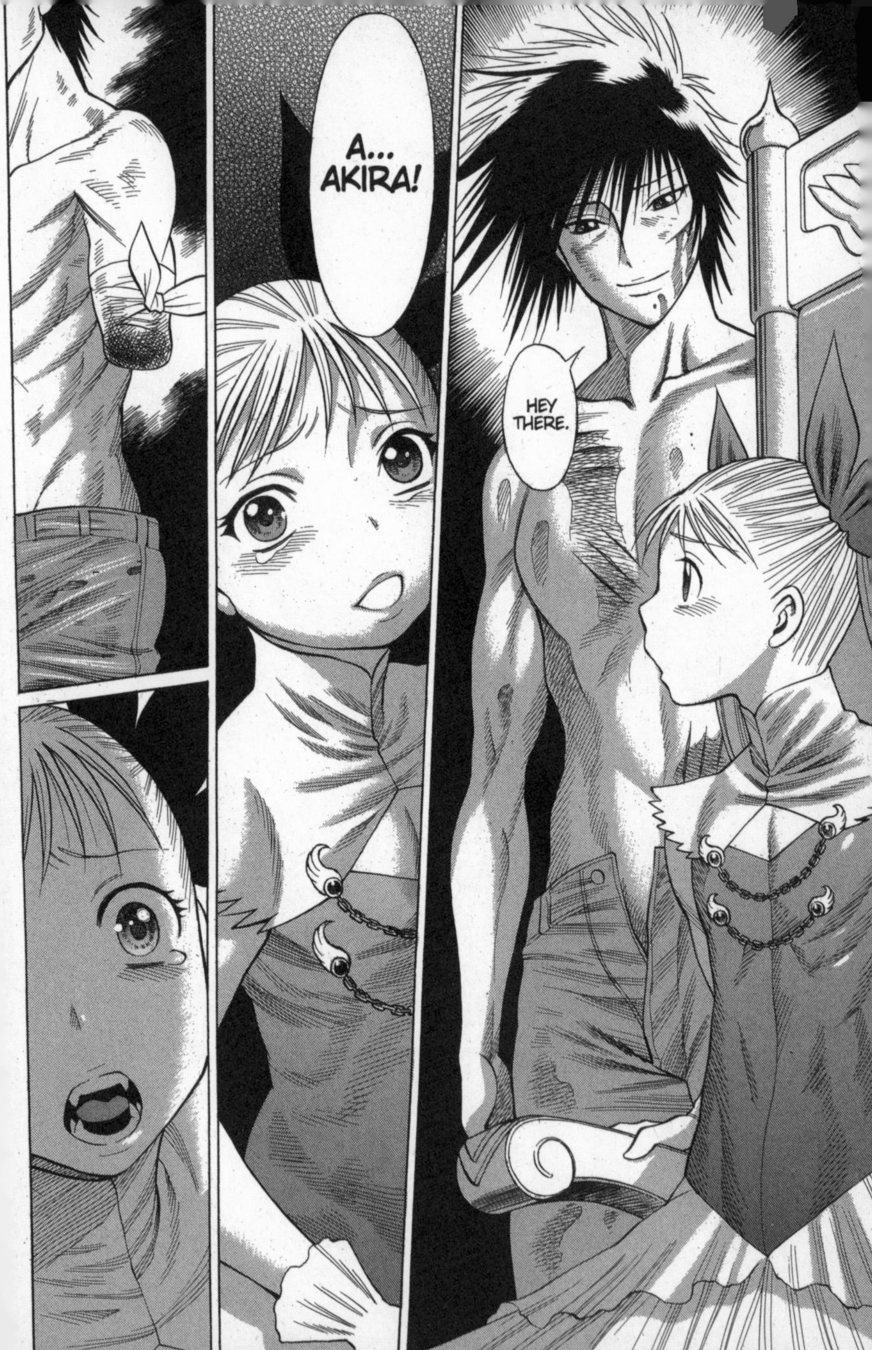
HEY THERE.
A... AKIRA!

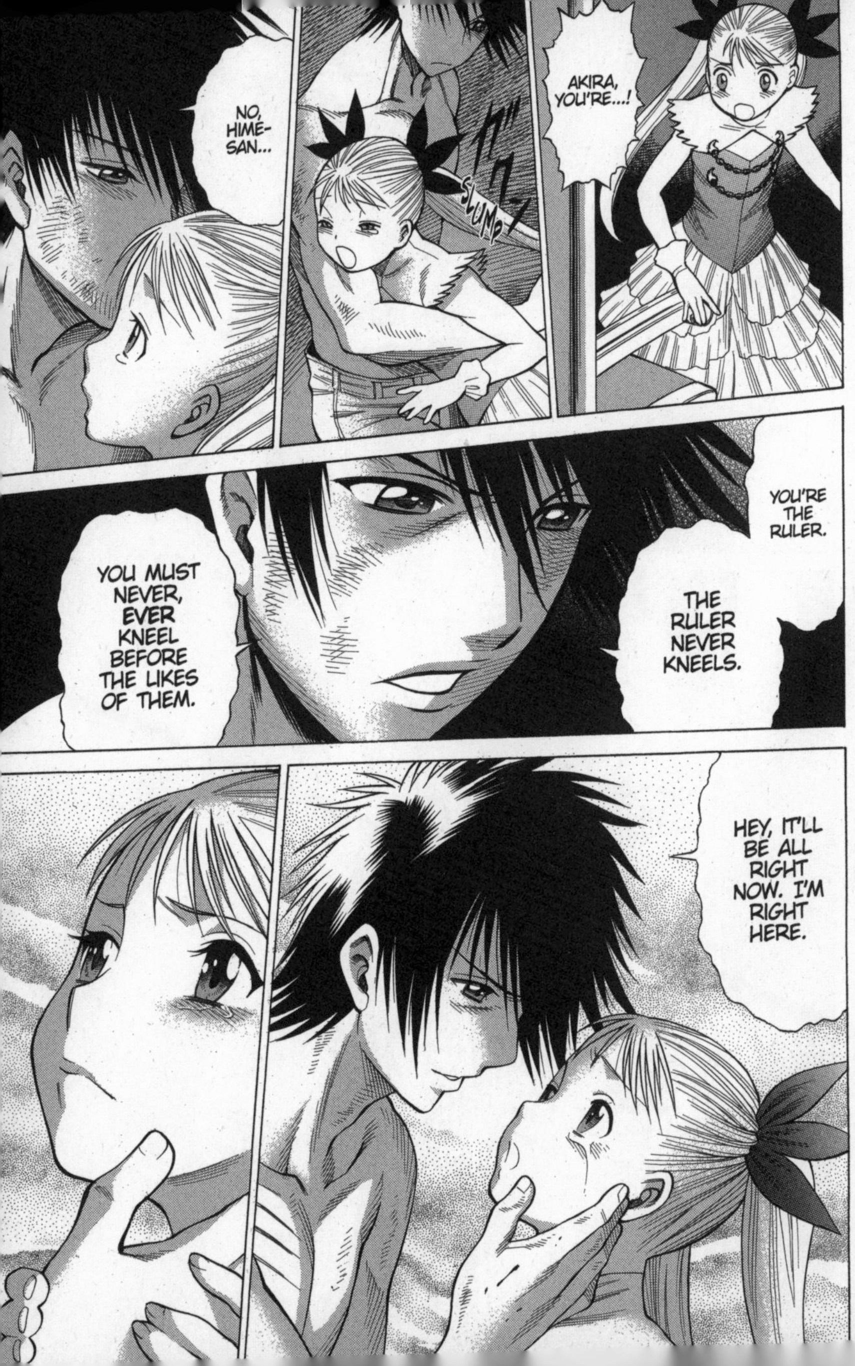
AKIRA, YOU'RE...!
SLUMP
NO, HIME-SAN...
YOU'RE THE RULER.
THE RULER NEVER KNEELS.
YOU MUST NEVER, EVER KNEEL BEFORE THE LIKES OF THEM.
HEY, IT'LL BE ALL RIGHT NOW. I'M RIGHT HERE.

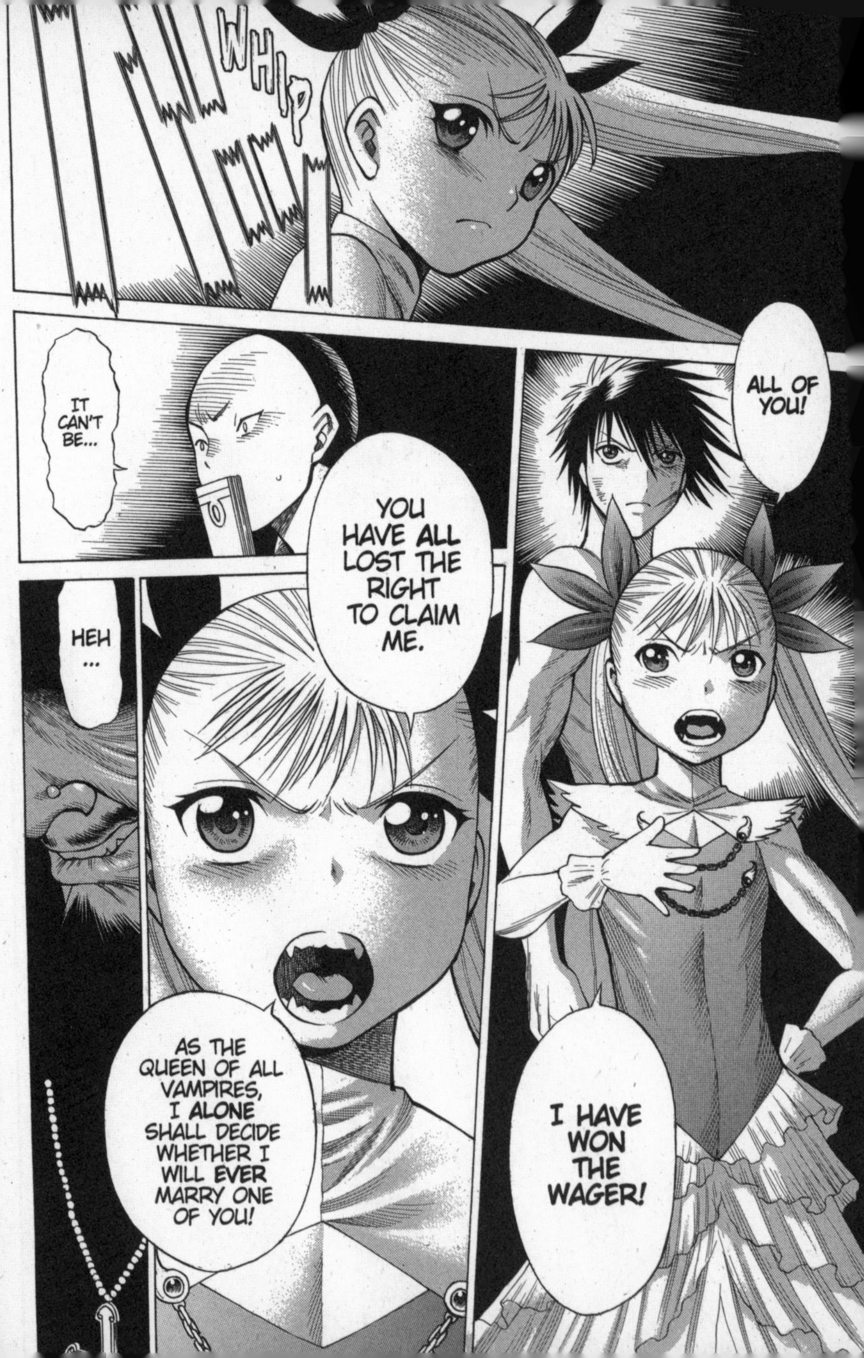
WHIP
ALL OF YOU!
I HAVE WON THE WAGER!
IT CAN'T BE...
YOU HAVE ALL LOST THE RIGHT TO CLAIM ME.
AS THE QUEEN OF ALL VAMPIRES, I ALONE SHALL DECIDE WHETHER I WILL EVER MARRY ONE OF YOU!
HEH ...

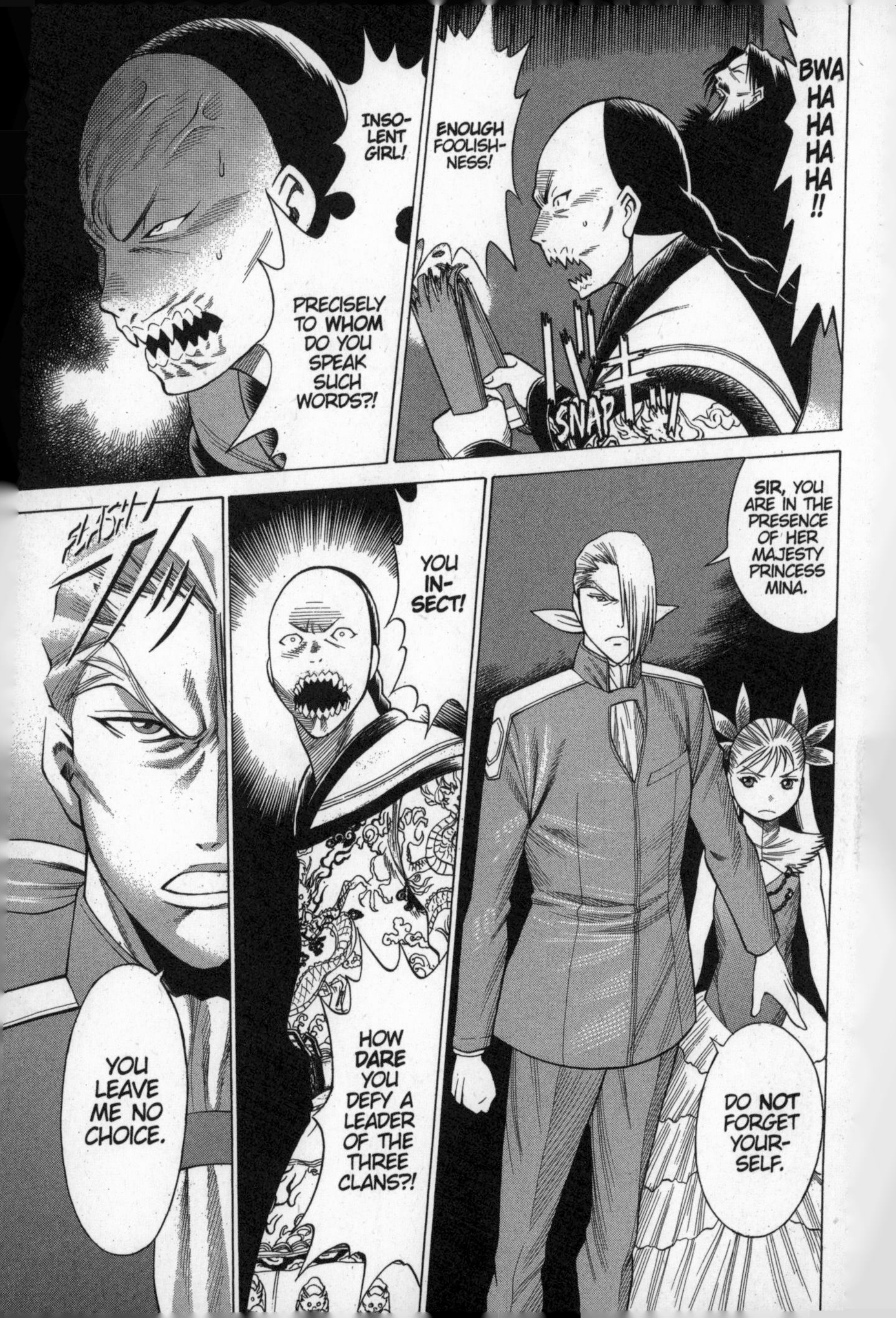
BWAHAHAHAHAHA!!
ENOUGH FOOLISHNESS!
SNAP
INSOLENT GIRL!
PRECISELY TO WHOM DO YOU SPEAK SUCH WORDS?!
SIR, YOU ARE IN THE PRESENCE OF HER MAJESTY PRINCESS MINA.
DO NOT FORGET YOURSELF.
YOU INSECT!
HOW DARE YOU DEFY A LEADER OF THE THREE CLANS?!
YOU LEAVE ME NO CHOICE.

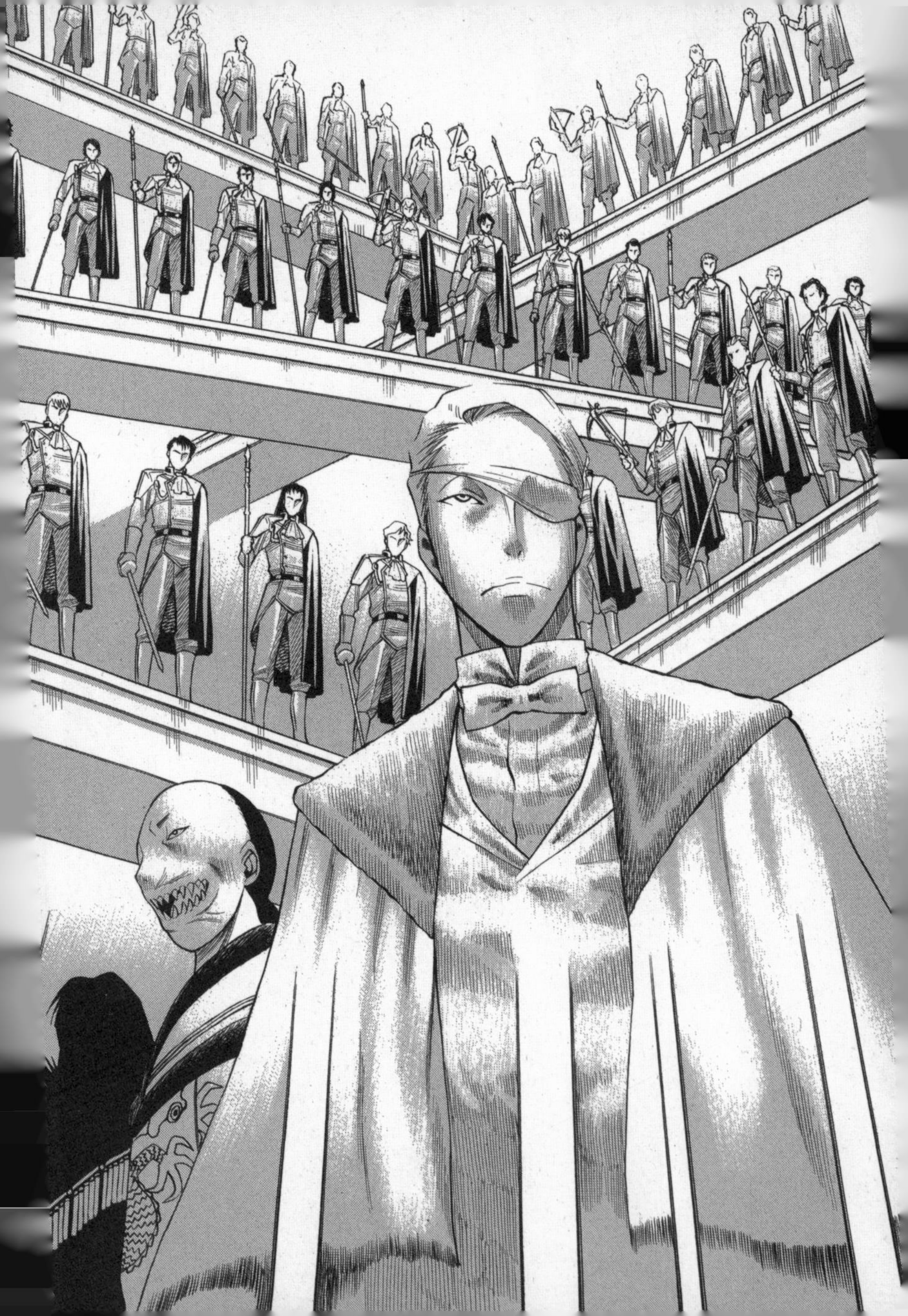

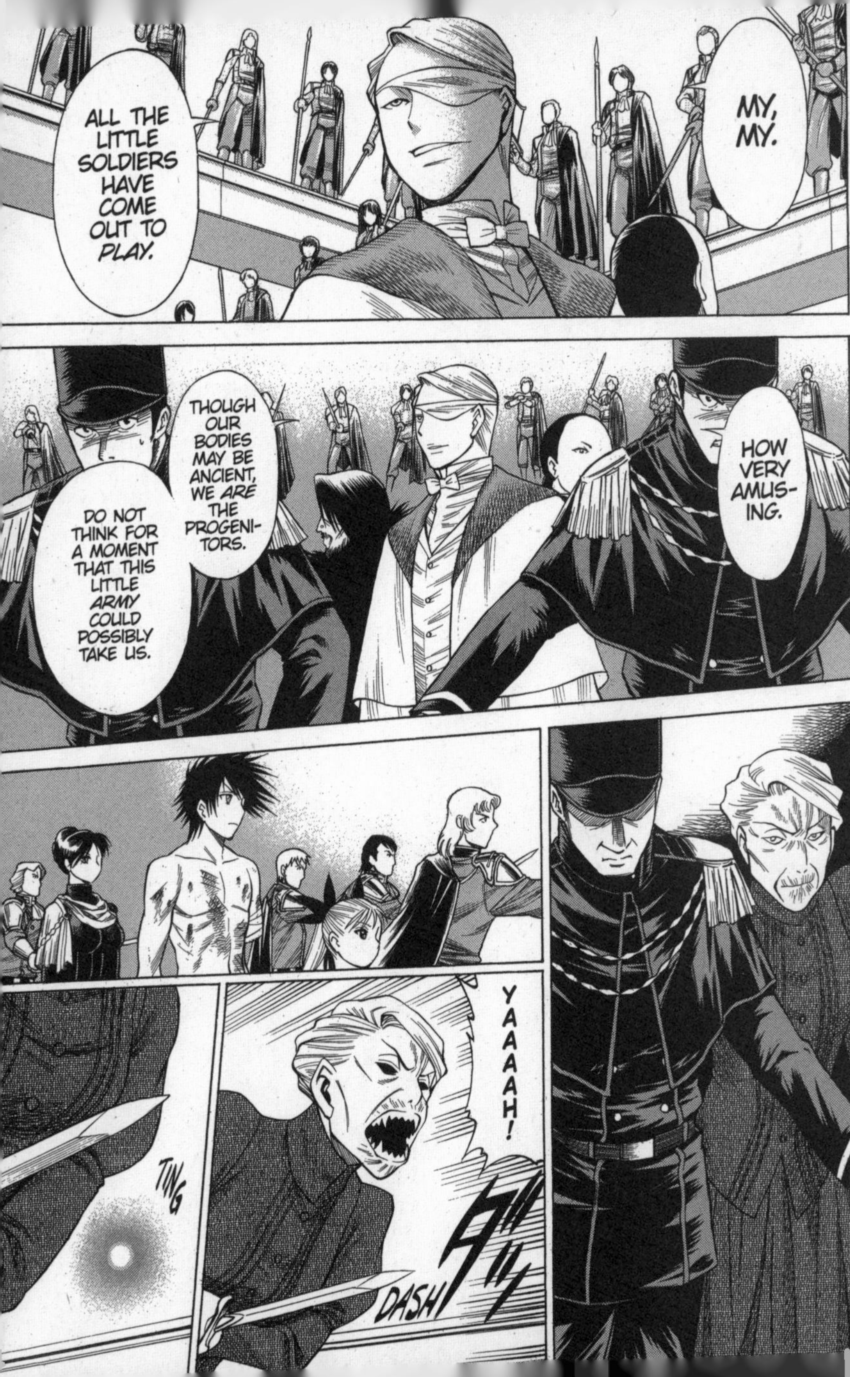
MY, MY.
ALL THE LITTLE SOLDIERS HAVE COME OUT TO *PLAY.*
HOW VERY AMUSING.
THOUGH OUR BODIES MAY BE ANCIENT, WE *ARE* THE PROGENITORS.
DO NOT THINK FOR A MOMENT THAT THIS LITTLE *ARMY* COULD POSSIBLY TAKE US.
YAAAAAH!
DASH
TING

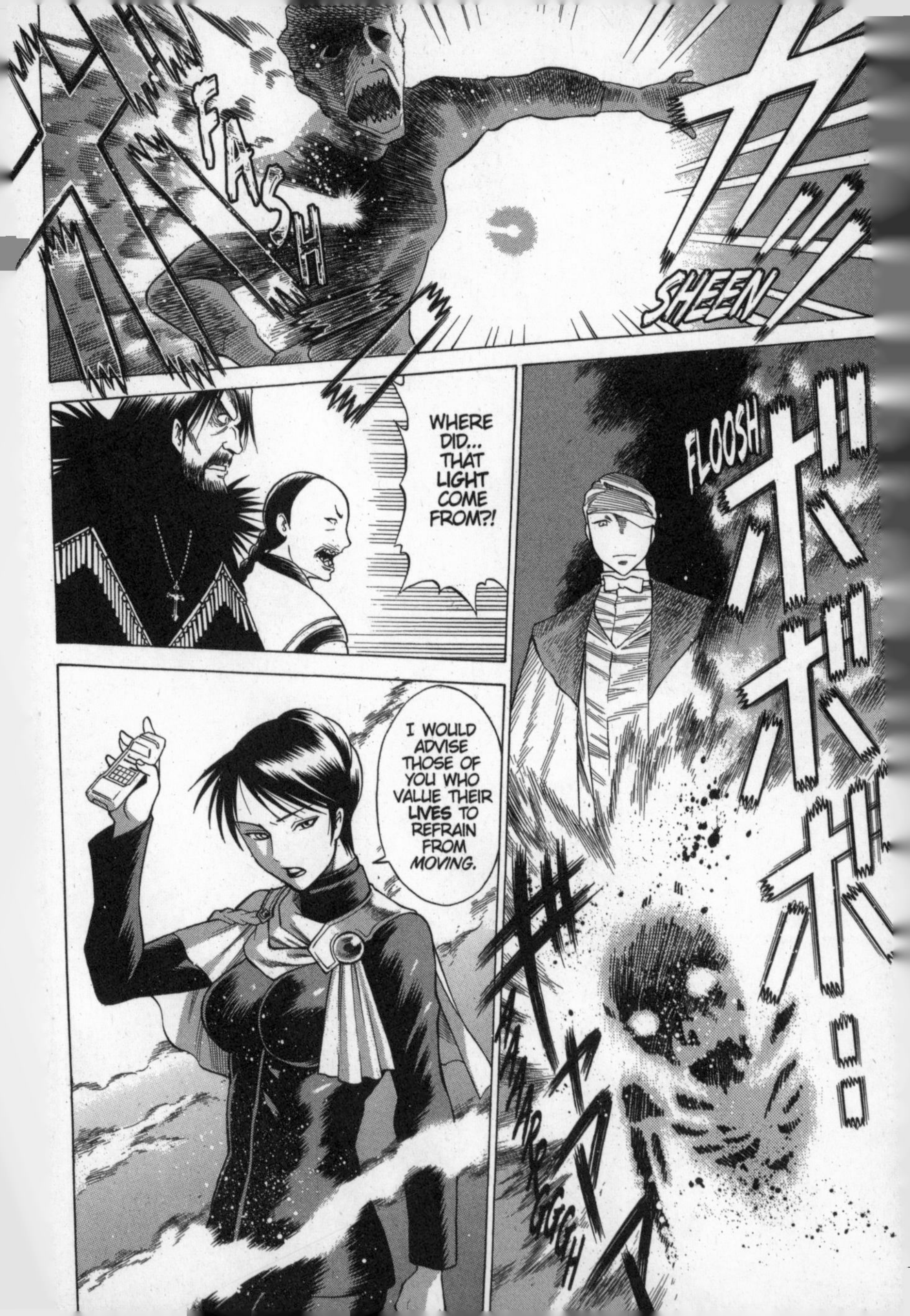
SHEEN
FASH
FLOOSH
WHERE DID... THAT LIGHT COME FROM?!
I WOULD ADVISE THOSE OF YOU WHO VALUE THEIR LIVES TO REFRAIN FROM *MOVING.*

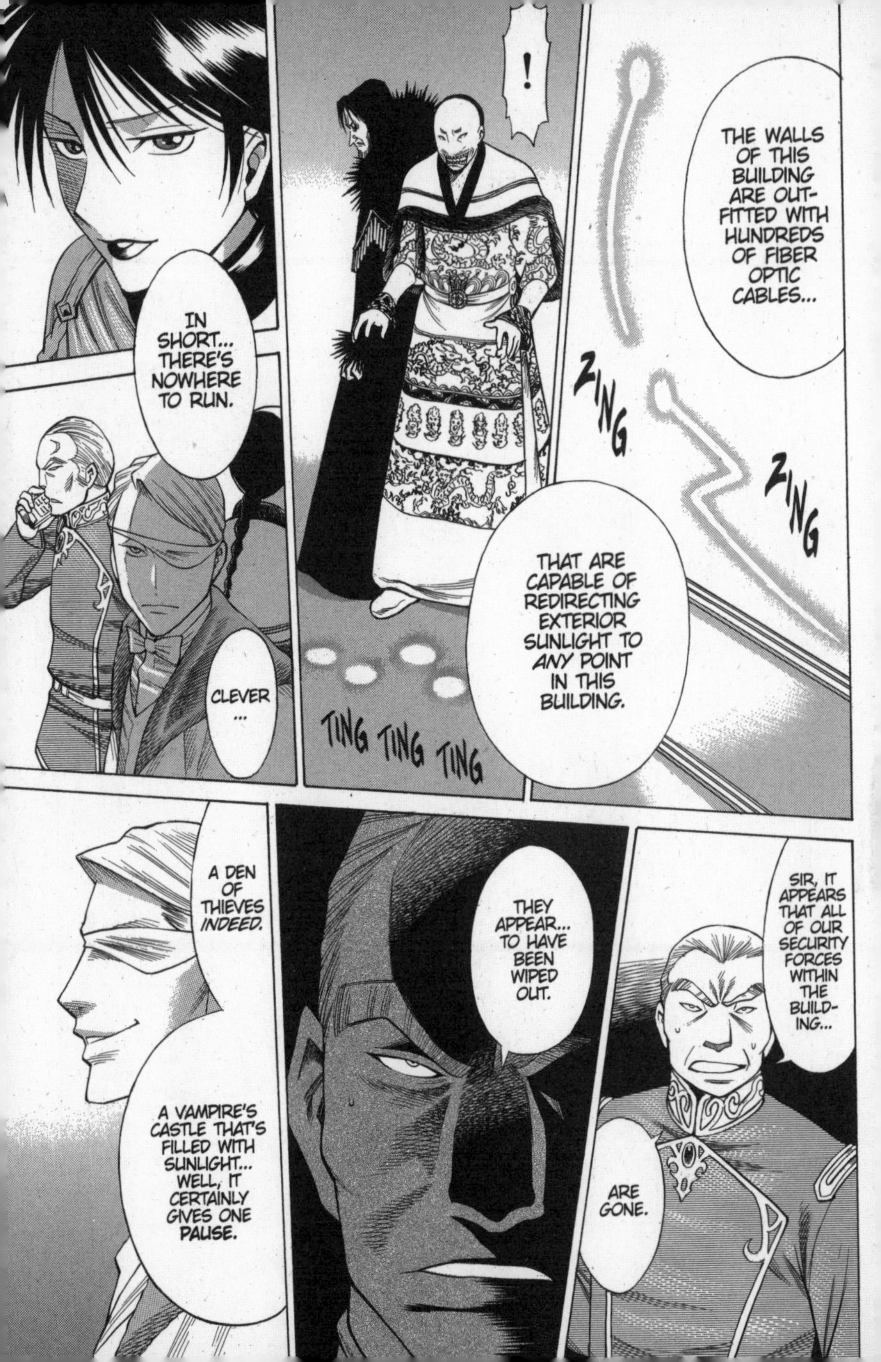
THE WALLS OF THIS BUILDING ARE OUT-FITTED WITH HUNDREDS OF FIBER OPTIC CABLES...
ZING
ZING
THAT ARE CAPABLE OF REDIRECTING EXTERIOR SUNLIGHT TO *ANY* POINT IN THIS BUILDING.
!
TING TING TING
IN SHORT... THERE'S NOWHERE TO RUN.
CLEVER ...
SIR, IT APPEARS THAT ALL OF OUR SECURITY FORCES WITHIN THE BUILD-ING...
ARE GONE.
THEY APPEAR... TO HAVE BEEN WIPED OUT.
A DEN OF THIEVES *INDEED.*
A VAMPIRE'S CASTLE THAT'S FILLED WITH SUNLIGHT... WELL, IT CERTAINLY GIVES ONE PAUSE.

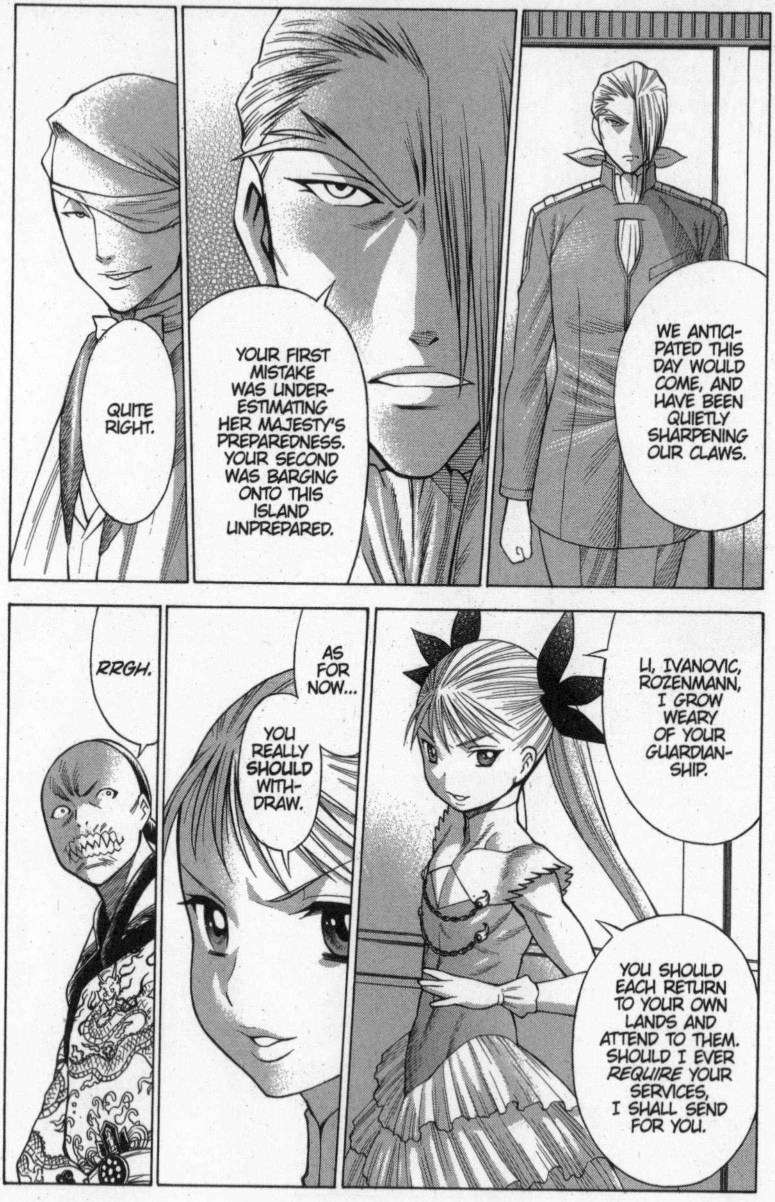
WE ANTICIPATED THIS DAY WOULD COME, AND HAVE BEEN QUIETLY SHARPENING OUR CLAWS.
YOUR FIRST MISTAKE WAS UNDERESTIMATING HER MAJESTY'S PREPAREDNESS. YOUR SECOND WAS BARGING ONTO THIS ISLAND UNPREPARED.
QUITE RIGHT.
LI, IVANOVIC, ROZENMANN, I GROW WEARY OF YOUR GUARDIANSHIP.
YOU SHOULD EACH RETURN TO YOUR OWN LANDS AND ATTEND TO THEM. SHOULD I EVER *REQUIRE* YOUR SERVICES, I SHALL SEND FOR YOU.
AS FOR NOW...
YOU REALLY SHOULD WITHDRAW.
RRGH.

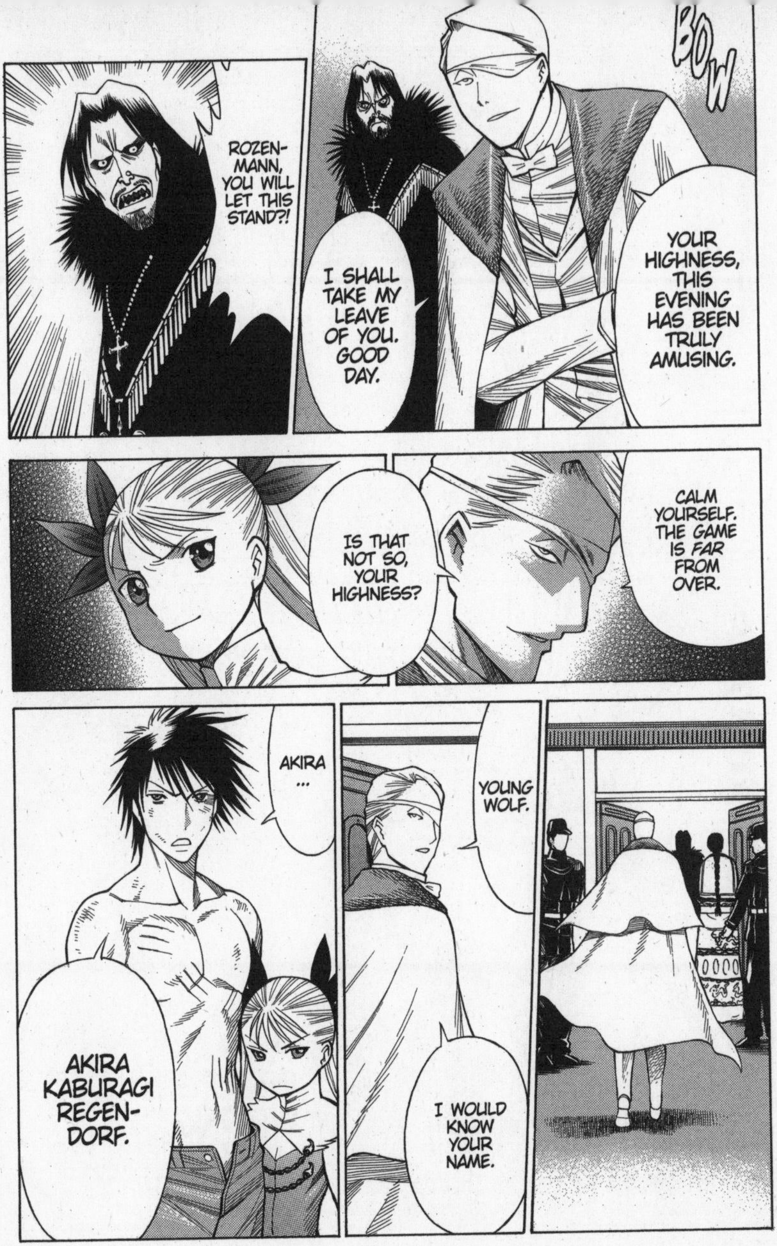
BOW
YOUR HIGHNESS, THIS EVENING HAS BEEN TRULY AMUSING.
I SHALL TAKE MY LEAVE OF YOU. GOOD DAY.
ROZEN-MANN, YOU WILL LET THIS STAND?!
CALM YOURSELF. THE GAME IS *FAR* FROM OVER.
IS THAT NOT SO, YOUR HIGHNESS?
YOUNG WOLF.
I WOULD KNOW YOUR NAME.
AKIRA ...
AKIRA KABURAGI REGEN-DORF.

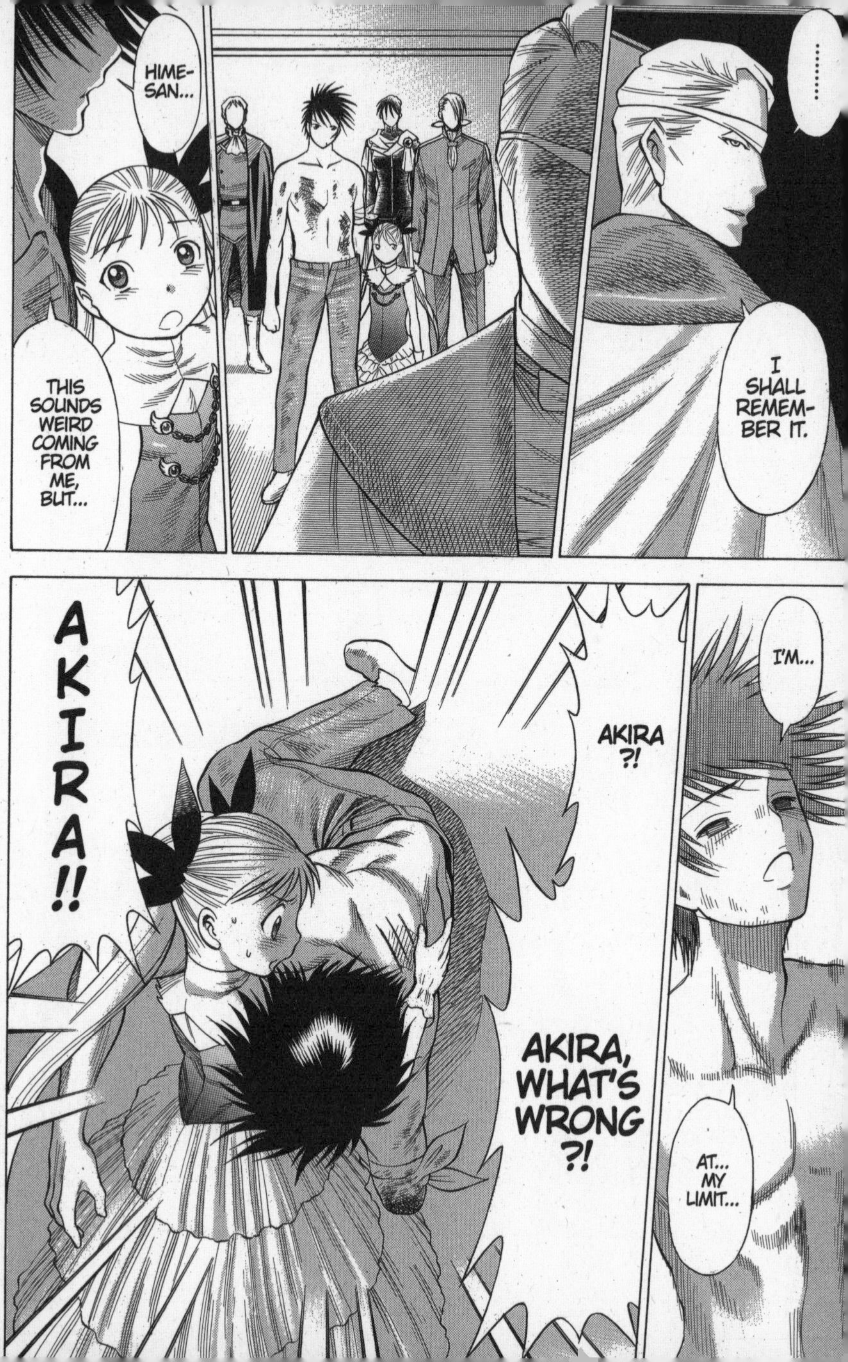

……
I SHALL REMEMBER IT.
HIME-SAN...
THIS SOUNDS WEIRD COMING FROM ME, BUT...
I'M...
AT... MY LIMIT...
AKIRA ?!
AKIRA, WHAT'S WRONG ?!
AKIRA!!

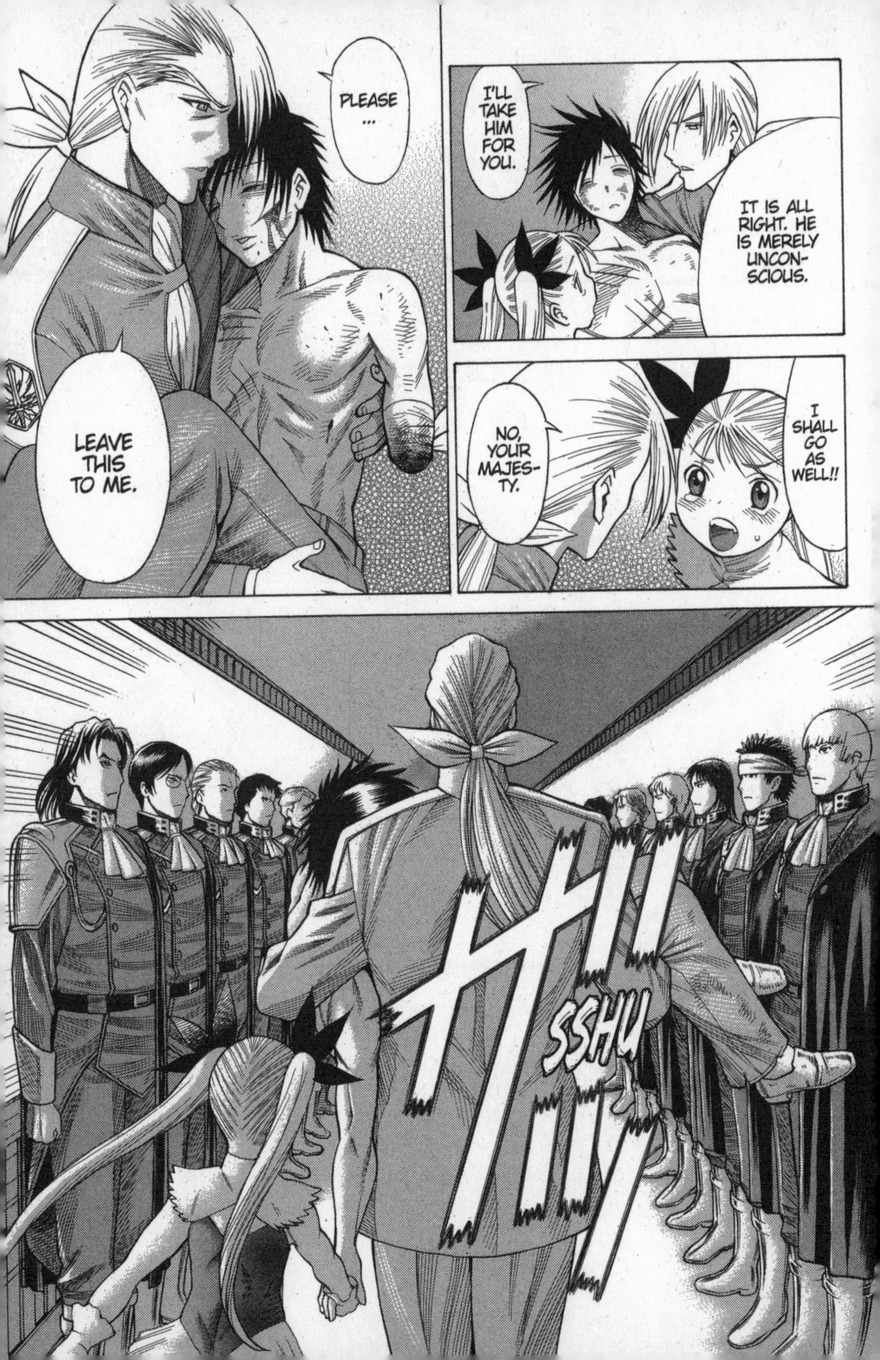
IT IS ALL RIGHT. HE IS MERELY UNCON-SCIOUS.
I'LL TAKE HIM FOR YOU.
I SHALL GO AS WELL!!
NO, YOUR MAJES-TY.
PLEASE ...
LEAVE THIS TO ME.
SSHU

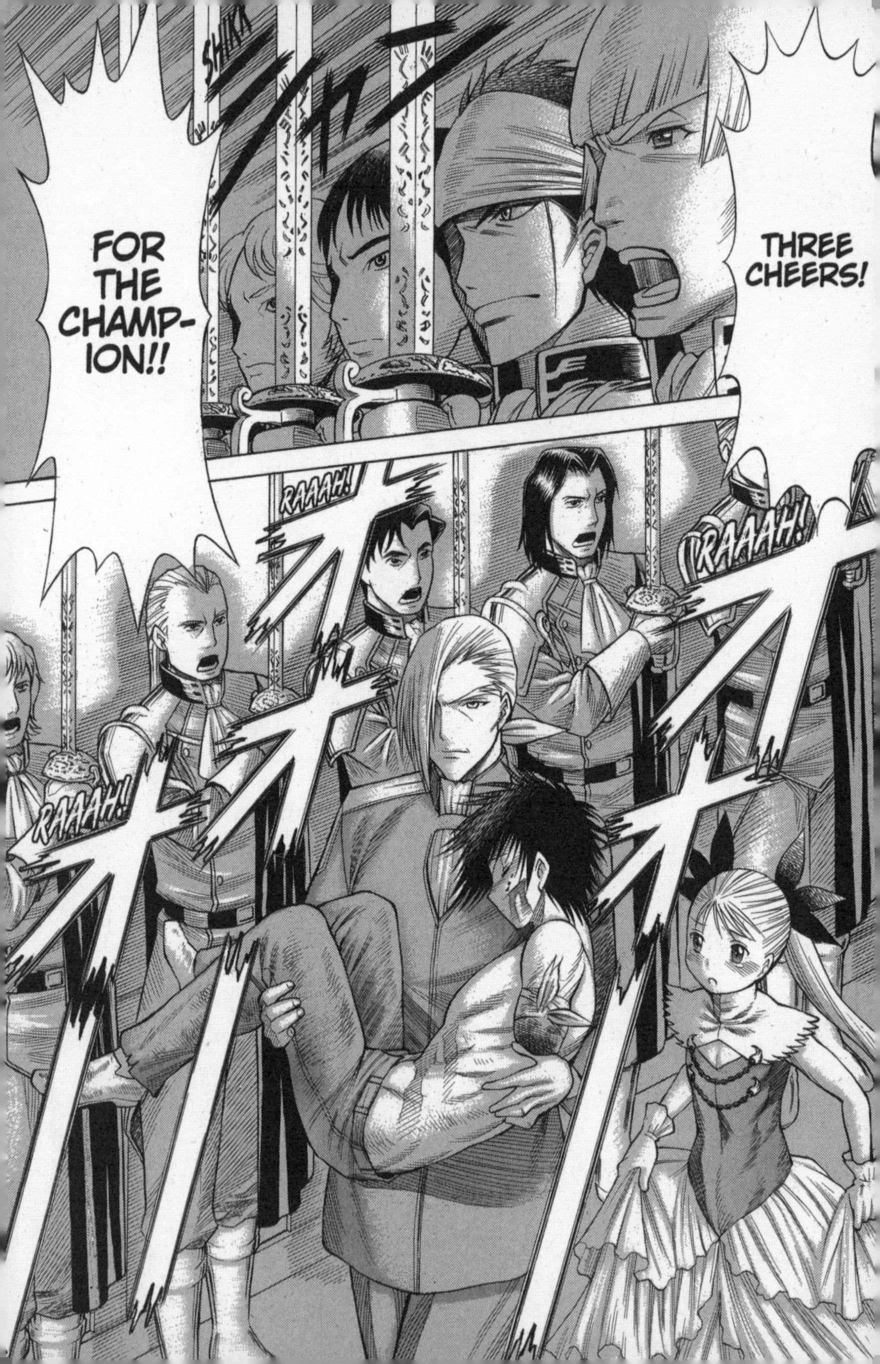
THREE CHEERS!
SHIKA
FOR THE CHAMPION!!
RAAAH!
RAAAH!
RAAAH!

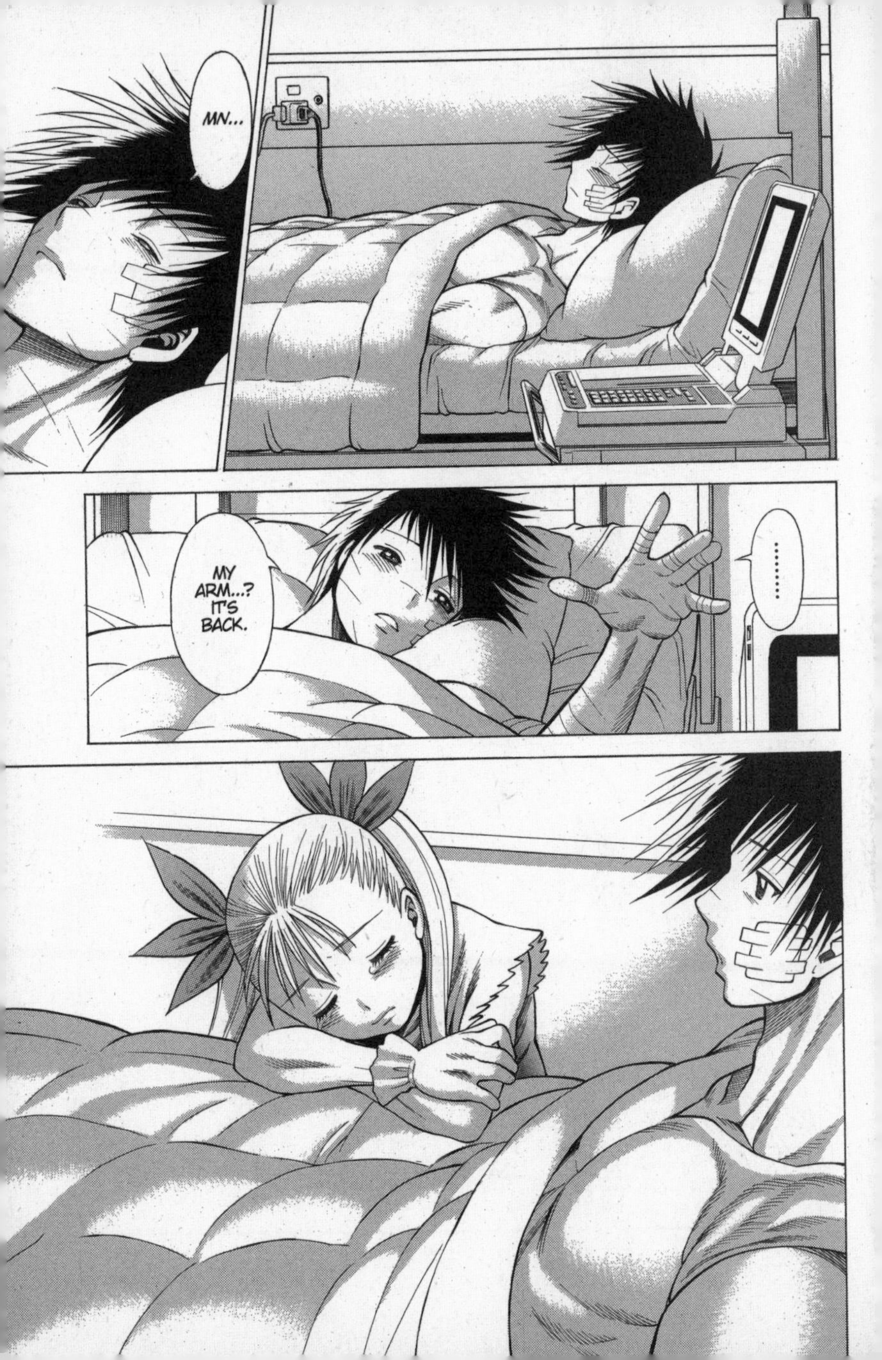
MN...
MY ARM...? IT'S BACK.
....

HEH ...
HOWEVER YOUR HEARTS ARE BOUND TOGETHER...
YOU AND HER MAJESTY SHARE A PECULIAR KARMA...
FATED TO BE STAR-CROSSED, EVERMORE.

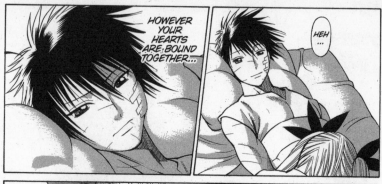

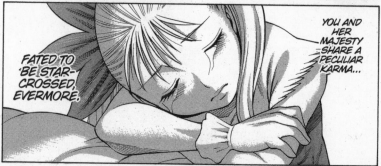

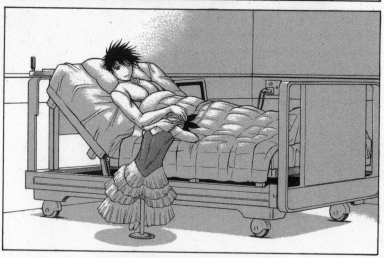

TO BE CONTINUED IN VOLUME 6

STAFF

JUGGERNAUT

TAKASHI KOMATSU

KENICHI NAKAMONO

RYUSUKE TAKIGUCHI

SPECIAL THANKS

HIROSHI YAGUMO

KAORU ARATANI

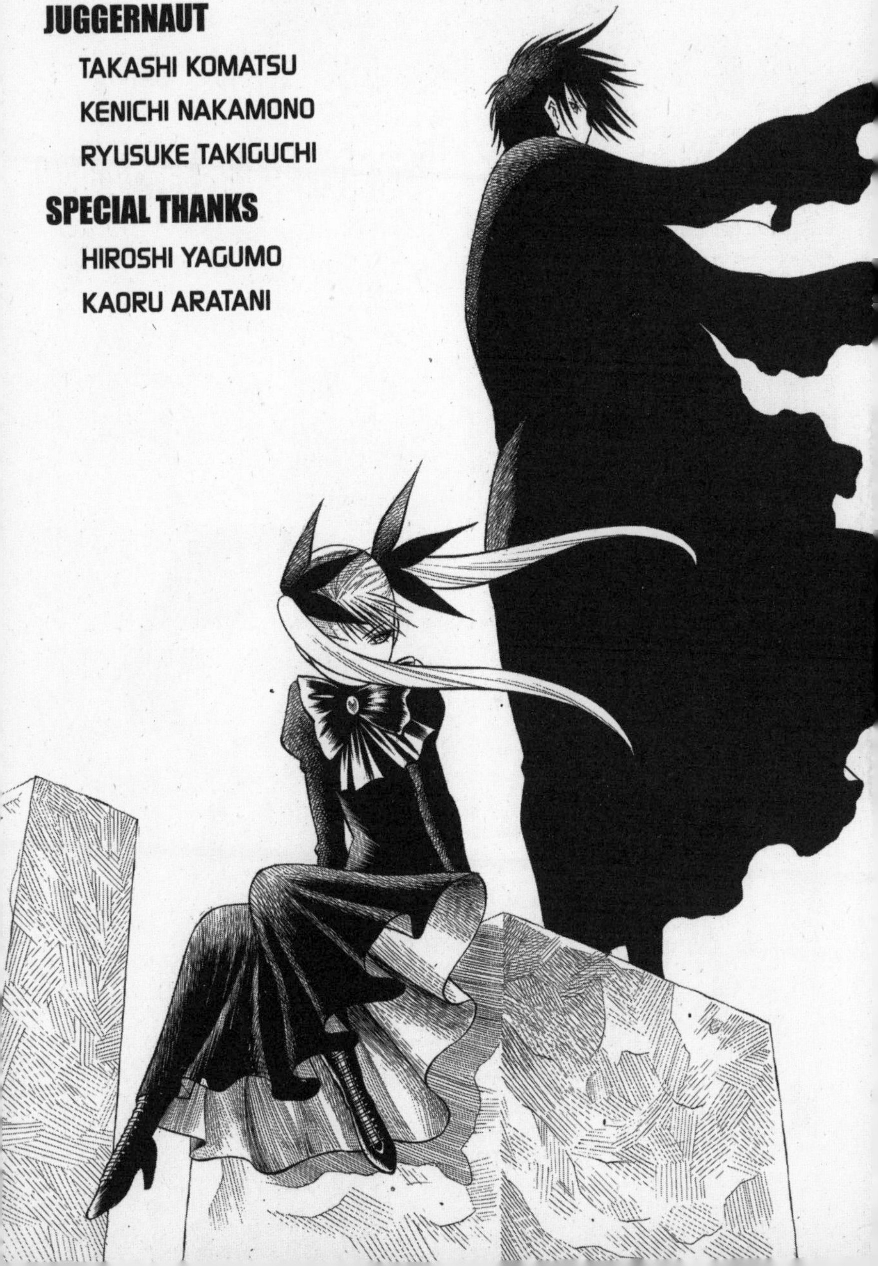

DANCE with the VAMPIRE MAID

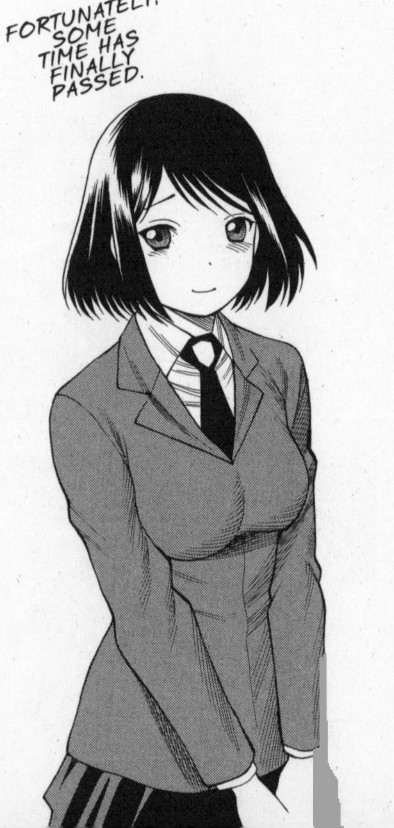
FORTUNATELY, SOME TIME HAS FINALLY PASSED.

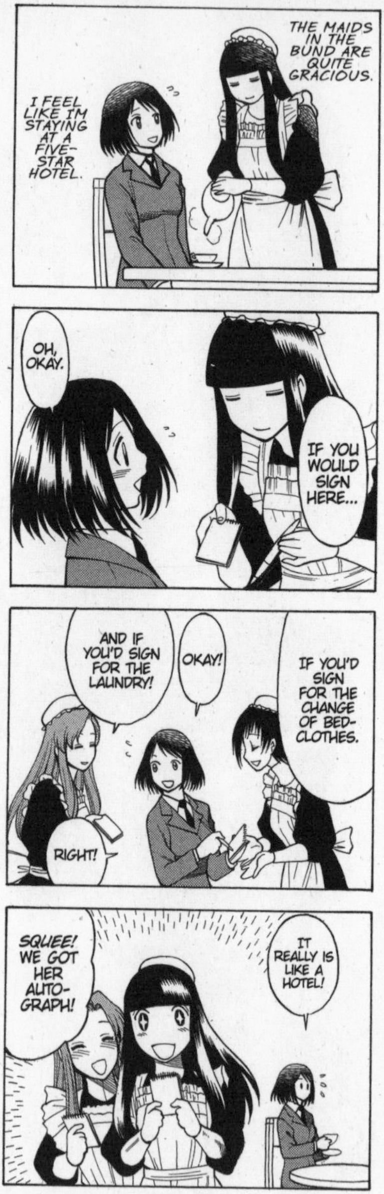
THE MAIDS IN THE BUND ARE QUITE GRACIOUS.
I FEEL LIKE IM STAYING AT A FIVE-STAR HOTEL.
IF YOU WOULD SIGN HERE...
OH, OKAY.
IF YOU'D SIGN FOR THE CHANGE OF BED-CLOTHES.
OKAY!
AND IF YOU'D SIGN FOR THE LAUNDRY!
RIGHT!
IT REALLY IS LIKE A HOTEL!
SQUEE! WE GOT HER AUTO-GRAPH!

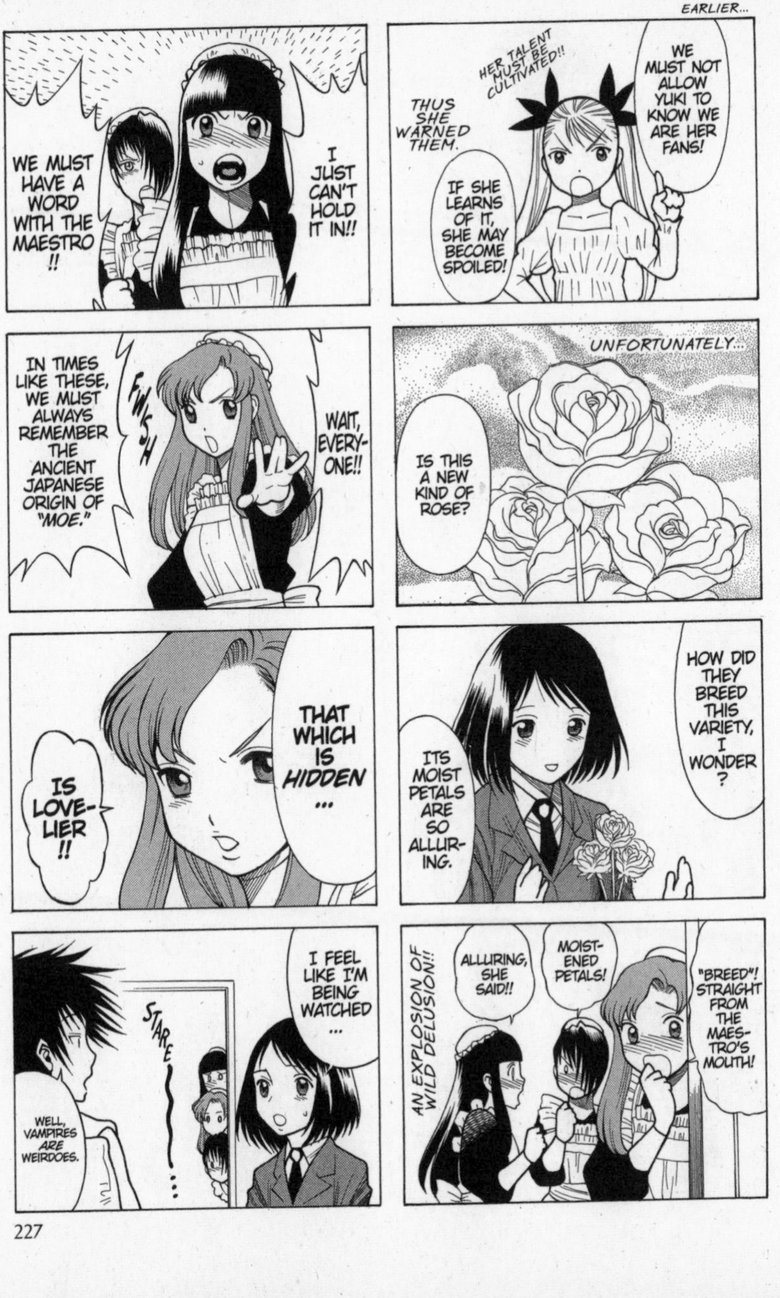
EARLIER...
HER TALENT MUST BE CULTIVATED!!
WE MUST NOT ALLOW YUKI TO KNOW WE ARE HER FANS!
THUS SHE WARNED THEM.
IF SHE LEARNS OF IT, SHE MAY BECOME SPOILED!
I JUST CAN'T HOLD IT IN!!
WE MUST HAVE A WORD WITH THE MAESTRO !!
UNFORTUNATELY...
IS THIS A NEW KIND OF ROSE?
WAIT, EVERY-ONE!!
FWISH
IN TIMES LIKE THESE, WE MUST ALWAYS REMEMBER THE ANCIENT JAPANESE ORIGIN OF "MOE."
HOW DID THEY BREED THIS VARIETY, I WONDER ?
ITS MOIST PETALS ARE SO ALLUR-ING.
THAT WHICH IS HIDDEN ...
IS LOVE-LIER !!
"BREED"! STRAIGHT FROM THE MAES-TRO'S MOUTH!
MOIST-ENED PETALS!
ALLURING, SHE SAID!!
AN EXPLOSION OF WILD DELUSION!!
I FEEL LIKE I'M BEING WATCHED ...
STARE~~~...
WELL, VAMPIRES ARE WEIRDOES.

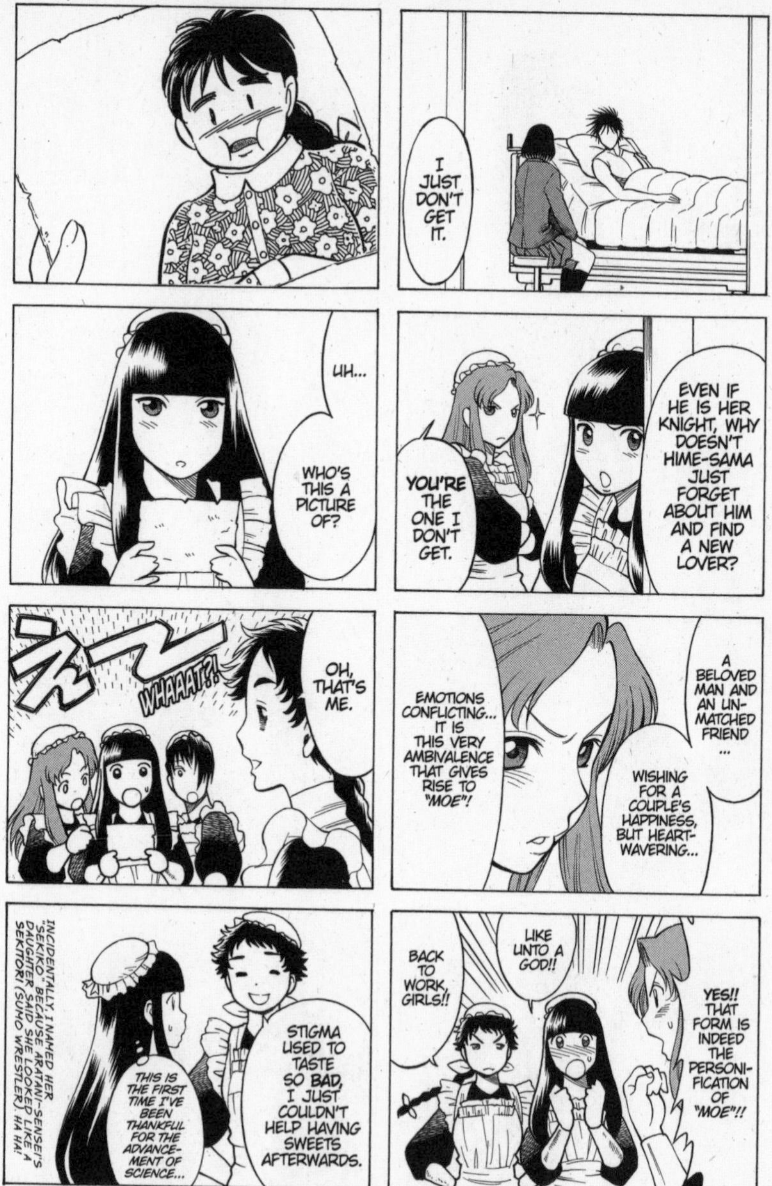
I JUST DON'T GET IT.
EVEN IF HE IS HER KNIGHT, WHY DOESN'T HIME-SAMA JUST FORGET ABOUT HIM AND FIND A NEW LOVER?
YOU'RE THE ONE I DON'T GET.
UH...
WHO'S THIS A PICTURE OF?
A BELOVED MAN AND AN UN-MATCHED FRIEND ...
WISHING FOR A COUPLE'S HAPPINESS, BUT HEART-WAVERING...
EMOTIONS CONFLICTING... IT IS THIS VERY AMBIVALENCE THAT GIVES RISE TO "MOE"!
OH, THAT'S ME.
えーー
WHAAAT?!
YES!! THAT FORM IS INDEED THE PERSONIFICATION OF "MOE"!!
LIKE UNTO A GOD!!
BACK TO WORK, GIRLS!!
STIGMA USED TO TASTE SO BAD, I JUST COULDN'T HELP HAVING SWEETS AFTERWARDS.
THIS IS THE FIRST TIME I'VE BEEN THANKFUL FOR THE ADVANCEMENT OF SCIENCE...
INCIDENTALLY, I NAMED HER "SEKIKO" BECAUSE ARATANI-SENSEI'S DAUGHTER SAID SHE LOOKED LIKE A SEKITORI (SUMO WRESTLER). HA HA!

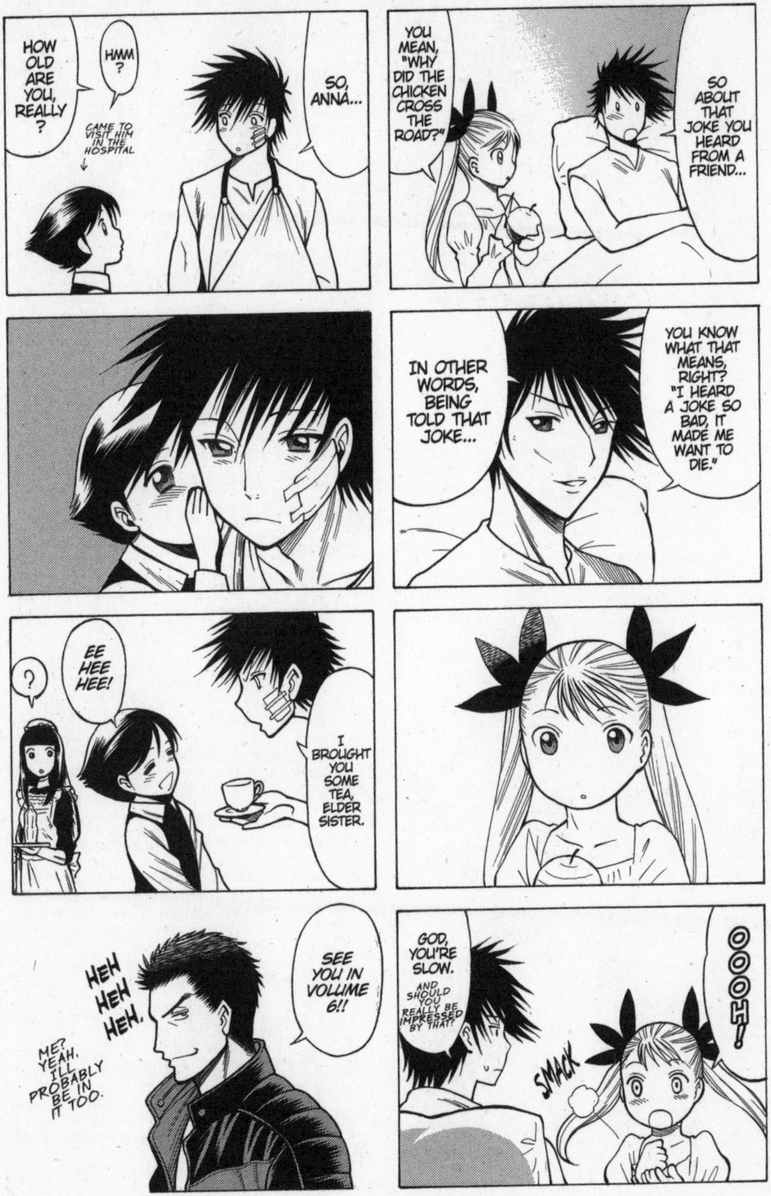
SO ABOUT THAT JOKE YOU HEARD FROM A FRIEND...
YOU MEAN, "WHY DID THE CHICKEN CROSS THE ROAD?"
YOU KNOW WHAT THAT MEANS, RIGHT? "I HEARD A JOKE SO BAD, IT MADE ME WANT TO DIE."
IN OTHER WORDS, BEING TOLD THAT JOKE...
OOOOH!
SMACK
GOD, YOU'RE SLOW.
AND SHOULD YOU REALLY BE IMPRESSED BY THAT?
SO, ANNA...
HMM?
HOW OLD ARE YOU, REALLY?
CAME TO VISIT HIM IN THE HOSPITAL
I BROUGHT YOU SOME TEA, ELDER SISTER.
EE HEE HEE!
?
SEE YOU IN VOLUME 6!!
HEH HEH HEH.
ME? YEAH. ILL PROBABLY BE IN IT TOO.

Dance in the Vampire Bund

Volume 5

story & art by Nozomu Tamaki

STAFF CREDITS

translation	Paul Tuttle Starr
adaptation	Janet Houck
retouch & lettering	Roland Amago
cover design	Nicky Lim
layout	Bambi Eloriaga-Amago
copy editor	Shanti Whitesides
editor	Adam Arnold

publisher **Seven Seas Entertainment**

DANCE IN THE VAMPIRE BUND VOL. 5
© 2007 Nozomu Tamaki
First published in Japan in 2007 by MEDIA FACTORY, Inc.
English translation rights reserved by Seven Seas Entertainment, LLC.
Under the license from MEDIA FACTORY, Inc., Tokyo.

Visit us online at www.gomanga.com

ISBN: 978-1-934876-65-7

Printed in Canada

First printing: November 2009

10 9 8 7 6 5 4 3 2 1

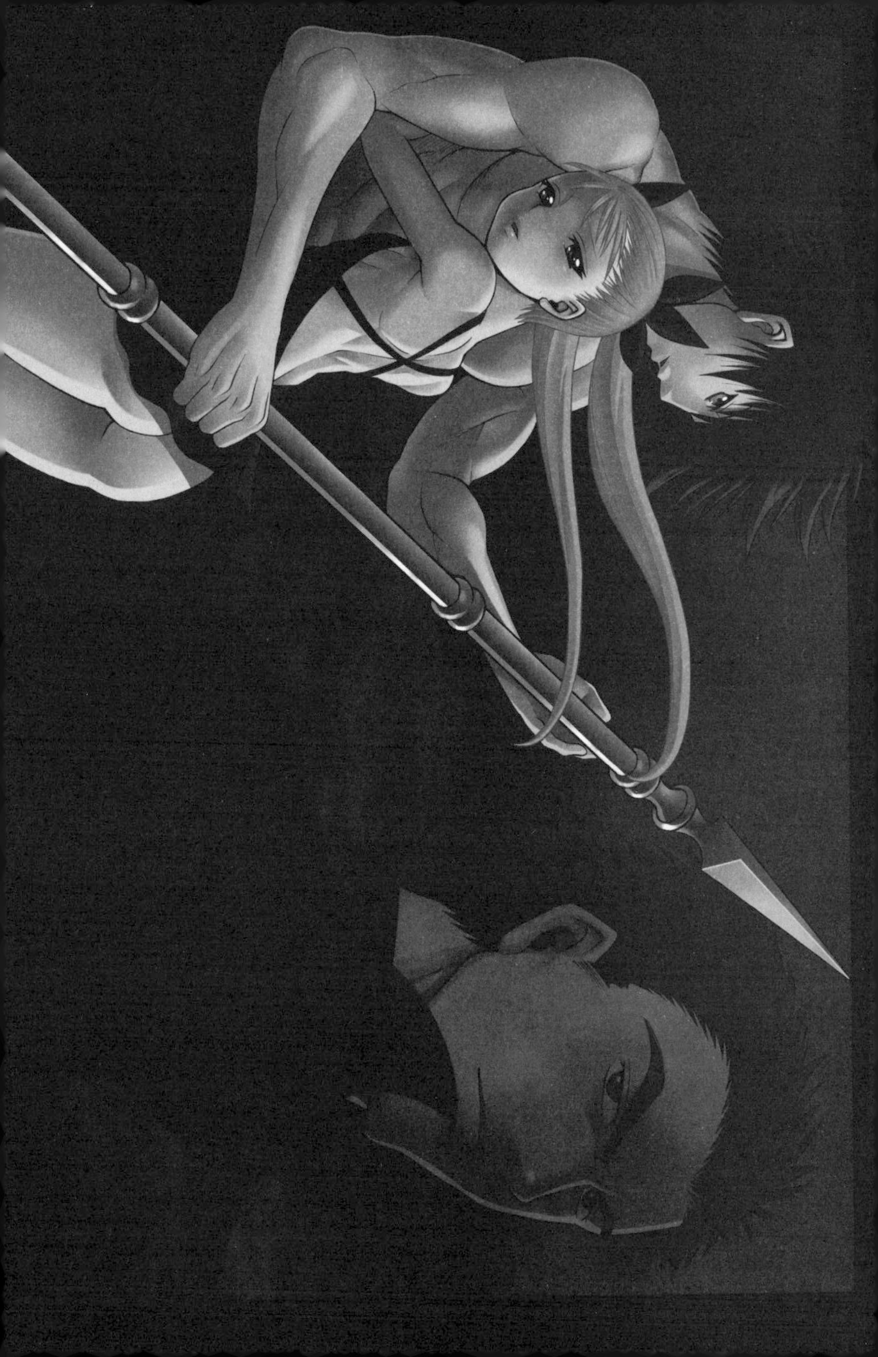

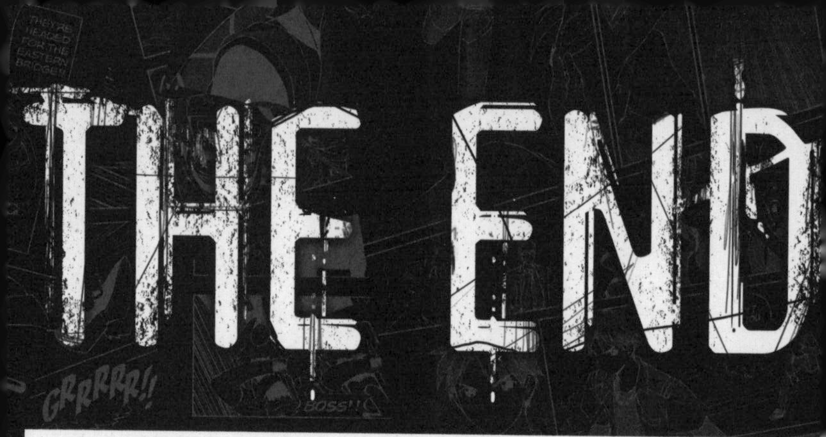
THEY'RE HEADED FOR THE EASTERN BRIDGE!
THE END
GRRRRR!!
BOSS!!

YOU'RE READING THE WRONG WAY

This is the last page of
Dance in the Vampire Bund
Volume 5

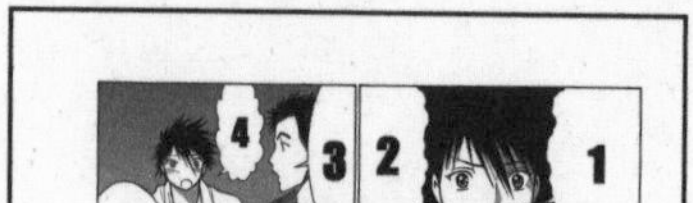
1
2
3
4
5
6
7
8
9
10

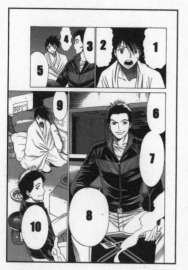

This book reads from right to left, Japanese style. To read from the beginning, flip the book over to the other side, start with the top right panel, and take it from there.

If this is your first time reading manga, just follow the diagram. It may seem backwards at first, but you'll get used to it! Have fun!